CUSTER AND HIS WOLVERINES

CUSTER AND HIS WOLVERINES

The Michigan Cavalry Brigade, 1861-1865

Edward G. Longacre

COMBINED PUBLISHING
Pennsylvania

PUBLISHER'S NOTE

The headquarters of Combined Publishing are located midway between Valley Forge and the Germantown battlefield, on the outskirts of Philadelphia. From its beginnings, our company has been steeped in the oldest traditions of American military history and publishing. Our historic surroundings help maintain our focus on military history and our books strive to uphold the standards of style, quality and durability first established by the earliest bookmakers of Germantown and Philadelphia so many years ago. Our famous monk-and-console logo reflects our commitment to the modern and yet historic enterprise of publishing.

We call ourselves Combined Publishing because we have always felt that our goals could only be achieved through a "combined" effort by authors, publishers and readers. We have always tried to maintain maximum communication between these three key players in the reading experience.

We are always interested in hearing from prospective authors about new books in our field. We also like to hear from our readers and invite you to contact us at our offices in Pennsylvania with any questions, comments or suggestions, or if you are having difficulty finding our books at your local bookseller.

For information, address:
Combined Publishing
1024 Fayette Street
P.O. Box 307
Conshohocken, PA 19428

E-mail: combined@dca.net
Web: www.dca.net/combinedbooks
Orders: 1-800-4-1860-65

Library of Congress Cataloging-in-Publication Data
Longacre, Edward G., 1946-
   Custer and his wolverines: the Michigan Cavalry Brigade, 1861-1865/Edward G. Longacre
      p. cm.
     Includes bibliographical references and index.
     ISBN 0-938289-87-X
   1. United States. Army. Michigan Cavalry Brigade (1862-1865). 2. Custer, George Armstrong, 1839-1876. 3. United States—History—Civil War, 1861-1865—Regimental histories. 4. United States—History—Civil War, 1861-1865—Cavalry operations 5. Michigan—History—Civil War, 1861-1865—Regimental histories. I. Title.
E514.4.L66   1997
973.7'474—dc21   97-26963

Printed in the United States of America.
Maps by Paul Dangel

For
Jacob and Jonathan Campbell

Acknowledgments

Over the past twenty years I have accumulated debts to many who helped me research the Michigan Cavalry Brigade. Those most deserving of recognition include:

Marilyn Blackwell of the Vermont Historical Society; Phyllis Burnham, University Archives and Regional History Collections, Western Michigan University; Marie T. Capps, United States Military Academy Library; Mr. Lou Clark, Sharpsburg, Maryland; William H. Combs and Frederick L. Honhart, University Archives and Historical Collections, Michigan State University; Alice C. Dalligan, Burton Historical Collection, Detroit Public Library; John C. Dann, William L. Clements Library, University of Michigan; Connell Gallagher, Guy W. Bailey Library, University of Vermont; John Hinz and Paul G. Smithson, Kalamazoo College; William Miles, Clarke Historical Library, Central Michigan University; David J. Olson, State Archives of Michigan; Mary Jo Pugh, Michigan Historical Collections, Bentley Historical Library, University of Michigan; Richard J. Sommers, U. S. Army Military History Institute; Mr. Charles Van Adder, Forked River, New Jersey; Mr. Alva B. Van Dyke, Nappanee, Indiana; Larry A. Viskochil, Chicago Historical Society; and Valerie Wingfield, New York Public Library.

Special thanks go to three of my Air Force colleagues: Lieutenant Colonel Al Mackey, Civil War cyberspace monitor; Lieutenant Colonel Mark Thompson, authority on Yellow Tavern and Trevilian Station and the living-history personification of James H. Kidd; and Major Mike Riggleman, cavalry reenactor and tactics interpreter. For support throughout this project I thank Bob Pigeon, my publisher; Ken Gallagher, my editor; Paul Dangel, my cartographer; and Ann Longacre, my research assistant, business manager, and wife.

Contents

Illustrations appear on pages 167 through 174.

Maps

Introduction

When Major General Joseph Hooker, commander of the Army of the Potomac, coined his celebrated jest that "no one ever saw a dead cavalryman," he had not heard of the Wolverine Brigade. Formed just after Hooker and his humor departed the army, this command—consisting of the First, Fifth, Sixth, and Seventh Michigan Volunteer Cavalry Regiments—was destined for glory, but glory won at great price. By war's end it had established itself as the hardest-fighting cavalry brigade of the war, as well as the most prone to casualties: its battle losses included 425 officers and men killed or mortally wounded, significantly higher numbers than suffered by any force of comparable size, Union or Confederate.

The mounted brigade's fame was based on more than battle scars. Many of its troopers wielded the most formidable cavalry weapons of the day, the seven-shot Spencer rifle and Spencer carbine. From Gettysburg to Appomattox, the command saw action in every battle and campaign waged by the mounted forces in the eastern theater of operations. In many of these engagements the Wolverines held the post of honor, spearheading advances through disputed territory, carrying the fight to the enemy. And through the greater part of its existence, the brigade was led by George Armstrong Custer, the war's most publicized "boy general" and, after J. E. B. Stuart, its most flamboyant and colorful horseman.

While forming a cohesive, close-knit force, the brigade's components boasted distinctive personalities. Well before the command was formed, the First Michigan gained a reputation as one of the savviest and most tenacious regiments of horse in the East. Under Colonel Thornton F. Brodhead and his successors, Charles H. Town

9

and Peter Stagg, the First was especially formidable in a saber charge. As an admirer in another Wolverine outfit observed, "when the First Michigan could not stand before a storm of bullets, no other regiment in the cavalry corps need try."[1]

The Fifth and Sixth Michigan, formed in the autumn of 1862 and immediately equipped with repeating arms, supported and complemented the First by fighting primarily on foot. These regiments differed mainly in the qualities transmitted to them by their most influential commanders: the dashing, sometimes impetuous Colonel Russell A. Alger of the Fifth, and the capable but unostentatious Colonels George Gray and James H. Kidd of the Sixth.

The Seventh Cavalry, the junior component of the brigade (organized in the winter of 1862-63) and for a time also its smallest (until the latter stages of the Gettysburg Campaign it mounted ten rather than the normal twelve companies of horsemen), was considered an "understudy to the First Michigan." Generally employed as a saber regiment but able to fight skillfully afoot, the Seventh, under the direction of Colonel William D. Mann, Lieutenant Colonel Melvin Brewer, and Major Henry W. Granger, evolved from an awkward gaggle of would-be troopers into a poised, polished outfit able to stand proudly alongside its more celebrated comrades.[2]

The Wolverine quartet saw more than its share of service. Following the early-war experiences of the First Regiment in the Shenandoah Valley and at Second Bull Run, the brigade participated extensively at Hanover and Hunterstown; at Gettysburg, where on the climactic third day of battle it played a leading role in defeating Stuart's cavaliers; in pursuit of Lee's army from Pennsylvania to Virginia; at Newby's Cross Roads, Brandy Station, Culpeper Court House, and elsewhere during the bloody autumn of 1863; in the Wilderness and at Todd's Tavern; on Major General Philip H. Sheridan's raid to Richmond (north of which a member of the brigade killed General Stuart); at Trevilian Station (where Custer's men, surrounded on all sides, fought a desperate battle that prefigured their leader's stand at the Little Bighorn); in the Shenandoah Valley clashes at Front Royal, Kearneysville, Winchester, Tom's Brook, and Cedar Creek; at Dinwiddie Court House, Five Forks, and in the final pursuit toward Appomattox Court House.

As if they had rendered insufficient service to their army and nation, the Wolverines were not permitted to return to civilian life after Lee's surrender. While thousands of their comrades went home, the Wolverines were sent to the far frontier to guard the routes of westward settlement. Although outraged at being kept in service and tempted to mutiny, the majority of the brigade served faithfully and well on outpost and expeditionary duty in Indian-infested corners of the Nebraska, Colorado, Dakota, and Utah Territories. Not until March 1866—almost a year after the guns had fallen silent in Virginia—were the Wolverines mustered out and permitted to entrain for Michigan and a long-overdue homecoming. Few troopers were so deserving of a hero's welcome.

CHAPTER ONE

"A Fine Body of Men"

When South Carolina artillery bombarded the U.S. Army garrison at Fort Sumter, Charleston harbor, in April 1861, twenty-year-old James Harvey Kidd of Ionia, Michigan, was anything but surprised. Kidd, a freshman at the state university at Ann Arbor, had seen the hostilities coming. Politically aware, attuned to the menace of sectionalism and disunion, for months he had been distressed by the tendency of the government to let the ship of state drift on, "making slight, if any, efforts to put her up against the wind and keep her off the rocks." The inevitable consequence was civil war, and now he and thousands of other youngsters would have to pay for the shortsightedness of national officials.

In the days following receipt of the news out of Charleston, Kidd attended a series of campus rallies in support of the war effort. He listened intently as Chancellor Henry P. Tappan ("a magnificent specimen of manhood, intellectually and physically") stated the university's policy toward students who wished to enlist. The school would place no obstacles in their path, "but, on the contrary, would bid them God speed and watch their careers with pride and solicitude." Tappan echoed the words of other campus officials in praising the patriotic motivations of would-be soldiers. At the close of his oration, however, the tall, dignified educator sounded a theme that struck a responsive chord in James Kidd: "He advised against haste, saying that the chances were that the country would be more in need of men in a year from that time than it was then."

Tappan's advice made the youth from Ionia resolve to continue his studies for at least another year, until mature enough to handle the responsibilities army life would thrust upon him. Kidd reasoned that to rush off to enlist "was to give up cherished plans and ambitions" and to interrupt an education barely begun. Conversely, a year of preparation would stand him in good stead if the early volunteers failed to put down the rebellion. Thus he took to heart not only the words of Dr. Tappan but those of another university spokesman, Professor A. D. White, who predicted that a "protracted and bloody struggle" lay ahead.

If the war waited for him, young Kidd would prepare himself to heed its call. In common with dozens of fellow students, he joined one of several quasi-military units organizing on campus. To his surprise and gratification, he was elected its second lieutenant. To prove himself worthy of the honor, he began to pore over tactics manuals such as that compiled by Major William J. Hardee (now a general in the Confederate service) and to participate in, and occasionally lead, dress parades and close-order drill. The student-soldiers wore a hodgepodge of attire; few possessed the proper accoutrements; and they carried hunting-pieces or family-heirloom firearms in place of regulation-issue muskets. What they lacked in raiment and weaponry, however, they made up in enthusiasm and determination.[1]

By August, the student companies had been drilling for four months and had adopted a semblance of polish. By this point, the war to save the Union had made only spasmodic progress. The previous month had seen the great Confederate victory at Bull Run (or Manassas) in northeastern Virginia, but Federal forces had gained a few victories in the western reaches of the state. At Wilson's Creek, Missouri, in the Trans-Mississippi Department, Rebel armies had defeated a small force under the feisty but unfortunate Brigadier General Nathaniel Lyon. Amphibious forces were poised to capture strategic outposts along the coast of North Carolina. Professor White's prediction of a protracted, uncertain conflict had come true.[2]

Certain that he would soon join the fighting, James Kidd gave careful thought to which branch of the service he should enter. Weary of marching, he may already have considered the prospect of fighting in the saddle. It was in August, however, that the idea of cavalry service began to mature. In company with other students,

Kidd, then about to embark on his sophomore year, made the forty-mile journey from Ann Arbor to Detroit to watch a much-publicized parade by members of the First Michigan Volunteer Cavalry, then organizing in the city. Although all but the ranking officers of the regiment lacked uniforms and horses, even those afoot seemed imbued with martial splendor; Kidd pronounced them "a fine body of men." He was especially impressed with the "tall, commanding figure and military bearing" of the regiment's newly commissioned commander, Colonel Thornton Fleming Brodhead, a resident of the Detroit suburb of Grosse Isle.[3]

A native of New Hampshire, a Harvard graduate, the thirty-nine-year-old attorney had long been a prominent figure in the political and military history of his adopted state. As an officer of regular infantry he had won two brevets for gallantry during the Mexican War, after which he served in the Michigan legislature and as postmaster of Detroit. Through education, experience, and inherent leadership, Brodhead would be primarily responsible for the enviable record the First Michigan acquired during its first year of service.[4]

Brodhead was supported by a number of talented subordinates, some of whom caught James Kidd's eye as they marched up Jefferson Avenue on that midsummer afternoon. The sophomore singled out Brodhead's lieutenant colonel, Joseph Tarr Copeland, a lumberman from Pontiac and a retired judge of the St. Clair County Court, properly sagacious with his patriarchal beard and hooded eyes. He also scrutinized two ruddy-faced and rugged-looking captains, William D. Mann of Detroit and Melvin Brewer of Almont. In sharp contrast to this pair was the balding, sallow-complected Major Charles H. Town of Marquette, an early-stage consumptive whom Kidd would come to regard, despite his frail physique, as "a modern Chevalier Bayard" remarkable for his energy, his mastery of mounted tactics, and his "superb courage."[5]

The soldierly bearing of Brodhead and his subordinates and the almost swaggering gait of the men in mufti who followed them up the avenue had a marked effect on James Kidd. Having enjoyed the responsibilities and prerogatives of a student-officer, he had decided to seek a commission in the army. Now he knew in which service he wanted to serve. Barring unforseen obstacles, he would ride to war.

* * *

Colonel Brodhead's regiment was the product of a recruiting program unique among the states of the Union. That program had gotten off to a slow start. Four months after the outbreak of war, few outfits of volunteer cavalry were forming anywhere in the North. This situation was at least partially the result of the tradition-bound (others might say fossilized) officers who formulated military policy. Aged officials including Commanding General Winfield Scott, Adjutant General Lorenzo Thomas, and Secretary of War Simon Cameron—who lacked the military experience that should have been a prerequisite for his position—thought mounted volunteers a superfluous commodity as well as a waste of taxpayers' money.

The triumvirate's opposition to volunteer cavalry was multi-faceted. They considered the cost of organizing, arming, equipping, mounting and maintaining horsemen—upwards of $14,000 a year per regiment—a luxury the government could not afford. According to a popular axiom, it took at least two years to develop a capable trooper. It might take even longer to produce volunteers able to oppose on equal terms the born-to-the-saddle youngsters in the Confederate cavalry. On the other hand, few in the War Department were willing to predict that it would take two years to suppress the rebellion; thus, cavalry training would only go to waste. Finally, the theater of operations in Virginia, where the major part of the war was expected to take place, was too heavily wooded, too hilly, too riven with watercourses, to permit large-scale cavalry operations.

Under these circumstances, the Union would be better served by relying on an existing resource, the Regular Cavalry. So believing, in early May Congress had authorized the formation of a sixth regiment of Regulars to supplement the two of cavalry, two of dragoons, and one of mounted riflemen (all redesignated as "cavalry" outfits) that had been formed between 1833 and 1855.[6]

Even the most optimistic observer should have realized that 6,000 cavalry would not suffice for the various armies organizing across the North. That number would barely satisfy the needs of the major Union command in the East, eventually known as the Army of the

Potomac. The 36,000-man advance contingent of this army, which Brigadier General Irvin McDowell led from Washington toward Richmond in July 1861, learned the hard way. When McDowell attacked Confederate defenses across Bull Run on the twenty-first, he commanded barely 500 horsemen—five companies of Regulars, no volunteers.

This contingent was so small that McDowell relegated it to guarding artillery and the flanks and rear of the infantry. To perform even those duties, the Regulars were stretched thin. Meanwhile, the thousands of horsemen at the disposal of McDowell's opponents, General Joseph E. Johnston and Brigadier General Pierre Beauregard, assumed the offensive, reconnoitering enemy positions, spearheading advances, and at battle's end pursuing their beaten enemy so closely, harassing them at every step, that orderly retreat became panicky rout.[7]

In the aftermath of the debacle, Northern newspapers clamored for volunteer cavalry. Many echoed the sentiments of the *New York Times*, which in June had called the dearth of horse soldiers "an element of weakness... to which adequate attention has not yet been paid." The *Times* observed that "cavalry is the right arm of active, open warfare. Without cavalry the great army of the Union, now upon the march to crush rebellion, is crippled and imperfect." Lawmakers heeded the warning; the day after Bull Run, Congress approved a bill that empowered President Abraham Lincoln to call 500,000 volunteers into service for terms ranging from six months to three years. The act stipulated that the recruits should include cavalrymen.[8]

Armed with official authority, would-be commanders began to recruit mounted companies and regiments, hoping to enlist enough volunteers to guarantee themselves high rank and political patronage. Men who fancied themselves cavalry material appeared to be especially active in Michigan; the Wolverine State took an early lead in raising units of horse. Perhaps because Michigan had only recently been carved out of the wilderness (it had joined the Union in 1837) and lacked an extensive network of internal improvements, transportation by horseback was as much a way of life there as it was below the Mason-Dixon Line. A generation of equestrians-by-necessity ensured that ample cavalry resources existed within Michigan's borders. In fact, proportional to its population Michigan would supply more mounted volunteers than any other state in the Union.[9]

* * *

Within a fortnight of Bull Run, Thornton Brodhead opened the state's first cavalry recruiting stations in Detroit and Grand Rapids. He quickly discovered he had tapped a fertile source of manpower. A few days later a Grand Rapids weekly was reporting that "this arm of the service seems to be quite a favorite with the men.... they are rushing from all quarters to join the Colonel's standard." Brodhead and his subordinates were pleased with the material at their disposal; in Grand Rapids Captain Brewer made a special effort to enlist backwoodsmen, whom he considered "not only first class riders, but also crack shots."

The lure of mounted duty—which promised an improvement over the mundane, footsore service that infantry recruits could expect—ensured that the regiment would be filled in record time. As early as 13 August, Brewer and other Grand Rapids recruiters had procured enough enlistees to form a company. That very evening, the members of this initial component of the outfit elected their officers.[10]

The following day the nucleus of what would become Company G of the First Michigan Volunteer Cavalry assembled at the rail depot at Pontiac, where its men would entrain for the regimental rendezvous in suburban Detroit. Corporal-to-be Henry S. Cox recalled the festive atmosphere that prevailed at Pontiac. He and his fellow-enlistees believed "we were in for a good and easy time... being relieved from the laborious and slavish occupation of the farm." They soon discovered, however, that much work awaited them and that few recruits were born soldiers. When Second Lieutenant Fordyce Rogers tried to assemble Company G in marching formation, chaos ensued. "We started out all right, left foot first," Cox remembered, "but before we got to the depot we were all broken up like a flock of sheep, so green were we as to a military step."[11]

When the raw recruits reached Detroit, they were assembled at the downtown depot where they were joined by Colonel Brodhead, his ranking lieutenants, and the nucleus of other companies, recently disembarked from trains that had come in from all corners of the state. Brodhead and his staff arranged the civilians into some semblance of a column and led them—whichever foot first—up Jefferson Avenue. At first the men loped along at an unmilitary gait, heedless of the few onlookers. Word of their coming, however, had preceded them, and as the blocks went by the crowd lining the street grew to impressive proportions. Spurred by the cheers and applause that greeted their passing, many of the would-be troopers mimicked the professional attitude of their officers. By the time they had passed out of the city and into the farmlands beyond, the men were fatigued, footsore, dust-covered, and thirsty—but at least a few had begun to think of themselves, in some small way, as soldiers.

The improbable parade did not end until Henry Cox and his comrades reached the old Hamtramck Racetrack, three miles above the city line. A recruit from Marquette, Edward Watson, soon to be appointed a corporal in Company B, described the training facility as "nothing more... than a wide road running round a large field perfectly level, and fenced in by a board fence ten or twelve feet high, with only one gate, which is guarded night & day by two sentinels." The site, which would soon feature rows of wooden barracks and canvas "doghouses," had been christened Camp Lyon to honor the martyr of Wilson's Creek.[12]

Farmboys, lumbermen, store clerks, and day laborers—a few of whom had military experience dating from the Mexican War but most of whom knew nothing of the profession on which they had embarked—swarmed over this place that smelled of new-cut pine and freshly turned earth. Newcomers mingled with those who had preceded them: the lanky and the diminutive, the barrel-chested and the sunken-chested, graybeards who had lied to the recruiters, and sixteen-year-old Johnny Phillips of Bay City, the youngest enlistee, who, swept away by patriotic fervor, had fled a one-room schoolhouse to join Company H.[13]

If the recruits expected accommodations superior to those they had left behind, they were promptly disabused. Conditions at Camp Lyon were spartan, if not downright primitive; the new arrivals were not immediately issued uniforms, equipment, or even bedding. "Night came on before we were well prepared for it," recalled Henry

Cox, whose only warmth that evening came from the body heat of his tentmates. The next day he and his comrades were each issued a blanket and mess equipment including a tin plate, knife, fork, spoon, and cup. Later they learned to their indignation that the cost of the cutlery would be deducted from their first month's pay—thirteen dollars.[14]

While free, the rations issued to Cox were nothing to write home about: for breakfast, they consisted of the army biscuit known as hardtack, a cup of lukewarm coffee, and half-boiled beef from a can; for noonday dinner, some thin soup and a piece of pork abounding in fat; for supper, beef, perhaps a vegetable, and more hardtack. "Not very inviting," the youngster declared, "for an epicure." Cox and company could supplement the meager fare with the wares of sutlers, civilian purveyors who had set up shop on the fringes of the camp. These merchants, however, charged dearly for their goods, which included such delicacies as lobster salad and prune pie. The ubiquitous vendors gave such dissatisfaction that when they appeared to overrun the camp Lieutenant Colonel Copeland, commanding the regiment in the absence of Colonel Brodhead, threatened to evict them all.[15]

For some days, while waiting for the rest of the regiment to assemble, the early occupants of Camp Lyon had little to do. Within forty-eight hours of their arrival, they were issued uniforms: light blue kersey pants with double-lined seats; dark blue, single-breasted jackets trimmed with the yellow piping of the cavalry; high-crowned hats with the numeral "1" above crossed sabers of silver; and knee-length black boots. Then the recruits queued up at the surgeon's tent where Doctor George Johnson of Grand Rapids administered a physical examination so perfunctory that only the obviously unfit were denied a soldier's life.[16]

For days afterward, those company officers in camp—several others, to Colonel Copeland's displeasure, were absent without leave—mounted guard details and made half-hearted efforts to teach the men the basics of drill pending the full-scale training that awaited the issuance of weapons and horses. By rights, that training should have been long and demanding because, as an officer in another Michigan regiment observed, "the duties of cavalry are as arduous, complex and diversified as it is possible for any branch of the military service to be." Those duties ran the gamut of vidette (i.e., mounted guard) duty, scouting, reconnoitering, skirmishing in the saddle and on foot, and a variety of battlefield evolutions. To master the demands thus imposed upon him, a cavalryman "must pass through a long course of drill training, both mounted and dismounted; and if any one imagines that even a hard and thorough course of drill training entirely fits a trooper for active campaign service, he will find himself much mistaken."[17]

At least in the early going these responsibilities, numerous as they were, did not consume every waking hour in a recruit's day. When not on the drill-field, the men had much time on their hands. A German immigrant, thirty-eight-year-old Frederic Schmalzried, wrote a friend back in Washtenaw County that the days passed slowly, monotonously, "especially when it rains," trapping the regiment under canvas. The lack of meaningful activity left Schmalzried, whose shaky grasp of the English language complicated his ability to make friends, longing for the farmhand's life he had left behind.[18]

As September came in and the camp population neared the personnel level—1,200 officers and men—authorized for a regiment of volunteer cavalry, the pace of activity quickened noticeably. With an eye for detail and some quiet humor, Corporal Watson described for a hometown correspondent the daily routine into which he and his comrades had settled:

"At five o'clock every morning we are awakened by the orderly singing out turn out to wash. After every body gets dressed & out, they form into line (for nothing is done here without forming into line) and march down to the river, where every one washes & combs his head. Then we form into line again & march into the camp, & drill an hour or two before breakfast, then march into a large tent along with three or four hundred other soldiers, as we have over a thousand men in camp. They have to Set three tables. Sometimes we have to wait until eight or nine o'clock before our turn comes [to eat].

"After breakfast we lounge about until nine, when we drill until eleven, then rest until noon when we march in to dinner where we get meat of most all kinds, cooked all ways & most of it as tough as Marquette steaks. Potatoes, Beefs & Bread, & sometimes beans with Butter, vinager [sic] & salt to season with, which, taken altogether, is more than we will get when we draw rations, & cook it ourselves, as we will have to do when we start south.

"So much for dinner. At three we have drill again until five. If the weather is very warm, we taken [sic] off our coats and drill only half an hour or so at a time, and then rest in the shade until we get cool, when we try it again.... When the after noon drill is over, the men do whatever they please except going out [of camp] but most of them go to bed, for it is rather tiresome work to drill. Some play ball, some cards, & others get up a subscription & buy a water mellon, or a basket of apples or pears, or any thing that they may wish except liquor, which is not allowed in camp.

"At six, if our turn at the table comes we take supper, if not, we have to wait until after dress parade.... at half past six, all the soldiers have to march out in the middle of the field and stand in a line two deep, with the captains & lieutenants in front, and the colonel in the centre out about a hundred yards, so every one can hear him as well as see him (come to think though he gives his orders to the Adjutant who gives them to the whole regiment in general, & the officers in particular so we see the Col. but dont hear him).... When the orders are given for the next day, the parade is dismissed, and, if we have had supper we go to quarters.... At half past nine the order is given to extinguish the lights, which is the last order of the day, unless we have the misfortune to be on guard...."[19]

Camp life took on a brisker pace after 5 September when Brodhead, who had been in Lansing to recruit and to confer with Governor Austin Blair and Adjutant General John Robertson, reached Camp Lyon and assumed command. Finding the regiment still shy of its full complement, he continued to advertise for recruits in newspapers throughout the state. He also sought the mounts his outfit critically needed, an effort in which he was aided by Senator K.S. Bingham. Before the middle of the month, colonel and senator received approval to inspect and purchase $200,000 worth of horesflesh, the mounts to be supplied wholly from within the state. By the end of September animals were being purchased at an average price of $110 a head at Detroit, Kalamazoo, Grand Rapids, and other cities with the necessary holding facilities.[20]

By 13 September the regiment, though fifty-six recruits shy of its authorized strength, was large enough to be accepted into federal service. On that day Colonels Brodhead and Copeland stood proudly at the head of their half-trained and horseless troopers as a Regular Army officer supervised the mustering-in process. The act of signing the muster rolls brought home to many recruits the full significance of their situation: they were entering into a contract with the government that would bind them for three years of soldiering. As the men understood it, they would be released sooner if the war should end before their enlistment term was up. While that prospect was worth considering, by the late summer of 1861 few recruits counted on a swift termination of hostilities. Most went into the service with eyes open and nerves steeled, pledging themselves for their full term of service, and longer—as long as need to restore the embattled Union to peace and prosperity.[21]

Not everyone at Camp Lyon on muster-in day could be considered a typical recruit. At least two who took on the duties of a soldier were female. While not carried on the official rolls, they would remain with the regiment for months to come, sharing with their male comrades the hardships of service in camp, on the march, and even in combat. One of these women, the wife of Private Richard C. Ostrander of Company M, had accompanied her husband from their hometown of Dowagiac. By mid-September Mrs. Ostrander had set up house in her spouse's tent, defying the efforts of regimental authorities to evict her. In time the officers would come to regard her as a member of the outfit, a New World version of the French *vivandiere*. Entering fully into the role, the lady donned a specially tailored uniform and clasped a brace of pistols around her waist. For the next two years (until accompanying him on his abrupt desertion to Canada), Mrs. Ostrander followed her husband in and out of battle. In 1864 a reporter with the *Detroit Free Press* described her admiringly: "Always cheerful and happy, she drove away the tedium of the camps, and was as much respected by the soldiers for intelligence and social worth as for daring in the face of the enemy."[22]

Another distaff member of the regiment was "Michigan Bridget"

Divers, supposedly the wife of another enlisted member of the First but one whose name cannot be found on the rolls. A "true, brave, loyal, and unselfish woman," who possessed "the hearty good will, the vigorous sense, and the unwearied industry of the laboring class," Ms. Divers served the First as cook, nurse, and matriarch. Her devotion to the regiment won the sympathy and respect of her comrades and dissuaded the authorities from expelling her. Like Mrs. Ostrander, Bridget Divers entered battle. A contemporary chronicler noted that "sometimes when a soldier fell she took his place, fighting in his stead with unquailing courage. Sometimes she rallied retreating troops—sometimes she brought off the wounded from the field—always fearless and daring, always doing good service as a soldier."[23]

Another nineteenth-century historian extolled Michigan Bridget's role as mother-confessor: "She knew every man in the regiment, and could speak of his character, his wants, his sufferings, and the facts of his military record. Her care and kindness extended to the moral and religious wants, as well as the health, of... her regiment, as she always called it. In the absence of the chaplain [Jonathan Hudson, frequently on leave from the First and for two months a prisoner of war] she came to the Christian Commission for books and papers for the men, saying that she was the acting chaplain, and appearing to take a very deep interest in the moral and religious well-being of them all."[24]

Unlike Mrs. Ostrander, Michigan Bridget served throughout the war; later she "joined" the same Regular Army regiment in which her husband enlisted. While the First Cavalry was not the only Michigan regiment with a *vivandiere*—at various times Annie Etheridge served openly in the Second, Third, and Fifth Infantry—the First appears to have been the only state outfit to feature two women in arms.[25]

* * *

The training period of the regiment was short even by the standards of the day, which saw many units rushed to the "seat of war" out of dire necessity. Dismounted training consumed at most a couple of weeks. For the most part it involved squads of ten to twenty men drilling in isolation under noncommissioned officers who were fortunate to keep one or two steps ahead of the men in their assimilation of tactics. By mid-September, however, Corporal Cox could report that he and the other non-coms had gained "considerable proficiency" in drilling the men afoot.[26]

Then the other half of the curriculum was added to the drill program. Shortly before month's end the first consignment of horses, fresh from the quartermaster's corrals, reached Camp Lyon. A scramble ensued as men tried to cull out the finest specimens. Once riders and horses were united, the former learned how to care for the latter with the curry-combs, feed bags, and tack recently issued to them. One of the first lessons they absorbed was that each trooper must water, feed, and groom his mount before attending to his own wants—a regimen that would prove especially burdensome after a long day's march.

Once they became familiar with the upkeep of their animals, the raw recruits—some of whom had never sat a horse in their lives—were introduced to the joys of equitation. For several days their lessons were confined to bareback riding, no saddles having been assigned to the regiment. Instructors placed a pole between two tree crotches and the men practiced jumping the barrier. In making the attempt many riders toppled from their mounts, although in time a majority of the would-be horsemen managed to clear the pole at heights of up to six feet. Some of the more proficient took their animals out onto the racetrack, where they exercised them at top speed.

In the main, however, as Corporal Cox observed, "we drilled very little on horseback" even after drawing saddles. Private Schmalzried agreed that the mounted exercises were brief and "not strict." No time was devoted to saber or pistol practice, for those weapons had yet to be obtained. It soon became clear that the greater part of the training program would be conducted not in Michigan but in Virginia, Tennessee, Missouri, or the numerous other venues where rumor-mongers claimed the First to be heading.[27]

Speculation about the regiment's ultimate destination ended in the last days of September when it became general knowledge that the men were bound for Washington, D.C. On the twenty-eighth officers and troopers were formed afoot in a hollow square as a delegation of citizens from Springwells, a Wayne County hamlet southwest of Detroit, presented Colonel Brodhead with a regimental banner, a ritual that often signified the imminent breaking of camp. The presentation of the blue silken flag was accompanied by an oration by Congressman H. T. Backus (father of Captain Frederick W. Backus of Company E), to which Brodhead responded with "a telling speech, full of burning eloquence and patriotism."[28]

The presentation complete, the regiment was dismissed, to reassemble before daylight the next morning. Members of the nine companies that could be accommodated aboard the only available troop train—a total of 862 men—marched on foot to Detroit. Upon arrival, Brodhead and Copeland placed them aboard a train bound for the nation's capital. After a series of vexing delays, the cars began moving southeastward, at what seemed like breakneck speed, toward Toledo, Ohio.[29]

Although few of the passengers had ever passed Michigan's borders, most found the early stages of the trip uninspiring. The Buckeye State struck them as flat, barren, and lacking in character. Not even the big-city ambience of Cleveland, through which they rolled on the second day, impressed the travelers. Once they entered Pennsylvania, however, they met the "beautiful scenery of the Alleghanies," which produced sighs of admiration. The scene turned bleak again when they jounced through Pittsburgh; a bookish recruit from Jackson observed that "the coal fires that send their dismal smoke towards the sky reminds one of Milton's description of the regions below."[30]

Continuing east, the anonymous critic found Harrisburg "a very pretty city," although when the train veered southward he took a dimmer view of secessionist Baltimore. If not picturesque, at least the city was quiet: the streets where anti-Union mobs had fired on the first troops bound for Washington were now patrolled by sentries in blue uniforms. Animation was confined to a well-dressed woman who waved to the passing troops and shouted, "God bless you all!"[31]

Reaching the environs of Washington, the passengers disembarked, reassembled in marching formation, and trooped through the streets, past scattered groups of soldiers and civilians, to Camp Rucker, a training-ground along the Potomac River about a mile east of the Capitol Building. Camp Brodhead, as the site was quickly renamed, was a cheerless place, lacking even the few amenities offered by the Hamtramck racecourse. Perhaps because of its proximity to the seat of war, however, some recruits found it "much more soldier-like here than at Camp Lyon." The surroundings left Private William S. Arnold of Company B in fine "sperets," fueling his determination "to fite for my countries rights" against the planter aristocracy.[32]

For a full month the nine companies of the First Michigan remained in these bleak quarters where they received the same low-level training given them at home. By early October Brodhead was bragging to his mother of his "fine command," but even he admitted that his men were far from combat-ready. Through government foot-dragging the men had yet to draw sabers, pistols, carbines, or the last of their horse equipments; meanwhile, for want of transportation, their mounts remained in Michigan. Private Schmalzried expressed the prevalent belief that nothing was expected of the regiment in Washington: "I do not believe that we will ever be called to make a field campaign, or to take part in a battle, so we simply have to be satisfied with lying around until they send us home again."[33]

Days filled with long stretches of inactivity and listless drill in which the regiment merely imitated cavalrymen began to take their toll. Disgruntled recruits began to pose disciplinary problems, and some officers began to neglect their duties. Early in October Brodhead had to arrest Captain Backus for drinking while on duty as officer of the day. Backus's conduct prompted the colonel to remind everyone that "it is not in the field of battle that the highest and best qualities of a Soldier are developed." He stressed that "the careful observance of the etiquette of the camp... can only be learned by instructions and example of officers sober, moral & competent." Perhaps mindful of Backus's family connections, Brodhead restored him to command hours after his arrest. The captain, however, may have considered himself under a cloud he could never evade, for he resigned his commission two months later.[34]

In late October two events breathed life into the regiment's training program. On the twenty-ninth the remaining three companies arrived in camp, followed a few days later by boxcars carrying 1,200 horses. At about this same time the troopers drew pistols, sabers, a panoply of horse equipment, and their primary weapon, the Burnside carbine, a breechloading percussion firearm that fired a 54-caliber metallic cartridge. Named for a Union general who would later command the Army of the Potomac, the Burnside was easy to fire and reload, was light enough to use in the saddle, and packed a wicked punch. A trooper in another regiment described the carbine as "convenient and pretty as well as destructive..." Exaggerating somewhat, he added that "one can load and fire them 10 times per minute... through a sheet iron bar."[35]

Fully armed and accoutred at long last, the regiment began to drill with a degree of enthusiasm previously lacking. The training pace did not slacken when, on 26 November, the regiment mounted up and moved to a new Camp Brodhead. Led out Seventh Street through Georgetown, then along the road to Rockville, Maryland, the ungainly column halted on a partially wooded tract astride the western outskirts of the District of Columbia. Breaking ranks, the men began to construct what rumor said would be only a temporary home. Within hours Frederic Schmalzried could report major results: "The tents are put up in rows, each Company starting a new row, with the officers' tents on the upper end of each row and the kitchen at the lower end.... The horses are tied between the rows. How long we are going to stay here, I do not know. I hope, though, that it will not last long.... It seems to be a healthy place, but not a very pretty spot for a company to be in."[36]

The young immigrant was made happier a few days later, when the outfit was mustered for its first pay, covering two months' service. With money in his pocket, Schmalzried proclaimed that "I never had it better since I've been in America than I have it now." Reading over what he had written, he begged his family not to consider him a mercenary: "You may think this war is [fought] for the sake of money. It is truly so in a way but it is also to preserve the Union," a goal to which all patriots should commit themselves.[37]

The regiment's stay along the Rockville Road proved to be as brief as the rumor mill had predicted—barely two weeks. The interval was insufficient to bring the First to an acceptable level of proficiency and deportment, but it provided an additional lesson in roughing-it. The camp lay in an isolated area bereft of good drinking water and any creature comforts whatever. In this cheerless experience, Brodhead and some of his subordinates refused to share. While thin canvas protected the men against late-autumn winds, the colonel and his staff enjoyed warm beds courtesy of neighboring Unionists with whom they lodged. Few of the enlisted men appear to have complained about the situation, chalking it up to the prerogatives of rank.[38]

On the morning of 10 December, the regiment relocated for the fourth time in its brief existence. Striking camp in the pre-dawn darkness, the men trotted eastward, Colonel Brodhead in the lead, a long line of supply wagons, ambulances, and travelling forges in the rear. Retracing its route through Georgetown, the column turned sharply north in the heart of Washington. The new heading took the First up Pennsylvania Avenue past President Lincoln's residence. Some of the troopers wondered if Old Abe were at the window to see them go by, admiring their soldierly bearing. In point of fact, bystanders told Brodhead that his outfit was the finest body of horsemen to pass up that storied thoroughfare. Considering the thousands of troopers—including those spit-and-polish fellows in the regular army—who had trod those cobblestones since the outbreak of the war, such compliments left the First Michigan feeling justly proud.[39]

The march, which took the regiment above the city and across the Potomac River, was by far the longest the recruits had made. It covered sixty miles, consumed more than twenty hours, and ended with the First in the Maryland countryside. En route, the regiment had some adventures. Some of the wagons broke down and had to be repaired on the spot; others became inextricably mired in the mud that coated stretches of the Frederick Pike. The first night out, the regiment bivouacked in a farm field. Several troopers sought protection from the December winds by lying close to a haystack that collapsed as they slept, nearly suffocating them.[40]

The next morning, as the again-mobile column passed through the village of Hyattstown, Corporal Cox and a comrade from Company G dropped out of ranks to seek a libation that would ease the fatigue and monotony of travel. From a local farmer they purchased "a pint of the vilest whiskey that ever passed a person's lips." Repressing an urge to spit it out, the men drank until they found themselves "in good trim for any kind of a joke." Upon rejoining the column they fabricated a report that two regiments of Rebel cavalry had crossed the Potomac for the express purpose of cutting off the First Michigan. Corporal Cox noted happily that the tale "was not long in going from one end of the marching column to the other, and the rumor actually got to be believed by nine-tenths of the regiment." Cox and his partner in deception shared a guffaw when Quartermaster James I. David issued extra rounds of ammunition to ward off the pursuers. After some hours of unmolested marching, however, everyone "relapsed into our wonted carelessness and composure."[41]

The second night on the march found the regiment at the southern extremity of its destination, a high, wooded plateau two miles from Frederick City. The venue, which brought the troopers much nearer to their enemy than ever before, told them their active service had truly begun. Frederick housed the field headquarters of Major General Nathaniel P. Banks, commander of an army corps assigned to the Department of the Potomac. One of the most celebrated political-generals in the Union ranks—the Massachusetts legislator had risen to Speaker of the U.S. House of Representatives—Banks occupied an advanced position in the foothills of western Maryland, an area teeming with Confederate regulars, guerrillas, and bushwhackers. The most recent offering of the rumor mill was that the First Michigan had been sent here to serve as the corps leader's personal escort. While many scoffed at the notion, others smiled to think that an elite assignment might be conferred on a regiment so new to the field.[42]

Suspicious that Rebels lurked nearby, the troopers were especially wary the next morning as they made their way into Frederick. But nothing untoward marred their passage through streets where the local populace (most of it pro-Unionist) was going about its daily business as though war were a distant memory. Only at intervals did warlike reminders come into view: blue-clad sentinels, defensive works, artillery emplacements.

The march, which took the First out the northern end of the city, continued for another four miles. Brodhead finally halted the column on open ground fringed by "a beautiful piece of timber" owned by a farmer named Worman. Despite the reported proximity of the enemy, the area appeared defensible enough to ease the mind as well as pretty enough to please the eye. Neighboring farms overflowed with other regiments of all arms, the rear echelon of Banks's command.

At a signal, the horsemen dismounted, hobbled their mounts, and dug into the supply wagons. Within an hour or so the meadow that sloped gently towards Worman's woods abounded with "doghouses." A bit later, company streets had been laid out, and the latest incarnation of Camp Brodhead had taken on a semi-permanent look. That look made the troopers believe they had reached a place where they would stay a spell, a place they might even come to regard as home.[43]

The early indications were valid ones: the First Michigan would remain on Farmer Worman's property for the next two months. The period would encompass the truly formative stage of the regiment's existence, an interval during which the First Michigan would evolve from an aggregation of untutored youngsters on some improbable adventure into a cohesive body of veterans familiar with every facet of their mission and looking forward to their baptism of fire.

CHAPTER TWO

Active Operations

More than a thousand miles west of the First Michigan's camp-site—back in the state it had left on the day it went to war—a young officer who would figure prominently in the fortunes of the regiment was dreaming desperately of martial glory. Much luck would be needed to make the dreams come true, but twenty-two-year-old Second Lieutenant George Armstrong Custer—then on leave from the army, visiting his stepsister in Monroe, Michigan—was an optimist of the first rank.

Already his brief military career had been blessed with such good fortune it seemed the stuff of fiction. Scion of a working class family—his father had operated a smithy shop and had farmed in New Rumley and Wood County, Ohio, as well as briefly in Monroe—young Custer had forged political connections strong enough to gain appointment to the U.S. Military Academy. An indifferent student, a fun-seeker addicted to escapades that cost him privileges and lowered his academic standing, he nevertheless man-aged to graduate with (although at the foot of) the Class of June 1861. And despite his lowly status as junior officer in the Fifth United States Cavalry, he had attracted the attention of powerful superiors including Brigadier General Philip Kearny, on whose staff Custer had served since August 1861. Under Kearny the young subaltern had rendered such conspicuous service that he had reason to anticipate promotion and even a field command of his own.[1]

Originally, Custer had hoped to avoid war. As the offspring of staunch Democrats, he did not embrace a conflict directed by a Republican administration. At West Point his upbringing and his natural inclination had drawn him to Southern-born cadets, whose political, social, and economic values he shared. Custer had dreaded the portents raised by Abraham Lincoln's election to the presidency. "You cannot imagine how sorry I will be to see this [disunion] happen," he had written his stepsister, Lydia Ann Reed, "as the majority of my best friends and all my room mates except one have been from the South." Late in his Academy career, as the country slid inexorably toward war, Custer had been torn by conflicting attachments—his cadet friendships and empathy with the Southern way of life; and his allegiance to Ohio, Michigan, and the Union.

In the end, he suppressed misgivings and opted to fight for his region and his nation. Once in the fray, he found he possessed a natural aptitude for field service as well as the ability to ignore the terrors of the battlefield. In time he shed his aversion to civil strife, informing a cousin that although he abhorred the misery and suffering it produced, "I shall regret to see the war end. I would be willing, yes glad, to see a battle every day during my life...."[2]

War was, of course, a springboard to career advancement, something Custer pursued with the zeal of an old Regular. His Academy record notwithstanding, he considered himself qualified to command. Physically, at least, he was warrior material. He stood only three inches below six feet tall, and his erect bearing and athletic physique—he weighed a trim 176 pounds—made him look even taller. His muddy blonde hair, which he wore long and occasionally in ringlets, framed a cherubic face that he sometimes disguised behind a fierce mustache.

Custer affected the carriage and demeanor of an older, more experienced soldier, brimming with maturity and confidence. And yet he could not repress the exuberance and impetuosity of youth. An incurable romantic, he could look past war's carnage to view it as something grand, even ennobling. Perhaps because he was so young, a sense of invincibility freed him from concern over his physical safety. A studied disregard of danger was one of the qualities that distinguished his mentor, General Kearny, whom Custer considered "a very gallant leader." The New York-born soldier-of-fortune, veteran of wars on several continents (one of which had cost him an arm), stressed that a leader "must never be frightened of anything."[3]

Custer's association with Phil Kearny, while close and cordial, was also brief. In late 1861, when army headquarters forbade Regulars from serving on the staff of a general of volunteers, Custer reluctantly rejoined his regiment, which remained attached to the Army of the Potomac. In October, however, he abruptly returned to Michigan on sick leave. The nature of his illness remains unknown, but it was severe enough that after his recovery Custer told a West Point friend that he nearly died of it.

There is a rather strong possibility that Custer's medical problems were the result of amorous indiscretions. Since youth he had been attracted to, and been attractive to, the opposite sex. In his late teens and early twenties he had carried on a romantic (and probably a sexual) relationship with at least a couple of young women from his Ohio hometown. Evidently his libido remained active during his career at the Military Academy; in the summer of 1859, while on a furlough in New York City, he contracted a venereal disease, recurrent symptoms of which appear to have plagued him through the remainder of his life. The infection may have rendered him sterile.

Perhaps the severity of the malady that sent him home in October 1861 wrought a change in his personal habits. There are no indications that Custer engaged in dalliances during the following year. Later, he would turn his attention to a handsome young woman of virtue and decorum to whom he would pay serious court, Elizabeth ("Libbie") Bacon, daughter of Judge Daniel Bacon of the Michigan Circuit Court.

A second major change occurred late in 1861. Soon after recovering from his mystery illness, the young lieutenant—once a regular customer of Benny Havens's Tavern, West Point's fabled watering hole—came staggering back to Lydia Ann Reed's home after a long night of drink. Unamused by her brother's condition, Lydia lectured him so sternly that he became a convert to temperance. Thereafter, as far as can be determined, he avoided liquor.

Custer passed the remainder of his Michigan furlough in good health and sobriety. Although no evidence confirms it, it seems likely that, given his strong ambition and his unassigned status, he sought a position in some Michigan volunteer regiment, a berth that would gain him more of the rank and authority he craved. If so, his quest ended inconclusively, for in February 1862 he entrained for the East to rejoin his regiment.

He made the trip as a lowly lieutenant without prospect of promotion. Still, he must have been excited by what the future held for him. By all indications, his life and career were in transition. If the war lasted long enough, he might become a captain—dare he hope, even a major—some day.[4]

* * *

Custer was not alone in viewing active campaigning as an agent of desirable change. Lolling in Camp Brodhead in the meadows outside Frederick, Maryland, Frederic Schmalzried wished that the First Michigan Cavalry would "fight a battle, and bring this thing to an end.... Laying around all day is not very pleasant." The German-American believed that timidity and vacillation on the part of the high command was postponing the inevitable. Since war meant fighting, better to meet the Rebels sooner rather than later. A good many of his comrades—most had been in service for more than three months without hearing shots fired in anger—shared Schmalzried's sentiments.[5]

Technically, a few troopers had seen action. One day after the First reached Frederick, a Rebel patrol crossed the Potomac, slipped through a crease in the regiment's picket line, and made for the corrals in the rear of the camp. Guards fired on the intruders, keeping them from the horses and chasing them across the water. The repulse gratified the regiment, but since so few had been engaged the First Michigan remained untested.[6]

The situation had not changed by year's end. The troopers continued to perform picket duty along the river and escort service at General Banks's headquarters, to scout the countryside for stray Confederates, and, as time permitted, to continue the drill they had last practiced in the suburbs of Washington. Camp life had settled into a monotonous routine that wearied many recruits. The camp itself had become "a slavish place," in the opinion of Trooper Joseph Gillet, "all scrub and scour." The collective impatience with the status quo increased everyone's longing for action.[7]

Even so, there was something to be said for remaining out of combat. For one thing, the horses of the regiment, many of them only recently broken to riding, might respond to gunfire by endangering their riders. Private Schmalzried believed that battle would be extraordinarily dangerous "with such horses as we have. They would start running, possibly right into the hands of the enemy, and if shooting should begin, nobody could hold or lead them."[8]

Another, more disquieting, reason for the regiment's unreadiness was that many of its ranking officers were not with it. The commander and namesake of Camp Brodhead had returned to Michigan to attend to regimental and personal business. For physical reasons, Major Town had joined him early in 1862. Frail from the outset, the major's health had deteriorated after he received in mid-November the news of his wife's death. On 27 January, Assistant Surgeon Alfred Nash feared that Town's pulmonary condition would kill him unless he received medical treatment and rest. At the doctor's urging, General Banks granted Town a two months' furlough. Meanwhile, several company officers were serving on detached duty, many at brigade and division headquarters. Others had tendered their resignations for health reasons. Still other officers, unequal to the demands of their position or hopelessly incompetent, had been forced to surrender their commissions.[9]

Ready or not, in the early weeks of 1862 the regiment appeared on the verge of active operations. On the fifth, with Camp Brodhead blanketed with a five-inch snowfall, orders came to pack two days' rations, sharpen sabers, and "be ready to march at a moment's notice." According to reports, another band of invaders—this one estimated at a thousand strong—had forced its way across the Potomac to strike an outpost near Hagerstown, twenty-five miles northwest of Frederick. A breathless letter from Sergeant Delevan Arnold of Company I ("maybe the last that I ever shall write") informed his mother in Kalamazoo that "we are waiting with horses saddled and every thing ready for the word to march on Hagerstown where there is, or is to be, a battle."[10]

The sergeant's anxiety soon subsided. Reports of the Rebel incursion proved to be overblown, and the majority of the regiment advanced no farther than its picket lines. Two companies, however, were temporarily detached from the main body for special service.

One was sent to Hagerstown, the other to Hancock, two dozen miles to the west. In both places the troopers guarded turnpikes, railroads, and telegraph lines. A rumor sprang up that the rest of the regiment would join them; instead, the estranged companies returned to Frederick.[11]

The First remained in place for the next six weeks, virtually immobilized by snow-covered earth and frozen roads. The weather affected the outfit in a number of ways. It prompted an issuance of weatherproof clothing as well as whole uniforms to men whose original attire had worn too thin to ward off the elements. Precipitation and plunging temperatures played hob with the regiment's health. Several troopers came down with fever and chills, and on 4 February Sergeant Everett W. Lusk of Company I succumbed to typhoid after a week-long illness. Lusk's was the first death in the ranks since the First took the field. Sergeant Arnold, who commanded the squad that escorted the remains to the local depot, observed that "he and myself were fast friends, always sharing with each other like two brothers, and I feel his loss keenly. I should rather he had died upon the field of battle."[12]

* * *

In the final days of February the First Michigan at last embarked on active operations. The movement had its roots in the strategy of Major General George B. McClellan, who not only had superseded Irvin McDowell at the head of the Army of the Potomac but had replaced the aged Winfield Scott as commanding general of the armies of the United States.

As the winter entered its final month, "Little Mac" determined to end his hibernation and lead his 112,000-man army against perhaps half as many Confederates ensconced in the Bull Run-Manassas Junction area. Aware that an earlier advance toward Richmond had ended disastrously, McClellan vowed to avoid his predecessor's mistakes. To ensure that enemy forces in the Shenandoah did not link with their comrades in northern Virginia, he ordered Nathaniel Banks to neutralize any threats the Valley Confederates might pose to his offensive. Banks's initial objectives included Harpers Ferry, Charles Town, and Winchester, as well as the Rebel army that for the past three months had been operating in those parts under Major General Thomas Jonathan ("Stonewall") Jackson.[13]

When the bugles sounded throughout Camp Brodhead on the morning of the twenty-fourth, the notes brought a sense of relief to many Michiganders. They had been prevented from earning their pay for too long; the oft-delayed expectation of field service had become unnerving. The order to mount up also quashed rumors of the regiment's imminent disbanding. Even those, like Frederic Schmalzried, who had grown weary of cavalry service and wished to go home, found marching orders preferable to mindless routine.

Once arranged in marching formation, the regiment started for the Potomac and the recently reoccupied Union garrison at Harpers Ferry. Under the scrutiny of Thornton Brodhead—just returned from his sojourn in Detroit—the men moved south at a brisk pace despite the slowness of the wagons, ambulances, and forges that accompanied them. The day was frigid and windy but the ground was no longer frozen; the result was "a cold muddy march."[14]

This day the regiment was not at full strength: only the battalions of Majors Town and Angelo Paldi of Brockway, formerly commander of Company G, made the journey toward Harpers Ferry. A few days ago, Banks had dispatched the First Battalion—Companies A, C, D, and E, under the regiment's junior major, twenty-one-year-old William S. Atwood of Ypsilanti—to the Potomac in advance of the main body. There Atwood's troopers would join an infantry column under Colonel John White Geary of the Twenty-eighth Pennsylvania Volunteers. Banks had directed Geary—a seasoned troubleshooter dating from his prewar stint as governor of the volatile and violent Kansas Territory—to occupy the disputed region around Harpers Ferry. Once Banks reached that point, Geary was to secure other enemy-occupied regions, clearing opposition from the path of the army.

Atwood's battalion would serve apart from the bulk of the First Michigan for nearly five months. For most of that period it would help Geary's foot soldiers safeguard Banks's communications as the latter moved south against Jackson. After Harpers Ferry, Geary's primary mission would be to patrol the vast sector of northeastern Virginia known as Loudoun County—a haven for Confederate

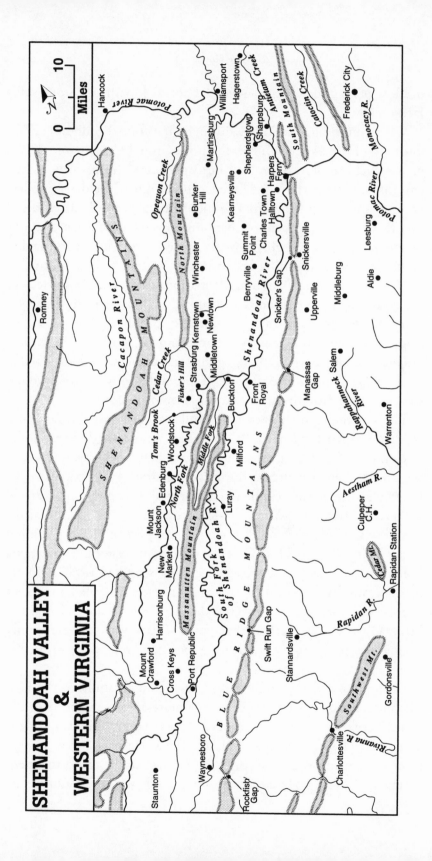

regulars and partisans. Geary's area of operations would run south from the Potomac crossings to the Manassas Gap Railroad, a critical supply route that was vulnerable to attack by raiders operating on both sides of the Bull Run Mountains. Whenever these destroyers eluded interception, Atwood's troopers and their infantry comrades had to repair the damage they inflicted on tracks, ties, and rolling stock.[15]

The work demanded of the First Battalion, which involved riding from one threatened point to another dozens of miles apart, would prove extremely taxing. From late February until the outset of May, Atwood's horsemen would operate near Harpers Ferry and Sandy Hook, Maryland, as well as in such Virginia locales as Lovettsville, Leesburg, Waterford, Middleburg, Snickersville, Upperville, Aldie, White Plains, Warrenton Junction, Catlett Station, Piedmont, Rectortown, Salem, Markham, and Linden. Such service would give the battalion—and by extension the First Michigan Cavalry—what one Wolverine called "a mad and roving commission—here today and gone tomorrow."[16]

On their march to Harpers Ferry, Town's and Paldi's battalions encountered few of the hazards that Atwood faced. For support Atwood could call on a regiment or two of foot troops, but the main body of the First marched south in company with 25,000 comrades: three brigades of infantry, five batteries of light artillery, and 350 other troopers. And whereas every Loudoun County ridge and woodlot might conceal the enemy, Nathaniel Banks expected to meet no troublemakers until well inside the Valley. He was not mistaken; his journey to the Potomac was unimpeded save for some burned bridges that a retreating Jackson had left behind.[17]

Most of these obstacles cropped up after the invaders reached Harpers Ferry on the twenty-fifth. That morning Banks's advance ground to a halt on the upper bank of the Potomac, prepared for an indeterminate stay. The First Michigan went into bivouac for two days, its men watching intently as engineers struggled to throw a pontoon bridge over the choppy river. The culmination of this effort—which reached from shore to shore just above the ruins of the old railroad bridge—struck Delevan Arnold as "one of the nicest pieces of work that I ever saw." The regiment crossed the floating span on the twenty-seventh. In its rear trudged the dozen other outfits that comprised Banks's vanguard. On the far side, Sergeant Arnold pronounced himself "fairly in the land of *Secesh.*"[18]

Feelings of gloom and unease buffeted the troopers as they trotted through the village where, three years before, John Brown had tried to foment a slave rebellion. The place appeared deserted. Streets lay awash in rubble, and the local armory and arsenal, in which Brown had taken refuge before forced to surrender, had been stripped of materiel valuable to the Confederacy. The ambience of bleakness and desolation troubled some of the more sensitive members of the First. Over the next three years they would recognize the same characteristics in many another town whose fate it was to be caught between the contending armies.

After bivouacking for the night in the heart of town, the regiment was roused before dawn on the twenty-eighth. In feeble daylight the troopers started southwestward toward Charles Town, seat of Jefferson County, Virginia, and site of "Old Osawatomie" Brown's appointment with the gallows. As Charles Town was thought to be held in force, the eight-mile jaunt was a study in caution and deliberation. Not until Banks's force reached the outskirts, however, did it come under fire, at long range, from sharpshooters perched in downtown buildings.[19]

By then the expeditionary commander had positioned two battalions of the First, sabers drawn, at the head of his column, supported closely by two regiments of artillery and two batteries. As the troopers poised on the edge of town, Colonel Brodhead called up a squadron composed of Companies F (commanded by Captain Henry K. White) and G (First Lieutenant Frederick A. Copeland, twenty-five-year-old son of the regiment's executive officer). When the dispositions were complete buglers signalled the regiment's first mounted charge of the war. "Down we came," wrote Sergeant Arnold, "the horses at a dead run, right through the centre [sic] of the town. But the birds (that is the secesh cavalry) had flown, so we took possession of the town, and waited for the Infantry and Artillery to come up and hold the place...."[20]

When the supports arrived, Captain White's squadron pursued the fugitives along two roads out of town. Eager to close with their quarry or at least come within carbine-range of it, two detachments of the First kept up the chase for several miles until "the running qualities of the Southern chivalry" prevailed. Disappointed Wolverines returned to Charles Town with their only captures, two wagonloads of Rebel flour and a few discarded firearms. While the haul was a meager one, the regiment could take satisfaction in having forced the foe to scatter in panic and confusion. The dash through Charles Town would become a source of pride for everyone in the regiment as well as for their families and friends at home. Michigan newspapers would pay tribute to the "dashing charges and gallant behavior" of the regiment during its first—albeit brief—experience under fire.[21]

* * *

When Banks's main body closed up on Charles Town, it established a fixed camp. For the next week the First Michigan did provost duty throughout the region, picketed the roads out of town, and scouted toward the Blue Ridge Mountains in the direction of Winchester, where Stonewall Jackson was reported to be plotting something nefarious. All elements of the regiment earned their pay. The military police kept Banks's camps in good order, the pickets nabbed upward of a dozen Rebels lurking in the countryside, and the scouts reported that Jackson would offer little opposition should Banks force the mountain passes.

Satisfied with his prospects, Banks renewed his advance on the morning of 10 March, the First Michigan in the lead. Late that day the invasion column waded the Shenandoah River to Berryville. At that point Banks's advance lay ten miles from Winchester, a strategic road center at the bottom (i.e., on the northern flank) of the Valley. Banks intended to make Winchester his base of operations; the only question was whether Jackson would remain to greet him or would depart early. Deciding to remain in Berryville until able to answer that question, Banks encamped most of the Michiganders on the outskirts of the town while detachments of their outfit probed southward.[22]

When, on the evening of the twelfth, the scouts returned word that Winchester appeared on the verge of evacuation, Banks prepared to move. To preserve the advantage of surprise, he led his column on a moonlit march to Bunker Hill, twelve miles north of his objective. Then, early on the thirteenth, he pushed forward to Jackson's headquarters with the infantry of Brigadier General Charles S. Hamilton, screened by Companies K and L of the First Michigan plus thirty men of Company H. The mounted force was led by Captain Mann of Company K, who despite his youth—he was not yet twenty-three—was known for both initiative and prudence.

Reaching the entrenchments that Jackson's men had dug a mile east of town, Mann's advance found them empty. The captain also discovered that a band of Jackson's cavalry under the celebrated Turner Ashby had taken post on the far side of Winchester, as though daring the Federals to come on. Although his infantry friends halted short of town, Captain Mann responded to the challenge. Leaving Company H to secure his flanks, he sent Company L around the town to make a display that would draw Colonel Ashby's attention. This tactic held the enemy in place, whereupon Mann rode to the head of his own company and led it, shouting and shooting, through the rutted streets of Winchester. Startled by the offensive, the Confederates held their ground only briefly. Well before the charging Wolverines reached them, the Southerners wheeled about and galloped off. A triumphant Company K pursued for five miles. Although most of the Rebels had too great a jump to be overtaken, Mann's people snatched half a dozen stragglers. Later in the day, after Brodhead brought up the main body, Captain Brewer renewed the pursuit at the head of Company L. Brewer found some grayclads lingering a few miles out; he put them to flight, chased them down, and took four prisoners at no cost to himself.

Like the sprint through Charles Town, Mann's and Brewer's attacks gave the regiment a sense of satisfaction and accomplishment, one out of proportion to its field experience. The thought began to spread through the ranks: if Ashby's troopers—regarded as the most tenacious in Confederate service—could not stand against the massed might of the First Michigan, who could?[23]

* * *

Once Banks secured Winchester, detachments of the First Michigan and allied regiments ventured up the Valley. They returned word that Jackson had retreated—lock, stock, and rear guard—toward

Strasburg. Banks reacted curiously. Instead of following up his initial success, he remained in the lower Valley as though convinced that Jackson had been cowed, overawed—beaten into submission short of a pitched battle.

For the next several days, the Massachusetts general deployed his troops—members of the new V Corps, Army of the Potomac—around Winchester and its environs, including the hamlet of Kernstown, two miles to the south. He also prepared to assimilate reinforcements, the 12,000-man division of Brigadier General James Shields, an Irish-born veteran of the Mexican War whose busy political career included a term as governor of Illinois and stints as U.S. Senator from Oregon and Minnesota. Formerly commanding in western Virginia and along the upper Potomac, Shields had reached Martinsburg, twenty-three miles above Winchester, on 11 March, before advancing to meet his fellow-Democrat, Banks.[24]

Linking with Shields two days later, Banks finally extended the pursuit beyond Kernstown, sparring listlessly with the Rebel rear guard along the Valley Pike. Sensing his enemy's tentativeness, "Old Jack" was far from intimidated by their advance; even so, he kept moving. By the twentieth his vanguard was at Mount Jackson, almost forty miles south of Winchester.

That day, his pursuers shuddered to a halt outside Strasburg, then countermarched as though unwilling to devote more time to a needless chore. Part of Shields's division remained at Kernstown but the rest of the Union column returned to Winchester. To provide an early-warning system, Shields stationed Major Paldi with his old unit, Company G of the First, in advance of the infantry.

Neither Paldi's men, who began picketing the trails south of Kernstown, nor the rest of the regiment, stationed outside Winchester, expected to remain in the Valley for more than another day or two. Fast-flying rumors said that the entire army soon would head east to join McClellan on the Peninsula. As Sergeant George Kilborn of Company F informed a correspondent from Lapeer, Michigan, "we are still advancing slowly but surely on Richmond."[25]

The return to Winchester paid dividends for the main body of the regiment. Colonel Brodhead had been detached from the First to command all the cavalry under Banks: several companies from

Pennsylvania, Ohio, and western Virginia in addition to his own regiment. Brodhead's absence left the First in the hands of Lieutenant Colonel Copeland, who appears to have been less the disciplinarian than his superior. While Copeland averted his gaze, the regiment began to forage off the land with a thoroughness previously lacking. Sergeant Kilborn wrote of the "gay old times" he and his comrades enjoyed while "bringing in... lawful plunder" from local farms. Kilborn observed solemnly that "the boys think... too much raw meat, poor coffee & hard bread are not good for the stomach, unless it be seasoned with a little chicken broth & honey & such fixings."[26]

The gay old times ended abruptly on 22 March when Paldi's scouts observed large numbers of cavalry advancing down the Valley Pike from Strasburg. At Banks's direction, at about two P.M. Brodhead dispatched Joseph Copeland, with a battalion of the First, to join Company G, which had fallen back to a point midway between Kernstown and Winchester. Copeland dismounted his companies; deployed them, along with Paldi's unit, behind underbrush, fences, and farm buildings; and had them bang away at the head of Ashby's column. The brisk fire brought the latter to a halt and initiated two hours of long-range skirmishing.[27]

Some time after four o'clock General Shields came up to Copeland's position at the head of a small infantry column, accompanied by his cavalry leader. Brodhead continued to delegate operational authority to Copeland, to whom he assigned four companies of the First (West) Virginia Cavalry and two companies of a Pennsylvania unit known as the Ringgold Battalion. While Copeland fed the newcomers into his skirmish line, Shields and Brodhead rode forward to select positions for the infantry. Topping a ridge perhaps three-quarters of a mile below Kernstown, the two gained a clear view of the Valley Pike, which swarmed with dismounted Rebels. Brodhead cautioned Shields against advancing farther; a line of hills opposite them held a unit of horse artillery. Rejecting this sound advice, the brigadier continuing south toward the rising tumult of combat. Suddenly an artillery round burst beside his horse, mangling Shields's shoulder and hurling him to the ground.[28]

After the general had been carried to the rear, still accompanied by Brodhead, the now-outflanked Confederates broke contact and drew off. Wary that they might return, Copeland picketed southward toward Front Royal and westward toward Romney with the West Virginia and Pennsylvania companies. When Brodhead sent back for it, Copeland returned the First Michigan to Winchester, with instructions to report at cavalry headquarters come morning.[29]

Dawn held the promise of an eastward movement. Discounting the possibility that Ashby's advance signalled Jackson's intention to retake Winchester, Nathaniel Banks saw no reason to postpone his march toward Richmond. In fact, that movement was already in progress; the infantry division of Brigadier General Alpheus S. Williams, with Brigadier General John J. Abercrombie's brigade well in advance, had started for the Blue Ridge on the twenty-second. The Michigan cavalry appeared fated to join the exodus at the next opportunity.

It was not to be. No sooner had the First reported to Brodhead early on the twenty-third than Shields's temporary successor, Colonel Nathan Kimball, ordered most of it back to Kernstown in response to the ominous booming of artillery. Confounding his enemy, Jackson had sent infantry—the vanguard of his storied "Stonewall Brigade"—to support Ashby in an attempt to regain Winchester. Anxious to prevent Banks from opposing Joe Johnston near Richmond, Jackson was determined to keep his enemy in the Valley; the best way to do so was to strike hard at Banks's rear.[30]

At first, Jackson's aggressiveness achieved success. The few Federals near Kernstown, including the cavalry companies Copeland had stationed outside town, retreated under the pressure of Ashby's main body. The Rebel drive took on added weight at about ten A.M. when the advance contingent of the Stonewall Brigade reached the scene. Soon Copeland was being pushed through Kernstown and Ashby's troopers were occupying high ground to the north.[31]

Shortly before noon, Kimball's advance, including the five companies of the First Michigan that had been engaged the previous day, reached the scene of action, and the tide quickly reversed. Kimball's infantry, supported by well-positioned cannon, thrust Ashby's troopers back up the pike and reclaimed the lost ground. Backed by the Virginia and Pennsylvania horsemen lent them previously, as well as by three companies of the First Maryland Cavalry and a squadron of the First Ohio, Copeland and Paldi guarded the flanks and rear of the infantry, covered some of the more exposed artillery units, and resumed picketing south of Kernstown.

Having regained the initiative, Kimball moved to sweep the enemy from his front. Leaving Company F of the First Michigan, under Lieutenant William H. Freeman, to guard batteries along the Union right, Lieutenant Colonel Copeland prepared to support Kimball's advance with every other trooper at his disposal. These he stacked in close column of squadrons immediately in rear of the infantry.

When the line, several thousand strong, lurched southward some time after four P.M., it lacked coordination; consequently, it suffered a repulse. Realigning his forces, Kimball went forward again under a heavier barrage than before. This time he dislodged Jackson's forces not only along the Valley Pike but farther west, between the Middle Road and Opequon Creek. Overwhelmed, the Stonewall Brigade fell back slowly, then hastily and in some confusion.

The troopers under Copeland helped turn repulse into rout. Guiding his squadrons through a woodlot that fringed the Middle Road, the lieutenant colonel made contact with the Confederate left, blistered it with carbine fire, and threatened it with a mounted charge. When the enemy began to melt away, Copeland ordered a full-tilt pursuit. He reported proudly that "this order was received with enthusiasm and executed with alacrity," especially by the Michiganders under Captain Josiah B. Park and Lieutenants W. W. Gray, Michael F. Gallagher, and William M. Heazlit.

Charging across farm fields, topping wood and stone fences "under a shower of balls," the men of Michigan swarmed over the Stonewall Brigade, lashing the fugitives with carbine fire and saber strokes, capturing a couple hundred of them. The pursuit continued up the pike, horsemen screaming in amazed delight as they ran their quarry to earth. Thanks to their opponents' demoralization, the attackers absorbed few casualties, the most serious being a disabling wound to Captain Park.[32]

By sundown it was over. Working frantically, Ashby's men cobbled together a rear guard whose delaying tactics saved their comrades from annihilation. But the belated heroics could neither prevent the Michigan cavalry from savoring its first battlefield victory nor save Stonewall Jackson from his first defeat.[33]

CHAPTER THREE

Hard Fought Fields

*A*fter bivouacking on the ground they had won, the five companies of the First Michigan engaged at Kernstown took up the pursuit early on the twenty-fourth in the direction of Strasburg. They expected to be joined en route by Companies H and I, which had spent the previous day in Winchester, but in this they were disappointed. Already bereft not only of Atwood's battalion but of Captain Brewer's Company L, which had been on escort duty at corps headquarters since before Kernstown, the regiment now lost its rear-guard squadron to the same mission. This day both companies started eastward from Winchester under the senior commissioned officer, Captain Thomas M. Howrigan of Company H. At Manassas Junction they would join General Abercrombie's brigade, which had departed the Valley shortly before Kernstown. For the next few weeks the squadron would serve as bodyguard to Abercrombie, whose troops were guarding sections of the vast rail network that connected Banks's and McClellan's forces.[1]

Although distressed by this latest drain on regimental strength, the companies under Copeland and Paldi were buoyed by the accolades bestowed upon them throughout the twenty-fourth by comrades who had witnessed their performance at Kernstown. Such praise would be echoed by General Banks in a general order, disseminated throughout his corps, commending the "activity and bravery of the 1st Michigan Cavalry." The First was the only mounted unit to be honored in this way.[2]

Not everyone appeared to be impressed by the army's horsemen. The day before Banks published his praise, General Shields, still in Winchester recovering from his wound, telegraphed departmental headquarters that the cavalry supporting his division "is not efficient in the field." Later that day, Shields wired the newly appointed secretary of war, Edwin McMasters Stanton, to complain that "my cavalry is very ineffective. If I had had one regiment of excellent cavalry... I could have doubled the enemy's loss" at Kernstown.[3]

Since Shields was not on the field during the twenty-third, his conclusions are open to dispute. Nevertheless, his criticism appears to have been detrimental to Colonel Brodhead. The colonel had not served actively at Kernstown owing to feeble health; immediately after the battle he reported himself so debilitated that he could not remain on his feet. Shields may have considered Brodhead's inactivity the result of moral rather than physical weakness. At any rate, on the twenty-eighth Brodhead learned he was to be superseded in command of Banks's cavalry by a transferee from McDowell's corps, Brigadier General John Porter Hatch. Upon Hatch's arrival, Brodhead would reassume command of the First Michigan.[4]

Before Hatch could take over a force that would eventually comprise five regiments and twenty-four separate companies, Banks's vanguard had halted at Strasburg, nine miles from Winchester, where the Manassas Gap Railroad came in from the east. On the first day of April, elements of the occupying force, including a squadron of the First Michigan under Copeland, advanced down the railroad in the direction of Edenburg. A few miles out of Strasburg bands of Ashby's horsemen appeared astride the Valley Pike, precipitating what one Wolverine called "the usual running skirmish."[5]

The fight continued for nine miles. At Woodstock, just above Edenburg, Copeland took Company M of the First through the streets under fire from horse arillery that Ashby had positioned south of the town. Thankfully, the salvo passed over the heads of the troopers, who quickly pulled back into Woodstock. Under Captain Rollin C. Denison, they held the place until infantry and artillery arrived to drive away the foe.

Late in the day the pursuit resumed to Edenburg, where distant smoke indicated that Ashby, now augmented by infantry, had fired foot and railroad bridges spanning the North Fork of the Shenandoah River. At this juncture Colonel Brodhead, having regained his strength and still acting as Banks's cavalry chief, suddenly appeared, assumed command, and led Denison's company in a dash toward the nearest bridge, hoping to save it from destruction.

The rescue attempt was equally impulsive and hazardous. Along with Ashby's troopers and horse artillerists, at least a regiment of infantry had dug in on the south bank, concealed from view by the smoke. On Brodhead's approach, the combined force swept the road to the span with musket and carbine fire, shrapnel and canister. Looking on from the rear, Copeland and the remainder of the First feared disaster. When the salvo slackened, they were immensely relieved to see Brodhead leading the still-intact unit back from the river at breakneck speed. As at Strasburg, the enemy had fired too high to inflict more than a couple of casualties; Company M's luck was holding.[6]

Brodhead's men occupied Edenburg throughout the night. Come morning they were relieved by Banks's lead-footed infantry. Irked by the glacial pace the main army had kept up since Kernstown, Brodhead set a brisker gait when the pursuit resumed, the Confederates having evacuated Edenburg.

Over the next two weeks, the fight-and-fall-back tactics of Ashby, covering Jackson's retreat, ensured that the outfits under Brodhead saw action on almost a daily basis, often in the rain. An especially sharp encounter occurred near Mount Jackson, a Rebel concentration point astride the meandering Shenandoah River, on the morning of 15 April. The First Michigan gave a strong account of itself this day, expertly guarding the flanks as the suddenly active infantry forced the Confederates across the river and into positions near Rude's Hill.[7]

Early on the seventeenth Banks renewed the pursuit, an operation dependant on a successful crossing of the rain-swollen Shenandoah. To ensure that success, his cavalry rushed down to the unfordable stream, only to experience a reprise of the situation at Edenburg: the Confederates had set fire to the sole remaining bridge in hopes of slowing their pursuers if not to stop them altogether. The First Michigan, leading the advance, would have none of it. At Brodhead's order, a detachment of the regiment, supported by two companies of the First Ohio, charged the flaming structure under a fusillade from the opposite shore. At a critical moment the detachment found itself leaderless; stepping in to fill the void, Corporal George R. Maxwell of Company K ordered his comrades to dismount at river's edge, scoop up water in their high-crown hats, and douse the flames.

Thanks to a cover fire from the Ohioans, which forced the nearest Confederates to hug the earth, Maxwell's unit saved the bridge. Looking on from the rear, now-Brigadier General Kimball praised the "splendid dash" and "gallant charge" that had salvaged the pursuit. His commendation, seconded by Colonel Brodhead, would mean sergeant's stripes for Maxwell. The promotion would set the diminutive non-com on a meteoric course: he would end the war as a lieutenant colonel and regimental commander, with the brevet rank of colonel for gallantry in action.[8]

* * *

From Mount Jackson the game of foxes and hounds proceeded up the pike at an accelerating pace. By 23 April Banks had occupied New Market, near the top of the Valley. By this point Stonewall Jackson's once-invincible army had been all but driven from the Shenandoah, and the political general who had brought this to pass was celebrating "the permanent explusion of the rebel army" from its base of operations of the past four months.[9]

The First Michigan had carried its share of the pursuit, skirmishing with Jackson's rear guard along the pike, in roadside fields, atop rock-studded ridges. The extended combat took a heavy toll of men and horses. Even after Banks halted at Harrisonburg on the twenty-sixth to await the untangling of his attenuated supply lines, the cavalry continued to see action. During the last days of April the Wolverines probed toward Jackson's new perch at Swift Run Gap, twenty miles to the east. The intermittent skirmishing that flared up there drained regimental strength even further.[10]

The First was mightily relieved when, in early May, the army began to pull back. Alarmed by the assault on Kernstown, unmollified by Jackson's overthrow and subsequent withdrawal, on the first of the month the War Department directed Banks to return to the lower Valley. The army leader was to hold the Strasburg-Front Royal area with a single division while sending Shields east of the Blue Ridge. Washington had come to an appreciation of its vulnerability;

on the near side of the mountains Shields could parry any thrust by Jackson toward the capital.[11]

Shields's transfer would also aid George McClellan, then completing his siege of Yorktown. Via Front Royal and Manassas Gap, Shields would move to Fredericksburg to join the corps of Irvin McDowell. Shields's arrival would trigger McDowell's long-planned march to the Peninsula, an operation that Kernstown had postponed. Even the worrywart McClellan, given to downgrading his own strength and magnifying his opponents', believed that McDowell's 40,000 effectives would enable him to overwhelm Joe Johnston's pesky secessionists. That done, "Little Mac" would advance to Richmond to conclude the war before the close of spring.[12]

For his part, Nathaniel Banks liked the troop-transfer strategy not at all. After petitioning in vain to launch a full-strength offensve in coordination with the 10,000 troops operating in western Virginia under Major General John C. Fremont, the politician-general reluctantly obeyed the 1 May order. Five days later he began withdrawing to Strasburg and on the twelfth started Shields along the road to Fredericksburg.

As Banks fell back, his vanguard protected by the First Michigan (other horsemen under Hatch brought up the rear), Banks worried that he would be unable to guard adequately his new post—the fifty-mile plain that stretched from Strasburg north to the Potomac—with his reduced force of 9,000. Another concern was that his evacuation of the upper Valley would permit a reinforced Jackson—credible reports had him strengthened by 8,000 troops under Major General Richard S. Ewell and Brigadier General Edward Johnson—to operate more freely to the south, threatening the Federals from many directions. Only one bit of intelligence lessened Banks's sense of unease. Secretary Stanton had informed him that Fremont's command would enter the Shenandoah from the west to cooperate with what was left of the V Corps. The combined Union force should be a match for the 17,000 Confederates now in the theater.[13]

Although reinforcements were at hand, Banks truly had cause for concern. His retreat gave Jackson's resilient command a boost to morale and a strategic opportunity. The Union commander improved that opportunity by placing the majority of his reduced force (and the greater part of the First Michigan) at Strasburg, while attempting to hold Front Royal, on the east side of an intervening network of ridges known as Massanutten Mountain, with a thousand troops under Colonel John R. Kenly. Kenly's force was composed almost exclusively of infantry; its mounted support consisted of Companies H and I of the First Michigan, which had been released from escort duty to patrol that stretch of the Manassas Gap Railroad that passed through Front Royal.[14]

A deluded Banks convinced himself that Kenly's garrison held no allure for Jackson. Sergeant Arnold of Company I of the First agreed, believing his unit in "no danger.... We are kept here to hold the town and neighborhood in check, and have nothing to relieve the monotony of camp life" except picket duty. Occasionally, the sergeant's squadron also foraged off Southern-sympathizing farmers, many of whom were amateur brewers. During a three-day period early in May Arnold and his comrades "visited seven distilleries and destroyed over one hundred and twenty barrels of poor whiskey. We wont let the rebels have the fun of drinking it and it will not do to let our soldiers have much if any of it...." His ability to gauge the quality of the product suggests that the sergeant sampled it before stanching its flow.[15]

Lulled like Banks into a false complacency, Colonel Kenly's garrison failed to keep a sharp watch over the roads entering Front Royal from south and west. Not even news, received on 8 May, that a part of Jackson's command had defeated Fremont's vanguard deep in the mountains near McDowell, heightened Kenly's vigilance. When later intelligence indicated that the victors were heading for Strasburg instead of Front Royal, Kenly seems to have relaxed.[16]

The result was all too predictable. Early on the twenty-third Old Stonewall, having crossed the Massanutten behind Ashby's cavalry screen, struck the isolated outpost, overwhelmed its slender garrison, and threatened to cut off its retreat. After a stubborn stand that cost him heavily, Kenly ordered a withdrawal toward Winchester. Having departed the day before on a scouting mission toward the village of Markham, Companies H and I were not swept along in the rout. Hundreds of other soldiers were, their confused flight made more chaotic by Ashby's pursuit. A wounded Kenly fell into enemy hands along with scores of fugitives.

The survivors retreated north with as much speed as their artillery, wagons, and ambulances would permit. Apprised of the rout, Banks at first determined to hold Strasburg. Early on the twenty-fourth, however, he succumbed to better judgment and sent Williams's division toward the half-finished defenses south of Winchester.[17]

* * *

While the majority of Hatch's cavalry operated in the rear and on the flanks, the First Michigan, which had been attached directly to Williams's division, scouted the roads north of the withdrawal. For the past ten days Colonel Brodhead had been suffering from a serious illness—he described it as "lung fever and hemorrhage"—that had confined him to his quarters. This day, despite his affliction, he was in the saddle at the head of five companies of the regiment (the sixth apparently had been detailed to brigade or division headquarters). Poor health had forced the colonel to miss the fighting at Kernstown; it would not interfere today.[18]

While scanning the retreat route, Brodhead sent Major Paldi, with detachments of three companies, to assess the situation at Front Royal. In the company of a Pennsylvania infantry regiment added for the occasion, the Italian-American officer proceeded five miles toward Kenly's outpost, at which point he encountered Rebel pickets, mounted and on foot. As per his orders, Paldi turned north toward Middletown, where he overtook a fleeing supply train under siege by Ashby's outriders. A series of attacks in which even the regimental surgeon, Dr. Johnson, took a "most gallant" part, drove off the assailants and saved the wagons.[19]

After the secessionists fled north, Michiganders and Pennsylvanians escorted the train toward Winchester. Their chosen route lay through the village of Newtown, where many of Ashby's displaced riders had rallied. Determined to prevent them from harrasing Banks's retreat as they had Kenly's, Paldi contained them until Banks's advance reached Newtown and chased them away.

Learning that Paldi's detachment was progressing well, Brodhead led the balance of the First to Winchester, which, to his immeasurable relief, he found free of the enemy. His men secured the works outside town until Banks's infantry came up and filed inside. Then, by direct command of the corps leader, Brodhead placed Major Town and a single squadron on "grand-guard duty" along the road to Front Royal. Holding such a strategic position, this force ordinarily would have been commanded by Joseph Copeland, but today the lieutenant colonel was even sicker than his superior, and unable to do duty.[20]

Town, certainly no stranger to illness, gave a healthy account of himself that evening and the following morning, by which time Jackson had reached Winchester in force. Throughout the night the major's dismounted detachment, supported by an infantry outfit from Maine, repulsed numerous advances by much larger but less resolute forces. Only at seven A.M. on the twenty-fifth, when they finally sized up their opponent, did the Confederates force Town to withdraw and rejoin Brodhead.

At dawn Paldi's detachment, having escorted the beleaguered supply train to safety, also rejoined the colonel. Brodhead had the new arrivals occupy a hill on the western outskirts of Winchester, from which they could scout the Valley Turnpike. Just before Town was driven in, Paldi spied infantry pickets rushing back from the front lines at the dead run, pursued by Rebels on the pike. To save them from capture and to give the main body time to improve the earthworks it had occupied, Paldi located a light battery and persuaded its commander to sweep the road with his guns.

Supported closely by the Michiganders, the artillery unit took position as Paldi instructed. By rapid and accurate firing its guns halted the drive. Colonel Brodhead noted that Paldi "remained in this position, under a severe fire of musketry and artillery, until the retreat of both infantry and artillery from the hill," whereupon he and his men disengaged safely.[21]

No sooner had the hill been evacuated than the enemy resumed its advance, threatening to overtake the infantrymen Paldi had saved. General Williams, just arrived at the threatened sector, observed the troops' plight and resolved to reoccupy the hill. Only a fast-moving force—meaning cavalry—could get there before the Rebels. Because Hatch's command was occupied at the other end of the line, only the First Michigan was available to help. The division commander ordered the regiment to retake the evacuated position and, if possible, charge the advancing enemy.[22]

Brodhead's illness having laid him low at last, Major Town, as the senior officer still on his feet, received Williams's order. He saluted smartly, re-formed Paldi's battalion, augmented it with other elements of the regiment, transformed the whole into a 200-man column, and led it toward the high ground. When within observation range of his objective, Town found it already occupied by gray infantry. Against the fire of half a dozen regiments, his column kept moving with what General Williams called "great promptness and gallantry," blazing away with Burnsides and pistols. About twenty rods from the hill, however, the first rank began to reel from one fusillade after another. As casualties mounted in front, Town suddenly found his right flank under attack by Rebel horsemen.

Before his command could disintegrate, the major shouted: "Left about, wheel!" and the column swung to the rear with parade-ground precision. Squinting through field-glasses, General Williams marveled at the orderliness of the retrograde. The feat was magnified by the terrain that obsructed it, including a stone wall which the troopers topped with minimal loss of alignment. Despite having suffered more than two dozen casualties—an unusually heavy loss for any mounted unit in proportion to the number engaged—the Wolverines retired in good spirits as well as good order. They had a right to feel proud. As Brodhead later noted, their determined advance had delayed the enemy a "full ten minutes, giving our retreating infantry time to gain the cover of the town."[23]

After reaching safety in the rear, Town's and Paldi's troopers were sent to the far side of Winchester to link with General Hatch. There they salved their wounds as fighting raged on all sides, the tide of battle slowly but steadily beating against the defenders. There, too, Lieutenant Colonel Copeland, although so weak he could barely remain in the saddle, temporarily assumed command of the outfit.

To Copeland's chagrin, he found himself heading a retreat column. By midday it had become obvious that Winchester could not be held against Jackson's reinvigorated army. Most reluctantly—fearing the political as well as the military repurcussions of abandoning a fixed position—Nathaniel Banks had ordered a full-scale withdrawal.[24]

The troops began to pull out just as their assailants crushed the Union right flank. Mirroring its steadfastness along the Valley Pike, the First Michigan remained in place east of the town until Banks's other flank could fall back and clear the area. Brodhead noted proudly that his was "the last regiment that left the field." Just before Jackson's advance could swallow it up, the troopers put spurs to their mounts and raced to overtake their infantry and artillery, whose rear they guarded as far as the Potomac crossings.[25]

Not everyone withdrew with the equanimity of the First Michigan. When Banks's main body streamed through Winchester, it lost cohesion, many units milling about in the streets and alleys. Those who struggled on through to the Martinsburg Road bunched up in confusion behind the First, Hatch's horsemen, and the supply trains that Banks had waited too long to evacuate. Chaos dogged the main body all the way to the Maryland line, prompting one of Banks's aides to dub the retreat "another Bull's Run panic."[26]

*   *   *

Jackson's triumph at Winchester accomplished more than his opponents' expulsion from the Valley; it drove the Washington authorities into panicky miscalculations that adversely affected not only subsequent operations in the Shenandoah but also McClellan's campaign on the Peninsula. Although a bloodied and bewildered Nathaniel Banks remained above the Potomac until the second week in June, Lincoln and Stanton immediately dispatched Irvin McDowell to the Blue Ridge to avenge Winchester and prevent Jackson from riding the tide of victory as far north as Washington.[27]

The move infuriated McClellan, who, fearing that the loss of McDowell's corps was permanent, conducted the critical phase of his advance on Richmond even more cautiously, more timidly, than before. The upshot was that when he got to within five miles of the Confederate capital, a series of unexpected assaults by Joe Johnston's successor, Robert E. Lee, forced him into a retreat just as abject and ignominious as Banks's flight from Winchester. The effect of this reverse on Union morale was bad enough, but early in June Stonewall Jackson piled insult upon injury. Through hard marching and hard fighting he not only prevented McDowell from linking with Fremont as the War Department had intended, but he whipped elements of both commands, capping his stunning campaign with victories at Cross Keys and Port Republic, 8-9 June. By mid-month Stonewall had accomplished his purpose in the Valley and was hastening eastward to help put the final touches to McClellan's debacle.[28]

Throughout June, the several elements of the First Michigan continued to serve apart from each other. Colonel Brodhead, with the greater part of Town's and Paldi's battalions, remained with Banks's force, reshoeing and resupplying at Williamsport, Maryland, until his commander regained enough poise and confidence to revisit the Valley. Recrossing the Potomac on the twelfth, the six companies under Brodhead led Banks's march, via Martinsburg, to Front Royal. From that scene of recent disaster, Town and Paldi guided detachments in seeking the troops Jackson had left behind.[29]

They covered a great deal of ground. By 20 June the Wolverines were at Orleans, Barbee's Cross Roads, and Sandy Hook; the next day they were at Milford and Luray. Turner Ashby had been killed while the First refit at Williamsport, but his command remained pugnacious enough, exhanging much carbine- and pistol-fire with the invaders. On at least one occasion the Michiganders were also fired on by stragglers from Jackson's command, who fled toward the mountains when the First took after them. On other occasions Ashby's men likewise failed to linger, as on the last day of June when Companies F and G, under Paldi, "bravely and gallantly" drove them through the dusty streets of Luray.[30]

While the companies under Brodhead, Town, and Paldi scoured the country east of the Shenandoah, the other half of the First Michigan was roving through the suburbs of Washington, D.C. Late in May, now-Brigadier General Geary, having ended his operations in Loudoun County, led his peripetetic command, including Major Atwood's Wolverines, to Manassas Junction. There the battalion linked with Captain Howrigan's squadron. Companies H and I had been operating under Geary's remote direction since early April. The combined force totalled 419 officers and troopers.[31]

Manassas lay within the jurisdiction of Irvin McDowell, who on

28 May came upon the Wolverines quite unexpectedly. The corps commander was ignorant of Atwood's and Howrigan's recent operations (how they came to be at Manassas "I do not know"), but he could use their help. Then preparing to join Fremont in the Valley, McDowell wished to add the Michiganders to his own mounted force, the understrength brigade of Brigadier General George Dashiell Bayard.[32]

The rub was that the new arrivals' recent exertions had hobbled them badly; McDowell found them "in unserviceable condition... the horses all requiring shoeing." And no sooner did he see to their refit than he lost control of them. At Secretary Stanton's order, McDowell sent all 419 to report to Brigadier General James S. Wadsworth, commander of the Military District of Washington. Three days later a regretful McDowell asked Wadsworth to return the Wolverines if able to do so without displeasing the government: "I do not wish to run the risk of a censure for stripping Washington." When his petition was rejected, McDowell trudged westward without them.[33]

Under General Wadsworth, Atwood and Howrigan resumed their roving ways. Throughout June they journeyed back and forth between Washington and its environs, scouting from Leesburg halfway to Richmond. Among other places, they visited Centreville, Dranesville, Waterford, Dumfries, and Alexandria. The gyrations prompted Delevan Arnold to wax philosophic: "How changeful is the life of a soldier, and how little he can tell one day where he will be the next."[34]

If there was a strategy, a master plan, behind their movements, "I dont know," Arnold admitted, "and as far as I can learn, nobody else does. But I do know one thing, and that is that we were marched until we could barely sit in our saddles." Not only the troopers were experiencing hard times; local citizens had suffered heavily at the hands of both armies. Trotting through a burnt-over section of Culpeper County, Private Alfred Ryder of Company H noted that "the mien of war everywhere meets the eye and... convinces me of its very foul character."[35]

The uncertainty that came of wandering far from the rest of one's regiment disappeared early in July, when General Banks massed his cavalry east of the Valley. On the sixth, Atwood's and Howrigan's men left the capital for the final time. Loping through Culpeper, they reached Warrenton on the tenth, where they went into bivouac. There, the following day, they were joined by Colonel Brodhead and the main body of the First. Men who had not seen each other in five months shouted greetings, pumped hands, and clapped one another's shoulders.[36]

To mark the restoration of corporate identity, Brodhead issued a message expressing "heartfelt thanks for the bravery and soldier-like bearing exhibited by officers and men" throughout their period of estrangement. He praised all three battalions, each of which had experienced "hard fought fields—successful marches and endurance... beyond even the energies of the best and bravest." And he rejoiced that "we are again together as a Regiment... [to] live with, or die under, the Old Flag."[37]

The colonel's words had a prophetic ring. The grouping of the mounted arm suggested that a new round of campaigning was imminent. It seemed a good bet that, not many days hence, members of the First Michigan would die beneath the banner of their divided nation.

CHAPTER FOUR

From the Rapidan to Bull Run

*A*nother result of Stonewall Jackson's success in the Valley took effect two weeks before the First Michigan's reunion. Reasoning that fragmented command had caused the failure to bag Jackson, on 26 June the War Department grouped the forces of Banks, McDowell, Fremont, and Shields. The result, dubbed the Army of Virginia, was assigned to forty-year-old Major General John Pope of Illinois.[1]

The new leader was a recent transferee from the Mississippi Valley, where he had won small victories that hero-hungry journalists magnified beyond recognition. He had the swagger and strut, however, of the successful commander, and he lacked an appreciation of the effect his braggadocio had on his enemy—or on his own army. On 14 July, as he prepared to leave Washington for the field, Pope issued an address to his new troops that struck a discordant note: "I have come to you from the West, where we have always seen the backs of our enemies; from an army whose business it has been to seek the adversary and to beat him.... I have been called here to pursue the same system...."[2]

The First Michigan and the other regiments that had recently closed up on the Warrenton-Culpeper Court House vicinity had a right to take offense at such words. The implication that the Army of Virginia reeked of defeat and defeatism was an unfair rebuke. The general consensus was that any commander who tried to elevate himself by downgrading his own men while making light of his enemy's prowess had far to go to prove himself worthy of his rank and authority.[3]

In the near term, Pope proved only that he was a poor judge of subordinates. The best that could be said of General Hatch during the Valley Campaign was that he had displayed flashes of competence. Ignoring his spotty record, Pope named him commander of the army's cavalry and conferred on him great responsibility. To assist Pope in his mission to disrupt Robert E. Lee's westward communications, Hatch was ordered to advance toward Gordonsville, near the point at which the southward-running Orange & Alexandria Railroad met the Virginia Central from out of Richmond. With McClellan's army stationary along the James River, the War Department feared that Lee might make a break for Washington. But if Hatch could destroy enough track on the Virginia Central, the southern commander would have to remain on the Peninsula for want of mobile supplies.[4]

At four A.M. on 16 July, the First Michigan stumbled out of its camp near Culpeper, mounted up, and headed south under a leaden sky. The regiment expected to become part of a large column under Hatch, but it was joined only by the Fifth New York of Colonel Othneil De Forest. After starting south, the First learned that Hatch had decided to move in two columns across the Rapidan River. Below that stream, the Michiganders and New Yorkers, under overall command of Colonel Brodhead, would move on Gordonsville by way of Orange Court House. Meanwhile, Hatch, at the head of a larger column that included infantry and a wagon train—neither of which he was authorized to take—would approach the common objective farther to the west via Madison Court House. Somewhere above Gordonsville the forces would unite for a strike on the town and the nearby Virginia Central.[5]

Whatever happened to Hatch, Brodhead was determined that his demi-brigade would perform its share of the mission despite unseasonable weather. Rain drenched the troopers, "the wind howled fiercely through the forests, and large trees snapped like pipe stems." Late in the day the wind gave way to "hail stones as large [as] plums," which "pelted us unmercifully." After two hours of such treatment, the men welcomed the dismal drizzle that fell the rest of the day.[6]

Reaching the Rapidan in late afternoon, Brodhead found the stream too swollen to cross safely in the fading light. The men spent the night on the north bank in fields awash in mud and water. Next morning, they carefully forded the river and pushed on to Orange Court House, ten miles from Gordonsville. As another cloudburst broke, the regiments charged through the seat of Orange County, expelling thirty or forty Confederates who had set up an outpost in the town.

After securing the area, Brodhead scouted toward Gordonsville, where, local informants told him, a sizable force of the enemy had congregated. The reports proved correct; at midday bands of Rebels sauntered up to evict the Wolverines. Intermittent skirmishing consumed the balance of the day. Thanks to the fortitude of his own regiment, especially Captain Howrigan's Company H and Company E, under feisty young Captain Peter Stagg, Brodhead held his position.[7]

From a captive sergeant, Brodhead learned that as many as 75,000 Confederates under Jackson's old subordinate, Richard Ewell, had massed above, as well as in, Gordonsville. Fearing their proximity would kill any chance of meeting Hatch, the colonel drew in his outposts and departed Orange Court House early on the eighteenth, his pull-out covered by a six-company force under De Forest. Finding the Rapidan even higher than it had been two days ago, Brodhead took several hours to get his regiments across. They reached dry ground none too soon; less than half an hour afterward Ewell's advance guard appeared on the south bank.[8]

Not until early on 20 July, while en route to Culpeper, did Brodhead and De Forest meet the main column. Fatally slowed by his infantry and wagons, and cowed by the reports of Ewell's nearness, General Hatch had not even reached Madison Court House before declaring his expedition a failure and calling it off. Frustrated and disappointed, Brodhead and De Forest followed their superior northward and went into camp beside him along the Hazel River.[9]

When he learned that Hatch had accomplished so little—largely through disobedience of orders—General Pope demanded he try again, and quickly. A sheepish Hatch sought to comply, this time at the head of a single column composed of all his regiments but no impedimenta. The concentration of strength and mobility counted

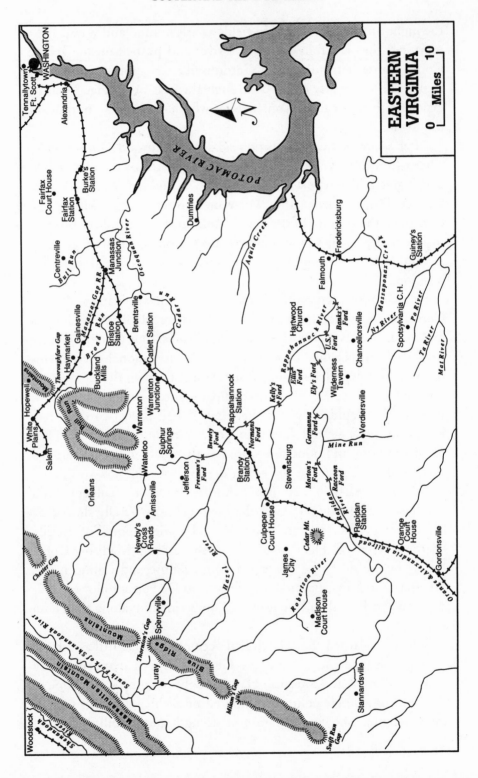

for nothing. Old obstacles—roads turned into lakes by the rain and nerves turned to jelly by new reports of Rebels on the advance—drove Hatch to abort the mission twenty miles short of his objective. Back at Culpeper by the twenty-fifth, Sergeant Arnold of the First Michigan wrote his mother a brief account of the recent raids, calling the experience so unpleasant that "I dont like to dwell upon it."[10]

* * *

Hatch's lack of fortitude cost him his command. On 27 July he was transferred to the infantry while the newly promoted Brigadier General John Buford took over the horsemen attached to Banks's command (now known as the II Corps, Army of Virginia). The newcomer, most recently a staff officer at army headquarters, was a native Kentuckian with fourteen years' experience in dragoon and cavalry service. Squat, stocky, and anything but a dandy, he quickly impressed his new command with his no-nonsense, plain-speaking style. In contrast to the his predecessor, Buford exuded self-confidence without betraying a hint of self-importance.[11]

Under the Kentuckian, the Wolverines were soon off on another expedition below the Rapidan—but not before they met a Confederate force on a raid of its own. The presence of large numbers of the enemy between Gordonsville and the Rapidan signalled that Robert E. Lee would not remain near Richmond, keeping watch over his beaten opponents. Already, in fact, Lee had dispatched Jackson, with many of the troops that had helped defeat McClellan, to confront the new army under Pope and bring it to battle. Less than a week after Hatch's return from his second unaccomplished mission, Jackson's infantry and cavalry pushed across the Rapidan at several points, driving toward Madison Court House, Sperryville, and Pope's headquarters at Culpeper. Vedettes on the north shore, including those of the First Michigan, quickly found themselves fighting for their lives.[12]

For General Buford, who had inherited Hatch's picket line, it was a most inauspicious way to begin field command. At first intent on remaining at the river, by midday of 7 August the new brigadier found both of his flanks in danger of collapse. Prudently, he ordered a pull-out toward the northwest while setting up a delaying action that slowed Jackson's progress and stoked his ire. The fight-and-fall-back tactics of the First Michigan and its comrades bought General Pope enough time to place Banks's infantry in the Rebels' path near Cedar Mountain. There Jackson slugged it out with his old adversary throughout 9 August. The encounter, which cost thousands of casualties on both sides, ended as a tactical draw but prompted Jackson, his progress checked, to turn about and recross the Rapidan.[13]

Only one squadron of the First Michigan was present for Cedar Mountain, Companies L and M having been detailed to escort Generals Banks and Williams, respectively. The balance of the regiment withdrew with Buford's main force to Woodville, fifteen miles west of the battlefield. The brigade remained there, absorbing late arrivals from the Rapidan, until it moved to Culpeper the day after the fight.[14]

A small portion of the First postponed its retreat to land a blow. With Buford's permission, the detachment teamed with some squadrons of the First Virginia in attacking the bivouacs of two of Jackson's infantry regiments along the road to Madison Court House. After lashing the startled Rebels with carbine fire, the troopers held an exposed position until the reinforced enemy threatened their flanks. At the last minute they pulled out, galloped north, and joined their regiments at Woodville.[15]

Buford's respite from combat lasted until the eleventh, when Jackson's retreat turned pursued into pursuer. Late that day, at Pope's command, Buford's brigade raced back to the Rapidan, snatching up dozens of stragglers. Meeting Jackson's rear guard on the north bank, the First Michigan and its supports—some mounted, some afoot—advanced with enough verve to convince the Rebels to join their commander on the opposite bank. Taking custody of hundreds of wounded whom Stonewall had left behind, the horsemen reestablished the picket lines they had withdrawn the previous week.[16]

They would not guard the river for long. By 14 August the greater part of Pope's army, still nursing wounds from Cedar Mountain, had advanced to within supporting distance of the cavalry. So too had advance elements of McClellan's army, which the War Department had dispatched by transport from the Peninsula to enable Pope to throttle Jackson and any supports Lee might send him. Unaware that a reinforcement operation was already underway—on the tenth Lee had begun to move his main army, under Lieutenant General James Longstreet, to the Rapidan—Pope intended to probe Jackson's position with Major General Jesse Reno's division of the IX Corps, Army of the Potomac. He sent Reno, Buford's brigade in advance, to locate and if possible sever Jackson's eastward communications.[17]

The mission carried Buford's people toward a familiar but never-reached objective, the Virginia Central. Early on the sixteenth the brigade made a wide detour to the east and crossed the river at Rapidan Station, an Orange & Alexandria depot beyond Jackson's right flank. Heading south, late that day it skirmished outside Orange Court House. After securing the place, Buford patrolled in the direction of Jackson's position. At the same time he dispatched Brodhead, with his regiment and De Forest's, toward the Virginia Central via Louisa Court House. Officially, Brodhead's mission was a reconnaissance. The Colonel was aware, however, how badly Pope—and therefore Buford—wanted the railroad broken.[18]

Late in the day, a few miles short of his objective, Brodhead bivouacked in a cornfield, on the far side of which his vedettes discovered a Confederate cavalry patrol heading their way. The Federals captured the entire unit, whose members testified that several regiments under J.E.B. Stuart lay only a mile or so away, near Verdiersville. This was startling news: no one in Pope's army knew that Lee's cavalry had left the Peninsula. Stuart's nearness suggested that Lee was planning to assault the Army of Virginia.

Before dawn on 17 August Brodhead's column, the Fifth New York in advance, cautiously approached Verdiersville, just north of the railroad. In advance of the main body rode perhaps a dozen Wolverines under Lieutenant Rogers, who had helped organize Company G and was now adjutant of the First Battalion. As the sun spread its light over acres and acres of pastureland, Rogers spied two gray-clad riders moving through the fields on his left. With a shout, he spurred after them, his men close behind.

The Confederates raced to a farmhouse where they shouted a warning to some comrades inside, then galloped off. When the Michiganders reached the house minutes later, they saw a hatless soldier leap from the porch, vault a fence, and vanish into an adjacent woods. Two other men raced out of the house, mounted waiting horses, and galloped off.

As his men took after the riders, Rogers, pistol drawn, entered the house. Inside he found an officer who identified himself as Major Norman Fitzhugh of Stuart's staff. Rogers also discovered some personal articles the fence-jumper had left behind: a knapsack, a brace of pistols, and a slouch hat with an exotic plume. Rogers donned the elegant headgear, causing his alarmed prisoner to inquire: "Where is the man who wore that hat?" When Rogers explained that the fugitive had escaped Fitzhugh exclaimed, "Thank God for that, that's Jeb Stuart's hat!"[19]

* * *

To surprise and nearly capture the most famous cavalry leader of the war would have been enough of a feat for most raiding forces, but the knapsack Stuart left behind proved an even greater catch. It contained dispatches from Lee, fixing Jackson's and Longstreet's positions and detailing an operation to join their commands in the face of an unsuspecting foe. The critical stage of Lee's plan to "suppress" General Pope was to begin next day with a united crossing of the Rapidan.

After Colonel Brodhead scanned the papers, he redirected the column to Orange Court House, his railroad mission forgotten. Rejoining Buford in the Orange County seat, the First Michigan and Fifth New York hastened north with the rest of the Cavalry Brigade, II Corps, Army of Virginia. Couriers galloped ahead to rush the captured intelligence to army headquarters. Even before Buford reached the Rapidan an alarmed and angry Pope was issuing orders for a full-scale withdrawal. By the nineteenth much of his army had occupied high ground above the wide and fast-running Rappahannock River, with Buford's troopers guarding the army's flank at Kelly's Ford.[20]

Enraged by the security lapse that had permitted the Yankees to slip Lee's trap, Stuart mounted a ferocious pursuit. On the twentieth he overtook Bayard's brigade, which had been guarding the crossing of Pope's rear echelon at Brandy Station, northwest of Kelly's Ford. In a several-hour set-to, Stuart severely handled the blue horsemen.

Due to strict orders, Buford's command was not engaged this day, though the following morning his main body joined General Reno in reconnoitering the south bank of the Rappahannock near Stevensburg. In this mission the First Michigan did not participate; the regiment had returned by a circuitous route to picket duty on the Rapidan. This time, the Wolverines guarded Barnett's Ford, west of the enemy's latest position, where they screened the camps of a newly arrived brigade from McClellan's V Corps.[21]

When enough reinforcements reached him from the Peninsula, Pope planned to retake the offensive. While he consulted his maps, however, he surrendered the initiative. Surreptitiously Lee split his army and dispatched its components toward the Union rear by similar routes but hours apart. Stuart, seeking redemption for Verdiersville, and Jackson, seeking revenge for Cedar Mountain, circumvented the Union right via gaps in the Bull Run Mountains beyond the view of Pope's cavalry. By 26 August Stuart was looting Yankee quartermaster's and commissary stores at Catlett Station; Jackson was making for the old Bull Run battlefield; and 26,000 troops under Longstreet were hitting the mountain roads to join their comrades farther north.[22]

Dimly aware that something was afoot to the west, Pope on the twenty-sixth had his ranking subordinate, Irvin McDowell, order Buford's brigade to reconnoiter beyond the Bull Run Mountains. Augmenting his own command—including the First Michigan, which had quit picketing the Rapidan—with horsemen from another of Pope's corps, Buford started west early the next day. Although concerned by the evident weakness of his command—officers, men, and mounts were woozy from incessant marching and countermarching—he led it through the mountains, then across a clover-rich valley toward Jackson's portal to the Union rear.[23]

At the outset the journey had a pleasant resonance for one of Buford's outfits. Passing as it did through the Milford area, scene of their successes against Jackson and Ashby, it rekindled fond memories in the men of the First Michigan. A bit farther north, however, signs that the column was following the track of a large infantry force placed the First in a more somber mood. Near the valley town of Salem, stragglers materialized along the road; interrogated by

Buford, they disclosed that Jackson had pressed on to Thoroughfare Gap without them. The tired Federals were thankful for the news. They now had the information their army needed; they could return home without further ado.

They began to breathe easily too soon. Early in the afternoon, as they prepared to depart Salem, the rear guard detected the approach of Rebel infantry, the forefront of Longstreet's corps. Realizing that he had interposed between the major segments of Lee's army, both of which appeared to be heading for Pope's rear, Buford hastened his men in the direction of White Plains. As the main body cleared Salem, he positioned the First Michigan, supported by elements of other regiments, to conduct a delaying-action.[24]

Here was a clear indication of Buford's regard for the Wolverines, whose strong showing at Kernstown and elsewhere in the Valley inspired respect throughout his command. Under Brodhead, Town, Paldi, and Atwood (Lieutenant Colonel Copeland was on leave in Michigan), the First Michigan met Buford's expectations, keeping Longstreet's advance at arm's length by the tried and true process of fighting, withdrawing, and fighting again. From successive positions behind ridges, fences, and farm buildings, they sprayed the Confederate vanguard with carbine fire, then hustled along the road to White Plains. Many deferred retreating till the last moment, galloping north with rifle balls singing in their ears.

Buford's tactics succeeded. Time and again Longstreet's infantry would halt, deploy, and move forward, slowly and deliberately, to gouge the Wolverines from their nooks and crannies. The delays meant that Jackson would be without Longstreet's aid much longer than either general had anticipated.[25]

From White Plains Buford turned homeward via a southeasterly route through the mountains toward Warrenton. The heading enabled him to clear Longstreet's path and avoid further stress to his column—a fortunate circumstance, since exhausted horses were collapsing in the road. In advance of his return to McDowell, Buford dispatched couriers, on the freshest mounts, to spread the word of Jackson's advance into the Union rear. As it turned out, the intelligence had already reached Pope's headquarters from other sources; in response, the Army of Virginia had begun to withdraw toward Gainesville and Manassas Junction.[26]

Curiously, Buford's more significant discovery—Longstreet's imminent passage of Thoroughfare Gap—prompted a half-measured response. The following morning McDowell attempted to block the pass with a force large enough to delay, but not to prevent, Longstreet's reunion with Jackson. With his main body, the corps leader moved to link up with Pope.[27]

Buford's weary riders completed their return-trip to Warrenton at nine P.M. on the twenty-seventh. Discovering that McDowell's corps had already quit the area, they stayed there overnight. Fortified by hours of uninterrupted sleep, early on the twenty-eighth the First Michigan and the rest followed Buford up the Warrenton Turnpike toward the army's point of concentration. The march consumed most of the day, which saw combat off to the west at Thoroughfare Gap as well as to the east at Groveton, where Jackson's command was tangling with one of Pope's wings.

After bivouacking his command short of the railroad, Buford led it toward Thoroughfare Gap—now free of combatants—on the morning of 29 August. In the village of Haymarket the brigade leader took up a position just off the road that was carrying Longstreet toward Groveton. Through most of the morning the First Michigan remained quietly in the rear, grabbing additional rest, as forward regiments observed the enemy's rapid passage through the area. By ten o'clock, having counted several thousand foot soldiers and artillerists, Buford broke contact with Longstreet's flankers and headed south to Bristoe Station, McDowell's last known whereabouts.[28]

As usual, Buford sent his boss advanced word of his findings. McDowell responded to it in a manner that defied logic. While he shared Buford's report with some subordinates as well as with Major General Fitz John Porter, commander of the recently arrived V Army Corps, McDowell failed to relay it to army headquarters. Here was another link in a long chain of mistakes and failures that had encircled the corps leader since July 1861. His record would prompt some critics to brand McDowell not only a poor general but a traitor to the Union.[29]

While the latter assertion was untrue, the effect of McDowell's latest omission would be calamitous. John Pope concentrated his attention and his army against Jackson in his rear, while remaining ignorant of the disaster approaching from the west.

* * *

Reaching Bristoe Station on the Orange & Alexandria late on 29 August, Buford again found McDowell gone. The infantry's rear guard informed the new arrivals that the main body had moved up the railroad to join the balance of Pope's army, then engaged with Jackson near Bull Run. The men of Buford's column had suspected that a full-scale battle was in progress; throughout the day Alfred Ryder and his comrades in the First Michigan had listened to a "constant roar of artillery" from the east.[30]

After bivouacking for some hours, Buford guided his brigade up the railroad on the morning of the thirtieth. By early afternoon, the cavalry had taken position along the far left of Pope's army about two miles below Manassas Junction, where they supported Porter's corps. When visiting army headquarters for his orders, Buford learned that the previous day's fighting had ended indecisively. This day, however, Pope intended to strike Jackson a fatal blow with his infantry and artillery; the cavalry could sit back and watch.

Until or unless it was needed, Buford dismounted most of his brigade. Troopers sprawled in the meadows that skirted Dawkins's Branch. A few miles away elements of Pope's army saw furious fighting, but the only active troops on the left were small patrols Buford had stationed along the road from Warrenton to Washington, D.C. These units experienced what Surgeon Johnson of the First Michigan called "spasmodic and localized fighting."[31]

The pace of operations quickened in midafternoon, when Pope paid the price for his limited vigilance. Shortly after four o'clock Longstreet's corps, having settled into place opposite the Union left without alerting its opponents, attacked. Within minutes, Pope's flank dissolved in human splinters and Longstreet began to roll up the Union line like a thin blue carpet.

The offensive surprised but did not paralyze Buford. Reining in his squadrons, he pulled back to Lewis Ford, just west of the point where the Warrenton-Washington road crossed Bull Run. He sheltered his main body behind a low ridge almost half a mile in advance of the ford, keeping some units in the saddle, placing others on foot. The First Michigan remained mounted, as did bands of skirmishers sent forward to scout the enemy.[32]

Some time after five P.M. Buford received a report from an outpost with a better vantage point that a column of Rebel horsemen was approaching Lewis Ford, a heavier force of infantry to its rear. As the riders hove into view and an accompanying artillery unit trained its pieces on the ford, Buford turned to his senior subordinate and called for a charge. At once, Colonel Brodhead led his regiment over the ridge and formed columns of attack. One of his enlisted men, new to this brand of warfare, recorded the nerve-jangling upshot:

"The order came, 'By fours front into line!' The men came up in fine style, and then came the order, 'By platoons, right about wheel! Draw sabres!' The rebel battery and cavalry were in front of us. I held my breath for a moment, for this was our first charge. I thought of home and friends. The bugle sounded the charge, and away we went...."[33]

The oncoming Confederates—a portion of a single regiment that had been driving Buford's skirmishers back upon his main body—tried to wheel about, but too late. In seconds "the lines crashed together, and men and horses went down and rolled over in the dust." The opposing forces fused into a kicking, rearing tangle amid the cracking of pistols and the slashing of swords, until the First Michigan staggered out of the pile-up. Before the Wolverines could re-form, however, the balance of the attacking force, the Second Virginia, came up at the gallop and hurled itself into the fray.[34]

With many of its horses and riders down, the First Michigan was in no condition to absorb a counterattack. Fortunately, Buford had already committed a regiment on loan to him, the Fourth New York. Charging in from the east, the New Yorkers bowled over the Second Virginia, scattered it, and forced it to retreat.

Once the pressure eased on the First Michigan, Brodhead and his subordinates separated their men from the intermingled squadrons of the Fourth New York and fought to regain a semblance of formation. Suddenly, two more regiments of Virginians, charging under cover of their artillery, sliced through the Federal lines. Thanks to their momentum and the stationary pose of their opponents, the Confederates battered the Michiganders and New Yorkers as well as their general, who took a disabling wound.[35]

The First Michigan suffered grievously. Endeavoring to mount a counterattack, Colonel Brodhead made a target of himself. Before the horrified eyes of his men, he toppled from his saddle, shot through the lungs. Near him, Major Town took five wounds, three inflicted by pistol balls, two by saber strokes. None of the injuries was life-threatening and Town kept to the saddle, but six officers and troopers fell dead or mortally wounded and a dozen men received injuries of varying severity.[36]

The regiment's greatest loss was in captured. When the Virginia regiments struck, they cut off the forward squadrons of the First and initially took 113 prisoners. A number managed to escape, but the majority were conducted to Gainesville, then to Leesburg, and finally to prison camps outside Richmond. The POWs included two of the Wolverines' ablest officers, Major Atwood and Captain Howrigan, as well as Lieutenant Herman E. Hascall of Company I. While the First Michigan would recover from the beating it received at Lewis Ford, the physical and psychological effects of the fight would linger for months.[37]

Thanks to the inertia of the other regiments in Buford's brigade, Colonel Brodhead also fell into enemy hands. After being overpowered, the First Michigan and Fourth New York expected to be rescued by the First (West) Virginia and First Vermont. Instead, through miscommunication or deficient leadership, these outfits failed to come up in support. In fact, they abandoned the field, accompanying their hobbled general to the rear. Thus unencumbered, the Confederates secured their prisoners, paying special attention to the fallen colonel, whom they found coughing up blood.[38]

Carried to a farmhouse inside enemy lines, Brodhead received as much medical assistance as his enemy could spare, although neither he nor his captors doubted that his wounds were fatal. On 2 September, three days after Longstreet and Jackson completed their second triumph along Bull Run in little over a year, the man who had raised and organized the First Michigan Cavalry succumbed to his injuries. He left behind a letter addressed to his family, stained with his blood. In his final words he gave way to frustration and despair, blaming his demise and that of his army on the obtuseness of one superior and the perfidy of another:

".... Before I die let me implore that in some way it may be stated that General Pope has been outwitted and that McDowell is a traitor. Had they done their duty, as I did mine; and had led, as I had led, the dear old Flag [would] have waved in triumph.... Our Cause is just. And our Generals—not the Enemy's—have defeated us. In God's good time he will give us Victory. And now, Good bye, Wife and Children...."[39]

* * *

On the day Brodhead died, a bloody and demoralized Army of Virginia limped toward the safety of the Washington defenses. As the troops neared the outermost forts, General McClellan rode out to meet them. Having effectively lost his command when it went to Pope's department, Little Mac now reclaimed it along with the army that had been throttled at Bull Run. The national authorities trusted McClellan neither as a soldier nor as a political figure, but with a victorious Lee heading toward the Potomac River and Maryland, the government had no option but to reinstate a general who had already come out second-best to "Marse Robert."[40]

The crisis atmosphere gripping Washington toppled the morale of many Northerners in and outside the army. It infused other men with a sense of excitement, purpose, and anticipation. One who perceived opportunities in the present situation was Brevet Captain George Custer of the Fifth Cavalry, since May a member of McClellan's staff.

As his position indicated, the youngster with Ohio roots and Michigan ties had made the war work to his advantage. After losing his place on Phil Kearny's staff early in the year, Custer had returned to his outfit but thereafter stood out among the anonymous faces of his comrades. Early in March, when the Confederates fell back from the lines they had held since First Bull Run, Lieutenant Custer led a fifty-man detachment in harassing their rear south of Manassas Junction. The imprudent offensive involved him in a fight with six times as many antagonists. Although "the bullets rattled like hail...

close to my head," Custer held his ground until withdrawing in good order, having suffered only three casualties. His coolness in a tight spot, observable from the rear, impressed McClellan's chief of cavalry, Brigadier General George Stoneman, as well as several news correspondents, who eagerly interviewed the young officer.[41]

Custer added to his fighting reputation throughout the Peninsula Campaign. During the siege of Yorktown, in April, he took part in two dangerous reconnaissances, on one exposing himself recklessly while everyone near him "got behind a tree" and stayed there. The revocation of statuary prohibitions brought him staff assignments during the latter stages of the siege, including one at the divisional level. His new duties ranged from copying paperwork and transmitting battle orders to manning observation balloons, an experience he found both harrowing and exhilarating.[42]

Returning to earth, on 4 May he led the way into abandoned Yorktown as the Confederates retreated out the other side. The following day, as fighting raged outside Virginia's colonial capital, Williamsburg, Custer led an infantry column around the enemy's flank via a route he had brought to his superiors' attention. On that field he also distinguished himself by capturing a half-dozen Confederates and one of their flags. When the Rebels fled toward Richmond, Custer spearheaded the pursuit across the bridgeless Chickahominy River near Mechanicsville. There, by his initiative and daring, he helped capture fifty prisoners. Impressed by this feat, McClellan soon afterward made the lieutenant his aide-de-camp.[43]

The prestigious position was everything Custer could have hoped for at this stage of the war. He was especially happy to serve under a commander whose military abilities, personal habits, and political leanings he could admire: he would follow McClellan, he told his parents, "to the ends of the earth." His trust and admiration were reciprocated, the general expressing a fondness for the "reckless, gallant boy" who had joined his headquarters family.[44]

Custer maintained a high place in the army leader's regard. As McClellan's front-line emissary, he won distinction at Beaver Dam Creek on 26 June and the following day at Gaines's Mill. In early July, in the aftermath of the rear-guard action at Malvern Hill, he helped guide the army in its retreat to the James River at Harrison's

Landing. Although the campaign had ended in failure and frustration, Custer continued to distinguish himself, winning rank commensurate with his achievements. Early in August, as a newly minted first lieutenant and brevet captain of Regulars, he commanded a 300-man scouting party from the James to White Oak Swamp. On this mission he shot an enemy officer (his first confirmed victim of the war), dispersed the man's cavalry unit, and brought army headquarters valuable intelligence. Again he was commended for his "gallant and spirited conduct."[45]

Before John Pope failed disastrously at Second Bull Run, McClellan's uneasy relations with his civilian superiors and his uncertain status as commander of an army stripped of its troops raised doubts about his continued tenure. The possibility that he would suffer should Little Mac be relieved must have troubled the ambitious, career-conscious Custer. Although loyal to his commander, at this point Custer appears to have begun actively seeking a position in the volunteer forces.

His preference would have been for a cavalry command, and his instincts told him to cultivate relations with officials in Ohio or Michigan. While few mounted units from the Buckeye State served in the Army of the Potomac, Custer was aware that Michigan had contributed a regiment of horse to McClellan's army and that others were on the way. Following the collapse of the Peninsula Campaign, Abraham Lincoln—persuaded that the war would be long and its future uncertain—had put out a call for 300,000 volunteers to save the Union. In response to this petition, by mid-July what would become the Fifth, Sixth, and Seventh Michigan Volunteer Cavalry regiments were in process of organization. Bearing this in mind, Brevet Captain Custer contacted Governor Blair and other officials (including state Republican leaders) in hopes of parlaying a reputation as a "reckless, gallant boy" into a position of rank, authority, and tenure.[46]

CHAPTER FIVE

Three More for Michigan

By the time Lincoln called for 300,000 three-year troops "to bring this unnecessary and injurious civil war to a speedy and satisfactory conclusion," Michigan had already contributed more than her share to the fight to save the Union. As of the first of July 1862, the lightly populated state had raised, organized, equipped, and placed in the field three cavalry and sixteen infantry regiments as well as eight batteries of light artillery, totalling more than 20,000 officers and men; a fourth cavalry outfit and another infantry regiment were in training camp. Under the new call, Michigan would raise an additional six regiments of foot soldiers (one in each of her congressional districts), plus three regiments of horsemen.

As befit the state's location, most of the new units would serve in the western theater of operations. Curiously, the three new mounted units would follow the lead of the First Cavalry, being assigned to the Army of the Potomac. This circumstance was a result of the close cooperation between Michigan's congressional delegation (especially Senator Bingham and Representative Francis W. Kellogg of the Fourth Congressional District) and the War Department, which appeared to pay special attention to the needs of the main Union Army in the East, the guardian of the capital.[1]

One of the perceived needs of "Mister Lincoln's Army" was more cavalry. Speculation about the causes of McClellan's failure on the Peninsula took many directions, but one theory that developed a following was his relative lack of horsemen. From its advance out of Fort Monroe to its retreat to Harrison's Landing, McClellan's command had consisted of some 6,000 cavalrymen, less than 6 percent of its total strength of 105,000 effectives. Many military theorists declared that to be truly effective a typical army should maintain 10 to 14 percent of its manpower in cavalry. However much credence was given to the cavalry-poor argument, government officials determined that McClellan's mounted arm should be substantially increased.[2]

Soon after Lincoln's call went out, Congressman Kellogg returned to Lansing with authority from his friend Edwin Stanton (from whom, claimed James Kidd, he "received favors such as were granted to but few") to raise two regiments of horsemen for service in the East. Kellogg had a reputation as a supporter of volunteer cavalry, having played a major role in raising the Second and Third Michigan regiments. Both outfits had served creditably in the western theater under commanders that included future Generals Philip H. Sheridan, Gordon Granger, Russell A. Alger, and Robert H. G. Minty. Now the congressman would lend his services to recruiting what would become the Sixth and Seventh Michigan.[3]

The first of the mounted outfits to be raised under Lincoln's call, the Fifth Michigan Cavalry, was already organizing by the time Kellogg journeyed home. Yet the recruitment periods of the Fifth and Sixth would overlap to a considerable degree, just as the recruiting of the Sixth and Seventh Michigan would run concurrently for a time. Thus the fortunes of all three regiments were fated to entwine.

Several officers who had served conspicuously in other regiments had helped recruit the Fifth Cavalry under grant of higher rank and authority. The prime mover was William D. Mann, who, though not a permanent resident of Michigan, had made a name in state military circles through his service with the First Cavalry. Armed with endorsements from superiors including John P. Hatch, Mann had obtained from Secretary Stanton authorization to raise a regiment of cavalry in some undesignated state. Hoping to play his Michigan connections, he severed his ties with the First early in July and travelled to Lansing to seek Austin Blair's approval to recruit in Detroit. To enhance his prospects, Mann decided to take second place in the regiment, offering the colonelcy to his old superior, Joseph Copeland, a close friend of the governor's and an officer known to be seeking promotion.[4]

Both Copeland and Blair accepted the offer, and by late July Mann had opened recruiting offices in the Detroit area. Soon he was joined by other colleagues in the First Regiment, including Lieutenants Wellington Gray and Frederick Copeland, who would command, respectively, Companies A and M of the Fifth. These and a few noncommissioned officers who later transferred from the older regiment provided the new outfit (unofficially known as "Copeland's Mounted Rifles") with a nucleus of experience that would ease its transition from camp to field.[5]

The contributions of these veterans would be augmented by the efforts of talented newcomers who fit Mann's and Copeland's standard of eligibility: "gentlemen of character and ability." Such men included Majors Freeman Norvell and Luther S. Trowbridge of Detroit and Ebenezer Gould of Owosso; Captains Allyn C. Litchfield of Blendon, Crawley P. Dake of Armada, Noah H. Ferry of Grand Haven, and John E. Clark of Ann Arbor; and Lieutenants Samuel Harris of Rochester, Myron Hickey of Davisburg, and Smith H. Hastings of Coldwater. In fact, the Fifth Cavalry would compare quite favorably with the First in the calibre of its officers; most of its non-coms and troopers would also prove to be of sturdy material. Especially in mastering the science of horsemanship, the Fifth would concede honors to no other regiment.[6]

The drive to fill the Fifth by midsummer went smoothly, although probably not as quickly as Mann later boasted ("in eight days from the time I arrived in Detroit I had mustered in... full to the last man allowed by law"). Men rushed to enlist with an enthusiasm not observed since the opening days of the war, as if Lincoln's proclamation had freed from restraints those who had resisted earlier calls due to family or professional responsibilities. Recruits arrived in Detroit in groups of fifty or more, ready to form whole companies on the spot. Such was the response that by 26 August, barely six weeks after the camp at Detroit opened its gates, more than a thousand would-be troopers were in training. Three days later, an influx of 200 more forced Mann and Copeland to halt recruiting, but not before they had an overflow on their hands. In mid-September, according to one recruit, a cook, the camp was home to "thirteen hundred men, some singing, some swearing, some hollering, some playing cards, and some dunning me for something to eat."[7]

Closing the regimental rolls left many youngsters with cavalry aspirations out in the cold. In addition to the one hundred or more superfluous men in camp, another 200 or so would-be enlistees had been turned away. Among the eager but unlucky was James Kidd, then closing out his sophomore year at the university. Having turned down a commission in an infantry regiment encamped near Ann Arbor, the youngster had held out for a berth in any mounted regiment that drew his fancy. That outfit had finally come into existence. The "Mounted Rifles" nickname of Copeland's regiment—a title reminiscent of the Regiment of Mounted Riflemen of Mexican War fame—had captivated Kidd's imagination. "The name," he later wrote, "had a certain fascination which entwined it around the memory." In late August this fascination led him and three college chums to travel to the crossroads village of Muir, just east of Ionia, to enlist—only to learn from the local recruiter that the regiment had been filled. The rejected patriots rode back to college "with heavy hearts at the lost opportunity."[8]

Kidd, convinced that the time to enlist had come, got an earlier start on exploiting the next opportunity to confront him. His father's prominence in Ionia and his support of the Republican party gained the elder Kidd an audience with Representative Kellogg. Within a week of his dispirited return from Muir, the industrialist's son had written authorization to recruit a company for the Sixth Michigan Cavalry, he to be commissioned its captain if he enlisted the minimum number of troopers—seventy-eight—within a fortnight.[9]

Overflowing with enthusiasm, Kidd threw himself into the process of recruiting from among the student body at Ann Arbor and the farmers and small businessmen in the towns surrounding Ionia. It proved to be—as he knew it would—a formidable task. The locality had been thoroughly scoured during the war's early months, and again recently by Fifth Cavalry recruiters. Then, too, three other men, all older and with more extensive connections than he, had been promised the same captaincy if they beat Kidd at the recruiting game.

Fortunately, cavalry aspirants were likely to be more numerous than candidates for infantry units such as the one Kidd had snubbed. And although Governor Blair and the legislature refused to authorize a state bounty, federal bonuses unavailable to the war's early recruits promised to be an effective inducement. A bounty of twenty-five dollars would go to every recruit on the day his regiment was mustered in, while a stipend of up to fifteen dollars per month would be paid his family. Finally, Kidd's contacts in Ann Arbor and his home village ensured him a sizable fund of manpower. As he proclaimed in Ionia on the day he received authorization to recruit, "I can get quite a mob of boys, right here in town."[10]

His primary method of luring young men to his standard was both simple and effective. At every crossroads village for miles around his recruiting base, he would hold a well-advertised war rally in the local schoolhouse. Drawing on his college contacts, he secured the services of an eloquent speaker who would stoke the patriotic fires of the audience while Kidd and his classmates—two of whom would also become officers in the Sixth Michigan—passed enlistment forms up and down the aisles. Sometimes this labor-intensive and time-consuming process would draw gratifying results, with impressionable farmboys vying with one another to be the first to pledge three years of their lives to Uncle Sam. Other meetings were hardly worth the effort involved. Once, Kidd and his speaker drove sixteen miles, presented an hour-long program before a large crowd, and found one youngster willing to "jine the cavalry."

Although prospects sometimes looked bleak and other candidates for captain boasted of enlisting more men than they could accept, Kidd beat his every rival. By mid-September—at about the same time that General McClellan was repulsing Lee's thrust into Maryland during a day-long bloodbath known as the Battle of Antietam—Kidd was leading into training camp at Grand Rapids more than enough men to fill Company E of the Sixth Michigan. He thus received the coveted commission, while his most formidable competitor, Edward L. Craw of Lyons, settled for the position of first lieutenant. Two other residents of Ionia and Lyons—Franklin P. Nichols and Ambrose L. Soule, respectively—were commissioned second lieutenants. Soule's was a supernumerary position that existed in every company of the regiment as also throughout the Fifth Cavalry.[11]

* * *

When Kidd's company arrived in camp, recruiting for the Sixth had been in progress for almost three weeks not only in the western part of the state but in Detroit and other areas that had provided numerous recruits for Copeland's Mounted Rifles. So many, in fact, had enlisted in the Fifth that Copeland and Mann sent the overflow to Grand Rapids to fill understrength units of the Sixth. Copeland also used his influence to obtain for the new regiment (as for his own) the most modern arms and equipment, including the Spencer repeating rifle. Prized by infantrymen and troopers alike for its rapid rate of fire, this 56-caliber shoulder arm contained within its stock a tube that held seven cartridges; an eighth round was in the firing chamber. Armed with the Spencer, the Fifth and Sixth Michigan would gain a reputation for power and tenacity enjoyed by few other cavalry units.[12]

The prominence Copeland had won in the First Michigan prompted state officials to tap his expertise on personnel matters. His advice influenced the composition of several cavalry outfits including the Sixth Michigan. Thus, the colonel can be held at least partially responsible for the quality of the field officers assigned to James Kidd's regiment.

The highest-ranking officers to receive Copeland's endorsement—Colonel George Gray and Lieutenant Colonel Russell Alger—were men of ability but also of contrasting personalities and leadership styles. Kidd described the thirty-nine-year-old Gray, an Irish-born attorney from Grand Rapids, as educated, polished, witty, and a good orator. Although neither a West Point graduate nor a career officer, Gray was also a martinet who took swift action against those who violated his code of discipline and deportment. More than once he planted a spurred boot on the backside of officers and men guilty of "untidy dress or shabby habiliments." Kidd remarked that "once or twice I felt the sting of his tongue, myself," though "on the whole he was very kind and courteous...."[13]

Gray's effectiveness in command was compromised by a glaring weakness. Known as "a leader at the bar of Western Michigan," for years he had patronized bars of another sort. In camp at Grand Rapids he could disguise his fondness for alcohol but after his regiment took the field the vice would render him erratic and undependable. To worsen matters, his poor relations with the reporters who covered the outfit's operations—he barred newsmen from his camp and censored the letters his soldiers wrote to hometown editors—ensured Gray a poor press. Frequent rumors of his inebriation, spread by resentful newsmen, may have played a role in Gray's resignation from the army in early 1864.[14]

Despite his harsh brand of discipline and his addiction to the bottle, Gray cut a popular figure among his officers. For the greater part of the Sixth's period in training camp, he was its lieutenant colonel. According to reports, he would ascend no higher, the colonelcy being reserved for a Regular officer. Although personally favoring a more experienced commander, Kidd signed a petition to promote Gray to the top position, as did every other company officer. The petition was duly forwarded to the governor, and on 13 October Gray received his silver eagles.[15]

Not long after he moved up, it was learned that the position he had vacated would be filled by the experienced field officer Kidd preferred, though not by a member of the regular service. As a company officer in the Second Michigan Cavalry, Russell Alger had acquired a reputation as a savvy and energetic soldier. Among other feats ascribed to him, the previous July he had led fewer than a hundred men in routing a Confederate force thirty times as large. The exploit outside Boonville, Mississippi, brought him a wound and a major's leaf, while bestowing a star on his regimental commander, Phil Sheridan.[16]

The twenty-six-year-old Alger, a lawyer and lumber magnate who had survived the financial panic of 1857 through what Kidd called "the dash and self-reliance that were marked features of his subsequent career," was, unlike the balding, ruddy-faced Gray, the beau ideal of a cavalryman, "tall, erect, handsome..." He was scrupulous about his attire—behavior Colonel Gray doubtless appreciated—and his body language was that of a man used to command, with no need to swagger. An expert horseman and tactician, he quickly took over the training of the Sixth while his commander confined himself to "executive management." Early on, Kidd decided that "as a battalion commander Colonel Alger had few equals and no superiors. He was always cool and self-poised, and his clear, resonant voice had a peculiar, agreeable quality. Twelve hundred horsemen formed in a single rank make a long line but, long as it was, every man could hear distinctly the commands that were given by him."[17]

Despite Kidd's tribute, Alger was not perfection incarnate. In combat he tended to be impulsive and impetuous. This trait had gained him honors and promotions in the West, but it would sometimes prove a liability in Virginia. Sometimes, too, Alger sought favors in a manner that bent—if it did not break—regulations. This habit would land him in trouble two years hence, to the detriment of his civilian career. Finally, he was a budding politician. On the surface, there was nothing objectionable in this—politics was the staff of life of every Civil War Army—but occasionally Alger's political skills warred with his responsibilities as an officer. At times he could be a martinet like his superior. On other occasions he would seek the goodwill of officers and the obedience of men through soft words and conciliatory gestures that some observers considered prejudicial to good order and discipline. Appropriate or not, such behavior was successful and personally rewarding. The skills it polished helped launch a postwar career that would include terms as governor of Michigan, commander of the powerful veterans organization known as the Grand Army of the Republic, Secretary of War, and United States Senator.[18]

Their flaws and failings notwithstanding, Gray and Alger would work well in tandem, and they would be supported by capable subordinates. The original majors of the regiment—Thaddeus Foote and Elijah D. Waters of Grand Rapids, and Simeon B. Brown of St. Clair—served ably enough, and two of them proved worthy of higher rank. Their influence on the Sixth, however, would be relatively short-lived. Each would leave the regiment within fifteen months, Foote and Brown to command, respectively, the Tenth and Eleventh Michigan Cavalry, and Waters because of disability.[19]

Among the line officers of the Sixth, only three had prior military experience: Captain Peter A. Weber and Lieutenant Don G. Lovell of Grand Rapids, and Lieutenant Phineas G. White of Lapeer. Weber and Lovell had gone to war as corporals in the Third Michigan Infantry; Lovell had been wounded during the Peninsula Campaign, while Weber, a former seaman from Connecticut, had won a lieutenancy in Alger's Second Cavalry. James Kidd considered the twenty-three-year-old Weber one of the finest talents in the regiment, "fitted by nature and acquirements for much higher rank than any he held." Lieutenant White, another cavalry veteran, had been quartermaster sergeant of the First Michigan before trading his staff position for a line command.[20]

An entire unit of the regiment might also be considered veterans, for they had served—albeit briefly—in the Fifth Cavalry. Part of that regiment's excess manpower, these men formed Company A of the Sixth under Captain Henry E. Thompson and Lieutenants Manning D. Birge, Stephen H. Ballard, and Joel S. Sheldon, all of Grand Rapids. All but Sheldon would leave a lasting mark on the Sixth; and Thompson and Birge would rise to field command. Ballard would be deprived of promotion only because he would spend half the war in a prison camp.[21]

Other company officers would rise to distinction, including James Kidd, who would perform conspicuously in virtually every action his outfit saw. The Ionia youth would take two wounds, rise to command his regiment, and win the brevet of brigadier general "for gallant and meritorious services." Honorable records would also be made by Captains Wesley Armstrong of Lapeer, David G. Royce of Burns, Detroit's George A. Drew, Henry L. Wise of Caledonia, and Charles W. Deane of Pentwater; as well as Lieutenants Charles Storrs, Charles E. Bolza, Harvey H. Vinton, and Benjamin F. Rockafellow (a distant relation of the New York Rockefellers).[22]

The Sixth also boasted several eminent members of the regimental staff. From Surgeon Major Daniel G. Weare of Pentwater and his assistant, Lieutenant David C. Spaulding of Grand Rapids, the regiment received excellent medical care in camp and field. Kidd characterized Surgeon Weare as "an elderly man with iron grey hair and beard which became towards the last almost as white as snow.... He looked like a preacher, though he could swear like a pirate."[23]

Weare's assistant was, like him, "a capable physician and surgeon," though destined to leave the regiment in mid-1863 to become chief surgeon of the Tenth Michigan Cavalry. Kidd remembered Dr. Spaulding as responsive to any request made of him, however unorthodox. On one occasion, he asked Spaulding's help in dealing with a member of Company E who would feign illness whenever active duty loomed. The next time this man pled illness he remained under the assistant surgeon's care for barely a week before rejoining his company—pale, sickly-looking, and willing to do anything that would keep him out of the hospital. When Kidd asked Spaulding what had caused the transformation, the doctor replied that, having found nothing physically wrong with the slacker, "I began a course of heroic treatment. He was purged, cupped, blistered, given emetics, until life really became a burden and he ran away...."[24]

In the Reverend Stephen S. N. Greely, pastor of Grand Rapids' leading Congregational church, the outfit had what James Kidd called "a unique character.... a powerful pulpit orator, a kind-hearted, simple-minded gentleman of the old school...." Although he gave untiringly of himself in ministering to the spiritual needs of the Sixth, Doctor Greeley "was more like a child than a seasoned soldier and needed the watchful care of all his friends to keep him from perishing with hunger, fatigue, and exposure." Kidd added fondly that "I always forgot my own discomforts in commiseration of those of the honest chaplain."[25]

Finally, the quartermaster's department was in good hands. Lieutenant Charles H. Patten of Grand Rapids was, in Kidd's words, "a good quartermaster, honest, energetic and capable, and that is saying a good deal for him." Patten fit Kidd's description of a model member of his much-maligned but highly important profession: full of energy, initiative, industry, tact, and administrative ability. As Kidd noted, the highest praise that could be bestowed on any quartermaster was descriptive of Charles Patten: "His wagon trains never failed to reach the front... when it was possible to get them there."[26]

* * *

The material available to the Fifth and Sixth Cavalries was shaped largely by enlistment standards: in the main, white males in their early or mid-twenties, few of whom possessed even a rudimentary military education or professional experience beyond a militia muster or two. A company selected from the descriptive rolls of the Fifth and Sixth Michigan—Company C of the Fifth, recruited from the farming villages around Detroit—is probably representative of the two dozen companies that composed these regiments. The average age of this particular unit was twenty-four, although it also contained a couple of sixteen-year-olds who disguised their youth and a few recruits fifty and above. The extreme age of some enlistees—the oldest with sixty—attests to the company's formation during a period in which settled, married men were heavily recruited.

The typical enlisted man of Company C was blue- or brown-eyed, had light-colored hair, stood just under five feet, eight inches tall, and weighed approximately 130 pounds—pretty close to the ideal size for a cavalryman, whose arm required light-weight, agile men. Of the 150 enlisted men who served, at one time or another, in Company C, fewer than fifty listed their occupation as something other than farmer—these were joiners, millers, coopers, wheel-wrights, laborers, and members of other skilled and semi-skilled professions. Because Michigan had long been a haven for immigrants, it should be no surprise that only a little more than half the members of the company were born in the state. The rest came from Ohio and the East Coast, mainly New England, New York, and Pennsylvania. A couple dozen identified themselves as natives of foreign lands: Canada, Germany, Ireland, England, Scotland, and Switzerland.[27]

Despite great variations in their physical and mental capabilities—and despite their ignorance of the profession they had adopted—most of these men would acquit themselves admirably. As James Kidd observed, "at first they were not soldiers at all.... With few exceptions, they were not accustomed to the use of arms and had everything to learn." With pardonable prejudice, he added that "for personnel and patriotism, for fortitude and endurance, they were never excelled."[28]

To activate these native talents through professional education, the Fifth and Sixth Michigan underwent almost three months of training in their camps at Detroit and Grand Rapids. In most respects, their formative weeks mirrored the experience of the First Michigan the previous year: long periods of inactivity as the camp population climbed toward regulation size, followed by days crowded with mounted and dismounted drill on the company, battalion, and regimental level, as departure day drew near.

Despite the heightened pace of activity toward the end, training camp provided a mere glimpse at the fundamentals (and a few of the nuances) of cavalry service. By the close of camp, as they stood clad in their jackboots, reinforced pantaloons and natty jackets, their caps and slouch hats at a rakish angle, they looked something like cavalrymen. At this point, they would be conversant with the care and function of their horses, if not, perhaps, with their weaponry. Thanks to experienced drillmasters like Copeland, Alger, and Mann, the recruits might even wear a patina of professionalism. Kidd claimed that by the time it broke camp his outfit had come to be "a very well drilled organization," especially in dismounted fighting, which would prove to be, tactically, its strong suit.[29]

Still, even he would have admitted that the officers and men of his own and Copeland's regiments were not soldiers by any accepted definition of the term—far less were they horse soldiers. Only experience in the field and under fire would confer such distinctions upon these would-be cavaliers.

* * *

Although the Fifth and Sixth Regiments were mustered into federal service several weeks apart—30 August in the case of the Fifth, 13 October for the Sixth—both broke camp in early December. Delays in procuring arms and equipment for Colonel Copeland's regiment accounted for the differential. In fact, when the Fifth left for Washington, D.C., most of its men continued to lack Spencer rifles as well as pistols, sabers, and a full set of accoutrements. The outfit was, however, properly attired and fully mounted. Moreover, it travelled with its own artillery support: the Ninth Michigan Battery, which had been organized and trained in conjunction with the regiment. Later the unit would be separated from the Fifth and redesignated Battery I, First Michigan Light Artillery. Under Captain Jabez J. Daniels of Hudson, formerly second lieutenant of Company E, First Michigan Cavalry, it would become a mainstay of the First Horse Artillery Brigade, Army of the Potomac.[30]

In addition to arms and equipment, the Fifth Michigan lacked field officers. When it left Detroit, it had neither colonel nor lieutenant colonel. Early in its training period, Joseph Copeland had returned to Washington, where he remained (according to some critics) to lobby for promotion. Thanks to his military, political, and judicial connections, he would be successful in this effort. A little over a month after the Fifth arrived in the capital, Copeland would part from it for good to accept a brigadier generalship in the volunteer service.[31]

In early November, Lieutenant Colonel Mann, who had commanded the regiment during its formative weeks, also departed. Although reluctant to break with an organization he had almost singlehandedly trained, Mann accepted Governor Blair's offer to become the colonel of one of the two regiments Congressman Kellogg was raising. Thus, when the Fifth Cavalry left Detroit, it was led by its senior battalion commander, thirty-five-year-old Major Norvell. Soon after it reached Washington, Norvell would move up to lieutenant colonel and, less than a month later, to colonel. Following his promotion, however, the lieutenant colonelcy would remain vacant for another two months.[32]

On the bright moonlit evening of 10 December, one day after Norvell and his outfit reached Washington, Colonels Gray and Alger led the Sixth Cavalry to the depot at Grand Rapids. Unlike the Fifth, no members of the Sixth had been issued Spencer rifles. The outfit did have its full complement of equipment and tack, and its horses were not only abundant but aesthetically grouped, Company A being mounted solely on bays, Company B on browns, C on grays, D on blacks, and so on.[33]

On the fifteenth, after a journey marked by delays and difficulties but also by what Captain Kidd called "hearty and affectionate greetings," the memory of which would forever follow the troopers, the color-specific assortment of men and animals arrived in Washington City. Forming a column at the Baltimore & Ohio depot, the regiment rode through soldier-clogged Fourteenth Street to Camp Copeland, situated atop Meridian Hill, across the city from the Fifth Michigan's camp on East Capitol Hill.[34]

The ride to war may have furnished happy memories for the Fifth and Sixth Michigan, but journey's end brought to their attention some grim realities. On 13 December, members of the Fifth heard the thunder of artillery wafting north from Fredericksburg, Virginia, where the Army of the Potomac was advancing to disaster under Major General Ambrose E. Burnside, successor to the slow-moving and politically troublesome McClellan. In later days a trickle of wounded from the fighting front became a flood of mangled men, many of whom were received at Columbia College, just south of the Sixth's camp, which had been converted into a hospital. The sights that met the eye and the cries that assaulted the ears told the new arrivals that the war they had just entered was not yet over, its outcome very much in doubt, its thirst for suffering and destruction far from quenched.[35]

* * *

Just as excess recruits from the Fifth Michigan provided the nucleus of the Sixth Michigan, the Seventh gained its initial members from the overflow of enlistees in the Sixth. The first of these—mainly residents of the Niles and Battle Creek areas—were mustered into service on 13 October along with others who had been accepted into Colonel Gray's regiment. In time they formed Company A of the Seventh, under Captain Alexander Walker.[36]

The new outfit's training camp did not get fully underway until the first week of November, when William Mann, sporting newly embroidered eagles, reached Grand Rapids and assumed command. He was joining his fourth regiment in as many months. Having served as a line officer in the First Michigan and founder and executive officer of the Fifth, Mann had recently left the Sixth Cavalry after a stormy twenty-four-hours as its commander. One day after accepting Austin Blair's offer to fill that position, he had been called to the governor's office in Lansing, where he found his patron besieged by Grand Rapids officials incensed over his appointment. Mann quoted the delegation of congressmen and judges as admitting that he "might be a good sort of a fellow, possibly a good soldier and a competent commander, but he was not a Michigan man, nor a Grand Rapids man."[37]

The governor's visitors very much wanted the local legal eagle, George Gray, for the coveted position; they suggested that Mann take, instead, a cavalry regiment whose colonelcy Blair had yet to fill, the Seventh Michigan. That outfit, he was assured, already had a thousand recruits in camp and would obtain the requisite 200 more within the week. The callow officer recalled his reaction to the situation: "Boy as I then was, somewhat diffident of my own ability and impressed by the age, character and position of the men surrounding me, I, in what I sometimes thought afterwards was a foolish moment, assented to the arrangement and accepted the Colonelcy of the Seventh...."[38]

Only after he had arrived at Grand Rapids did Mann realize that the promises made him—including the opportunity to organize a supporting unit of horse artillery, as he had for the Fifth Cavalry—were emptier than a ghost town. Including Captain Walker's company, a total of 237 recruits were in camp, and no efforts were underway to enlist anyone else. It was a dead certainty that the Sixth Michigan would be taken into service before the Seventh, negating Congressman Kellogg's pledge that Mann would gain seniority over Colonel Gray. "My first impulse," Mann admitted, "was to throw up my commission and retire from the service."[39]

After spending an unhappy night at the camp known as Lee Barracks, Mann tried to adjust his mood. Finally he decided that "my ambition, tastes, nervous energy, or patriotism," would not allow him to flee in the face of adversity: "I determined to go to work, trusting to the same luck that had given me the Fifth Regiment so quickly to fill up the Seventh, determining to make it as good as the Fifth or Sixth, and if possible better."[40]

By all indicators, it would be a long, hard climb. Looking back years later, Asa B. Isham, a Detroiter who had become the regiment's historian, detailed some of the obstacles facing the colonel: "Enlistments lagged; for so many recruits had already gone [into the army], that men could not well be spared from the farm, the workshop, the counting-house, and other departments of industry." By now, too, recruiting inducements had lost much of their power. Compared to those of other states, the bounties offered to Michigan enlistees were rather paltry; and rumors of a state draft, which had received currency earlier in the conflict, no longer rang true.[41]

Isham continued: "The war had progressed far enough to make it plain to everyone of average intelligence that it was to be continued and bloody. Therefore, those that went in at this time faced the prospect of three years of battle and peril for... thirteen dollars a month, hard tack and bacon included. With the hazard so out of proportion to the compensation, it is not remarkable that there was not the same impulsive patriotic ardor to fill up the ranks of organizing regiments that was exhibited in the first year of the contest, when the war was regarded more in the light of an ephemeral frolic...."[42]

What patriotic ardor there was, Mann resolved to activate, as did his second-in-command, Allyn Litchfield, formerly captain of Company B, Fifth Cavalry. Much as James Kidd had scoured the hamlets of Ann Arbor and Ionia, these officers, along with members of the embryonic regimental staff, canvassed western Michigan in a fervid search for manpower. They ranged along the banks of the Grand River and even ventured toward Lake Michigan, beating the tocsin and treating the populace to speeches that appealed to men's better instincts even as they played to their dread of disunion and distaste for treason.

Slowly, gradually, these tactics produced results. As wintry winds skipped across the Grand River Valley, Lee Barracks (which, despite the congressman's inability to keep his promises, Mann redesignated "Camp Kellogg") began at last to fill up. By mid-December, the rendezvous held enough horses and riders to initiate dismounted drill. The results were predictably dismal. While some of Mann's subordinates threw up their hands in disgust each time a recruit missed a step in skirmish formation, Lieutenant Bradley M. Thompson of Company C would dig into his pocket and fling a fair-sized rock at the man's head along with "a volley of blood-curdling oaths."[43]

Such punishment could be an effective motivator; even so, to much official dismay the men learned the cavalryman's art with painful deliberation. Many could not even master the simplest dismounted tactics, provoking the principal drillmaster, an elderly captain named Bothan, to exclaim: "Oh, stupid! stupid! even an ox may be taught to know right from left, but ye will never learn!"[44]

The recruits' troubles were not confined to the drill-plain. When not fumbling through the day's exercises, they were fighting the

January weather. The structures erected for their accommodation offered little protection; winds whistled and howled through cracks in the barracks' walls. In the mess hall "it was too cold to sit down," reported Sergeant Isham, "and meals were therefore eaten standing, with every muscle in the body undergoing exercise. At night blanketed forms huddled around the red-hot stoves, giving no heed to the demand for sleep, in the endeavor to keep warm...."[45]

By early February, the Seventh, if not fully manned, was adequately mounted. Its horses were especially fine specimens ("never was a regiment sent out of Michigan," Isham boasted, "with better mounts)." Their high quality was owing to the keen-eyed resourcefulness of four subalterns, all of them experienced horsemen: Captains Lynus F. Walker of Royalton (Company B), George A. Armstrong of Eaton Rapids (Company D), and Richard Douglas of Ross (Company H), and Lieutenant Farnham Lyon of Grand Rapids, the regimental quartermaster.[46]

With a full complement of horseflesh, drill achieved a new level of zeal, one intensified by the approach of the muster-in process. But a faster pace did not translate into greater proficiency. For one thing, many of the handsome-looking beasts proved fractious. "Biting, kicking, rearing, and bucking horses made life a burden to those who had drawn them," noted Sergeant Isham, "while they occasioned a high degree of hilarity among those that bestrode more decorous beasts; but the wayward were gradually toned down and brought into subjugation."[47]

As January waned, state authorities took note that Camp Kellogg held the minimum number of companies—ten—required to form a regiment of volunteer cavalry. These they rather hopefully designated as members of the Seventh Michigan Cavalry. To mark the occasion, Colonel Mann proclaimed that "we now have a place and name among the many hundreds of gallant bands... that compose the great armies, the bulwarks, the defenders of our beloved country in this its dark struggles. We are hereafter to be reckoned among the noble Michigan regiments which have so often distinguished themselves in a manner to call forth praise from the entire land...." Here was oratory worthy of a student of the late, eloquent Thornton Brodhead.[48]

The regiment's next milestone occurred on 27 January, when

Lieutenant Colonel James Oakes of the Fourth United States Cavalry swore the men into federal service. The ceremony indicated that the Seventh's time in camp was drawing to a close. The fortunes of the Union demanded that even raw recruits hasten to the front. In the western theater, where Federal forces under Major General William S. Rosecrans had recently won a major victory in Middle Tennessee, the outlook was promising, even bright. In Virginia, however, the Army of the Potomac was still reeling from the debacle at Fredericksburg. Ambrose Burnside's successor, "Fighting Joe" Hooker, had vowed to restore his command's health and confidence—he had made a special pledge to reorganize and upgrade George Stoneman's mounted arm—but to attain his goal he required a new fund of manpower.

Under these circumstances, the Seventh Michigan was fortunate to be allotted a few more weeks to reach a minimal level of effectiveness. By the third week in February, it was time to go. On the twentieth, the horses of Companies A through E, accompanied by a twenty-man detail, were loaded onto an eastbound train. The next day the animals of Companies F through K were placed in another set of boxcars. Under the supervision of Colonel Mann, Lieutenant Colonel Litchfield, and Majors John S. Huston of Lyons and George K. Newcombe of Owosso, early on the twenty-second the main body of the regiment, some 700 strong, boarded a third train to start the tortuous journey to Virginia. The departing men left behind a few dozen comrades under Major Henry W. Granger of Grand Rapids to perform caretaker duties at Camp Kellogg and to recruit Companies L and M.[49]

Asa Isham described the low-key sendoff given the regiment that would provide the fourth and final piece of the Michigan Cavalry Brigade:

"No ladies appeared upon the scene to present us with [gifts]... no lunches were spread. Our martial ardor was not fanned by flag and sword presentations. No soaring orator pointed us to the achievements of antiquity.... The near and dear ones of the few that belonged to Grand Rapids and its immediate vicinity were there to bid us Godspeed and a safe return, and pathetic partings were not wanting."[50]

CHAPTER SIX

Hunting Stuart and Mosby

While Michigan's newest cavalry regiment chuffed and chugged toward Washington, eager for the fray, the state's oldest lay in camp outside the capital, mired in snow and gloom. The First Michigan had been stationed near Fort Scott, midway between the District of Columbia and Alexandria, since retiring, with the rest of Pope's army, from Second Bull Run. The crushing defeat its army had suffered at the hands of Lee, Longstreet, and Jackson had demolished regimental morale, and nothing that occurred during the next six months had rebuilt it.[1]

Not even the news of McClellan's strategic victory at Sharpsburg, Maryland, had improved the collective frame of mind. The mid-September victory along Antietam Creek had been won without the Wolverines' help; moreover, it had come to be regarded as an aberration, a short-lived success in a long line of enduring defeats. The war continued, and no end was in sight. Lincoln's call for more troops had come too recently to improve the situation, and the only result of Ambrose Burnside's succession to command had been another disastrous battle.

A faint hope had appeared in the guise of Burnside's successor, who promised better days; but with the third spring of the war fast approaching, "Fighting Joe" Hooker had yet to redeem his pledge. George Kilborn of Company F (recently promoted to second lieutenant) summarized the popular perception as of February 1863: "We are not gaining much ground. The defeat at Fredericksburg... overshadows every thing. Confidence in the Civil & Military Leaders is below zero. As matters go now this *great Army* will be used up in detail—the Government ruined and at last a dishonorable and ignoble peace made with rebels on their own *terms*." It was enough to make any man who had enlisted out of patriotic motives feel downright foolish.[2]

More than a bleak military picture was behind the decline in morale. No one in the regiment had received so much as a dollar in pay over the past four months. Another factor was evident to any visitor to snow-clogged "Camp Buford": the ranks of the regiment were terribly thin. Since taking the field just over a year ago, the First had lost thirty men killed or mortally wounded, sixty dead of illness, almost as many wounded in action (many of them still in the hospital), and almost 200 others taken prisoner, the majority on 30 August. Early in November the Bull Run POWs had been exchanged for an equal number of Confederates, but three months later most had yet to return to action. Then, too, in late November Company D had been permanently detached from the regiment to do provost duty at Alexandria, Virginia. Adding to these numbers the dozens of officers and men incapacitated by illness or on detached duty and the regiment, once 1,200 strong, could count fewer than 700 available for duty.[3]

In the wake of Second Bull Run, regimental command had undergone change. To replace Thornton Brodhead, Major Town had been promoted colonel on 30 October. Town was a popular choice to succeed a much-mourned superior, but his health remained a concern, especially after his wounding at Lewis Ford. Lieutenant Colonel Copeland's successor, though not the logical candidate, was also well received. Instead of Major Paldi, the senior battalion commander, Peter Stagg had been promoted to second-in-command of the regiment early in December, having risen to major less than a month earlier. To fill the vacancies created by Town's promotion and the recent resignation of William Atwood, the dashing Melvin Brewer had been promoted to major, as had Captain Howrigan, about to rejoin the First after six months in prison and parole camp. Much shuffling also took place in the company ranks, among both officers and non-coms.[4]

Promotions might lend the regiment stability, but there appeared little likelihood that the gaps torn in the ranks by debility, illness, and wounds would soon be closed. Although a perfunctory effort at recruiting had been made back home, the manpower drives of the Fifth, Sixth, and Seventh Michigan had all but denuded the state of cavalry material. Governor Blair and Adjutant General Robertson seemed more interested in stocking the new outfits—green as they were and thus less likely to make a contribution to the war effort—than in restoring to peak operating condition a presumably more valuable commodity: a body of seasoned veterans.

To be sure, the First Michigan—what remained of it—was a veteran outfit. Having been thoroughly trained, having been tested at Kernstown, Winchester, Bull Run, and in numerous skirmishes and small unit engagements, and having been steeled by the thousand and one hardships of field duty, the regiment had become efficient and proficient. Its men had acquired many skills: how to function as individuals and also as gears in a mighty machine; when and how to fight in the saddle and on foot; how to mount an attack and how to support other attackers; how to locate the enemy, how to draw his fire, and how to suppress that fire. Above all, each trooper had learned how to protect himself—and how to cover his comrade's backside—in any given situation.

Given the high state of their development, the men felt they had earned membership in a major field command. But the Army of the Potomac, which had given them a home back in 1861, no longer seemed to want them. Instead of retaking the field under McClellan with the opportunity to overcome their unhappy experience with the Army of Virginia, the troopers of the First had languished as components of the XXII Army Corps, Department of Washington. While strategically important to the war effort, this force seemed destined to serve well behind the front lines. As though to emphasize its backwater status, the corps was led by Major General Samuel P. Heintzelman, a septuagenarian considered unfit for field duty. Heintzelman's command was peopled largely by infantrymen and heavy artillerists, but it included a large contingent of cavalry—not only the First Michigan but other regiments that had served under John Buford: the Fifth New York, First Vermont, and First (West) Virginia. The brigade these outfits comprised, which also embraced the Second and Eighteenth Pennsylvania, plus detachments of the

First New Jersey and First Ohio Cavalry, was commanded by Colonel R. Butler Price.[5]

The First Michigan and its comrades had not sat idle since Second Bull Run. In addition to manning some of Washington's forts, Price's brigade had been guarding the countryside between Leesburg, on the upper Potomac, and the mouth of the Occoquan River, an area that took in such major outposts as Centreville, Chantilly, Dranesville, and the village of Occoquan. In these and other locales the troopers had tangled not only with regular Confederates—mainly raiding forces from J.E.B. Stuart's division—but with guerrillas, bushwhackers, and the partisan rangers of Lieutenant (soon to be Major) John Singleton Mosby, who bedeviled the occupiers of eastern Virginia as though by divine decree.

Mosby's men posed an omnipresent menace. When not attacking Price's camps, picket posts, and horse herds, they were slipping through the lines—sometimes in disguise, sometimes boldly in Rebel gray—to gather critical intelligence. Price and his colleague, Colonel Sir Percy Wyndham of the First New Jersey, an English soldier-of-fortune with continental notions of warfare, often blasted the partisans as horse-thieves. The slight, soft-spoken Mosby merely replied that any horses he took came with riders armed to the teeth.[6]

Through the fall of 1862 and the winter that followed, the First Michigan saw combat on an intermittent basis, as well as much scouting. In mid-November portions of the regiment scouted from Camp Buford to Leesburg, thence to Aldie and other points in the Loudoun Valley familiar to the veterans of Atwood's battalion. Throughout December other detachments scouted from the Washington suburbs northward and westward to Gum Springs, to Hernden and Guilford Stations on the Loudoun & Hampshire Railroad, and to an Occoquan River village with the mellifluous name of Frying Pan. As the New Year came in, the main body reconnoitered farther north to Lewinsville and Dranesville, scene of the war's earliest skirmishing.[7]

From the last week in December through the latter part of February the regiment conducted a running war with the troopers of Stuart and Mosby. The small size of their detachments ensured that the Wolverines came off second best most of the time. Three days before year's end, Lieutenant Maxwell of Company E—whose heroics near Mount Jackson the previous April had started him on the through route to promotion—rendered "efficient service" in opposing Stuart's raiders at Selectman's Ford on the Occoquan. The more numerous Rebels, bent on striking neighboring supply depots, eventually muscled their way across the river, compelling Maxwell's unit and supports from the Second Pennsylvania to retire under "a perfect shower of bullets." While the First escaped this perilous situation without casualties, one week later Maxwell and three of his people were captured by Brigadier General Wade Hampton's brigade of Stuart's division at Brentsville, eleven miles from Select-man's Ford. Three days after that, however, the captives were liberated by a roving band of regular cavalry from the Army of the Potomac.[8]

Early in the new year other elements of the First, while patrolling the Occoquan line, fell prey to surprise attacks. On 31 January Mosby's men swept down on a picket post along the Leesburg and Alexandria Turnpike near Frying Pan, snatching up twenty-five members of Companies C and I. And on 13 February three scouting detachments under overall command of Captain Charles F. Snyder were ambushed, one after another, while on patrol near Brentsville. One trooper was killed, two were wounded, and twenty-one others, including Frederic Schmalzried, were taken prisoner. Schmalzried—who blamed Snyder for deserting the men at a critical time—remained in a Richmond POW camp for only three days before he and his comrades were sent to a parole facility at Annapolis, Maryland. It would be three months, however, before any of the captives rejoined the regiment.[9]

The First Michigan attempted to gain some measure of revenge late in February, after a large segment of Stuart's cavalry, under Brigadier General Fitzhugh Lee, attacked the distended picket line of the Army of the Potomac northwest of Fredericksburg. Near Hartwood Church the raiders drove in detachments of Brigadier General William W. Averell's cavalry division, ransacked their camps, captured 150 defenders, and repulsed hundreds of others who attempted to interfere.[10]

While Averell organized a pursuit, his boss, Joe Hooker, sought assistance from the Washington defense forces. General Heintzelman responded by sending upwards of 2,000 troopers, including a large detachment of the First Michigan under Lieutenant Colonel Stagg, down the Orange & Alexandria toward potential routes of enemy retreat. A hoped-for confrontation never materialized: Lee's men slipped back across the Rappahannock next day without opposition. Still, Stagg's men performed their duty so well under such miserable conditions—rain, mud, and bone-chilling wind—that he presented each of the companies involved with two canteens filled with whiskey. (This was in keeping with the lieutenant colonel's style; he always seemed to have on hand liquid refreshment of the sort denied his men by regulations.)[11]

A gift libation did not adequately compensate the First for the hardships it had endured through the winter now crawling to a close. As March came in, dozens of troopers, their endurance weakened by near-constant picket and scouting duty in inclement weather, were moved to the hospital at Camp Buford for treatment of various illnesses, mainly upper respiratory complaints. To offset the man-power loss, Colonel Town and his subordinates made excessive demands on the healthier members of the regiment. Some began to hope, as Alfred Ryder put it in a letter home, that Stuart would attack again, this time to "gobble up some of our stylish officers."[12]

The worsening relations between the shoulder straps and the rank-and-file appeared to come to a head on 5 March. That afternoon Peter Stagg ordered the main body of the regiment, which had grouped at Wolf Run Shoals on the Occoquan, to fall in for inspection of arms, followed immediately by a dress parade. The onerous routine led to catcalls and complaints. To punish the grumblers, Stagg compelled the men to fall in three times more—a tactic that prompted several to break ranks and shout out their displeasure. An enraged Stagg placed the loudest offenders under arrest, which only provoked their comrades. As Private Dexter Macomber of Company C noted in his diary, "the boys not liking to be worsted by whisky drinking Officers continued shouting untill [sic] 10 Pm," when the regiment finally fell into an uneasy sleep.[13]

The small-scale mutiny of 5 March did not recur. The captives were soon released, and the trouble appeared to blow over. Yet the incident pointed up growing tensions in the ranks that boded ill for the regiment's future. Until the daily workload lessened—perhaps until progress in the war effort became evident—Michigan's first and finest regiment of volunteer cavalry might collapse under the weight of sagging morale.

* * *

In sharp contrast to the lot of the First Michigan, life tasted sweet and the future looked bright for the new arrivals of the Fifth and Sixth Regiments. To be sure, camp life in the capital was no more entertaining than camp life in Detroit and Grand Rapids; with the exception of a few government buildings, Washington was a most unimpressive place. In James Kidd's words, the city consisted mainly of "wide streets of mud, through which teams of army mules, hauling heavy wagons, tugged and floundered." The more sensitive troopers recoiled from local monuments to foulness, including the capital's notorious red-light district and its noxious canal, which reeked of human waste and other refuse.[14]

There were some advantages to service in Washington. When not on duty, the enlisted men could sightsee. Sergeant Edwin B. Bigelow of Company B, Fifth Cavalry, enjoyed an outing at the Capitol, "which is by far the grandest building I ever saw.... Afterward I visited the Smithsonian Institute situated on 7th St. The building is of brick and contains a museum which contains specimens of *almost* everything man can think of, besides a gallery of Indian portraits which are very fine...."[15]

In viewing the local attractions, officers fared better then their men. In mid-December, a delegation from the Fifth Cavalry visited the White House as guests of Congressman Kellogg. James Kidd recalled a similar visit a few weeks later by officers of the Sixth. One by one, Mr. Kellogg introduced the visitors to President Lincoln, who offered each an hospitable if diffident handshake. Writing of the occasion years later, Kidd recalled "the terrible strain under which he [Lincoln] seemed to be suffering; the appearance of weariness which he brought with him to the interview; the pale, anxious cast of his countenance; the piteous, far-away look of his eyes...."

Kidd felt especially sorry for his host when Lincoln turned to leave, only to be halted by a rather pompous address by Mr. Kellogg, who praised the officers as "Wolverines... on the track of 'Jeb' Stuart, whom they propose to pursue and capture...." With a weary grin, the president assured his visitors that "it would give me much greater pleasure to see 'Jeb Stuart' in captivity than it has given me to see you." A moment later he was out the door.[16]

In subsequent weeks, emissaries of both regiments continued their political rounds. Sometimes escorted by Congressman Kellogg, sometimes by Brigadier General-to-be Copeland, they met political luminaries including Secretary of War Stanton, Navy Secretary Gideon Welles, and Secretary of the Treasury Salmon P. Chase. They also called on Major General Henry W. Halleck, McClellan's successor as Commanding General of the Army, as well as Quartermaster General Montgomery C. Meigs and Brigadier General Silas Casey, to whose division in the Defenses of Washington the Wolverines had been assigned.[17]

Meeting the great men of the nation was an exciting experience, but it constituted a sideshow to the training mission of the Fifth and Sixth Michigan. Many duties occupied the regiments between five A.M., when reveille was blown, and nine P.M., when the lights were extinguished, but at least six hours out of every day were spent on the drill plain. Inevitably, drill took on a vigor, an earnestness, it had never captured in Michigan. It appeared particularly realistic in the camp of the Fifth, many of whose men had been armed and accoutered before leaving home. Between 10 and 18 January the remainder of the outfit received its Spencer rifles and entered fully into the training regimen.[18]

During this same period, the Sixth Cavalry was finally issued enough sabers to begin practicing with them. Not until 10 February, however, did the Sixth take receipt of its small arms: Colt revolvers and a combination of Spencer rifles and Burnside carbines. Armed with such formidable tools of war, both regiments practiced fighting in line and in column, on horseback and on foot, trotting forward in light skirmish order and pounding across the drill field at full gallop, everyone shouting at the top of his lungs.[19]

By the last week in January, field service appeared imminent—at least for the Fifth Michigan, which had been training a few weeks longer than its sister regiment. Private William Ball of Company M informed his parents in Algansee that despite the ever-present snow and mud, "we have every thing ready to leave here... [at] a minute['s] warning and go to the front lines near the enemy." Most would welcome that warning. In a letter to his brother in Detroit, Major Ferry described his frame of mind succinctly: "I want to fight."[20]

Many members of the Sixth Cavalry, despite lacking shoulder-arms, were similarly inclined, wishing to escape a camp that one member of Company C likened to a maximum-security prison. The restrictions placed on one's ability to come and go, the trooper complained, violated "our former notions of American liberty." Other members of the Sixth were too ill to travel. Writing to the editor of the *Grand Rapids Daily Eagle* on 2 February, Sergeant James Somerville, a regimental saddler, described his comrades as ravaged by pneumonia, rheumatism, typhoid fever, and measles; he also reported a few cases of the dreaded smallpox.[21]

If not in peak physical condition, the regiment appeared to be morally healthy. Presumably after consulting with Chaplain Greely, Sergeant Somerville observed that "there is not so much boisterous conduct or profanity [in the ranks] as at an earlier day." Neither were there as many cases of drunkenness or absence without leave. One possible reason was that religious services were held on a regular basis before large congregations. Moreover, the good chaplain received excellent support from the regimental staff; Somerville reported that he had never heard either Colonel Gray or Lieutenant Colonel Alger utter a curse word. He added, however, that "I wish I could say as much about all the officers."[22]

* * *

In the ranks of the Fifth and Sixth, it was generally assumed that field service would commence by the end of January. On the twenty-seventh, however, the latest in a series of snowstorms to hit Washington trapped both regiments in their camps. Not until the first days of February did the men venture forth and when they did they had to navigate seas of mud.[23]

On 1 February, Companies D and H of the Fifth became the first element of either regiment to leave the capital, marching up the river road to Poolesville, Maryland, north of Edwards Ferry. At Poolesville the squadron patrolled the Potomac just above the upper flank of

Colonel Price's picket line. The new arrivals undoubtedly exchanged greetings, and perhaps visits, with the troopers of the First Michigan, on the lower bank. A few days later the squadron was joined by Companies I and M of the Sixth, under Captain Charles W. Deane. Armed only with sabers and sidearms, Deane's men had been sent to break up a network of civilians smuggling medical supplies and war goods to the enemy. Although Companies D and H would soon rejoin their regiment, Deane's people were fated to remain in the Harpers Ferry region, tracking guerrillas and chasing down bands of raiders, for several months.[24]

According to rumor, the departure of Companies D and H presaged a general movement by the Fifth Cavalry. A native of Cheshire, Michigan, Corporal William H. Rockwell of Company I, informed his family that soon after the squadron left camp the remainder of the regiment got ready to move, no questions asked, "for that is the first duty of a soldier." But the day passed without a further exodus. Rockwell observed that "there was lots of the boys that was sick this morning on account of the [expected receipt of] marching orders but some was rejoiced to think we were agoing to leave this mud hole...."[25]

On the morning of Sunday, the eighth, Colonel Norvell at last ordered the Fifth to strike tents and move out. As the regiment formed column south, Noah Ferry could hardly believe they were going forth so soon after being hit with rain and snow, "thinking... that we should have to swim most of the way." Though the roads proved to be drier than he feared, the trip to and across Long Bridge was lengthy and tedious, prolonged by the fits and starts common to inexperienced travelers.[26]

Soon after reaching Virginia, the slow but eager horsemen met a party from Price's brigade which they joined in trolling for Rebels as far west as the Shenandoah Valley. The three-day expedition, which proved largely uneventful, was a good way for a rookie outfit to break into field service. The column wended its way through the Loudoun Valley, past Aldie and Upperville where the lead regiments captured a half-dozen stragglers, and on to Ashby's Gap in the Blue Ridge. By the eleventh, when the Fifth Michigan returned to Camp Copeland, it reported itself "unable to find any large body of troops."

The regiment's only casualty was a member of Company I, wounded in the leg by the accidental discharge of his Spencer.[27]

In fact, the only memorable feature of the expedition was the disgraceful conduct of Freeman Norvell. The second day out Sergeant Bigelow found his commander "*very* drunk." A comrade complained that "the little hound... was so beastly drunk that two men had to hold him on his horse." Two days later Norvell was again inebriated, so much so that he made the homeward jaunt in an ambulance.[28]

Placed under arrest soon after reaching Washington, the mortified colonel tendered his resignation, which was accepted on 27 February. His departure would leave the regiment in the hands of Lieutenant Colonel Gould, who probably expected to wear the eagles his predecessor had relinquished. If so, he was doomed to disappointment: the colonelcy would lie vacant for more than three months and when it was filled it would go to someone other than Gould.[29]

After returning to the all-too-familiar confines of Camp Copeland, the Fifth remained there for two weeks, drilling and picketing. On the evening of 26 February came orders to leave Washington on another expedition. Next morning at two o'clock Colonel Gould was leading sleep-dulled troopers across the Potomac to Fort Scott, there to rejoin the main body of Price's brigade, today under the foppish Colonel Wyndham.[30]

This operation also provided the Sixth Michigan with its introduction to active campaigning. Just after midnight on the twenty-seventh James Kidd returned from liberty in the capital, "completely tired out and nearly sick," to find his regiment's camp "all bustle and confusion." At fifteen minutes after two the regiment was heading south across the Potomac, Kidd reeling in the saddle from fatigue and a pounding headache, possibly the result of off-duty drinking. Whatever the nature of his ailment, a several-hour march seems to have cured it. By the time his column reached Fort Scott Kidd was back to health—thanks in part to numerous cups of coffee brewed from a sack of beans sent him by his mother.[31]

The Sixth reached Fort Scott a few hours before the Fifth Michigan. By sundown on the twenty-eighth men of both regiments were greeting each other warmly. From now on, with infrequent exceptions, they would serve side-by-side. Their attachment to Price's brigade, however, was only temporary; a few weeks ago they officially had been grouped into a demi-brigade under General Copeland. That officer was not with his command on this occasion, possibly to avoid overslaughing Colonel Wyndham, whose sensitive pride would not tolerate his being outranked on a mission he had some claim to lead.[32]

In addition to a stickler on seniority, Sir Percy was a showman who enjoyed orating to his troops on the march, which he viewed as a spur to morale. He attempted vocally to motivate his present command on numerous occasions over the next two days. By the time the fast-paced scout ended on the twenty-eighth at Falmouth, headquarters of Hooker's army on the Rappahannock, Lieutenant Harris of the Fifth Michigan had sized up the raiding leader as "a big bag of wind."[33]

Harris and many of his comrades also disparaged the raid itself, "which for hardships and barrenness of results," James Kidd declared, "will vie with any similar expeditions that ever attempted to bag the Rebel General Stewart [sic] or any other *Fox.*" Like Price's recent trip to the Blue Ridge, Wyndham's expedition fatigued his men and horses but failed to capture more than a handful of Rebels—none of them Stuart's men—either en route to Falmouth or on the return trip to Washington on 3 March. Adding to his misdeeds, in his after-action report Sir Percy appeared to blame the Michigan regiments for the disappointing outcome. He claimed that the Wolverines had been late in joining his expedition and had run out of forage midway through, causing it to end prematurely. By all indications, his criticisms were overdrawn and unwarranted.[34]

By nine P.M. on the third, tired men and blown horses had reached Washington, "safe," as Corporal Rockwell put it, "but not sound." From the camp on Meridian Hill, Colonel Gray vented his frustration over the conduct and results of the expedition. In a report to General Copeland he complained that "in consequence of the extraordinary condition of the roads and the rapidity of the march... the brigade has sustained great loss.... It will be many days before large numbers of the horses which reached camp can be used, and several, I fear, are rendered wholly unfit for future service." With more than a trace of sarcasm, he added: "Not having any knowledge of the object of the expedition, I am, of course, unable to say whether or not it was accomplished. We did not see the enemy, and our march from his supposed direction was generally at least as rapid as toward him...."[35]

For the next two weeks the Fifth and Sixth suffered the effects of Wyndham's recklessness. During this period rumors began to sweep Michigan that the Sixth was in complete ruin, its men and mounts broken beyond repair, Colonel Gray incapacitated by drunkenness. Chaplain Greely came to the regiment's, and the colonel's, defense. "It is untrue, every word of it," he insisted to the editor of the *Daily Eagle*.[36]

By mid-March, the clouds that had been hovering over the camps of the Fifth and Sixth began to lift. Charges that the Wolverines had somehow scuttled Wyndham's raid faded away after Sir Percy was relieved of his command and returned to his regiment in Hooker's army. The Englishman's demise had begun on the ninth when Mosby's raiders, whom the colonel so often promised to annihilate, slipped through his lines at Fairfax Court House, raided his head-quarters, and kidnapped Brigadier General Edwin H. Stoughton, commanding the post. To many observers, however, Wyndham's departure was a mixed blessing. His replacement was another pompous, overrated foreigner: Major General Julius Stahel. A Hungarian emigre who had transferred from an infantry command in the polyglot XI Corps, Army of the Potomac, Stahel had been assigned every cavalry unit in the XXII Corps, including Copeland's and Price's brigades.[37]

Soon after Sir Percy's leave-taking, the picture for the Union cavalry in the East brightened with news that General Averell's troopers had surprised and uprooted Fitz Lee's brigade near Kelly's Ford on the Rappahannock—retaliation for Hartwood Church. Suddenly the newspapers began to speak of a rejuvenated cavalry, one capable of giving as good as it got—or better—against the vaunted horsemen of J.E.B. Stuart.[38]

To further improve the mood of the Fifth and Sixth Michigan, their animals recovered from their recent exertions more quickly than anticipated. As a result, on 11 March both regiments returned to Virginia, spending three days of desultory scouting near Fairfax Court House under their new commander. Sent back to Washington on the fourteenth, they resumed drill in their respective camps until recrossing Long Bridge on the twenty-fourth and moving to Bailey's Cross Roads, midway between the capital and Fairfax, "hoping," as Sergeant Bigelow put it, "to do our distracted country some good by being nearer the enemy."[39]

The men did not know it, but they had left Washington for the final time. When they crossed to Virginia on the twenty-fourth, the camps on Meridian and Capitol Hills were broken up and all equipage, down to the travelling forges, was transferred to Stahel's headquarters in the Fairfax Court House-Vienna region. The Michiganders reached that locale on the twenty-sixth to find their camps separated only by a hillside and a brook. After several days under canvas the men realized that their relocation would be long-term.[40]

Most of the troopers applauded the change. In Washington they had been restricted to rear-guard service while other units, closer to the front, carried on the war. In northern Virginia, if not in sight of the guns, they were at least within earshot of them.

* * *

On 27 February, Colonel Mann and the Seventh Michigan climbed out of the cars that had carried them to Washington, stretched legs stiffened by a five-day journey with few rest-stops, and marched to a temporary barracks in the heart of the city. Freed from confinement two days later, they were escorted to the stables where the horses that had preceded them were corralled. Mounting, they trotted up Fourteenth Street to the camp awaiting them on Meridian Hill, just south of the home of the Sixth Cavalry.

Mud was so deep everywhere the men walked that eighteen-year-old Ed Harvey of Prairieville and Company A doubted the city contained a single paved street. Sergeant Isham recalled that within minutes of being tethered, the horses were "knee-deep in the cold ooze, without shelter." This was a most undesirable situation; to remedy it, a rude stable was erected in furtherance of Colonel Mann's injunction that the horses be protected from the elements even if the men were not. Mann also demanded that the animals be fed, watered, and groomed at least once a day and that the veterinary sergeant of each company regularly inspect his unit's mounts for loose shoes, saddle sores, and symptoms of equine diseases such as "scratches" and "grease-heel."[41]

The horses attended to, the next order of business was to pitch tents. But before all dwellings were up several inches of wet snow descended upon the camp. Warding off the chill proved difficult, for the Seventh lacked wood for fuel and for stockading the tents. Everything considered, it was a most inhospitable introduction to service in the eastern theater.[42]

The officers, at least, made the best of a bad situation. Within a few days of arriving, Colonel Mann named the new rendezvous, like the old, "Camp Kellogg," and published what was surely one of the most detailed duty schedules ever to guide a volunteer cavalry regiment. The daily routine included reveille at sunrise, stable call twenty minutes later, breakfast call at 7:30 A.M., sick call at eight, assembly of buglers at 8:15 and of guards five minutes afterward, adjutant's call at 8:30, and orders call at 8:45. The day's first drill began at 9:15, followed by dinner at 12:30 P.M., stable call at one o'clock, officers' and sergeants' drill at two, assembly of buglers at 3:30, general assembly at 3:35, dress parade at 3:45, supper at 5:15, officers' call at 6:30, second stable call at 6:45, tattoo at 8:30, and lights' out at nine P.M. The order warned that "no departure from the above schedule will be tolerated."[43]

From the first, the most popular call was the one that sent the sick, those who thought they were sick, and those who wished their superiors to think they were sick, to the surgeon's tent. That habitation, which Isham described as mired in "a sea of slush," received dozens of sufferers, many brought low by the weather. Neither Surgeon William Upjohn of Hastings nor Assistant Surgeon Adna Sherman of Lamont was immune to the ills that pervaded Camp Kellogg. Years later Isham could still see the doctors, "rheumy-eyed, with blue and dripping noses," as they dispensed their nostrums "with lavish hand, but... no words of cheer." The sergeant would avow that "if anywhere, during all our service, we were more thoroughly miserable than during the first weeks on Meridian Hill it had escaped the memory."[44]

Fortunately, the Seventh Michigan was not condemned to linger in this vale of squalor and sickness. A few days after arriving at Camp Kellogg—having barely reacquainted itself with the drill-field maneuvering it had begun at Grand Rapids—the regiment learned that, upon receipt of its arms, it would trade District of Columbia mud for the Virginia variety. On 9 March the men took possession of their sabers and Colt's single-action pistols along with some items of tack not issued in Michigan. Two weeks later their shoulder-arms arrived. Everyone had expected to receive the same rifles the Fifth and a part of the Sixth Michigan had been issued. Many were mildly disappointed when, instead of the Spencer, they were armed with the carbine Ambrose Burnside had designed.[45]

On the evening of the twenty-sixth the Seventh Michigan pulled up stakes and crossed the Potomac to Fairfax Court House on the Little River Turnpike sixteen miles southwest of the capital. Too new to campaigning to appreciate the importance of traveling light, the regiment was accompanied by no fewer than twenty-five wagons, each stocked to capacity. Every imaginable piece of paraphernalia made the trip, making the column look, as Sergeant Isham said, like "a caravan of junk-dealers."[46]

Throughout this, its first outing in enemy territory, the regiment moved warily. Advance guards and flankers eyed the dark woods on either side of the turnpike, imagining that they teemed with cutthroats under Stuart and Mosby. Isham called it "the most 'heart-in-the-mouth' march we ever made," though he and his comrades felt a bit sheepish when they later learned that the nearest enemy force was fifty miles away.[47]

* * *

Gradually, the Michigan Brigade was coming together. By the early morning of 27 March, the Fifth, Sixth, and Seventh Regiments were encamped within five miles of each other between the Loudoun & Hampshire and Orange & Alexandria Railroads. As soon as the Seventh arrived in the area, it officially joined the other outfits in Copeland's command, one of three brigades belonging to General Stahel.[48]

Less than a week after the Michiganders joined forces, they were off on an expedition that no snowstorm—not even a recent fall of ten inches—could postpone. Like his predecessor, Wyndham, and his subordinate, Price, General Stahel was determined to run to earth the partisans of John Mosby, whose exploits were already inspiring campfire tales among the Seventh Michigan. On 3 April, at Stahel's order, Copeland led his regiments into the Loudoun Valley, the most prominent expanse of the region known as "Mosby's Confederacy."[49]

For four days the regiments scouted as far west as Middleburg without encountering a coherent force of the enemy. Signs of Mosby's proximity were evident, however, everywhere the Wolverines went. They visited some of his haunts and took into custody citizens suspected of having aided the furtive Virginian. Yet the "Gray Ghost" continued to elude the dragnet, saddling the mission with an embarrassing incompleteness. Back at Fairfax, Major Ferry of the Fifth confessed that "had I been on trial in Michigan for whipping a lame idiot and stealing his dinner, I should not have been more mortified and ashamed then I was coming home yesterday...."[50]

On the eleventh, a new, expanded search effort got under way when the First Michigan reached Fairfax Court House after a long march from its camp along the Occoquan. On this day, for the first time, all four of the regiments that would form the Wolverine Brigade were serving within sight of one another. As their men exchanged three-way greetings, the half-dozen other outfits that comprised Price's brigade and that of Colonel De Forest also arrived at the courthouse. Evidently, a major campaign was about to begin.

To emphasize the importance of the concentration, regimental commanders addressed pep-talks to their troops. Colonel Mann called on his men, "now fairly launched out into the field of duty," to prove themselves team players while also maintaining the good name of their regiment: "Whatever reputation it [the Seventh] makes now will be exclusively its own...." For his part, Colonel Town thanked his officers and men for the support they had lent him since assuming command, and enjoined everyone to embark on "the campaign just opening before us fully determined to discharge our whole duty with the greatest zeal and alacrity." The coming weeks, he predicted, "will undoubtedly decide the fate of the contest."[51]

Such pronouncements proved very timely. The spring campaign—at least on the Army of the Potomac's front—began a few days after the colonels orated, though it got off to a rocky start.

After three months of plotting and preparing at Falmouth, Joe Hooker moved to cross the Rappahannock and engage the Army of Northern Virginia. In advance of his foot troops, he sent his revitalized cavalry—now a full-size corps more than 10,000 strong, under George Stoneman—to turn Lee's flank and destroy vital communications in his rear. Then came torrential rains to prevent most of the troopers from fording the river, thus delaying the opening act of the drama. Not till the twenty-eighth did the cavalry head south; at about the same time Hooker's infantry and artillery crossed with the intent of turning the enemy out of its formidable works near Fredericksburg.[52]

When Hooker's offensive got underway, so did the Michigan cavalry and their comrades in upper Virginia. On the twenty-seventh Stahel's main force set out to scour the Loudoun Valley yet again. For three days the several-thousand-man force sniffed around Aldie, Middleburg, and Upperville, before heading south to Salem and White Plains. Once again Mosby's Confederacy yielded no clues to its namesake's whereabouts although the First Michigan did engage a vicious little band of bushwhackers on the twenty-ninth outside Aldie. Side-expeditions by the Fifth Michigan toward Warrenton Junction and by the Seventh Michigan to Bristoe Station also failed to flush any prey. By dawn of 30 April Stahel's division was back at Fairfax with barely a dozen captives in tow, several others having escaped on the homeward leg of the journey. Once again, much time and energy had failed to produce comparable results.[53]

A few days later scouting missions resumed, including some toward Kettle Run and Warrenton Junction. On one of these the Seventh Michigan finally located some of Mosby's people—to the regiment's regret. On the morning of the fourteenth, four companies under Colonel Mann were fired on from concealed positions by a small band of rangers outside Warrenton Junction. Casualties included the regiment's first combat fatality as well as Asa Isham and another trooper wounded.[54]

A little over two weeks later, Isham's outfit exacted revenge. With its colonel again in command, a detachment of the Seventh, closely supported by the First Vermont of Price's brigade, cornered Mosby's unit near Greenwich, seven miles above Warrenton Junction. In what

Isham called "a spirited action," the Federals captured several partisans as well as two light cannon attached to their command. According to Isham, a member of Company C of the Seventh had Mosby himself in custody for several minutes until other rangers rescued their leader and captured the Federal. Although the Gray Ghost and most of his men got away after inflicting several casualties on their assailants, Isham pronounced the fight "a glorious victory... [which] put us in high feather." It was, at the least, a milestone in the early career of the Seventh Michigan.[55]

This limited success, however, provided about the only good news the Michigan cavalry heard that month of May 1863. It soon became known that both Hooker's and Stoneman's offensives had ended badly. Hooker's drive had stalled in the thick, foreboding woods below the Rappahannock, where Lee rushed up to pummel his enemy into helplessness near a crossroads called Chancellorsville. With Hooker's retreat to Falmouth suddenly a foregone conclusion, Stoneman's raid—though it did great damage to Confederate rail lines and supply depots—became a strategic failure that cost its leader his job.[56]

Assessing the outcome of a campaign that had raised so many hopes, Noah Ferry exclaimed: "Oh! it is aggravating to think what might have been done and was not...." With the Union effort in the East in a greater shambles than ever before, the major's lament sounded like an epitaph for a fatally wounded Army of the Potomac.[57]

* * *

As June came in, Mosby became less and less reluctant to show himself, with unhappy repercussions for his opponents. Just before daybreak on the fourth his rangers fired from a woodlot on the picket lines of the Fifth Cavalry near Frying Pan, wounding one man. Showing themselves, the Confederates confiscated outpost equipage and made off with several horses. Colonel Gray led three companies—one each from the First, Fifth and Sixth Regiments—in pursuit. He overtook his quarry, but in the ensuing fracas eight Wolverines were made prisoner. The pursuers took only one captive, a noncombatant (a surgeon) to boot.[58]

Two days later, a squadron of the First Michigan under Major

Brewer clashed with Mosby's men at Waterloo Bridge during a scout from Fairfax Court House toward the Shenandoah Valley. The fight ended inconclusively although it left both sides with casualties. On 11 June Mosby struck again, leading more than 200 men against one-third as many members of Captain Deane's squadron of the Sixth along the Maryland side of the upper Potomac. The early morning attack southeast of Poolesville routed Companies I and M and forced them to flee across Seneca Creek.

Making a stand near Seneca Bridge, Deane's men held on till their ammunition ran low and Mosby pressed them on three sides; the result was a second, longer, retreat. Mosby pursued briefly before returning to Deane's camp, which he burned, then withdrawing along the towpath of the Chesapeake and Ohio Canal. By then the Michiganders had lost four killed, one wounded, and seventeen missing as against two Rebel casualties. When he learned of the assault, General Stahel sent 400 men—including Brewer's detachment, just back from the Valley—in pursuit. All too predictably, the Gray Ghost got away.[59]

Thanks to Mosby, frustration remained the principal emotion among the cavalry of the defenses of Washington. Farther south, the mood was gayer. Even as Stahel's troopers pursued the phantoms of the recently designated Forty-third Virginia Battalion, they learned that their counterparts in the Army of the Potomac had gained a moral, if not quite a tangible, victory below the Rappahannock. On the ninth George Stoneman's replacement, Brigadier General Alfred Pleasonton, had surprised, battered, and almost destroyed J.E.B. Stuart in a day-long series of saber charges, dismounted clashes, and horse artillery exchanges near the Orange & Alexandria depot of Brandy Station. In the aftermath of the drawn battle horsemen in blue dared to wonder if the born-to-the-saddle Confederates who had beaten them to the point of humiliation over the past two years were no longer invincible.[60]

Hooker and Pleasonton believed that Brandy Station had preempted a raid into the North by Stuart's people. In reality, the battle delayed by a week Stuart's participation in a full-scale invasion by Lee's army, which had gotten underway on the third. The offensive caught Hooker by surprise, but it should not have. Many observers considered the time propitious for Lee to carry the war into enemy territory. In a 1 June letter to his mother, Captain Kidd predicted that "Lee may make a rapid march through the Shenandoah Valley, and thence into Pennsylvania and Maryland." Kidd was confident, however, that scouts and pickets would provide ample warning of the movement. This Pleasonton's men failed to do, forfeiting some of the credit they had won at Brandy Station. The head of General Ewell's column circumvented the upper flank of the cavalry's picket line via roads that Pleasonton should have covered.[61]

Not until the thirteenth, with one-third of Lee's army in the vicinity of Winchester, did Hooker gain concrete information about the invasion. At once he directed his army to fall back to a position from which it could assess Lee's progress and intentions. By the fifteenth, most of the Army of the Potomac was near Fairfax Station, only three miles south of General Stahel's headquarters.

While the infantry camped along the Orange & Alexandria, Pleasonton's horsemen trotted westward, passing through the Bull Run Mountains to the Loudoun Valley, seeking the head of the Rebel column. Instead it found Stuart's troopers, who had come up at last to screen Lee's march. The opposing cavalries clashed at Aldie on 17 June, at Middleburg two days later, and at Upperville on the twenty-first. Like Brandy Station, all were hard-fought contests in which each side gave as good as it took. But Stuart's counterreconnaissance barrier remained intact and the Confederate drive, which now involved all three corps of Lee's army, kept moving.[62]

CHAPTER SEVEN

Boy General of the Golden Locks

*H*ooker's entry into the area of operations of the XXII Corps drew the Michigan cavalry into the unfolding campaign. On 17 June General Heintzelman agreed to a request from Hooker's headquarters that while Pleasonton challenged Stuart in the Loudoun Valley, Stahel's division would probe toward Warrenton Junction to see if Lee's rear-guard remained on the Rappahannock. For the assignment Stahel selected Colonel De Forest, with two regiments; at the same time, he dispatched a smaller force to seek the enemy among the northern reaches of the Bull Run chain.[1]

De Forest found a portion of Stuart's cavalry, under Brigadier General Wade Hampton, near Fredericksburg—but no infantry, as Hooker had feared. The force Stahel sent north found no Rebels at all. While the report of the latter did not bother Hooker, he appeared unsatisfied with De Forest's findings, perhaps reasoning that two regiments could not have swept the Rappahannock country adequately. On the twenty-first Fighting Joe compelled Stahel to send his entire division back to Warrenton, where rumor continued to place a large portion of Lee's army, while also scouting about Waterloo, Sulphur Springs, Rappahannock Station, and other points toward Fredericksburg. Until Hooker got definitive word that the Rappahannock line was clear of troops, thus removing any threat to Washington, he would not commit himself to a pursuit into Maryland and Pennsylvania.

Although he probably believed that Hooker had enough cavalry to reconnoiter as well as engage Stuart, Stahel complied with the army leader's directive. In truth, he had no choice: on the twentieth the War Department had announced that Hooker enjoyed authority over the troops of other departments "which, as his army moves, fall within the sphere of his operations." By pitching his headquarters just below Fairfax Court House, Hooker had draped this authority over Stahel's bailiwick.[2]

Having already sent surplus stores to Fairfax Station and all unsound horses to Washington (where sick men would soon join them), Stahel broke camp before noon on the twenty-first. With the sounds of battle at Upperville clearly audible, his men expected to move westward to join the fight. Instead, all 3,500 riders were led south to Centreville and Manassas Junction, where they encountered no Rebels—only the too-shallow graves of Bull Run victims. Corporal John Farnill of the Sixth Cavalry informed his parents in Pittsfield that "the Dead had just been covered over with dirt.... it was no uncommon sight to see the Skeletons of Men lieing [sic] around and in one Place every little tree had Four and five shots in it." In addition to desecrated remains the troopers had to pick their way through a field pockmarked with unexploded ordnance.[3]

From Bull Run the division passed on to New Baltimore and Brentsville, arriving at Warrenton early on the twenty-second to find no enemy. After scouting fruitlessly as far south as Kelly's Ford, the troopers spent the night at Bealton Station. The following day they made a hectic return march to Fairfax Court House, which they reached early on the twenty-fourth.[4]

In addition to macabre sights, the reconnaissance was memorable for the hunger pangs it induced. "The march was so rapid," wrote Captain Kidd, that despite the finest efforts of Quartermaster Patten and his colleagues, "the trains were left behind and a good portion of the time we were without forage or food." Troopers made do by downing the limbs of cherry trees that lined their road and for hours enjoying the "ripe and luscious fruit."[5]

For Kidd's outfit, the expedition was notable for still another reason: it marked the first time the Sixth had moved in full strength without either Colonel Gray or Lieutenant Colonel Alger at its head; Major Foote guided the regiment throughout the operation. Three days before the trip began, Gray had been placed under arrest for drunkenness; he awaited possible court-martial. One of his men, who claimed an insider's knowledge of the situation, feared the charge "will hold good."[6]

Meanwhile, on 11 June Russell Alger had left the Sixth to fill the vacant colonelcy of the Fifth Cavalry. It was a welcome move for his new regiment, who greeted him warmly, as well as for Alger, who had hungered for an outfit of his own. As recently as late May he had considered applying for a colonelcy in the United States Colored Troops. Governor Blair, who dissuaded him from that course, had assigned him instead to the Fifth, largely on the strength of a plea by its officers that someone from outside the regiment be appointed to lead it. Clearly—though for unknown reasons—the petition was a slap at Lieutenant Colonel Gould, the logical candidate for promotion.[7]

* * *

After a day of rest in their now-tentless camps around Fairfax Court House, the Wolverines and their comrades under Stahel again hit the road, this time bound for Maryland. At daybreak, 25 June, the Hungarian led off in what Sergeant Isham described as "a covered spring wagon drawn by four white mules." The column's heading was toward the Potomac River at Harpers Ferry, where Stahel had been ordered to report to the garrison commander, Major General William H. French. From the outset, his division passed in rear of the moving wings of the Army of the Potomac, which had finally nerved itself to confront the defilers of Pennsylvania.[8]

On the leg to Dranesville, many Michiganders had a close-up view of their division leader in his headquarters vehicle; most were not impressed by what they saw. James Kidd, for one, decided that Stahel's "appearance was that of a natty staff officer, and did not fill one's ideal of a major general...." Reflecting a nativist tendency to identify all Europeans by a single nationality, Kidd thereafter thought of his leader as "a dapper little Dutchman."[9]

Model soldier or not, Stahel got a good day's march out of his men. By noon Price's brigade, including the First Michigan, was nearing Harpers Ferry, even though that place was no longer Stahel's destination. A recent communique from Hooker had instructed him to leave a mere detachment with French, who was having trouble dealing with a pesky band of gray horsemen north of the river. With his main force the Hungarian was to press on to Maryland and report to Major General John F. Reynolds, the Pennsylvanian who commanded the forward wing of the Army of the Potomac, its I, III, and XI Corps. Later Stahel was told to march east of Reynolds's infantry in the direction of Frederick.

Just shy of Edwards Ferry on the Potomac, Stahel found the twin pontoon bridges that had been laid there, some twenty miles east of French's garrison, crowded with the men of his old infantry corps. Although a few members of the Sixth Michigan trod the pontoons in early evening darkness, Stahel sent most of their comrades two miles downstream to cross the mile-wide river at Youngs Island Ford.[10]

Although the ford was usually shallow, tonight the water level was rising rapidly. Captain Kidd recalled that "by the time the Sixth reached the river the water was nearly to the tops of the saddles.... there was imminent danger of being swept away and few, except the most reckless, drew a long breath until the distance had been traversed and our steeds were straining up the slippery bank upon the opposite shore." Quartermaster Sergeant Andy Buck of the Seventh Cavalry added that "we crossed in safety, but our boots filled with water and our pants, thoroughly soaked to our knees, added none to our comfort." The rain-swollen waters were so treacherous that Stahel temporarily left his supply train on the south bank, guarded by a battalion of the Fifth Michigan under now-Major Dake.[11]

When the column hit dry ground, the march continued through a chilly drizzle to Poolesville, where the Sixth Michigan expected to find Captain Deane's battle-scarred squadron—only to learn that Companies I and M had been sent to join General French. At Poolesville all bedded down for the night, "wet, weary, hungry, and chilled." Next morning they lurched into motion, wending their way past Sugar Loaf Mountain (and past the head of Reynolds's column), then through the Monocacy River Valley to the village of Urbana.[12]

The rain, which had fallen through the night, quit in mid-afternoon. By early evening, as the troopers came within sight of the First Michigan's old home at Frederick City, they beheld what Kidd called an "enchanting vision.... The rain of the early morning had left in the atmosphere a mellow haze of vapor which reflected the sun's rays in tints that softly blended with the summer colorings of the landscape. An exclamation of surprise ran along the column as each succeeding trooper came in sight of this picture of Nature's own painting." Equally pleasing was the sight of United States flags flying from the homes of residents who showed, according to Sergeant George W. Barbour of the Sixth, "great demonstrations of Union feeling.... this is a beautiful place."[13]

Stahel's people spent an uninterrupted night in fields outside Frederick, awakening on the twenty-seventh "much refreshed" and ready to hit the road. It turned out to be a momentous day. As the cavalry later learned, Hooker was out, a victim of Chancellorsville and a tension-filled relationship with his military and civilian superiors. To replace him the War Department this day tabbed the erstwhile commander of the V Corps, Major General George Gordon Meade. With a confrontation on Union soil imminent the change appeared to suffer from poor timing. Still, it underscored the government's determination to evict the invader, a task it refused to entrust to a soldier in whom it had lost confidence.[14]

General Stahel's first action after crossing the Potomac was to fragment his command. Early on the twenty-seventh he ordered De Forest's brigade to Crampton's Gap in South Mountain, the northward extension of the Blue Ridge, beyond which Lee's infantry was reported to be on the march. Then he sent Colonel Mann and the Seventh Michigan toward the Antietam battlefield, to patrol lower South Mountain.[15]

Most of Price's brigade, including the First Michigan, remained at Frederick, as did General Stahel. The division leader apparently concluded that his present position between Reynolds's headquarters at Jefferson, eight miles to the southwest, and the Pennsylvania line was a good place from which to coordinate his mountain reconnaissances while supporting Meade's vanguard. But by not advancing toward John Reynolds's home state, Stahel left himself open to criticism as being lackadaisical. Such criticism would hurt Stahel in the hours to come.[16]

Like the Seventh Michigan, the Fifth and Sixth left their division leader behind. Early in the day, with horses groomed and fed and haversacks full, General Copeland detached Alger's and Gray's regiments from the hospitable citizens of Frederick and led them past the bivouacs of infantry regiments about to head north in their wake. Outside the city the Wolverines curved to the left, passing along the eastern rim of the Catoctin Mountains in the direction of Emmitsburg and, just beyond, Pennsylvania.

From Emmitsburg Copeland had been ordered to push across the Mason-Dixon Line. En route he was not only to seek Lee's whereabouts but to keep an eye on the roads to the east where, as reports had it, J.E.B. Stuart was again raiding in rear of the Army of the Potomac. Copeland's ultimate destination was a crossroads village and railroad depot seven miles inside the Pennsylvania border—Gettysburg.[17]

* * *

The Michiganders' stay in Emmitsburg was brief, an overnight bivouac. Their visit to Gettysburg—which was believed to lie in the heart of enemy territory—lasted only a few hours longer. Although meeting no organized enemy short of the town, the Wolverines cast glances in every direction, alert to any sign of trouble, as they entered the Adams County seat shortly after noon on Sunday, 28 June.

Having already seen enough trouble to last a lifetime—Ewell's cavalry and infantry had occupied the village only two days before—the citizens were ecstatic to find Union horsemen in their midst. For one youngster, Sally Myers, the new arrivals were a joyous contrast "to the dirty mean-looking rebels who call themselves 'Southern Chivalry'." Remembering the scene years later, another girl exclaimed: "Oh! how we did rejoice to see so many of our own men and how gladly we gave them everything we had to eat, bread and pies and coffee," all handed up as the troopers passed through town. The reception also presented a contrast for the Wolverines; many of the Pennsylvania Dutch folk they had encountered on the road from Emmitsburg had charged dearly for the food and forage they made available to the troopers. Another gift the people of Gettysburg showered on their visitors pleased both sight and smell. "By the time the center of town was reached," observed James Kidd, "every man had a bunch of flowers in his hand, or a wreath around his neck. Some even had their horses decorated...." Seventeen years later, Russell Alger recalled that "such demonstrations of joy... it has never been my privilege to witness either before or since."[18]

After establishing a command post in a center-square hotel, General Copeland met with townspeople who had information on enemy movements. He also reduced his regiments to companies, which he dispatched to cover the dozen or so roads that radiated from Gettysburg like spokes from a hub. At the head of Companies E and H of the Sixth Michigan, Captain Kidd picketed the northwestern approach to the town along the Cashtown Road. More than forty years later he observed: "A very vivid remembrance is yet retained of the 'vigil long'... during which I did not once leave the saddle, dividing the time between the reserve post and the line of videttes."[19]

When night came, men not on duty slumbered in the pastures that surrounded the town. While they dozed, General Copeland dispatched couriers to Frederick with important news. The brigadier had learned that Lee, with his main body, was just beyond South Mountain at Chambersburg, twenty-three miles to the west. Other elements of the Army of Northern Virginia were north of Gettysburg, at Carlisle, as well as off to the east, at York. This information, passed on by the locals, had been verified through dispatches carried by a Confederate courier whom Copeland's pickets had captured soon after entering the town.[20]

The intelligence must have concerned Copeland, whose men were camping in the midst of the foe. Before long, the general was not the only one aware of this fact. When comrades in Company C of the Sixth Michigan returned from scouting duty before midnight, they brought Trooper Allen Rice "news that thare [sic] was about 60 thousand of the Rebs about 2 miles from thare...." Copeland and his troops must have been relieved when Stahel ordered them to pull out before daylight. By two A.M. the Wolverines were riding out of Gettysburg. "We begged them to stay with us," a resident recalled, only to be told, ominously, "No, madam, we must go, but before long you will see more soldiers than you ever saw before in your life...."[21]

Copeland had done an effective job of intelligence-gathering; he expected a warm welcome at Stahel's headquarters. Instead, while on the march to Emmitsburg he met a courier bearing the news that both he and his superior had been relieved of command. The man announced that Meade had replaced Hooker at the head of the Army of the Potomac, adding that Meade, with War Department approval, had made organizational and personnel changes—changes that effectively ended Joseph Copeland's military career.

The horsemen of the XXII Corps had been merged into the Army of the Potomac as the Third Division, Cavalry Corps, under Brigadier General Judson Kilpatrick, a feisty little Irishman from New Jersey who had won notice at Aldie and Upperville. Kilpatrick had reorganized the division into two brigades which his boss, General Pleasonton, had assigned to brand-new brigadiers, former members of his staff. The first brigade, consisting of De Forest's regiments and most of Price's, was led by former Captain Elon J. Farnsworth of Illinois and Michigan. The second, comprising Copeland's men plus Colonel Town's regiment—and soon to be known, fittingly, as the Michigan Cavalry Brigade—had been entrusted to George Armstrong Custer.[22]

*   *   *

Custer may have gained his coveted star through a fortuitous reorganization, but he had labored to be in the right place at the right time. Stints on the staffs of Kearny and McClellan had failed to gain his advancement, and when Little Mac was relieved after Antietam it looked for a time as though Custer would be shelved, too, his heroics on the Peninsula all for naught. His early efforts to enter the volunteer ranks had failed largely due to his political affiliation, which denied him Austin Blair's goodwill. In the late fall of 1862, when the brevet captain applied for the colonelcy of the Seventh Michigan Cavalry, then in progress of organization, the Republican governor denied him serious consideration.[23]

According to Lieutenant Sam Harris, early in 1863 the persistent Custer had tried to outmaneuver Lieutenant Colonel Alger for command of the Fifth Michigan. By Harris's account, the "slim young man with almost flaxen hair" visited the camp of the Fifth at Fairfax Court House, announced his intentions to Lieutenant Colonel Gould and his subordinates, and asked them to petition the governor in his behalf—only to be rejected as too young for the position. The story may be apocryphal: such an attempt at self-promotion seems too blatant, too crass, for Custer. On the other hand, the regiment's known preference for an outsider to command lends the account some degree of credibility. Whatever the truth of the matter, Custer yet again failed to win a position he coveted.[24]

Even so, his luck had begun to improve. Over Thanksgiving, 1862, while on furlough in Monroe, he met the effervescent young woman whose hand he would win and whose disapproving father he would win over during a long and determined courtship. And in May 1863, back with the army in Virginia, he landed a position on the staff of Alfred Pleasonton, the flashy, foppish, man-about-war whose meteoric rise in the Army of the Potomac—fueled by his consummate ability to play politics and exploit contacts—far outstripped his modest abilities as a soldier.

It was Pleasonton who placed the young Buckeye-turned-Wolverine on the fast track to promotion, especially after Custer turned in conspicuous performances at Brandy Station and Aldie. When, after a mighty effort, Pleasonton maneuvered himself into the position vacated by George Stoneman after Chancellorsville, he importuned his new commander, Meade, to authorize the advancement of "officers with the proper dash to command cavalry." On Pleasonton's short list of candidates, Custer ranked just behind his fellow West Pointer, Kilpatrick, who had been a brigadier since early June.[25]

Custer's qualifications notwithstanding, the man he succeeded was far from pleased by his promotion. Leaving the Fifth and Sixth Michigan near Emmitsburg early on the twenty-ninth, General Copeland, his face an apoplectic purple, rode with his staff to army headquarters at Frederick. There he complained to Pleasonton about the circumstances of his relief, which, coming on the verge of a major campaign, appeared to impugn his character as well as his leadership. Embarrassed by the confrontation, Pleasonton sent his visitor to Middleburg, headquarters of the Second Cavalry Division, with an implied promise that its commander, Brigadier General David McMurtrie Gregg, would assign Copeland a brigade.

After a long and tiring ride through the Loudoun Valley, Copeland located Gregg and explained his predicament. The courteous, dignified commander listened respectfully until he learned that Copeland was his senior by date of commission, whereupon he sent the older man back to Frederick. Again face-to-face with Pleasonton,

Copeland began to rant about his loss of command, "an indignity and disgrace I should not and cannot quietly submit to." Pleasonton abruptly ended the interview by stating that "while he intended no disrespect nor reflection" on Copeland, he "must insist on giving the command to those best known to himself."[26]

And that was that. When the army started off for Pennsylvania, Copeland was directed to report to the Adjutant General in Washington. In later weeks the War Department gave him a series of minor assignments: establishing a draft rendezvous at Annapolis, Maryland, and another in Pittsburgh; commanding the post of Alton, Illinois. The judge-turned-soldier never again held a field command. Of greater personal regret, he never again served with the Michigan cavalry he had helped staff, arm, and bring to a high state of effectiveness.[27]

*   *   *

Having sought a commission in two of the regiments he now commanded, George Custer knew a few facts—but only a few—about his newly acquired brigade, the only one in the Cavalry Corps whose regiments all hailed from the same state. In time he would learn the details of their organization and personnel, and the strengths and limitations of their commanders. Of one thing, however, he was certain: as a fighting force, his command had unlimited potential. Although only one-fourth of it sported battle experience, each of its parts had been seasoned by months of campaigning and tested by hardship and adversity. Moreover, it had been strengthened by the recent addition of a unit of Regular artillery, a replacement for the volunteer battery that had been raised in conjunction with the Fifth Michigan and thereafter had served intermittently with Copeland's brigade. The new unit, Battery M of the Second United States Artillery, was commanded by an impressive young officer with an equally impressive name, First Lieutenant Alexander Cummings McWhorter Pennington, Jr. All in all, Custer's first command of the war was a plum assignment. As when catching the eye of Libbie Bacon, he vowed to make the most of the opportunity presented him.

Even before grouping his command—joining the regiments at Emmitsburg with those he had recalled from South Mountain late on the day of his appointment, 28 June—Custer acted to give himself, and by extension his command, a unique image. With the assistance of a Regular trooper of long acquaintance, Joseph Fought, he added some touches to a suit of clothing he must have assembled months ago, long before he enjoyed the rank that would permit him to wear it. More costume than uniform, the garish raiment would attract everyone's attention, stimulating esprit de corps and providing a rallying-point in battle.[28]

The principal items of Custer's ensemble were a black velveteen jacket of hussar type, five loops of gold lace on each sleeve; matching pants with a gold stripe running along the seam; and a dark blue sailor's shirt with a wide, turned-down collar—supposedly the gift of a gunboat crewman. At Custer's direction, Fought, who would become his orderly, had sewn silver stars on the collar points. Around the general's open neck hung a bright scarlet cravat, its long ends curling in the breeze. Custer topped off his attire with a brown slouch hat that a Rebel had left behind after a skirmish (some sources describe the hat as gray; others as a black, broad-brimmed felt hat adorned with another star, this encircled by a rosette). From the crown of his blonde head—his curly hair fell in ringlets almost to his shoulders—to his high-topped, gilt-spurred boots, Custer looked less a cavalry commander than—as one of Meade's staff officers put it upon seeing him for the first time—"a circus rider gone mad!"[29]

Clad in this outlandish garb, the baby brigadier rode out to take control of that half of his command—the First and Seventh Michigan and Pennington's battery—within marching distance of Frederick. According to an early biographer, from the first he adopted a stern and formal manner with the officers to whom he introduced himself. His officiousness appears to have been carefully staged, a contrivance—like the moustache and imperial he had cultivated—to offset the effect of his callow appearance on subordinates older than he.[30]

Having exchanged initial salutes, Custer hastily inspected his squadrons. While impressed by some of the sights that met his eye—especially by the grizzled veterans of the First, who proudly sat their mounts beneath bullet-gashed guidons—he decided that the discipline of his command was "lax," and its organization "incomplete" (detachments had noticeably thinned the ranks of both regiments). Custer had no prejudice against volunteer troops; he had served alongside them long enough to know that, properly led, they made good soldiers. Even so, on this occasion he vowed, when time permitted, to instruct his men in the nuances of tactics and the Regular Army's brand of deportment. He was determined that one day the men of the Michigan Brigade would be recognized as "unequalled in every trait essential to soldiers."[31]

At noon on the twenty-ninth, his evaluation over, Custer led the First and Seventh and Battery M out of the Frederick area—where army headquarters personnel were fast decamping—to join the Fifth and Sixth as well as the rest of the division. Custer's ultimate destination, as also Elon Farnsworth's, was York, which General Kilpatrick had been tasked to reconnoiter, confirming or disproving reports of Ewell's presence in the area.

By the time it had crossed into Pennsylvania, Custer's truncated brigade had made contact with Kilpatrick and Farnsworth, beside whom they spent the night outside Littlestown, six and a half miles southwest of Hanover. At or near the latter place Custer expected, by morning, to find the outfits that had advanced to Gettysburg. He looked forward to joining them to his force, although he may have anticipated some embarrassment in meeting his old rival for regimental command, Russell Alger.

The last day of June opened with a shower, through which the cavalry and horse artillerists rode to Hanover. By ten A.M. they had passed through the town, Custer's regiments in the lead, accompanied by the cocky, energetic Kilpatrick and trailed by Pennington's guns, then by the four regiments and the battery that made up Farnsworth's brigade. After being greeted and fed by the local citizens—who, though spared the invasion their neighbors in Gettysburg had experienced, hailed their visitors as deliverers—the troopers passed out the north end of town, heading toward Abbottstown and, beyond, York.[32]

Custer's men were within sight of Abbottstown when, just before noon, firing broke out in the rear. It was quickly apparent that Farnsworth's brigade had been attacked in the streets of Hanover. As Custer was to learn, the assailants were members of Colonel John

R. Chambliss's brigade of Virginians and North Carolinians, the vanguard of J.E.B. Stuart's raiding column, just up from Westminster, Maryland—a force that Gregg's division, not Kilpatrick's, had been expected to confront. Seeking the whereabouts of Lee's main army, from which they had been detached six days before, Stuart's men had been as surprised to find their path blocked at Hanover as Elon Farnsworth had been to block it.[33]

With Kilpatrick's permission, Custer, his adrenaline pumping, countermarched to Hanover. By early afternoon, when he arrived north of the town, he found that the erstwhile troops of Price and De Forest had been driven through the streets alongside terrified citizens. In the heart of town the Federals had rallied to begin a spirited contest, snapping away with carbines and pistols from behind breastworks made of fence-rails, wagons, hay bales, and other readily available material.[34]

With Farnsworth and Chambliss locked in a duel, Custer moved westward until opposite, and several hundred yards from, another large body of the enemy. This force, supported by horse artillery and with mounted and dismounted skirmishers in front, proved to be the Virginia brigade of Robert E. Lee's nephew, Brigadier General Fitzhugh Lee.

Scanning Lee's position from a ridge above the hamlet of Pennville, Custer spied a third enemy force well to the rear of the others: the brigade of Stuart's ranking subordinate, Brigadier General Wade Hampton of South Carolina. Even at long distance, Custer could discern the outline of a supply train in Hampton's midst—dozens of canvas-topped wagons of U.S. Army pattern. Later, Custer learned that more than 100 quartermaster's and commissary vehicles, intended for the succor of Hooker's army, had fallen into Stuart's hands outside Rockville, Maryland.[35]

While a notable prize, the slow-moving train had cost Stuart's column precious time on the road north, as had a brief but bloody encounter with ninety-five Union horsemen in the streets of Westminster. Casualties incurred in the 29 June fight had forced Stuart to linger in Maryland, paroling his prisoners, tending to his wounded, and burying his dead. These delays had prevented the cavalryman from linking with Robert E. Lee at a propitious time, forcing the Army of Northern Virginia to grope fitfully through lower Pennsylvania, ignorant of Meade's pursuit. Now Custer was about to disarrange Stuart's timetable even further.[36]

In fact, even before Custer moved to engage the foe, a portion of his brigade—a portion he had yet to lay eyes on—had gone nose-to-nose with Lee's brigade, and had blinked. Shortly after noon, the Fifth and Sixth Michigan had left Littlestown, which they had reached early that morning, the Sixth by the main road to Hanover, the Littlestown Pike, the Fifth via another road, apparently one that ran north of the pike. It was the Sixth that provided Fitz Lee with his first fight since crossing into Pennsylvania.[37]

There is some confusion as to who led the two regiments prior to their joining Custer. Years later, Russell Alger claimed that General Copeland, upon his relief, had turned both outfits over to him. Other evidence suggests that Gray, Alger's senior, succeeded to the command once Copeland left Emmitsburg for Frederick on the twenty-ninth. If so, Copeland must have released the Irishman from arrest and restored him to command; pardons of that nature were common when the offense was considered minor and the prisoner's regiment was on the brink of battle. Whatever the circumstances, Gray, and not his executive officer, now-Lieutenant Colonel Foote, was leading the Sixth Cavalry when it left Littlestown for Hanover.[38]

Gray may have regretted the timing of his reinstatement, for he quickly found himself outnumbered four-or-more-to-one. When within a mile or so of Hanover, he led his regiment off the pike and through a wheatfield, then up a tall, wooded ridge—and ran head-on into Fitz Lee's skirmishers. The encounter should not have surprised him, for residents of Littlestown had warned that a Rebel raiding force, just up from Maryland, was in the area. For that reason, Gray had sent Company A, under Captain Thompson, to scout along the road to Westminster.[39]

Despite making preparations to receive the enemy, when Gray dismounted part of his regiment and sent it to drive in Lee's skirmishers, it suddenly found a bank of horse artillery threatening its right flank. Behind the guns waited Fitz Lee's main body, fully mounted and apparently ready to attack. When the cannon started in, Gray hastily recalled his men and decamped for Hanover. The precipitate nature of the withdrawal bothered some of his men; one complained that his regiment "was obliged to skedaddle not very creditably to our Col[onel]."[40]

As Gray pulled out, he directed Companies B and F, under the able Peter Weber, to secure the rear. Immediately the Rebels pounced on the vulnerable squadron. Working their Spencers furiously, Weber's men repulsed two assaults before giving way before a third and withdrawing by a circuitous route to Hanover. The captain's stand had enabled the main body to disengage but at the cost of numerous casualties, including some twenty men captured. Others had barely escaped; one who did, forty-five-year-old Daniel Stewart of Company B, informed his wife that for a time the entire squadron "though[t] we were killed or taken pri[s]oners."[41]

Short minutes after breaking contact, the Sixth Michigan saw their new brigade commander approaching from Hanover, where he had been plotting strategy for the past hour or so. After sizing up his opposition, Custer had moved Pennington's battery to a commanding eminence north of town, Bunker Hill. From this position the lieutenant engaged horse artillery along Fitz Lee's right flank and Chambliss's left. At Custer's order, Colonel Town had deployed the First Michigan as battery supports, while Colonel Mann threatened both brigades in front. Eventually, a battalion of the Seventh, under Lieutenant Colonel Litchfield, advanced dismounted across farm fields, holding Rebel skirmishers in place and foiling any plans to attack Battery M. Later, Companies C, E, and H of the regiment, led by Major Newcombe, moved into Hanover to help man the barricades Farnsworth's men had erected in the streets and alleys.[42]

As fighting heated up along the length of his line, Custer peered at dust clouds rising in the direction of Littlestown, from which, presently, emerged the Sixth Michigan. Riding up to the head of the regiment, he reined in, went through the hastiest of introductions, and told Colonel Gray what he expected of him and his men.

His basic expectation was that they retreat no farther. While Pennington and his supports occupied Lee's right flank, Custer wished the Sixth to pressure the Rebels, members of Chambliss's brigade, farther east. At his command, Gray dismounted virtually the entire regiment, 600 officers and men. Minus the one man in

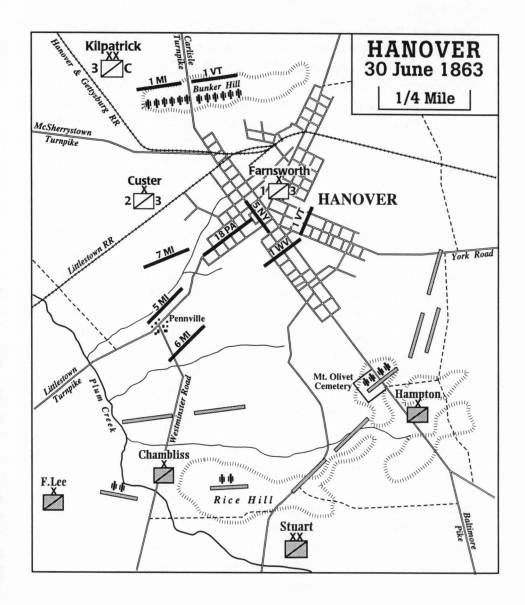

Kilpatrick
XX
3 / C

Carlisle Turnpike

Hanover & Gettysburg RR

1 MI   1 VT
Bunker Hill

HANOVER
30 June 1863

1/4 Mile

McSherrystown Turnpike

Custer
X
2 / 3

Littlestown RR

Farnsworth
X
1 / 3

HANOVER

5 NY

18 PA

1 VT

1 WV

York Road

7 MI

5 MI

Pennville

6 MI

Littlestown Turnpike

Plum Creek

Westminster Road

Mt. Olivet Cemetery

Hampton
X

Chambliss
X

F. Lee
X

Rice Hill

Stuart
XX

Baltimore Pike

every four left behind to hold his own horse and those of three comrades, the Sixth surged forward across the tracks of the Littlestown branch of the Hanover & Gettysburg Railroad, toward the enemy position.[43]

One of those advancing into his first battle was James Kidd. The Ionia youth heard an officer "giving directions for the movement, in clear, resonant tones, and in a calm, confident manner, at once resolute and reassuring." Looking around, he saw a gaudily dressed horseman "whose appearance amazed if it did not for the moment amuse me... an officer superbly mounted who sat his charger as if to the manor born. Tall, lithe, active, muscular, straight as an Indian and as quick in his movements, he had the fair complexion of a school girl."[44]

Custer quickly displayed his command of the situation. Thanks to the rapid firepower of their Spencers, his Wolverines drove the enemy steadily backward. Unlike their effort farther west, this time they did not withdraw as soon as they neared the ridge that held Lee's guns and main body. Instead, they crept ever closer, some on hands and knees, until at the foot of the high ground, only 300 yards from the artillery. At a signal, they rose up and sprayed riflefire across the crest, causing mounted men on either side of the guns to break for the rear in stunned surprise. Taking fifteen prisoners, the skirmishers turned their Spencers on the battery crews, inflicting so many casualties as to silence the cannon.[45]

Fearing the loss of his artillery entire, Fitz Lee rushed up a large part of his main body, which managed to retake the ridge. But while forcing a portion of the Sixth Michigan to withdraw, the new arrivals proved unable to dislodge dozens of Wolverines who remained within rifle-shot of the position even as shell and canister burned the air above their heads.

The Wolverines maintained their lodgement, threatening Lee's guns and making J.E.B. Stuart fear for his left flank, until sundown. In gathering darkness, they realized that the enemy had gone, taking their artillery with them. Soon they discovered the entire raiding force—men, guns, and wagons—in full retreat.[46]

Just before leaving, Stuart had landed a final blow—and took better than he gave. Throughout the day, while Gray's men fought, Colonel Alger's Fifth Michigan had been guarding their rear just north of Pennville, where the Littlestown Pike met the Westminster road. In that position Alger's men saw only intermittent, long-range action until the sun began to set, when a large force under Chambliss suddenly looped around the flank of the Sixth Michigan and presented the Fifth with "its first serious encounter with the enemy." Bolstered by Captain Thompson's company, which had fallen in with the Fifth after ending its reconnaissance toward Westminster, Alger's regiment counterattacked on foot. It pushed back the enemy, "driving him some distance... killing and capturing quite a number." Skirmishing continued until Chambliss and Fitz Lee cleared Hanover, joining Hampton in making a wide circuit to the east.[47]

The Michigan Brigade had fought stoutly in its maiden outing under Custer. The three regiments that had smelled battle-smoke for the first time had suffered dozens of casualties, and one, the Sixth Michigan, had been forced initially to retreat. Ultimately, however, each had stood firm, keeping Fitz Lee and Chambliss at bay, dislodging portions of both brigades from prepared positions, and coming within an ace of capturing several cannon. Along with Farnsworth's troopers (once they recovered from their early confusion), the Wolverines had kept Stuart on the defensive throughout the fight, making his withdrawal inevitable. Finally, by pinning the "Beau Sabreur" down all day, they ensured his inability to reunite with his army for almost forty-eight hours.

The day's results had given Custer's men a large helping of confidence in themselves and in their leader. Some had already begun to refer to him, fondly, as "the boy general of the golden locks," and they were looking forward to following his circus rider's costume into future battles.[48]

* * *

Considering his division fought out, Judson Kilpatrick elected to group his brigades, call in outlying detachments and patrols, tend to his casualties, and grant almost everyone several hours of unbroken sleep. Not until the early afternoon of 1 July did he start after Stuart; when he did he headed for East Berlin, almost ten miles above Hanover, which local informants claimed to be occupied by a large part of Lee's army. The report was spurious, and Kilpatrick should have known it. But his specialty was combat, not reconnaissance—he enjoyed being quoted to the effect that cavalry could fight profitably anywhere on land—and he accepted the tale of Lee's proximity as truth. Consequently, he spent the better part of the afternoon loping through Abbottstown and closing up on East Berlin.[49]

He should have marched, instead, in one of two directions. Stuart's raiders were sweeping well to the east of the Federal column, making for York via the village of Jefferson. Meanwhile, a dozen miles to the west, infantry had come up to relieve Pleasonton's First Cavalry Division, which, under the First Michigan's old superior, John Buford, had been tangling with Lee's vanguard outside Gettysburg since dawn. Sounds of battle were clearly audible to Kilpatrick's troopers throughout the day. Yet it was close to six A.M. on 2 July—with the main bodies of Lee and Meade on the field at Gettysburg, poised for another day of battle—before Kilpatrick moved to join his army in response to orders from Pleasonton.

Instead of hastening where needed, he moved his division at an easy gait, as though to belie the reputation for exhausting marches that had given him the nickname, "Kill-cavalry." He took a country road to the Baltimore Turnpike, thence south to the York Pike. Late in the morning his men turned west via New Oxford, before veering north toward Hunterstown, five miles above the battlefield.[50]

At about two P.M., Kilpatrick halted his column—Farnsworth's brigade in advance—beyond Hunterstown. There he learned he must countermarch. A courier from Pleasonton's headquarters at Gettysburg directed the Third Division back along the York Pike toward Abbottstown, a position from which it could guard the right and rear of Meade's army. The transfer to a far-off point threatened to deny Kilpatrick the battle-action he craved. Lips pursed in disappointment, he turned his column about and rode off in the direction he had come, Custer's troopers now in the lead.[51]

When the vanguard of the Michigan Brigade reached Hunterstown at about four o'clock, Kilpatrick saw that he would have his diet of combat after all. The town turned out to be occupied by a contingent of Wade Hampton's brigade, the main body of which had halted a mile or more to the south along the road into Gettysburg. At a word from Kilpatrick, Custer sent a detachment of his forward unit, the Sixth Michigan, toward the rear of the gray column. Meanwhile, a unit of Farnsworth's brigade, which Kilpatrick entrusted to one of his staff officers, Lieutenant Lewellyn G. Estes of Michigan, careened through the town in a saber charge that routed the occupation force, a squadron of Cobb's (Georgia) Legion.[52]

The troops Custer had sent south, led by Lieutenant Storrs, found Hampton's rear guard none too vigilant. Dismounting amid a woods along the Gettysburg road, Storrs's men opened up with their Spencers, sending Carolinians scurrying for cover. One Rebel officer on a light-colored horse, however, spurred toward the Federals' hiding-place. The rider, who proved to be General Hampton himself—expert horseman, swordsman, and pistol shot—singled out a trooper amid the foliage and exchanged gunfire with him at a range of 125 yards.

Hampton's opponent, who appears to have been twenty-five-year-old James C. Parsons of Company I, Sixth Michigan, squeezed off several shots before his repeater fouled. Appealing to his rival's sense of fair play, Parsons raised his hand to ask for time to clear the bore. The chivalric Hampton replied with a nod and waited patiently for the contest to resume. When at last Parsons raised his carbine, however, the brigade leader put a pistol ball through the trooper's wrist, sending him fleeing among the trees.[53]

As the victor disengaged from his improbable duel, he was attacked without warning by Lieutenant Storrs. Charging up from behind, the subaltern struck the back of Hampton's skull with his saber. Saved from quick death by his slouch hat and thick hair, the general whirled about and trained his pistol on the assailant, who abruptly galloped off. Angered and in pain, Hampton pursued at top speed, snapping his pistol at Storrs. A faulty percussion cap and a good headstart enabled the fugitive to gain the same shelter that had swallowed up Trooper Parsons.[54]

As an enraged Hampton went to the rear for medical attention, Custer digested the results of Storrs's reconnaissance and conferred with General Kilpatrick. About five P.M. the Union brain trust decided to challenge Hampton's force, which they feared meant to strike Meade's upper flank. Gingerly, Custer led his brigade south, the Sixth Michigan in front followed closely by the First.

The careful attackers found a bloodied but unbowed Hampton

waiting for them. About a mile and a half below Hunterstown, Stuart's lieutenant had positioned several ranks of Cobb's Legion, Colonel Pierce Manning Butler Young at their head, across a fence-lined stretch of road. Another Georgia unit, the Phillips Legion, had formed on Young's right flank and the First South Carolina Cavalry had taken position on his left. Despite the roadblock, Custer's people continued south in column of fours before halting just out of rifle-range. Following a brief conference, Kilpatrick ordered Custer to scatter the Georgians.[55]

Custer must have wondered how Kill-cavalry expected the deed to be accomplished. Hemmed in by the fences, even a small squadron would find itself too densely packed into the road to make headway south. Knowing no other course, Custer selected Captain Thompson's Company A of the Sixth and placed himself at its head. Companies C and D of Thompson's regiment as well as portions of the First and Seventh Michigan went into position, dismounted, in the rear and on the flanks, while Pennington's rifles unlimbered on the east side of the road to provide a heavier degree of support. Another detachment of the First, the squadron of Captain Andrew W. Duggan, covered roads leading into Hunterstown from the south and east.[56]

When all units were in position, Custer waved Thompson's men forward. In gathering darkness, a compact rank of horsemen pounded down the narrow road, absorbing a destructive fire from Young's riflemen and their comrades on either side. Additional opposition came from Thompson's own supports: under Kilpatrick's plan of action, they had been placed in such proximity to the attackers that they raked Company A with an errant but deadly crossfire. This was bad enough, but the supports also fired into one another. "It was a great wonder that we was not all killed," recalled Allen Rice of Company C, "for the Rebles ware [sic] firing on us from one direction and our men from the other." The tragic upshot included several men and one officer, Lieutenant Seymour Shipman of Company D, seriously wounded.[57]

Long before Company A reached its target, men and horses went down with wounds, clogging the road and making further progress impossible. The twenty-seven casualties that resulted included Captain Thompson, severely wounded, and his second-in-command,

Lieutenant Ballard, wounded and captured when his horse fell with him. Ahead of Ballard lay a long recuperation, followed by nearly two years in a prison camp.[58]

Almost joining Ballard in captivity was George Custer, thrown hard to the ground by his wounded horse. Slowly regaining his feet, the brigadier found himself the common target of numerous marksmen. Before a bullet or a captor could claim him, Trooper Norvill F. Churchill of Company L, First Cavalry, dashed up from behind, threw out an arm, and lifted the still-woozy general into the saddle. Under a fusillade from several directions, Churchill and his saddle-mate returned safely to the starting-point of the ill-considered charge.[59]

Two days after a successful introduction to brigade command, Custer—abetted considerably by his division leader—had involved himself in a disastrous, if limited, defeat. Immediately following the boy general's repulse, Wade Hampton, a much more experienced commander, proved just as impetuous and short-sighted as his opponent. At the South Carolinian's order, the troopers of Pierce Young, "yelling like fiends," counterattacked up the same road—now more constricted than ever—against not only rifle-fire but Pennington's accurate shelling. Young met an even bloodier fate than Thompson, suffering dozens of casualties before whirling about in retreat.[60]

With Custer still feeling the effects of his fall, Kilpatrick mounted no more attacks. Shortly afterward, Hampton brought up some guns of his own and the action below Hunterstown became an artillery duel, interspersed with long-range skirmishing. The fighting raged until eleven P.M., when word came that Kilpatrick was now wanted at the opposite end of the Union line.[61]

Kilpatrick, who never dwelt on his miscues, must have departed Hunterstown in high spirits, buoyed by the fighting spirit of his new command, especially the Michigan portion thereof. In two battles a day apart, Custer and his Westerners had won the advantage in a major action and had emerged from a fierce little skirmish on at least equal terms with a more seasoned enemy. Kill-cavalry had a right to expect even better things from those Michigan boys in the days to come.

CHAPTER EIGHT

"Come On, You Wolverines!"

Combat had swirled across the fields and ridges surrounding Gettysburg throughout 2 July. Thousands of men had gone down dead or wounded, regiments and brigades had been ripped apart, but the outcome of the struggle remained undetermined. While most of the day's fighting—as also that of the day before—had been carried on by the infantry and artillery of the armies, mounted forces had also seen action. Stuart's men, like Kilpatrick's, had only recently reached the battlefield, but Buford's division had been fought out and was now refitting well to the rear. The other one-third of Pleasonton's corps, David Gregg's division, had taken position east of Gettysburg about midday on the second; toward evening, it had tangled with Confederate infantry along Meade's upper flank. While Gregg had not been so heavily engaged as Buford, neither was he at full strength. One of his three brigades had been sent to Maryland to guard a supply depot, and the two that had fought on the second had taken some hard knocks. Thus, in ordering Kilpatrick's division out of Hunterstown shortly before midnight, Pleasonton had earmarked it to support Gregg. The latter remained along the Union right rear, a position army headquarters considered vulnerable to assault by either J.E.B. Stuart or his infantry comrades.[1]

From Hunterstown Kilpatrick proceeded directly south, Custer's brigade in the van. The journey took the blue column across the York Pike and the Hanover Road, then down the length of the Union rear. Between three and four o'clock on the morning of the third the long line of riders, most of them dead-tired after hours in the saddle, came to an unsteady halt southeast of Gettysburg, along the road that led back to Littlestown. At a crossroads known as Two Taverns, not far from the bivouac of Gregg's equally fatigued command, Custer's and Farnsworth's troopers were finally permitted to care for their horses, then grab what sleep they could.

The lucky ones got five hours' worth. By eight A.M., with the thump of artillery and the rattle of small arms' fire audible to the west, Kilpatrick ordered half of his command to mount up. Pleasonton had changed their destination from Gregg's front to the far left of the army, between the roads to Taneytown and Emmitsburg. Farnsworth's brigade would lead off; Custer's would be able to sleep a little longer before bringing up the rear.

Though no one knew it at the time, Custer's men would be heading north, not south in Farnsworth's wake. Two hours before Kilpatrick roused Farnsworth, a courier from cavalry headquarters had ordered General Gregg to move up the Baltimore Pike closer to Gettysburg. Gregg, however, believed that his original orders—to return to his battlefield along the road to Hanover, where he could continue to guard the Union right—was the better idea. He made sure the messenger conveyed his views to Pleasonton. Eventually word came back that Gregg had to move up as ordered but that he could direct Kilpatrick to send a brigade to replace him on the right.[2]

When Gregg's own courier carried this news to Two Taverns, he found that Kilpatrick and Farnsworth, as well as a small portion of Custer's brigade, had left for points distant. Custer, however, remained on the scene, and he was receptive to Gregg's initiative. Having fully recovered from his injuries at Hunterstown, the general was eager for action, and he sensed that more of it was waiting up north than in the other direction. At once he recalled that part of his command that had started off with Kilpatrick. Minutes later his buglers were sounding "Boots and Saddles," and not long after that his column was trotting north along farm trails, the Sixth Michigan up front.[3]

By the light of mid-morning, Gregg's man guided Custer into position astride the dusty intersection where the Hanover Road met the north-south-running Low Dutch (or Salem Church) Road. Nearby, the Second Division had fought stoutly twelve hours ago, preventing Rebel infantry from joining an attack on Culp's Hill, a vital position one and a half miles to the southwest.[4]

Unaware that Stuart's cavalry would soon move against him from above, Custer faced his lead regiments, the Fifth and Sixth Michigan, westward. There they awaited the coming of the balance of the brigade. They were still waiting when, just shy of noon, four artillery reports sounded from atop Cress's Ridge, a long, wooded elevation to the northwest. These salvos, which announced Stuart's presence in force, directed the Michiganders' attention in that direction. When a line of dismounted skirmishers began to descend the high ground, Pennington's guns also shifted front. David Gregg, who was responsible for this sector being covered, began to look like a seer.[5]

Studying his enemy through field-glasses, Custer decided to go forth and meet them. Already he had erected a line of widely spaced outposts that ran north along the base of Cress's Ridge, then eastward across a grassy plain toward the edge of a woodlot astride the Low Dutch Road. Now he supported that line with two battalions of the Fifth Michigan under Colonel Alger and Majors Ferry and Trowbridge, along with two squadrons of the Sixth Cavalry under Captain Weber and Lieutenant Storrs. Recalling how well these Spencer-wielders had fought on foot at Hanover, he confidently watched them thrash through the clover and wheat fields northwest of the road junction, where they took up skirmisher positions. Soon the men of both regiments were trading rifle-fire with their opponents at long distance.[6]

As noon came and went, each side fed in reinforcements but neither seemed inclined to bring on major fighting until able to develop the other's strength and position. For his part, Custer kept the regiments of Town and Mann in column near the road junction, ready for use in a crisis. No crisis developed, however, and the pop-pop of small arms continued at a mild pace.

Then, abruptly, Custer's job appeared over. Shortly before one P.M. General Gregg's lead brigade, under Colonel John B. McIntosh, moved up in rear of the Michigan units and prepared to relieve them all along the line. Infantry commanders had become aware of Stuart's advance toward the Union rear; they persuaded Pleasonton to return the Second Division to its old position. In agreeing to do so,

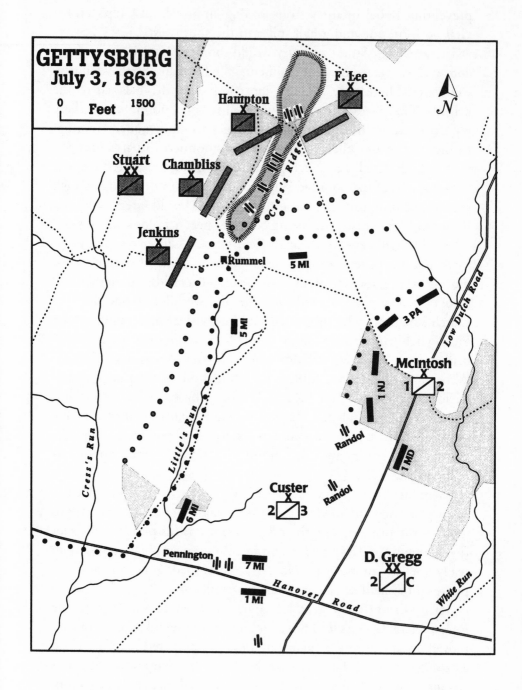

however, the cavalry commander demanded that Custer should join his own division on the opposite flank.

Though disappointed at having to leave, Custer received the order with good grace. He started off the First and Seventh Cavalry as well as the bulk of the Sixth, which had been protecting Pennington's guns. As the movement got underway the brigade leader provided McIntosh with a situation report, to which he appended a warning that the woods atop Cress's Ridge appeared to be teeming with graybacks. McIntosh merely nodded and saluted, then turned to an aide and ordered up his regiments.[7]

Trouble began as soon as the new arrivals pushed across the Hanover Road. Before they could exchange places with the riflemen of Alger and Weber, dismounted Confederates streamed down Cress's Ridge to block their path; behind them, horse artillery opened on Custer's outposts. Four of Pennington's guns returned the fire so accurately that Stuart's barrage slackened noticeably.

The diminished cannonade gave McIntosh the opening he needed. At his direction, the First New Jersey (Percy Wyndham's old outfit) moved to spell Custer's northernmost positions. The Jerseymen advanced toward John Rummel's farm, near the base of the ridge, adjusting their heading to confront a force holding a fenceline south of the barn. Before reaching the fence, however, the Federals found that the more numerous Rebels had curled around their flank, threatening them with capture en masse.[8]

Colonel Alger, whose large detachment stood nearest the action, came bravely if impulsively to the rescue. To the disputed site he ordered the companies under the quietly capable Noah Ferry. The major's unit hustled forward, but too late: well in advance of the fence they found the Jersey regiment pulling back before the reinforced enemy. A stream of Enfield bullets staggered Ferry's unit and sent part of it to the rear. To set an example of tenacity, Ferry picked up a rifle dropped by a wounded man, loosed a few shots at the enemy, then turned around and called after his troopers: "Rally, boys! rally for the fence!" Seconds later, another fusillade cut him down.[9]

His sacrifice was not in vain. Most of his men held their ground within rifle-shot of the Rummel property, pinning the Confederates to their fence and enabling other elements of McIntosh's brigade—chiefly Pennsylvanians and Marylanders—to advance in support. When a cluster of Stuart's men suddenly broke fire and advanced beyond the fence, Ferry's battalion, covered by the carbineers of McIntosh, chased them to their lines and kept them there while McIntosh completed his dispositions. Slowly, warily, the Fifth and Sixth Michigan relinquished their footholds on Cress's Ridge and fell back to the intersection. Rather than rejoin their brigade, some troopers remained within supporting distance of McIntosh's brigade should it need the special punch of the Spencer rifle.[10]

Firepower of a different sort suddenly claimed the attention of virtually every soldier for miles around. Open-mouthed troopers stared south in response to an artillery barrage so enormous that, though it originated below Gettysburg, it seemed to come from the next ridge. In preparation for a climactic attack, Robert E. Lee had begun to pound his enemy's center with 150 cannon, firing in unison. Later, many of Custer's troopers attributed a secondary purpose to the barrage, regarding it as a signal that Stuart should ready his men to hit the Union rear while the infantry struck from the other side.[11]

Under the heavier din, the fire generated by the men of Custer, McIntosh, and Stuart began to slacken. As if by prearranged agreement, a lull settled over the battlefield, albeit one that promised to be very temporary. While it lasted, General Gregg, who had come up to observe and, if possible, to control the unfolding situation, asked Custer to remain on the ground with those units that had yet to disengage. The youngster from Monroe required no persuading. A major fight was imminent, and his men appeared as eager as he was to see it through. Hell, yes, he would stay![12]

Soon after Custer sent back for his departed regiments, fighting flared near the Rummel farm. From Custer's position the firing sounded one-sided; soon it became obvious that many of McIntosh's men, low on ammunition, were trying to disengage. But as they started south, a new line of Confederates—some mounted, most on foot—left the foliage on Cress's Ridge. These were the Virginia regiments under Fitz Lee with whom the Wolverines had tangled at Hanover.

Artillery that had reached the field in company with General Gregg—four guns under Captain Alanson M. Randol—concentrated against the newcomers and forced them back to the high ground. But a half-hour later, about three P.M., Lee's brigade again emerged from the ridge and began to press McIntosh's skirmishers, most of whom still clung to positions within sight of the Rummel farm despite nearly empty cartridge pouches.[13]

Again Custer sought to help McIntosh, and again the Fifth Michigan was his medium of assistance. Again, too, Alger's regiment had a hard time moving up in support. The volume of fire from Lee's brigade compelled would-be rescuers under Major Trowbridge to seek refuge behind a post-and-rail fence that ran perpendicular to McIntosh's line. Suddenly, Trowbridge's men as well as the troopers they were trying to relieve came under attack from a new direction, the northwest, as John Chambliss's brigade moved toward them in unison with Fitz Lee's more northerly advance.

Despite their precarious position, Trowbridge's men held onto their fence, somehow keeping both Fitz Lee and Chambliss beyond the range at which their rifles would have done fatal damage. Toward three-thirty, however, one regiment of Lee's brigade not previously engaged—the First Virginia, one of the Confederacy's most heralded units of horse—emerged, mounted, from the northern slopes of Cress's Ridge. Through his glasses, an alarmed Custer watched the cavaliers prepare the first mounted attack of the day—an attack that threatened to scatter the Fifth Michigan like debris in a windstorm.[14]

Before the storm could break, Custer spied the Seventh Michigan returning to the road junction in column of fours. The regiment was not only green as grass, it was well below authorized strength: 461 officers and men present for duty in contrast to the 770 available to the Fifth Michigan, the brigade's largest unit. Still, Custer took heart at the sight of it. Reportedly, General Gregg was also gladdened by the outfit's arrival. Considering a countercharge imperative but fearing it would take a dreadful toll, the division commander preferred to commit a rookie regiment such as the Seventh, whose men would remain ignorant of the dangers until too late to turn back.[15]

Spurring south, Custer reined in at the head of the Seventh, where he imparted to Mann and his subordinates a few simple instructions. When the orders passed down the column, they were greeted by the sustained rasp of 500 men drawing sabers. Moments later Custer led the regiment forward at a trot that quickly accelerated into a limited gallop. Almost a mile to the north, the First Virginia came on at the same pace.

As the blue column rumbled across the grassy plain, dismounted men on either side scrambled out of its path. A few hundred yards above the Hanover Road the gait became an extended gallop, at which point Custer waved above his head the ornate kepi he had donned this day, shouting in a voice that made itself heard above the thunder of hooves: "Come on, you Wolverines!"[16]

For all its verve and enthusiasm, the Seventh Michigan failed to reach its target. It tore through the ranks of Chambliss's dismounted troopers, some of whom went down beneath the sabers of Mann's men and the flashing feet of their mounts. Other Confederates sprayed the head of the column with a deadly fusillade that caused many attackers to veer westward. The new heading caused the out-of-control detachment to slam into the post-and-rail fence that had sheltered Trowbridge's battalion. "It is useless to say," wrote Sergeant Edwin Havens of Company A, who took a wound in the charge, "that the regt. was thrown into confusion. No regt. could stand such a force." Halted by the barrier, some of Havens's comrades turned about and raced to the rear. Those left behind found themselves in a deadly pocket; "We... huddled together and the [enemy] was pouring a destructive fire among us. No wonder that we ran...."[17]

As the rear of the outfit accordioned into the group at the fence, Lieutenant John Clark of Company E followed a simple plan: "Kill all you can & do your best each for himself." Firing through the fence rails, Clark and other dismounted men finally struck at the First Virginia, which had dismounted on the other side; the pistol and rifle contest lasted a good thirty minutes. Still-mounted troopers, led by the regiment's newly appointed adjutant, Lieutenant George G. Briggs, managed to throw down sections of the fence. Through the gaps the horsemen went "pell mell," according to Captain George Armstrong of Company D, who added that "the enemy recoiled and withdrew only as we cut or shot them down or rode over them."[18]

Realizing he had lost much of his force, Custer, leading that portion of the Seventh which had not hit the fence, reconsidered his course. With the First Virginia engaged in the middle of the field, Mann's troopers needed go no farther. As it turned back to the Hanover Road, however, Custer's detachment was set upon by Chambliss's survivors as well as by supports from the only Rebel force thus far uncommitted, a regiment and a legion from Hampton's brigade. In turn, these troops were taken in flank by Trowbridge's remounted battalion. Regrouping, Hampton's force put much of the Fifth Michigan to flight and unhorsed Trowbridge, who barely eluded capture. The frantic succession of attack and counterattack ended when, for the third time this day, the Fifth Michigan advanced in support of embattled comrades. Its well-worked Spencers eventually forced Trowbridge's assailants to Cress's Ridge.[19]

Custer, Mann, and the other participants in the saber charge had barely returned home when the next, and final, episode of the battle began to unfold. Shortly after 3:30 P.M.—while nearly 13,000 infantrymen were assaulting the midpoint of the Union line at Gettysburg—the two regiments and one legion that remained to Wade Hampton passed down the ridge and formed an attack column between the positions of Fitz Lee and Chambliss. Like the First Virginia a half-hour earlier, Hampton's intentions were obvious: to sweep his adversaries from the field.

Sensing that Hampton would deliver Stuart's last blow, Custer determined to parry and riposte. Even as he planned, the weapon he needed came to hand in the form of the First Michigan, just now returning to the Hanover Road. Without hesitation, Custer galloped into place beside Charles Town. He found the colonel in especially poor condition, so weak from his chronic ills and from fatigue that he could barely remain in the saddle. When Custer explained his intentions, however, a light flashed in the dying man's eyes, for he desired nothing more than to fall at the height of a gallant charge. Here was an aspiration his superior could appreciate.[20]

Once again metal grated against metal as swords pulled free from scabbards—this time wielded by veterans who would not stumble over obstacles in their path. As Hampton's units neared the midpoint of the open plain, Custer spurred his charger forward; behind him, hard on his heels, came Colonel Town's troopers, shouting, cheering, twirling their sabers. Accelerating more quickly than had the Seventh Michigan, the First nearly crossed Pennington's and Randol's line of fire before the surprised artillerymen ceased shelling.

Spectators on all parts of the field watched open-mouthed as the blue column closed the distance to its enemy, taking a skirmish fire on both flanks without wavering or slowing. One of McIntosh's officers, whose company was stationed just east of Custer's route, would remember the attack as "the finest thing I witnessed during nearly three years" of fighting. Looking on from the other flank, Colonel Alger described it, simply, as "the most gallant charge of the war."[21]

When the charging columns collided, another observer in McIntosh's brigade likened the sound to "the falling of timber." So violent was the shock of Custer's and Hampton's meeting "that many of the horses were turned end over end and crushed their riders beneath them." For the rest of his life, this man would recall "the clashing of sabers, the firing of pistols, the demands for surrender and cries of combatants...."[22]

Although it had covered less ground than its opponents, the First Michigan had gained greater momentum; the result was a blue wedge driven deep into a gray column. Sabers flailing, Colt's revolvers making a fearful staccato, Colonel Town's troopers cut a long swath through their opponents, emerging well above the Rummel farm lane. Turning back to the main arena, they began to single out targets; soon individual combats spread to all corners of the field. "Such fighting I never saw before," wrote one of Town's men. A comrade, usually given to understatement, called it "the most furious dragoon fight I ever saw or engaged in."[23]

Like a majority of the regiment, Custer emerged unscathed from the tangle of men and horses—but just barely. Soon after merging with Hampton's column he had hurtled through space for the second time in twenty-four hours as his mount, "Roanoke," collapsed with a minie ball in the foreleg. This day no rescuer was close at hand, but Custer regained his feet—and his faculties—more quickly than at Hunterstown and thus avoided being shot or sabered where he lay. Vaulting onto a riderless horse, he resumed the fight, making life precarious for any Rebel who came within reach of his long Toledo blade.[24]

For several minutes the hacking, shooting contest continued between the lines, neither side giving or asking quarter. Then, suddenly, mounted supports added their weight to the melee, shifting the balance in Custer's favor. Detachments of McIntosh's brigade, including headquarters personnel, struck both of Hampton's flanks. On the left, they followed Russell Alger, who led his regiment's fourth advance of the day, an effort in which he was joined by small clusters of the Sixth and Seventh Michigan.[25]

Delivered at a critical time, these unexpected blows forced the Confederates to give ground, slowly, stubbornly, grudgingly. Assailed on almost every side, in danger of being surrounded, with no reinforcements at hand, and with their commander again gone to the rear with saber gashes, Hampton's troopers turned back to Cress's Ridge, retiring in good order and defiant spirits. Unwilling to pursue into the mouth of cannon, a bruised but alert Custer and an exhausted but uninjured Town let them go. Once able to disengage, the Federal leaders collected their able-bodied men and led them south in triumph.

Triumph it certainly was. Stuart's legions had been battered but not broken—overwhelmed on some quarters of the field but not undone. Tomorrow they would return to the fight with renewed vigor. Nevertheless, this day they had been decisively repulsed, largely as a result of two of the most dramatic saber charges of this or any other war. Stuart would not reach the Union rear in time to salvage the doomed attack against Meade's center that would become known as Pickett's Charge. And for that outcome, Custer's Wolverines could claim a heroic share of the credit.[26]

* * *

For the balance of 3 July and well into the following day, the opposing cavalries buried their dead, medicated their wounded, and maintained widely separated picket lines. At sundown Stuart left the disputed ground for the York Pike, as though conceding defeat. Following his pullback, General Gregg called Custer to his field headquarters, thanked him warmly for the service he and his brigade had rendered throughout the day, and directed him to report to Kilpatrick on the Union left.[27]

Custer accepted Gregg's tribute quietly and without comment, but he knew how deserving his people were of commendation. All four of his regiments, from the veteran First to the raw Seventh, had fought long and hard—sometimes brilliantly—against the best cavalrymen in North America. They had paid for their success. Of the 250-some Federal casualties on this field, Custer's outfits accounted for almost 90 percent. The First and Fifth had each suffered more than fifty, the lightly engaged Sixth (still smarting from Hunterstown), fewer than a dozen, and the Seventh an even 100: thirteen killed, forty-eight wounded including four officers, and thirty-nine missing or known to be captured—nearly a quarter of the regiment's effective strength on 3 July.[28]

The weary, grimy, bullet-riddled regiments deserved a rest, and Custer hoped to give it to them. But when he made contact with Kilpatrick along the Baltimore Pike that evening he found that his men were not the only members of the Third Cavalry Division to have suffered grievously. Some of Farnsworth's regiments had been roughly handled, particularly the First Vermont. The previous afternoon Farnsworth had led the Vermonters in a mounted attack that Kilpatrick ordered against well-fortified infantry and artillery. Farnsworth and sixty-six of his men had been killed, dozens of others wounded, on that suicide mission, which refuted Kill-cavalry's notion that horsemen could prevail under any conditions. The young general was widely mourned not only in his brigade but in Custer's. James Kidd, briefly a classmate of Farnsworth's at the University of Michigan, attributed his death to Kilpatrick's prolificate use of manpower: "So many lives were sacrificed by him for no good purpose whatever."[29]

The bivouac along the Baltimore Pike broke up soon after sunrise on the fourth. The Wolverines spent the early hours of Independence Day heading south in hopes of getting a jump on Lee's army. Meade believed that, having fought itself to exhaustion the previous day, the Army of Northern Virginia must return home to recuperate. The Union commander was correct, although his opponent did not depart Gettysburg until late in the day and only when convinced that Meade would not make a belated counterattack.[30]

Hours before ordering his main army to withdraw, Lee started toward the Potomac long columns of supply wagons carrying Pennsylvania food and forage and ambulances filled with shattered men. Although cavalry and artillery guarded these columns, they were vulnerable to the blows that fast-moving pursuers could deliver. These blows would have to come from the troopers of Kilpatrick and Buford; Gregg's division would be limited to short-range pursuit and protection of its own army. Alfred Pleasonton, forced to remain close to Meade, would also be denied front-line participation in the pursuit.[31]

By anticipating Lee's pull-out, Meade hoped to trap him north of the rain-swollen Potomac long enough to complete the destruction of the Confederate army begun at Gettysburg. Not only would Meade harass Lee's retreat with his horsemen; he would send General French to sever Lee's connection to Virginia. By 6 July mounted forces from French's command, including Captain Deane's squadron of the Sixth Michigan, would chase Lee's rear guard from the north bank of the Potomac. The troopers would then destroy the pontoon bridges Confederate engineers had erected near Harpers Ferry as well as several miles upstream at Falling Waters.[32]

Kilpatrick's pursuit enjoyed early success despite a steady rain and roads swallowed up by mud. At about three P.M. on the fourth, five hours after leaving Gettysburg, the brigades of Custer and Farnsworth (the latter now under its senior colonel, Nathaniel P. Richmond) reached Emmitsburg. There the Yankees linked with the brigade of Colonel Pennock Huey, which had been detached from Gregg's division three days before to guard a supply depot in northern Maryland. After assimilating Huey's men, Kilpatrick led the combined force, more than 5,000 strong, southwestward to Frederick, where the cavalry of John Buford was heading.

En route to Frederick, Kilpatrick learned from civilian informants that hundreds of wagons and ambulances from Lee's army—they proved to be the property of General Ewell—were still in Pennsylvania, trundling south via Fairfield Gap in South Mountain. Realizing that he had gotten well ahead of his target and aware that capturing or disabling a supply column would elevate his reputation (sagging just a bit these days), the general moved his column northwestward with trademark rapidity. The pace enabled him, by ten o'clock, to reach a road fork that led not only to Fairfield Gap but to Monterey Pass, farther to the southwest. At the fork he learned that Ewell's train had taken the upper road a few hours earlier and that he might head it off via the other defile. Kilpatrick led the main body toward Monterey while dispatching Colonel Town and the First Michigan to overtake the vehicles on the Fairfield road.[33]

When he reached the shank of the enemy column, Town found himself overmatched by opposing horsemen: a large brigade under Brigadier General William E. Jones, which Lee had assigned to protect the wagons. Despite the odds, Companies C and G, Lieutenant Colonel Stagg at their head, attacked the rear of the train. In the ensuing skirmish the assailants destroyed a few wagons but suffered heavily. Captain William H. Elliott was mortally wounded and First Lieutenant James S. McElhenny was killed instantly; six of their men also became fatalities. The several wounded included Stagg, injured when his dying horse threw him, and Lieutenant Maxwell, who would survive a minie ball to make captain the following month.[34]

The rest of the Wolverine Brigade cleared Monterey Pass in advance of the train's emergence from the gorge at Fairfield. Kilpatrick and Custer initially considered Ewell's wagons theirs for the taking, but they had not counted on the determination or the resourcefulness of the couple dozen members of the First Maryland Cavalry Battalion, holding the pass. Under cover of darkness, the Marylanders deployed themselves so well and generated such fire-power that the Federals believed they were facing several times as many sharpshooters, supported by artillery. The deception was assisted by a terrific thunderstorm. A *New York Times* correspondent at Kilpatrick's headquarters wrote that "the howling of the storm, the rushing of water down the mountain-side, and the roaring of the wind, altogether were certainly enough in that wild spot to test the nerves of the strongest...."[35]

The Fifth Michigan, now at the head of Kilpatrick's column, formed line of skirmishers, four companies on the left side of the mountain road, three on the right. Farther to the right, the Sixth Cavalry took cover amid rocks, trees, and underbrush adjacent to Monterey Springs, a mineral-water spa. From these positions they returned the Marylanders' fire and tried to mount an offensive. Colonel Gray's regiment twice or three times attempted to pry the Rebels loose from their rocky perch. Thanks to the darkness, the rain, and the foliage clogging the route of advance, every effort was reminiscent of blind man's bluff ("one had to be guided by sound," observed James Kidd, "and not by sight").[36]

A frustrated Custer finally ordered Alger's men to cross a bridge over a rain-swollen mountain stream. For a change, their colonel advanced cautiously, believing the enemy had unplanked the span. A time-consuming reconnaissance, made while his men lay face-down in the mud, convinced Alger that the structure remained intact. Even so, the job ahead looked formidable. One of his troopers, twenty-one-year-old Gilbert Chapman of Company E, observed that "it was a bad place for us to ride up, a narrow pass in the mountains with artillery planted in front of us and no chance for flanking the enemy."[37]

Just after midnight, Alger led his dismounted command against the enemy's position, visible only by the flashes of the antagonists' firearms. Close behind came the Seventh Michigan, also on foot, followed by the mounted First West Virginia of Richmond's brigade. Despite their strength, the attackers inflicted few casualties; when challenged, the Marylanders faded into the shadows and escaped. One who did become a statistic—thrown from his horse for the third time in three days—was George Custer, who could not resist going in beside Alger's men. This time, at least, he was not seriously injured.[38]

Upset by the realization that a handful of marksmen had held three brigades at bay for more than three hours, Kilpatrick re-mounted his column and headed for the mouth of Fairfield Gap. There his men swarmed over a segment of Ewell's train, which a trooper of the Sixth Michigan estimated at two miles in length. The attackers overturned scores of wagons, confiscated what they could among the contents, and set what remained on fire. They halted other portions of the train by shooting or sabering their teams and also many guards and drivers.

Before Jones's brigade came up from the rear to make them desist, the Wolverines destroyed or disabled upwards of 100 vehicles while making prisoners of more than 1,400 Confederates, most of them Gettysburg casualties. Riding past the debris, Allen Rice of the Sixth Michigan recorded his semi-literate impressions: "It put me in mind of a fourth of July spree to see the wagons all strung along the road, the wheals choped to pieces, tungs cut off, barels of liqer smashed in and the wagons set afire."[39]

Hampered by night and weather and concerned that Lee's army was approaching, Kilpatrick broke contact with Jones before dawn of 5 July and went looking for J.E.B. Stuart's main body. Dropping back into Maryland, he located his target some twelve hours later, just west of the South Mountain chain. This time the battle-weary Wolverines remained in the rear as Richmond and Huey contested Stuart's passage by two trails that converged toward the village of Smithsburg. Without Custer's participation, the fighting on both fronts went badly; about 6:30 P.M. Kilpatrick disengaged and headed south to Boonsboro "to save my prisoners, animals, and wagons."[40]

Reaching Boonsboro at ten o'clock, Kilpatrick permitted his command a good night's sleep. Early on the sixth he welcomed John Buford, who had been tracking a Confederate wagon train—a much larger one than Kilpatrick had attacked—that had reached the river at Williamsport, thirteen miles to the northwest. Instead of operating in unison, the commanders decided to go their own ways, Buford to surround the train and Kilpatrick to move up to Hagerstown, where Stuart was reported to have gone following the clash at Smithsburg.

Upon reaching Hagerstown, the expanded Third Division, Richmond's brigade now in advance, found Stuart's men approaching from the northeast. About noon, before the enemy could secure a lodgement, Kilpatrick attacked through the streets of town. Running hard aground against John Chambliss's Confederates, Richmond's lead regiment reeled backward, disorganized and demoralized. Comrades to the rear stiffened the column, launched heavier assaults, and chased Chambliss out of town.

In the melee, Charles Snyder of the First Michigan, who had been accused of deserting his scouting patrol the previous February, redeemed himself. The captain, this day serving on Kilpatrick's staff, led a detachment of a Pennsylvania regiment in one of the counterattacks. This day it was Snyder who found himself alone, surrounded by five or six pistol-wielding Confederates. He sold his life dearly, cutting down three of his assailants before taking a wound to which he would succumb two weeks later.[41]

Though victorious, the Federals fell back when the rest of Stuart's division, followed by the advance of Robert E. Lee's infantry, topped the hills above Hagerstown. Well before that time, however, Custer's brigade had left for the north bank of the Potomac. While Richmond and Chambliss dueled, John Buford had been making little headway against the escort of the wagon train at Williamsport, which consisted of two brigades of cavalry, two regiments of infantry, and two dozen pieces of light artillery. Hoping to improve his odds, Buford about midafternoon sent couriers to Hagerstown, seeking support. Although himself in a tough fight, Kilpatrick assented to the request.

Within an hour, Custer's command had halted a few miles outside Williamsport, where the Fifth Michigan drove enemy pickets into the village. Coming up to the Confederate position, Custer found that the compact defense line and the river bluffs that anchored it left little maneuvering room. As his men milled about in indecision, they came under a heavy cannonade. Through the rest of the day the Wolverines fought with "shells bursting over our heads." A fragment struck Sergeant Aaron Cone Jewett, the popular acting adjutant of the Sixth Michigan, killing him instantly. Running his guns into battery at the edge of town, Lieutenant Pennington replied to the barrage; the artillery duel continued until dark.[42]

Kilpatrick, who had accompanied Custer's column, was at a loss to break the stalemate. At first he ordered the Fifth Michigan, at the head of the line, to make a saber charge through the town. Then—possibly recalling Richmond's recent troubles in Hagerstown—he called it off and instead resorted to a dismounted advance. But when Alger's riflemen failed to get close enough to the wagons to do Buford any good, the latter asked Kilpatrick for additional help. Again, Kilpatrick agreed. This proved to be a mistake, for soon after Colonel Huey's brigade headed south to join the fight, Richmond's men lost their grip on Hagerstown under pressure from Stuart's cavalry, horse artillery, and infantry support.[43]

Concerned by Kilpatrick's eviction and forced to contend with newly arrived reinforcements including Fitz Lee's brigade, Buford called off the fight shortly after dark. Kilpatrick and he disengaged and fell back, Custer's men accompanying the First Division into camp at Jones's Cross Roads, seven miles east of Williamsport, and Kilpatrick, with Richmond and Huey, returning to Boonsboro. It had been a day of small accomplishment for the cavalry of the Army of the Potomac. Although pinned north of the Potomac, immobile and apparently vulnerable, Lee's advance echelon remained strong, defiant, and confident of its ability to survive. Buford, Kilpatrick, and Custer could only hope that more productive days lay ahead.[44]

* * *

Custer's command spent 7 July resting and recuperating in the fields near Jones's Cross Roads. Despite their inability to batter their foe into submission, many Wolverines thought the destruction of the Army of Northern Virginia a matter of, at most, a few days. Major Trowbridge assured his family that the Rebels were trapped: "Genl Meade is pressing them hard in the rear and upon their flanks, and I do not now see how that army can escape almost utter annihilation."[45]

Rain fell throughout that night, bringing misery to Kilpatrick's and Buford's men, who, out of fear that Stuart might strike their camps before morning, were kept awake, under arms, and "standing in mud to our knees." They did not fare much better the next day. About five A.M. Stuart came down from the direction of Funkstown at the head of four brigades, including Lee's and Hampton's. The Beau Sabreur was screening the transfer of his army's infantry from Hagerstown to the river. His opponents, however, believed he was trying to block the passes east of Boonsboro that Meade's main body intended to use, something Kilpatrick and Buford would not allow. For their own reasons, therefore, the cavalries clashed near Jones's Crossroads and Boonsboro, Buford's men in front and Custer, Richmond, and Huey directly behind the First Division.[46]

Stuart's initial attack, which consumed the morning, was strong enough to shake Buford's right flank and threaten other portions of his line as well. Just after noon, Kilpatrick sent Custer to stabilize Buford's center, which had begun to waver; meanwhile, Richmond's brigade shored up the sagging Union left. After hours of mostly dismounted action, the advantage swung to the Federals and they began to move Stuart backward along the Hagerstown Pike.[47]

Even with Stuart falling back, the Wolverines took many casualties, especially in officers. Colonel Alger fell with a minie ball in his left thigh; the brigade would not see him again until his medical leave ended in September. Meanwhile, Colonel Mann was thrown from the saddle by a round that burst just above his head. The enemy suffered even more. "It was a horidable [sic] sight," wrote Corporal Rockwell, "to see the miserable rebs lay[ing] mangled and wounded all over the ground."[48]

Even with regimental leaders *hors de combat,* Custer's men shoved their adversaries as far as Beaver Creek, three miles from Boonsboro, where Pennington's guns pounded them for the balance of the day. In early evening, Kilpatrick and Buford returned south in triumph. "This is the eighth fight we have had with the Rebs and have whipped them everry [sic] time," wrote one Wolverine. The Seventh Michigan ended the day on an especially high note, being joined at Boonsboro by Major Granger and 177 members of Companies L and M, ready to add their strength to what had long been the smallest component of the Wolverine Brigade.[49]

Like the day before Boonsboro, the day after was devoted to resting and refitting. The respite was critically needed, for the steady diet of combat was pushing men and horses toward exhaustion. "It would look strange to you," Lieutenant George W. Townsend of the Fifth Michigan informed the editor of the *Allegan Journal,* "to see officers and men as soon as [the column is] halted drop on the ground or pavement, but we are glad to get rest anywhere." Even so, as Townsend's fellow subaltern George R. Barse noted, tired soldiers were not necessarily demoralized soldiers: "Although much worn down by fatigue and need of rest, the cry is, 'No rest until the rebels are driven from the State'. We can whip them, and must do so, cost what it will.[50]

161

During the next two days, 10-11 July, Custer's people saw relatively little action, permitting Buford to keep Stuart occupied along Beaver Creek. While the First Division fought, Meade's army debouched from the passes beyond Boonsboro. "Our Infantry is now blackening the hillsides near us," reported Andy Buck, "signifying another great battle soon." The foot troops eventually established a line running north from Bakersville, about two miles from Lee's right flank at the river, to Funkstown, within sight of the Rebel rear guard at Hagerstown.[51]

Despite the infantry's appearance, the cavalry carried on the fight. Early on the twelfth, Kilpatrick's division—Custer's brigade in advance, Farnsworth's old command close behind—reached the outskirts of Hagerstown just as Lee's rear guard headed for the safety of the works that had gone up at Williamsport. Custer took post about a mile and a half below the town, where he could keep an eye on Lee's defenses and the replacement pontoons in process of construction at Falling Waters.[52]

With the streets all but free of uniformed Southerners, Kilpatrick expected no difficulty in occupying Hagerstown. About eight A.M. on the twelfth his men uprooted a handful of pickets two miles outside town, then chased them through the streets, making, as Sergeant John Morey of the Fifth Michigan put it, "all the screaming and yelling you ever saw or heard." After gobbling up some Rebels who had overstayed their leave, detachments of the First, Fifth, and Seventh Michigan proceeded out the road to Williamsport until halted by heavy lines of infantry and horsemen. While waiting for Meade's advance to come up, the troopers suffered several casualties including Lieutenant Colonel Gould, put out of action by a gunshot wound in his right leg, leaving the Fifth Cavalry in the hands of Major Dake.[53]

When Meade's advance finally appeared, the hard-pressed troopers fell back and formed in its rear. Custer's men had decided they had been unfairly monopolizing the pursuit business. They had been fighting every few days since leaving Gettysburg, but the infantry had not been engaged since repulsing Pickett ten days ago. No longer would the cavalry deny the rest of the army the opportunity to strike at General Lee and be struck by him in return.

* * *

Another lull in the fighting occurred after the set-to on the Williamsport road, as Meade and his lieutenants convened a conference to determine whether to attack Lee's defenses. The Michigan Brigade assumed that some sort of strike would be launched before the Confederates crossed their bridges to Virginia; otherwise, everything the army had achieved since day one at Gettysburg would be wasted. Instead of an assault, however, the meeting produced only a reconnaissance, which Meade made next day. Consequently, the thirteenth saw no fighting beyond localized, small-unit exchanges.

Meade's survey persuaded him to attack but not until seven o'clock the next morning. Well before then, Robert E. Lee decided to linger no more on Northern soil. After dark on the thirteenth, part of his army began to ford the now-receding waters at Williamsport, while other troops, horses, and wagons crossed on the downriver pontoons.[54]

At about three A.M. on 14 July, four hours before his scheduled advance, Kilpatrick's scouts outside Hagerstown discovered the enemy works nearest them to be empty. When a reconnaissance by Buford found defenses farther to the east evacuated and Lee's army in process of crossing, both divisions pursued slowly and cautiously toward the river. As the operation progressed, Buford notified his colleague that he would try to interpose between the river and Lee's rear guard. Apparently he expected Kilpatrick to assist him in this endeavor; if so, he was disabused of the notion shortly before six o'clock, when the Fifth Michigan, trailed by the balance of its brigade, reached Williamsport. The town held only a few stragglers from Ewell's corps. Frustrated at having reached the scene too late, Dake's outfit raced through the streets of town, waving their sabers wildly ("I never saw a madder lot of men than we were," wrote Sergeant Morey). Pressing on to the river, the Fifth drove numerous Rebels into the water and watched them paddle madly across under a covering fire from comrades on the Virginia side.[55]

While Dake remained at the ford, mopping up, Kilpatrick led Custer's main force toward the bridges at Falling Waters. There Kill-cavalry hoped to beat Buford to the punch, cutting off and capturing Lee's rear guard. About two miles from the bridgehead, the Sixth Michigan, riding well in advance of its comrades, accompanied by Generals Kilpatrick and Custer, encountered hundreds of Rebels and drove them steadily south. About seven-thirty Colonel Gray's regiment came up to a semicircular defense line that protected the pontoons. The fruit of several days' labor, the complex of breastworks and trenches not only occupied commanding ground but was defended by a large force of infantry and some cannon commanded by one of the principal figures in Pickett's Charge, Brigadier General J. Johnston Pettigrew of North Carolina.[56]

By all indications, the position should be approached carefully. Before attempting an attack, Custer wished to await the arrival of his main force. Kilpatrick, however, instructed him to strike at once with a battalion of the Sixth. Reluctantly, Custer dismounted 100 men and placed them under Captain Weber, whose great ambition—as he had recently confided to James Kidd—was to lead a saber charge. Weber got his chance when Kilpatrick had the men remount. Obediently and happily, Weber led his battalion toward the works at a brisk trot. Recalling the carnage at Hunterstown and reports of Farnsworth's doomed advance at Gettysburg, Custer may have remonstrated against his superior's choice of tactics; if so, he got nowhere. The best he could do was support Weber with the dismounted squadron of Captain Royce.[57]

Almost miraculously, Weber and his 100 men made it inside the first line of works before the Confederates—who had mistaken them, in their dust-coated uniforms, for comrades—unleashed a volley at point-blank range. Five minutes after the attack began, a Confederate reported "horses without riders... running in every direction." Weber and his executive officer, Lieutenant Bolza, fell dead, along with several others; almost thirty men were wounded or taken prisoner.[58]

When Pettigrew's marksmen trained their rifles elsewhere, they cut up Royce's squadron and killed its leader. In attempting to support Royce, Kidd's squadron also came under fire; the college man received a minie ball through his foot. The Confederates suffered an unknown number of casualties, the most notable being Pettigrew, mortally wounded by one of Weber's troopers as the general regained his feet after being thrown by his mount. An unknown Confederate fell beneath the sword of George Custer, who led a second attack wave.[59]

As part of the second offensive, Kilpatrick had Custer commit the just-arrived First and Seventh Michigan. The Seventh, its striking power diluted by its many recruits, withdrew precipitately when Pettigrew's men unleashed a volley that broke up a mounted charge headed by Lieutenant Colonel Litchfield. Major Granger, however, led some veterans in a dismounted attack against the left flank of the works that resulted in the capture of a 10-pounder Parrott rifle, which its captors turned against the Rebels. Meanwhile, the First Michigan, along with a re-formed portion of Weber's regiment, advanced so resolutely that they captured more than sixty members of the Forty-seventh Virginia Infantry along with the colors of that regiment and those of the Fortieth Virginia.[60]

All told, the Michigan Brigade took upwards of 500 prisoners along with a wealth of arms and ammunition. Many times as many Confederates might have been captured, however, had Kilpatrick coordinated with Buford and had he not attacked prematurely, a tactic that alerted the Rebel rear to imminent danger. As a result, the larger part of that force scrambled across the pontoons before either Kilpatrick or Buford, coming up from the east, could cut them off. Thus, the sacrifice of Weber, Bolza, Royce, and their many men appeared to count for nothing. It was a frustrating and tragic note on which to close a campaign that had witnessed some of the finest combat performances ever turned in by the cavalry of the Army of the Potomac.

General George Armstrong Custer

*Russell A. Alger (Lieutenant
Colonel, Sixth Michigan Cavalry;
Colonel, Fifth Michigan)*

167

Manning D. Birge (Major, Sixth Michigan)

Melvin Brewer (Major, First Michigan; Lieutenant Colonel, Seventh Michigan)

George G. Briggs (Colonel, Seventh Michigan)

Thornton F. Brodhead (Colonel, First Michigan)

Daniel H. Darling (Lieutenant Colonel, Seventh Michigan)

Henry W. Granger (Major, Seventh Michigan)

Edwin R. Havens (Lieutenant, Seventh Michigan)

Allyn C. Litchfield (Captain, Fifth Michigan; Colonel, Seventh Michigan)

Don G. Lovell (Major, Sixth Michigan)

William D. Mann (Captain, First Michigan; Lieutenant Colonel, Fifth Michigan; Colonel, Seventh Michigan)

Charles E. Storrs (Major, Sixth Michigan)

George K. Newcombe (Major, Seventh Michigan)

Alexander C. McW. Pennington, Jr. (Lieutenant, Battery M, Second United States Artillery) [far right]

Charles H. Town (Colonel, First Michigan)

Peter A. Weber (Captain, Sixth Michigan)

CHAPTER NINE

No Rest for the Weary

*T*he campaign in Pennsylvania had left the Michigan Brigade spattered with mud and blood, and tired to the bone. But even as the survivors rubbed aching muscles and mourned lost comrades, they exulted in the contributions they had made to the defense of the North, to the success of their army, and to the annals of mounted warfare. "Our cavalry is doing mighty things whereof we are glad," bragged Andy Buck of the Seventh Michigan, adding that "we are now practicing war—not theorizing it." In a letter to a Battle Creek newspaper, Adjutant Briggs of the Sixth Michigan observed proudly that "we have this to cheer and encourage us—the world has never seen such Cavalry fighting as we have done, which is the testimony of the best Cavalry officers in the service." Added Trooper Benjamin Clark of the First Michigan: "I think old Lee will remember Gen Killpatrick's [sic] Cavalry for some time."[1]

In trying to explain why the Wolverine Brigade had attained such prowess so early in its career, many troopers looked no farther than their leader. One who at Falling Waters had watched Custer "plunge his saber into the belly of a rebel who was trying to kill him," told his family that "you can guess how bravely soldiers fight for such a general." The Seventh Michigan's Edwin Havens described his young commander in glowing terms: "He is a glorious fellow, full of energy, quick to plan and bold to execute, and with us has never failed in any attempt he has yet made."[2]

Custer's letters reflected the same pride in his men that they expressed in him. To Lydia Ann Reed he outlined the composition of the brigade, pointedly referring to the Fifth Michigan as "the regiment of which I endeavored to obtain the Colonelcy.... I rather outwitted the Governor who did not see fit to give it to me." The command to which the Fifth belonged had become his prized possession: "I would not exchange it for any other brigade in the army."[3]

The Wolverines had ample cause to feel good about themselves and their future. Despite Lee's escape to Virginia, his once-invincible army had been decisively defeated on Union soil thanks as much to Michigan cavalrymen as to anyone else. At the same time, the war in the western theater appeared all but won. During the pursuit to the Potomac, Meade's troops had learned that the principal Rebel fortress on the Mississippi had surrendered to Major General Ulysses S. Grant, an outcome that effectively split the Confederacy in two. "Vicksburgh is ours with all it contained," William Rockwell wrote his wife, Polly. "They surrendered on the forth [sic] of July." Rockwell believed the news would demoralize and weaken Lee's army: "We think they will soon surrender here, then we will go and take Richmond. Then you may look for me [at] home...." Ed Havens put his praise of Vicksburg's captor into a pun: "I hope he will... come up and 'Grant' Lee and his army a Leave forever."[4]

Thoughts like these kept the brigade's spirits high as it led its army back into Virginia, where the outcome of the war would be settled. The initial strategy was to overtake Lee's command before it returned to its namesake region. That army had recrossed the Potomac near the western rim of the Blue Ridge; Meade's troops planned to head south on the other side of the mountains.

Two days after the fight at Falling Waters, the Michigan Brigade reached the river at Berlin, Maryland. The following day, the seventeenth, Custer's troopers crossed the pontoon bridge that had been laid there; on the Virginia side, they marched through Lovettesville, Morrisonville, and Wheatland, camping for the night at Purcellville, fourteen miles below the Potomac. Next morning they veered toward the Blue Ridge, seeking the head of Lee's column in the direction of Snicker's Gap and the town named for it.

By noon, as it approached the gorge at Snickersville, the brigade was no longer under Custer's immediate command. Worn down by the recent campaigning, General Kilpatrick had been granted twenty days' leave to visit his family in New York. In his absence Custer had assumed command of the Third Division, taking on responsibilities that forced him to "work night and day, usually get[ting] up before daylight [and] go[ing] to bed late." Custer's senior subordinate, Colonel Charles Town, had taken over the brigade, whose battle-thinned regiments were now commanded by Major Brewer, Major Dake, Colonel Gray, and Lieutenant Colonel Litchfield. Shortly after he replaced Custer, however, Town's health gave way and he too joined the casualty list. In his place Colonel Gray took over the brigade, leaving Lieutenant Colonel Foote—himself suffering from "physical weakness" of unknown origin—to lead the Sixth Michigan.[5]

The personnel changes appeared to have little effect on the command's field performance. When the head of its column reached Snicker's Gap early on the rainy afternoon of the seventeenth, the defile was found to be in the possession of a "considerable force" of Jones's cavalry which, after leading Ewell's wagons to safety, had assumed a position well in advance of its army. Hesitating not at all, George Gray sent a dismounted detachment of the Fifth Michigan, under Major Trowbridge, to clear away the rebels. Although the Confederates offered spirited resistance, the Spencer repeaters of Trowbridge's men finally drove them beyond the gap. They left behind more than a dozen wounded comrades. Trowbridge's loss amounted to two men slightly wounded.[6]

As it had the night after the fight at Boonsboro, the Wolverine Brigade spent the evening of the seventeenth standing to horse in a driving rain, alert to any reappearance by Jones. A thoroughly drenched Edwin Bigelow "suffered more" this night than at any time during his three and a half years of service.[7]

Late on the eighteenth, having held Snicker's Gap throughout the day without being challenged, the Wolverines were relieved by De Forest's brigade and went into camp. Next morning the Third Division saddled up and started for Upperville, along the western edge of Loudoun Valley. There the men spent another sleepless night, holding the reins of their still-saddled horses, ready for action at a moment's notice.

Early on 20 July Gray again led the brigade westward, this time toward Ashby's Gap in the Blue Ridge. Just short of the gap the

Fifth Michigan, at the head of the column, met Rebel pickets outside the village of Paris. As John Morey recorded, the regiment drove through the town "with drawn sabre[s], but we have no chance to use them as the enemy retreat, leaving the gap in our possession." The sergeant observed wryly that the enemy "seem to not like the seven shooters very well."[8]

Reaching the gap, Gray posted the First and Sixth Cavalries at its mouth, while sending scouts into the valley beyond to try to discern the position and heading of Lee's column. Meanwhile, eight miles to the south, John Buford's horsemen, a force of infantry under General French in their rear, were laboring to plug Manassas Gap before the Confederates could use it to exit the Valley. Farther east, Meade's infantrymen, preceded by Gregg's troopers, were also heading for the gap. If they reached the defile before Lee passed it on the other side, the Federals could strike his flanks, cut his column in two, and defeat both halves in turn. It was an ambitious plan, but if the various forces available to Meade moved quickly enough and cooperated precisely enough they might do more than end Lee's retreat—they might end the war.[9]

The Michigan Brigade played its role in this plan quite well. Through visual sightings and from information provided by a prisoner captured near Ashby's Gap, the Wolverines learned that the corps of James Longstreet, finding itself blocked by Custer, had moved south of the gap toward Front Royal. Even so, the cavalry picketed the gap well into the twenty-second, ensuring that no Rebels slipped through it to enter the Loudoun Valley. On the twenty-third, as French's slow-moving troops finally relieved Buford at Manassas Gap and passed into the Valley, Custer was directed to support the foot soldiers. Accordingly he looped south to Piedmont Station on the Manassas Gap Railroad, crossed the Rappahannock tributary known as Hedgeman's River, and spent the night at Amissville.[10]

En route to Amissville Custer learned that due to Meade's and French's lethargy the Confederates had slipped the trap set for them. By the morning of 24 July Longstreet had safely debouched from Chester Gap, seven miles below Manassas Gap, while the rest of Lee's column had passed the point at which French had hoped to intercept it. But if the Rebels were beyond reach of Meade's infantry, horsemen might still bring them to bay short of their destination, the area around Culpeper Court House. In response to orders from General Pleasonton, on the twenty-fourth Custer proceeded in advance of the main army to Newby's Cross Roads, four miles southwest of Amissville, the reported location of a portion of Lee's column.[11]

Upon reaching Newby's, where the trail from Sperryville intersected the southward-running road to Culpeper, Gray's brigade found an unexpectedly large force of infantry and artillery, members of Lieutenant General A.P. Hill's Third Corps, Army of Northern Virginia. Spreading Pennington's guns far apart to cover his advance, Gray attacked with the same imprudence that had brought on his meeting-engagement at Hanover. The blow appeared to stun the foot troops, who rarely took a body-punch from Union cavalry; in response, Hill carefully formed line of battle. For some hours Gray's dismounted skirmishers held their more numerous opponents in place, till it became clear that friendly infantry was too far away to lend them aid. Slowly but inevitably, the cavalry fell back.

At Custer's order, Gray tried to disengage, but before he could complete the maneuver Hill shifted two brigades toward the Union left and rear, hemming in Dake's Fifth and Foote's Sixth Michigan as well as a two-gun section of Pennington's battery. Pressed on three sides, the regiments worked their Spencers at a furious clip to stave off disaster. Thanks to their firepower, the support they received from the First and Seventh Michigan, and the accurate shelling of Pennington's other guns, Hill's men held back while most of the fugitives escaped through a dense woods. For this "display of great courage by both officers and men," Custer gave primary credit to Colonel Gray and to the officer in charge of the isolated section, Lieutenant Carle A. Woodruff.[12]

Having lost thirty men killed, wounded (including Captain Storrs of the Sixth), and missing, Custer and Gray led the survivors back to Amissville, where they again encamped. In his after-action report the image-conscious Custer tried to make his retreat look like a victory march. Not his troops, but Hill's, had withdrawn "hurriedly and in great disorder" once Custer's attack "spread great consternation" through them. Custer also claimed that although his casualties were many, Hill's loss "was known to be much greater."[13]

This was so much prevarication, and Custer and his men knew it. Having attacked a force of unknown size and composition without immediate prospect of support, the Wolverines had been reduced to fighting for their lives; they had extricated themselves through the sheerest good fortune. Until their last-minute rescue, John Morey of the Fifth Michigan feared "we were destined for Richmond. I said to myself 'how are you Libby prison?'" Days later the memory of his regiment's near-encirclement continued to unnerve Allen Rice: "I never want to be in as tight a place as we ware [sic] in in the last batle [sic]."[14]

* * *

Following Newby's Cross Roads the Michigan boys at last enjoyed the kind of respite to which their combat quotient of the past month entitled them. For the next week and more—as other belligerents carried on the eastward-shifting war—the Wolverines restocked haversacks and feed bags from the countryside as well as from their supply wagons. When pitching camp in that rich farming region, Custer had been deliberately contradictory in instructing everyone (as Trooper Rice put it): to "be shure [sic] and not steal anything but take all you want." The injunction was well received and closely followed; by the twenty-ninth, John Morey reported, he and his messmates were enjoying "plenty of chicken and all kinds of fresh meat that we confiscate."[15]

When not rifling the neighborhood for beef, fowl, or mutton, the troopers patrolled the roads toward Thornton's Gap in the Blue Ridge as well as eastward toward Warrenton and southward toward Culpeper. Patrols discovered few uniformed Confederates in any of those directions, although bushwhackers often attacked the brigade's picket lines. Before fatalities could result, Custer sent detachments to arrest local people suspected of engaging in that subspecies of warfare. A few of those so accused saw their homes and barns burned to the ground and their possessions confiscated. Considering such punishment insufficient to set a proper example, Custer petitioned Pleasonton for permission to apply more severe remedies, arguing that he could suppress bushwhackers "if allowed to deal with them as I choose." Pleasonton relayed Custer's request—a thinly veiled appeal to capital punishment—but General Meade refused to authorize the discretion that was sought.[16]

While at Amissville Custer culled from his brigades horses that had broken down during the recent campaigning as well as those showing symptoms of disease. Colonel Gray (who was in poor health himself, or wanted a furlough) was placed in charge of the troopers, drawn from each regiment in the brigade, who would accompany the worn-out nags to the remount camp maintained in Washington, D.C., by the recently created Cavalry Bureau.[17]

The first contingent of disabled mounts ("I think I never saw so many poor horses together," wrote a member of the escort) reached the capital on 28 July, followed by two other details several days apart. Because disabled horses diluted the brigade's fighting strength, the errand was a necessary one, but it cost Custer the services of many troopers for weeks to come. Some who travelled north were in no great hurry to return to the field; as Gershom Mattoon of the Sixth Michigan put it, the camp outside Washington was "the place where all the cavalry play outs stay to get out of going to the front."[18]

Moreover, the trip did not always produce desired results. Custer complained that one group of remounted men returned aboard "a more indifferent lot [of horses] than those sent to Washington as unserviceable." In another group of forty would-be returnees, seventeen never made it back because their remounts gave out on the way. Another complaint was that those sent to the capital, where they were free of the restraints that active service imposed, too often enjoyed "a grand spree" that landed them in trouble with the provost marshal. Not even field officers were immune to this behavior: late in August Major Granger, who had accompanied a party of the Seventh Cavalry to the remount depot known as Camp Stoneman, was arrested after being caught—while supposedly in the city on sick leave—in a brothel.[19]

If duty in the capital was a lark, service at Amissville was almost as pleasant. "We had it easy," a member of the Seventh Michigan recalled years later, "no fighting, no hurrying to and fro, and plenty of rations and time to eat them." Ed Bigelow agreed, writing in his diary that "we have comfortable quarters and easy times.... We are having a good rest."[20]

It was, of course, too good to last. On the evening of the twenty-eighth Meade ordered Pleasonton to either reinforce Custer's position, which lay only a few miles from one of Stuart's camps, or relieve the Third Division. Pleasonton chose the latter course; the next day a detachment of Gregg's division took up Custer's picket lines. Once relieved, Custer grouped his squadrons and guided them to Warrenton Junction, where the Manassas Gap Railroad met the Orange & Alexandria. There the troopers not only came within supporting range of the main army but had easy access to the rolling-stock that would carry their played-out horses north. There, too, on 4 August, Judson Kilpatrick, just back from his leave, reassumed command of the Third Cavalry Division. His return sent Custer back to the Wolverine Brigade, replacing Colonel Gray, recently returned from Washington.[21]

The brigade's new home along the railroad suffered by comparison with the old. Sergeant Bigelow criticized as "very poor" the camp that went up in a wooded area outside Warrenton late on the thirty-first. Presumably he was made happy in subsequent weeks when large portions of the command went off on detached service. Early in August, a 600-man force picketed southward toward Aquia Creek. On the fourth and again two weeks later much of the brigade headed down the Rappahannock on a reconnaissance to Falmouth, performing picket duty in sight of trigger-happy Confederates on the Fredericksburg side. By month's end parties of the Seventh Cavalry were patrolling the fords upstream from Falmouth, while Custer was leading the troopers of the Fifth and Sixth Michigan—as well as those from the First Vermont, formerly a part of De Forest's Brigade and a recent addition to Custer's—across the Rappahannock to Virginia's Northern Neck. Near King George Court House the reconnoiterers engaged Alabama infantry in a spirited skirmish, withdrawing in good order and without loss.[22]

At least two expeditions from Warrenton were devoted to the never-ending task of breaking up the partisan command of John Mosby. Early in August 300 picked men rode out to challenge the Gray Ghost, then operating north of the Manassas Gap Railroad.

Pleasonton informed Meade that Custer "has strong hopes they will either capture Mosby or drive him out of the country." The mission, however, ended in failure.[23]

A week later a similar operation involving 250 members of the Fifth and Seventh Michigan under William Mann (finally recovered from his post-Gettysburg wound) produced more tangible results. Mann's party tracked a force under Mosby to its lair at Gum Springs, north of the Bull Run battlefields. By spending three days in combing the vicinity, Mann captured perhaps a dozen partisans along with eighty horses and much equipage. Fruitful as it was, the expedition hardly fulfilled the goal Custer and Pleasonton had set for it: nothing less than Mosby's annihilation.[24]

In early September the Michigan Brigade in its entirety left Warrenton Junction for a clash with another old nemesis, J.E.B. Stuart. On the ninth, as both armies enjoyed a respite from combat, Lee detached thousands of troops to the western theater. The operation was designed to block an advance toward northern Georgia by Major General William S. Rosecrans, whose Army of the Cumberland had just occupied strategic Chattanooga. Late on the twelfth, after Meade learned of the troop transfer, he crossed the Rappahannock to exploit Lee's presumed weakness. Near dawn on the thirteenth, Kilpatrick's division, taking the cavalry's left, crossed at Kelly's Ford, then ranged down the Orange & Alexandria, spoiling for a fight.[25]

The trail led toward Lee's old headquarters at Culpeper Court House. Although the main body of the Army of Northern Virginia had slipped below the Rapidan River in response to Meade's advance, Stuart's horsemen remained about Culpeper, securing their comrades' withdrawal. Pleasonton's people located the Beau Sabreur on the morning of the thirteenth at Brandy Station, where after a brief skirmish he headed south. Later in the day the cavalries met again outside Culpeper, where Rebel troopers and horse artillerists checked the advance of Gregg, holding Pleasonton's right, and Buford, in the center.[26]

Coming up on the left of the line, Kilpatrick found himself in position to relieve the pressure being applied to his comrades farther west. At his order, the newly assigned commander of his First

Brigade, Colonel Henry E. Davies, placed himself at the head of his (and also Kilpatrick's) old regiment, the Second New York, and charged Stuart's artillery. Sensing the importance of this risky maneuver, Custer determined to pitch in. He called up a battalion of the First Vermont and led it in a charge in support of Davies. To occupy the Rebel right, Lieutenant Colonel Stagg led the First Michigan—which had just rejoined Custer after a flanking movement in the direction of Stevensburg—along the rim of Pony Mountain, southeast of Culpeper.[27]

The result was a multi-faceted success. Davies shoved the brigade of Brigadier General Lunsford L. Lomax through the town in headlong flight while capturing two of Stuart's Blakely rifles. Custer bagged a third cannon and numerous prisoners; he nearly added to his haul a train that had steamed into Culpeper at the height of the fighting. Meanwhile, Peter Stagg dislodged a body of Rebels from the forward slope of Pony Mountain, driving them all the way to the Rapidan. Coming up with his regiment in the wake of the offensive, Captain Daniel Powers of the Sixth Michigan "could see our cavalry charging with drawn saber[s] flashing in the sun, but we couldn't see the 'Rebs' for the dust they made" in retreating. Powers described the effort of Custer and the First Vermont as "one of the prettiest charges ever made" against artillery.[28]

When the Confederates retreated to a wooded rise southwest of town, Kilpatrick followed with mounted and dismounted skirmishers, including the First Vermont and Seventh Michigan. Rebel batteries let loose on the advancing troopers with fearful accuracy. Shell fragments struck Custer's gray charger, blowing it to bits and gashing its rider's foot. An amused bystander watched the general extricate himself from yet another fallen steed, then hobble up to Alfred Pleasonton. His "dry, flaxen ringlets" ajiggle, Custer saluted, drew attention to his foot, and suggested that he had fifteen days of medical leave coming. When his superior inquired about the severity of the wound, Custer flashed a grin: "They have spoiled my boots but they didn't gain much there, for I stole 'em from a Reb."[29]

Writing of the incident a few days later, the observer added that "the warlike ringlets got not only fifteen, but twelve [additional] days' leave of absence, and have retreated to their native [sic]

Michigan!" There the lame, hirsute officer would put the dangers of battle behind him while he closed out his well-crafted campaign to win the heart and hand of Libbie Bacon.[30]

* * *

Following the set-to in Culpeper, the Michigan Brigade, again under Colonel Gray, advanced to the north bank of the Rapidan, where it confronted not only Stuart but units of infantry and artillery. Along with Davies's brigade, Gray's men patrolled several crossing-sites—often while under cannon- and sharpshooter-fire—until Meade's army lumbered down to the stream to scrutinize the enemy's latest position.

While along the river, the command the absent Custer had left behind underwent personnel changes, the most notable being Gray's replacement by Colonel Edward B. Sawyer, commander of the brigade's newest addition, the First Vermont. Although Sawyer's reputation as a cavalry leader was rather weak, apparently none of the Wolverines resented the fact that the Michigan Brigade was now led by a Vermonter. Lieutenant Colonel Stagg continued to head the First Michigan, Colonel Town having gone home, like Custer, on sick leave—perhaps, concerned subordinates mused, for the final time. Meanwhile, Russell Alger, his post-Gettysburg wound healed, reversed the route of Custer and Town, journeying from Michigan to Virginia to resume command of the Fifth Cavalry. Gray returned to the Sixth, and William Mann retained command of the Seventh.[31]

Over the next month, the brigade moved in many directions on almost as many missions. On the twenty-first it patrolled to Madison Court House. Next day it crossed the Rapidan and moved downriver until it met a substantial force of the enemy; unwilling to risk a fight, the command promptly countermarched, Stagg and the First Michigan fending off an attack as the rear guard recrossed the Rapidan. Afterward the troopers went into camp at James City, a couple of miles below Culpeper Court House. For the next several days—into the first week of October, in fact—the brigade picketed Robertson's River, a Rapidan tributary, parrying the blows of roving bands of Stuart's newly formed cavalry corps.[32]

Early October brought brisk winds and other reminders of winter to the river country. It also brought Custer—fresh from Monroe, where Libbie had assented to his marriage proposal despite her father's misgivings—back to his command just in time to engage Stuart in a new round of charge and countercharge. The renewal of sustained combat was an indirect result of Lee's September troop transfer, which had enabled the western Confederates to defeat Rosecrans at Chickamauga and force his retreat to now-besieged Chattanooga. To rescue the Army of the Cumberland, Grant had been ordered to Tennessee with the troops that had captured Vicksburg as well as the XI and XII Corps, which Meade had shipped to him by train beginning 25 September. Lee's scouts detected the detaching and on 9 October the Army of Northern Virginia began to cross the Rapidan, forcing Meade back to Warrenton.[33]

For Custer's men, Lee's offensive began on the evening of the ninth with a heavy attack that dislodged a portion of the brigade picket line along Robertson's River near James City. Next morning, Lee's infantry, covered by a light battery, occupied the town, and in early afternoon Custer was directed to reclaim it. He began the task by having Pennington shell the enemy from a woodlot west of the place, then charged the battery with Major John Clark's battalion of the Fifth Michigan. Though the attack failed "for want of sufficient support" (an implied indictment of Custer's tactics), the Rebel guns limbered up, moved out of range, and troubled the Federals no more.[34]

Early on the eleventh, after resting on its weapons through the night, the brigade withdrew to Culpeper at a deliberate pace. Another commander might have opted for more celerity; Meade's retreat had left his horsemen virtually alone in enemy territory. The brigade's vulnerability was underscored by a young woman who shouted to the rear guard as it passed her Culpeper home: "You will catch it if you don't hurry!"[35]

True to her admonition, the end of the column, protected by portions of the Sixth and Seventh Michigan under Captain Lovell and Colonel Mann, soon felt the lash of Stuart's skirmishers. An unruffled Custer assumed a defensive position along ridges north of Culpeper. At this, the Rebels pulled back, permitting the brigade to resume its march to the Rappahannock where it hoped to rejoin Kilpatrick, Buford, and Pleasonton.

No sooner was the column in motion than Stuart, leading Wade Hampton's division, struck its rear. Custer left the fight in the capable hands of Don George Lovell, who, as James Kidd asserted, "greatly distinguished himself in the difficult duty of guarding the rear, meeting emergencies as they arose with the characteristic courage and coolness which distinguished him on all occasions...." Permitted to concentrate on what lay ahead, Custer presently discovered another column of horsemen—Fitz Lee's division—racing along his right flank as if to intercept him short of the river. Rather than stop and deploy, Custer kept the column moving along the trail to Brandy Station, its rear under continual assault.[36]

When he reached the depot, Custer discovered just how much trouble he was in: part of Lee's command, the brigade led by Custer's West Point classmate, Brigadier General Thomas L. Rosser, was now in front of the column, "thus cutting me completely off from the river." Forced to halt and take stock of his situation, Custer tried blasting a hole in Rosser's line with his battery, only to have Pennington absorb a heavier shelling than he delivered.[37]

In the midst of Custer's predicament, Alfred Pleasonton—as though to discredit rumors that he preferred commanding from the rear—managed to pass through the enemy's ranks to confer with his young subordinate. The hasty meeting of their minds produced a decision that the brigade should bull its way forward, using power and momentum to create a path to the river. Custer relayed the plan to some of the rank-and-file, shouting out: "Boys of Michigan, there are some people between us and home. I'm going home! who else goes?" An enthusiastic chorus responded, followed by the brandishing of sabers and pistols. The response was everything Custer could have desired. "It required but a glance at the countenances of the men," he would write in characteristic after-action prose, "to enable me to read the settled determination with which they undertook the task before them."[38]

Keeping the Sixth and Seventh Michigan in rear, Custer formed the Fifth Michigan and First Vermont on his right in column of battalions, the casualty-depleted First Michigan in column of squadrons on the left. As the recently organized band of the Michigan Brigade launched into a rousing rendition of "Yankee Doodle," the flank forces lurched forward, following the man in the gaudy uniform, capless today so that "his yellow locks floated like pennants on the breeze." Clustered about him rode staff officers, orderlies, and a flag bearer carrying a newly fashioned brigade banner, "soon to receive," Custer noted, "its baptism in blood."[39]

The men of settled determination got to within forty rods of the first rank of Rebels when the opposition appeared to melt away. "For some unknown reason," wrote Dexter Macomber of the First Michigan, "they wheel & run like so many sheep but as we come up with them they wheel again & charge with fury on our right flank & rear." Stuart's horse artillery added weight to the counterattack. Macomber saw one shell bowl over a row of eight mounts and riders: "In fact Men & horses are falling in every direction...."[40]

Responding to a natural law of battle, Custer's horse also fell to an artillery round, as did the brigade color-bearer's. Peeling himself from the turf for what must have seemed the hundredth time, the general mounted a fresh horse, only to lose it, too, to a marksman's bullet. Aboard a third animal, he formed his serried ranks into some semblance of a column, which he led against Stuart's main body, shouting (according to one listener) "Come on, you wolverine sons of bitches; now give 'em hell!"[41]

Only after three—some accounts say four—charges that cost many casualties could the Federals cut their way through the wall of gray. Meanwhile, at the other end of the column, the Sixth and Seventh Michigan continued to ward off Hampton's attacks until able to escape along the corridor their comrades had hewn. Reaching the river by eight P.M., all regiments crossed in good order. On the north bank they rejoined not only Davies's brigade but also John Buford, whose division Stuart had attacked near Brandy Station before turning on Custer.

Like Newby's Cross Roads, the fight of 11 October had brought the Michigan Brigade to the brink of disaster, but its people had survived to flirt with danger another day. Years later Lieutenant Briggs of the Seventh Michigan called this latest escape "little less than a miracle." He attributed the happy denouement to the brigade's "fighting qualities, its confidence in the leadership of the beloved Custer, and the failure of the enemy to take advantage of a great opportunity."[42]

* * *

The survivors of Brandy Station had little time to recover from their ordeal. Over the next week they accompanied Meade's infantry on a journey up the Orange & Alexandria to the north side of Bull Run, more than thirty miles from the Rappahannock. In that area a disgruntled Custer—who considered the retreat, in the face of a less powerful foe, tantamount to cowardice—protected the flanks and rear of his army's defenses while probing Lee's new position below Bull Run. One reconnaissance toward Gainesville was conducted by James Kidd, who, just back from the hospital, found himself for the first time in command of his outfit, all of his superiors being on the sick list. Custer described Kidd's maiden outing as "entirely satisfactory" in that it "showed the enemy to be in considerable force at that point."[43]

By the eighteenth Robert E. Lee, unable to flank Meade out of his works and still reeling from a disastrous attack on the Union rear at Bristoe Station four days before, turned back to Culpeper Court House. In midafternoon Meade ordered Kilpatrick to confirm reports of the withdrawal. Within the hour Custer's Michiganders and Vermonters were retracing their path to the river on a road parallel to, and east of, the Warrenton Turnpike; Davies's brigade took the pike itself. Near Gainesville, the First Vermont found Stuart lingering where Kidd had discovered him days before; he was coaxed into rejoining his army.[44]

After bivouacking at Gainesville, Custer's brigade assumed the advance early on the rainy morning of 19 October. Soon after starting out it again encountered the Confederate horse. Skirmishing continued as far south as Buckland Mills, just off the pike. Custer found his opponent "strongly posted" south of Broad Run, horse artillery anchoring his line. A time-consuming effort to cross the river in Stuart's front failed, whereupon Custer threatened his left with the Fifth Michigan. Leading a classic cavalry charge, Colonel Alger cleared that sector and opened a path south for his comrades.

After halting along Broad Run long enough to permit his men a noonday meal, Custer retook the road some time after three P.M.

and started after Davies's brigade. He had been in motion only a few minutes when he found his left and rear under attack from what he took to be a skirmish line of foot soldiers. In reality, his opponents were Stuart's men, an uncharacteristically large number of them advancing on foot with rifles and carbines instead of on horseback with pistols and blades. Custer spun about, placed the greater part of Pennington's battery in position supported by the First Michigan (today under Major Brewer), and tried to shell his foe into retreat. Though rocked by the cannonade, the Confederates held their ground, forcing Custer to deploy his entire force in opposition. He sent Major Kidd's regiment—which had made first contact with Lee—forward on foot and placed Alger's and Mann's outfits, also dismounted, on Kidd's right. He shored up the left with the mounted First Vermont and one gun of Battery M.[45]

Custer's dispositions not yet complete, Fitz Lee opened with his own artillery, then advanced an overwhelming force of footmen—a dozen regiments to Custer's five—along the length of the Union line, overlapping its flanks. What followed Major Kidd called "one of the gamiest fights against odds, seen in the war." Not surprisingly, the attackers broke through Kidd's line, forcing the Sixth Michigan to yield ground. His situation fast deteriorating, Custer finally registered concern. When the Rebels gained a foothold on his right and came within twenty yards of other portions of his line, he reluctantly gave the order to withdraw. At first in good order, later in some haste, his people remounted and hustled across a stone bridge that carried the Warrenton Turnpike over Broad Run, the First Michigan covering the pull-out.[46]

When they saw their opponents backtrack, the Confederates raced forward, thudding into Custer's rear. The veterans of the First Michigan turned back several blows, enabling most of their comrades to reach the north side before escaping themselves. One element of the brigade, however, failed to clear the scene of danger: Major Clark's battalion of the Fifth, which one of Kilpatrick's aides, without Custer's knowledge, had placed in an isolated position where it was surrounded and cut off from the bridge. Although Clark's men put up stiff resistance, "pouring volley after volley from their repeating rifles in[to] the ranks of the enemy," fifty-one officers and men were eventually forced to surrender.[47]

Even now, Stuart was not through. While part of Lee's division pressured Custer's retreat, the rest teamed with Hampton in over-taking Davies's brigade near Buckland Mills and squeezing it between pinchers. Facing overwhelming odds and no support, the First Brigade was a helpless victim. By late afternoon it was in tatters, fleeing toward Broad Run at such speed that its opponents termed its retreat the "Buckland Races." While the rout mortified Davies, it also had an impact on Custer, for in its flight the First Brigade abandoned the divisional train it had been escorting. Into Rebel hands fell, among other things, Custer's tent, desk, and personal papers—to which he had hoped soon to add letters from his fiancee.[48]

Davies's loss may have exceeded Custer's, but not by much. The casualties accruing from 19 October—which Custer called "the most disastrous [day] this Division ever passed through"—topped off a ten-day period in which his brigade had lost 214 officers and men killed, wounded, or captured, plus a hundred or more horses shot, lamed, or otherwise disabled. The brigade required an extended recuperation if it were to shoulder its burdens in the campaigning ahead. But no one could say how long Meade's and Lee's gyrations between the Rappahannock and Rapidan would continue. Looking to the future, Custer feared that more "long, arduous marches" and "hard-fought engagements" awaited his debilitated command.[49]

* * *

As November came in, Meade sauntered south to confront Lee, back in his snug defenses below the Rappahannock. As always, the cavalry took post closest to the front, inviting combat. But when the weather turned raw it appeared that Custer would get that period of inactive service for which he hankered.

One spate of campaigning happened to intervene. Upset by Meade's rather embarrassing withdrawal to Bull Run, President Lincoln and General-in-Chief Henry W. Halleck had announced that the Army of the Potomac should take the offensive before active operations ceased for the season. After considering and abandoning various plans, on 7 November Meade threw two corps south of the

Rappahannock preparatory to a deep penetration of enemy territory. The advance resulted in heavy fighting at Rappahannock Station and Kelly's Ford, forcing Lee to abandon his defensive position near Culpeper and Brandy Station and drop down below the Rapidan.

The fighting on the seventh involved few cavalrymen, none from the Michigan Brigade. But Meade was not finished. In obedience to his instructions from Washington, he planned to cut around the Confederate right flank via the lower fords of the Rapidan. If he stole a march on Lee, he could swing in behind Mine Run to strike unexpectedly from the rear.[50]

In preparation for the movement, for several days in November Custer's command and other bodies of cavalry tapped at Lee's new positions, gauging from the response how many troops held which parts of the line. The enemy resisted these intelligence-gathering efforts so staunchly that on 18 November Major Brewer, commanding the brigade pickets, complained that foot troops were "annoying him by constant firing" and occasionally sending troops across to threaten his flanks. Brewer managed to hold his ground, and the attacks subsided.[51]

Through the probing of Custer and other cavalrymen, Meade had gained, by the last week in November, a solid idea of his enemy's alignment. Believing Lee's eastern flank vulnerable to the turning-movement he had in mind, the army leader ordered his forces into action. Early on the twenty-fifth three massive columns crossed the river at as many places and tramped toward the Confederate rear. Each column was preceded by cavalry, consisting of every brigade in Pleasonton's command except Custer's. While the rest of the army moved south and west, the men of Michigan and Vermont would hold Lee's army in place through a series of attention-getting demonstrations at Raccoon and Morton's Fords, upriver from the army's crossing sites.[52]

Marching delays, the deplorable condition of the roads below the Rapidan, and other problems threatened Meade's offensive from the start, but the Michigan Brigade did its job thoroughly and effectively. On the twenty-sixth Custer—again commanding Kilpatrick's division in the latter's absence—struck camp near Stevensburg and headed for the river. He positioned Davies's brigade (recovered from its stampede at Buckland Mills) at Raccoon Ford and the Wolverines, under the temporarily healthy Colonel Town, at Morton's Ford. From Morton's, Town sent James Kidd and the Sixth Michigan farther upstream to guard Somerville Ford and other crossings along the left flank.

Dispositions complete, Custer had Pennington blast the Rebel-infested woods south of the river while the cavalry simulated a crossing at four divergent points. The feints were answered by what Custer estimated to be thirty cannon, under cover of which infantry suddenly occupied the works that stretched along the south bank. By late afternoon Custer could inform cavalry headquarters that he had "been entirely successful in deceiving the enemy to-day as to my intention to force a crossing. I have compelled him to maintain a strong line of battle, extending without break from Morton's to above Raccoon." He was confident that, at least along his front, the enemy remained ignorant of Meade's intentions. To strengthen the impression he wished his opponents to gain—that Meade intended to cross at Morton's and Raccoon rather than downstream—Custer had his men build rows of campfires and set his band to playing at several points along the river.[53]

Early the next morning, Custer found the works across from him empty—the Rebels had learned at last of Meade's turning movement—and so he moved to occupy them. Crossing the river, Town found a small force of cavalry dawdling inland; chasing after it, his men took thirty-two prisoners without loss of their own. One captive was secured in unusual fashion. A few days earlier, Captain Linus F. Warner of the Seventh Michigan had been placed in arrest by Custer, who accused him of feigning illness to avoid taking part in a skirmish; Warner had been stripped of his sidearms and forced to accompany his regiment under guard. When Town's pursuit began, Warner bolted from his escort and, despite his defenselessness, entered the melee. Overtaking one fugitive, he grabbed the man by the arm, hauled him onto his saddle, pinned him there, and confiscated his pistol. When the fight ended Warner went casually to the rear, his prisoner slung over his pommel like a sack of grain. "Needless to say," Asa Isham recorded, Custer "restored the Captain his arms and rescinded the order of arrest."[54]

The troopers remained along the river for another six days, skirmishing with roving cavalrymen and, on one occasion, with infantry. Early on the twenty-seventh, a portion of A. P. Hill's Corps came up to Raccoon Ford "with the seeming purpose," Colonel Town reported, "of capturing this command, or of driving it in confusion over the river." Through "determined resistance," his men foiled the plan, their Spencers and Burnsides keeping back the foot troops until retiring to the north bank in near-perfect order, having suffered only four casualties. Defiantly, Town recrossed next morning. When a small force of infantry assailed them, the colonel's men held their position: "Our line of skirmishers was not driven a rod from its original position, and the command did not retire to the other bank of the river until ordered to do so by the general commanding..." The brigade returned to Raccoon Ford, where it stayed until the afternoon of 3 December when Custer ordered it back to Stevensburg.[55]

Having heard nothing of Meade's movement except the sounds of distant cannonading, Custer suspected that his commander's strategy had gone awry. His suspicions were confirmed when he arrived at Stevensburg to find infantry all around. He learned that the army had moved so slowly into position, and Meade's subordinate commanders had carried out their assignments so poorly, that despite Custer's best efforts Lee had learned of the threat in time to bolster his right with infantry, artillery, and new and stronger fieldworks. These precautions effectively precluded assault. Two days later a frustrated and angry Meade aborted the campaign and headed north.[56]

And so another promising effort to finish the job begun at Gettysburg had been snuffed out by the winds of late autumn. Meade's next opportunity would not come till April or May. The failure at Mine Run assured the Michigan Brigade, as well as the rest of the army, a long recuperation. The thought gladdened the heart of many a Wolverine, even though the winter that lay ahead threatened to be a time of unrest, regret, and unhappy memories.

CHAPTER TEN

Riding with Little Phil

The wolverine thrives in winter; an adroit forager, he makes do nicely with the meager fare available in that season of hibernation. Pound for pound the strongest animal in the forest, he is also agile and wily enough to elude even the most formidable predator. Many of these same qualities defined another species of wolverine, genus *equites Michiganenses*. During a time of year that stressed the health, tried the patience, and assailed the morale of many a trooper, the Michigan Cavalry Brigade of the Army of the Potomac kept warm and fit, rested and recruited its strength, maintained its equilibrium, and in various ways—physical and mental—prepared for the role it must play when active campaigning resumed in the spring.

Throughout the winter, the brigade's primary goal was to regain the strength it had lost to wounds, illness, and the harsh demands of field service. Months of ceaseless duty had reduced it to skeletal proportions. James Kidd noted that before the October clash at Brandy Station his regiment had numbered fewer than 100 officers and troopers fit for duty, although the return of detached men raised the total to 250 (still, only one-fifth of its 1862 strength) by December. During the autumn campaigning in the Rappahannock-Rapidan basin, the Seventh Cavalry, despite its recent addition of two companies, had dwindled to 289 sabers. Although larger than its sister regiments, the Fifth Michigan had lost more than half of its original manpower.[1]

The most experienced member of the brigade was also a shadow of its former self. Early in December, with the end of its three-year term fast approaching, Colonel Town and his subordinates appealed to the men of the First Michigan to reenlist. Their efforts enticed

370 to sign on for another three years unless sooner discharged. This number was sufficient to confer on the First the status of a Veteran Volunteer Regiment, but not enough to guarantee that the outfit would retain the combat strength it had heretofore displayed.[2]

With the aid of state and national officials and friends of the brigade at home and in Washington, the manpower picture improved as the winter wore on. By late December, when the re-upping members of the First returned to Michigan on veteran furlough, an effort to recruit a new battalion for the regiment was well underway. An indication of the importance attached to the enlistment drive was its supervision by Lieutenant Colonel Stagg, who had been dispatched to the battalion's rendezvous at Mount Clemens, Michigan, in October. Thanks largely to Stagg's exertions, abetted by Governor Blair and the state's congressional delegation, the new unit garnered enough recruits to be mustered into federal service at year's end. By late January 1864, the battalion was at Camp Stoneman, outside Washington, undergoing training and equipping. In early March the returning veterans of the First, along with other recruits gathered in Detroit, Grand Rapids, and Kalamazoo, would join the raw levies at Camp Stoneman to form a new First Michigan, almost 1,000 strong.[3]

The other regiments of the brigade enjoyed some success in returning themselves to fighting strength. In early January enlistees in the Sixth Cavalry began to congregate at Grand Rapids; 200 of them reported to the camp at Stevensburg on 16 February. Another element of the Sixth recruited in the Harpers Ferry region as well as farther west. Companies I and M, still detached from the rest of the regiment and now led by Captain Harvey H. Vinton (Charles Deane, recently promoted to major, had rejoined the main body), tapped a fertile source of manpower, the staunch unionist enclaves of western Virginia.[4]

Late in January a recruiting detail of the Seventh Cavalry travelled to Michigan under command of Captain (soon to be Major) Darling; the party returned, as now-Lieutenant Asa Isham put it, with "some recruits, although not nearly as many as had been expected." A later drive brought in additional recruits by the middle of February. Finally, some time after the brigade pitched winter quarters, Colonel

Alger journeyed to the draft rendezvous at Grand Rapids to escort replacements to the Fifth Michigan, a task he completed in early January. While in the state, Alger oversaw the efforts of local recruiting agents such as Lieutenant Richard Bayles, who posted the following broadside—typical of enlistment propaganda specific to the brigade—around Tecumseh, Michigan, in January 1864:

Fifth Michigan
CAVALRY!
A Limited Number of
Able Bodied Recruits!
Will be received during the month of January to serve in this
GALLANT REGIMENT!
Under the DASHING ALGER.
This Regiment is in the "MICHIGAN BRIGADE" commanded
BY THE BRAVE AND DARING CUSTER,
"The boy General with the Golden locks"....[5]

Many gaps in the ranks at Stevensburg were caused not by combat attrition but by officers—many of field grade—on leave from their regiments or on detached service for one reason or another. Those whose health had given way to wounds, inclement weather, or the stress of campaigning, including Colonels Town and Gray and Majors Paldi and Storrs, were frequently gone from camp. Others were absent for less common reasons. Before the winter ended, Major Newcombe resigned his commission after being denied leave to visit his dying son and distraught wife in Michigan. Then there was Colonel Mann, who left his regiment at frequent intervals in early- and mid-winter to go to New York, Washington, and elsewhere to solicit financing for a device he had patented. Recent field campaigning had shown Mann a need for accoutrements that took the weight of knapsacks, cartridge boxes, and other waist-borne equipment off a cavalryman's loins and abdomen. Thus he had designed a network of adjustable straps and belts that slung equipment over a rider's shoulders and to which were affixed larger, fleece-lined cartridge boxes to accommodate and protect a trooper's metallic ammunition. Mann had patented his invention—which he had also adapted to infantry use—in early December; since then he had been trying by one expedient or another to interest the Ordnance

Department in his design. His unceasing efforts tried the patience of General Kilpatrick, who rejected Mann's "every excuse possible" to demonstrate his accoutrements to the right people.[6]

As a last resort the colonel tendered his resignation, effective 1 March 1864. This tactic, while drastic, redounded to his benefit, for the War Department thought the belts and straps promising enough to order 2,000 sets for field testing. Later, Generals Custer and Davies endorsed the device, while Ulysses Grant observed that "no one invention yet made will do more to promote the efficiency of the Army." In the end, however, Mann's equipment was found wanting for a number of reasons and was not adopted for army usage. The outcome left him not only out of the army but out the money he had put into producing and promoting his invention.[7]

Besides acquiring additional men and jettisoning officers more interested in personal gain than the well-being of their outfits, the Michigan Brigade benefited from the mid-winter receipt of thousands of remounts, a service grudgingly provided by a Cavalry Bureau that considered Custer's troopers "great horse-killers." Equally well-received was a weapons refit that resulted in all four regiments being armed with the seven-shot Spencer repeating carbine. Lighter in weight and eight inches shorter than its rifle version, the new arm could be operated much more easily from the saddle, meaning that the Fifth and Sixth Cavalries would no longer be employed (as it sometimes seemed) exclusively as foot soldiers.[8]

Along with the new weapon, the brigade was called on to assimilate new tactics. Since their muster-in the Wolverines had drilled and fought in a single-rank formation built around a maneuvering block of four riders. This system had been developed a few years before the war by then-Major (now-Brigadier General) Philip St. George Cooke of the Second U. S. Dragoons. Because of their newness, for the most part Cooke's tactics had been shelved in favor of the double-rank formation that had been the army standard since the 1840s. In fact, Custer's regiments appear to have been the only mounted units in the Army of the Potomac to have adopted the single rank. Now headquarters decreed that the brigade must use the older model. As James Kidd observed, "the utility of the change was, to say the least, an open question, and it necessitated many weeks of hard and unremitting toil on the part of both officers and men." On the other hand, the additional hours spent on the drill field only helped the brigade's many raw recruits.[9]

Kept busy with drill and target practice, the men had little time to brood over the past or complain about the less enjoyable features of winter camp: the poorly prepared rations, the infrequent leaves, the ubiquitous scout and picket duties that not even snow and sleet could cancel. Confounding the fears of some army observers, the Wolverines and most of their comrades survived the season in fine fettle. Better armed, better mounted, and better equipped than ever before, their self-confidence boosted by past success as well as by the respect and affection they felt for their commander—feelings symbolized by the red cravats that were springing up around Stevensburg like hot-house roses—the men of the Michigan Brigade looked forward to the coming of spring.

* * *

As the winter lumbered to a close, superiors much less well known than Custer drew the brigade's attention and embodied its hopes for the future. The most unheroic-looking of these was the greatest hero of all, Ulysses S. Grant, who in March had been given a third star to complement his new position as general-in-chief of the armies of the United States. Brought east shortly after raising the siege of Chattanooga and destroying the besiegers, Grant had decided to make his headquarters with the Army of the Potomac, prescribing grand strategy while George Meade made and implemented the tactical decisions. The relationship appeared fraught with difficulties and tensions, but Grant's reputation was so powerful that the Wolverine Brigade had reason to hope he would prove a match for his new opponents, the best commanders in the Confederacy. An anonymous enlisted man in the Fifth Michigan, writing in an Allegan newspaper, voiced the prevailing attitude of guarded optimism:

"As the war is not yet ended, it is best not to say too much yet [about Grant's appointment]. Idols may fall and get broken by being lifted up too high. What can be said with safety is that Gen. Grant has earned his way to his present position; and the way in which he has earned it, gives good hope of his keeping on...."[10]

Another new commander, successor to Alfred Pleasonton, would exert a major influence on cavalry campaigning for the balance of the conflict. A protege of Grant, who brought him east from Tennessee in April 1864, Major General Philip ("Little Phil") Sheridan was best known as an infantry commander, but back in mid-1862 he had been Russell Alger's superior in the Second Michigan. The Cavalry Corps would not miss Pleasonton, who had run afoul of Meade while running out of political supporters, but his successor was a mystery, an unknown quantity, to the troopers Pleasonton had left behind. All the Michigan Brigade knew of the bandy-legged Irishman from Ohio was how Colonel Alger remembered him: a restless, driven man with a great capacity for work, an impatience with slow-thinking, slow-moving subordinates, and a marvelous command of profanity.[11]

Two other newcomers to Meade's cavalry evoked no memories and inspired no deep impressions. In mid-December John Buford, generally regarded as the finest division commander of horse the army had ever known, died of an illness that had been aggravated by overwork and exhaustion. His successor—appointed by Meade, not Sheridan—was, like the latter, a transferee from the infantry, but with this difference: Brigadier General Alfred Thomas Archimedes Torbert of Delaware had no experience whatsoever in mounted service. Like Grant and Sheridan a West Pointer and a former Regular, Torbert was a handsome, well-spoken man who had accumulated a record of competence. He comported himself, however, like a genius forced to serve among cretins. James Kidd, for one, felt that Torbert's "arrogant bearing made him exceedingly unpopular with Buford's and Kilpatrick's veteran troopers, who had been accustomed to serve under men who could do harder fighting with less airs."[12]

Although most of Kilpatrick's people would not serve directly under Torbert, they too had to break in a new leader. This was Brigadier General James Harrison Wilson of Illinois, another Grant man—formerly an aide to the lieutenant general, more recently an army administrator (he had just ended a brief stint as head of the Cavalry Bureau). Like Torbert capable of vanity and arrogance, like Pleasonton a self-promoter, like J.E.B. Stuart addicted to success,

Wilson was a soldier of talent but a difficult man to like or even admire. His many enemies included George Custer, with whom he had jousted at West Point and who had come to regard the Illinoisan with envy and suspicion. When in April Grant handed Wilson the Third Cavalry Division, Custer made clear his unwillingness to serve under him. Apparently as a result, Sheridan shifted Custer and his Wolverines to Torbert's First Division. When Sheridan ruled that neither the First Vermont nor Pennington's battery would accompany the Michiganders, both units complained loudly and long, but to no avail.[13]

*   *   *

Wilson's arrival was a by-product of the only sustained operation launched from winter quarters. In early February Judson Kilpatrick had interested civilian superiors including Abraham Lincoln (but neither Meade nor Pleasonton) in a plan to raid Richmond, there to free Union prisoners and wreck Confederate communications and industry. That Kilpatrick's half-baked scheme was approved suggested Lincoln's desperation to shorten the war by any expedient. The result was a two-pronged offensive, begun on 28 February. Kilpatrick led 3,500 troopers against the enemy capital via Spotsylvania Court House and Beaver Dam Station. Simultaneously, a satellite force of 500 came in from the west and south under Colonel Ulric Dahlgren, an ambitious, reckless officer who seven months before had lost a leg helping lead the same charge through Hagerstown that had cost Captain Snyder his life.

Rain and snow, abominable roads, and a lack of coordination had doomed Kilpatrick's plan. So had the unexpected vigilance of Richmond's defenders and, at a critical hour, the fatal irresolution of Judson Kilpatrick. Beaten back from the city gates by a few hundred artillerymen and home guards, Kill-Cavalry had retreated to Union lines on the Virginia Peninsula, minus fifty-some men captured or left behind with wounds; charges that he had abandoned those troops would dog him for the rest of his career. Meanwhile, Dahlgren's force had been surrounded, cut to pieces, and its leader killed by regular troops and embattled farmers. Papers found on the colonel's body, suggesting that the raiders meant to kidnap or kill Confederate officials, had lent a macabre note to the disaster. Until cooler heads prevailed, the Confederates had talked of hanging the fifty captives in retaliation for their leader's flirtation with terrorism.[14]

Although only a small portion of the Cavalry Corps was involved in the debacle, the raid had a special interest for the Michigan Brigade. A couple hundred of its people were forced to take part, the highest-ranking being George Custer, just back with the army after being joined in wedlock with his beloved Libbie (an event that, according to a Detroit newspaper, had given "dull and unattractive" Monroe, Michigan, an air of "unusual liveliness and activity"). Instead of riding with Kilpatrick, Custer supported his superior by conducting a four-day diversion toward the Confederate left in the direction of Charlottesville. Although 1,500 troopers rode with him, most had been drawn from Buford's old division; none was a Wolverine.[15]

When Kilpatrick and Dahlgren chose men to ride with them, however, they had included detachments of the Fifth, Sixth, and Seventh Michigan under, respectively, Captain Hastings, Major Kidd, and Lieutenant Colonel Litchfield, as well as a large portion of the First Vermont under Colonel Sawyer. When fired into near Mechanicsville on the frigid morning of 2 March, each of these detachments suffered several casualties, especially in captured, the latter including Colonel Litchfield and Captain Clark of the Seventh as well as Sam Harris of the Fifth, who was also wounded. Incarcerated alongside the POWs they had set out to liberate, the captives would not rejoin their regiments for many months, if that soon.[16]

In the early days of April, after returning to Stevensburg from the Peninsula, Judson Kilpatrick was transferred to the western armies to appease the furor sweeping both North and South in the wake of the expedition. Newspapers everywhere applauded his departure. One of them, the *Detroit Free Press*, echoed James Kidd's assessment of Kilpatrick's character: "He cares nothing about the lives of men, sacrificing them with cool indifference, his only object being his own promotion and keeping his name before the public."[17]

* * *

Within a week or so of Kill-Cavalry's transfer, winter began to loosen the vice-like grip it had clamped on eastern Virginia. Inspired by the moderating weather, the members of the First Cavalry Division began to attend to the numberless duties incident to breaking camp and resuming the business of killing and being killed.

Built up by the recent recruiting, reduced again by the losses suffered under Kilpatrick and Dahlgren, the command comprised more than 2,000 well-mounted, well-armed, well-equipped officers and men. A considerable number—as many as 40 percent of the brigade's total—were unseasoned, inexperienced, and entirely unreliable in a crisis. And yet, enough two- and three-year men remained to give the command a veteran image that many another brigade coveted.

The First Michigan continued to wear the mantle as the brigade's elite regiment. This aggregation of old-timers had recently solidified its hard-drinking, hard-fighting reputation by starting a brawl that engulfed and nearly destroyed a section of Elmira, New York. En route to the army from Michigan in late February, the reenlisting veterans of the First had arrived in western New York to find that another regiment had appropriated the only through train to Pennsylvania. Angry troopers with too much liberty ranged through Elmira, sneering at her inhabitants, sampling the fare at every grog shop they spotted, and picking fights with anyone, citizen or soldier, who dared cross their path.

Incited by some of their officers, the troopers broke up several saloons, inflicting many hundreds of dollars' damage, before a detail of Invalid Troops (wounded but otherwise able-bodied veterans available for rear-guard duty) came out to arrest them. The troopers beat their would-be captors, confiscated their firearms, and started a new brawl "in which guns, sabres and bayonets were freely used." Before the police finally restored order, a member of the First had been shot dead, another had been mortally wounded by a bayonet, and several Invalids lay dead or dying. Confined for days at a local barracks, the regiment finally entrained for Virginia only after leaving behind several comrades charged with criminal conduct including Captain James Cullen of Company A and Company M's Lieutenant Edward L. Negus.[18]

Inspecting his regiments on the morning of 1 May, George Custer must have been impressed by rank upon rank of horsemen marching past his field headquarters, proudly bearing the scars of battlefield or barroom. Despite the long winter, the men looked neither dull nor flabby; they appeared rested, revived, and ready for field duty. Their ambitious brigadier hoped soon to impress his new superiors with the fighting spirit of these troopers and the might they could bring to bear on their enemy. Custer must have felt especially gratified to see so many scarlet neckties—testimony to the emotional bond that had sprung up between leader and followers.

The brigadier did admit to a few concerns. A mainstay of the brigade, Pennington's Battery M, was no longer a part of it, to the regret of its old comrades. In its place was combined Batteries B and L of the Second Artillery, led by Lieutenant Edward Heaton. Another potential problem was that three of Custer's four outfits were serving under officers who had never commanded a regiment on anything approaching a regular basis. Colonels Town and Gray, again on medical leave, would return to the brigade only briefly. Under the stress of the fall campaign, Town's health had shattered. Early in the year, when his furloughed veterans left home for Virginia, he had remained in Michigan. For a time he had commanded the draft rendezvous at Grand Rapids, but when that duty proved too much for his weakened constitution he took indefinite leave. In late June 1864 he would come east for one last stint of field duty but would be quickly hospitalized. He would resign his commission in August 1864, a few months before succumbing to the disease that had stalked him so relentlessly.[19]

Meanwhile, in late September Colonel Gray had developed lumbar pains that drove him to Washington for treatment. In December, still recuperating, he was appointed to a permanent court-martial sitting in the capital. Although some Michigan newspapers branded him a malingerer, Gray attempted on several occasions to rejoin his regiment; each time, however, pain would change his mind. He would resign from the service effective 19 May 1864.[20]

Fortunately, able officers were available to replace the missing. Lieutenant Colonel Stagg succeeded to the command of the First Michigan as he had on several brief occasions. The equally capable Major Kidd took over for Colonel Gray and the recently promoted

Lieutenant Colonel Thompson, who remained disabled by his Hunterstown injuries. Finally, Major Granger, who had been recalled from Washington in late March, headed the Seventh Michigan in the wake of the resignations of Colonel Mann and Major Newcombe.[21]

* * *

Short days after his troop review, Custer's men learned that there was life after winter quarters. At sunrise, 4 May, the Cavalry Corps broke camp and departed the Culpeper-Stevensburg area, never to return. Many Wolverines expressed disappointment that their initial field assignment under Sheridan was to guard the rear of Torbert's division, including its long, lumbering supply train. Most men, however, were happy to be in motion en masse.[22]

The march, which led to a bivouac at Stony Mountain, four miles south of Stevensburg, was unusually quiet. "Conversation was not indulged in to any great extent," recalled Lieutenant Isham, "every one being apparently occupied by his own reflections." That night the brigade, camped less than a mile above the Rapidan, was more animated. At Stony Mountain those units that had not replaced their outmoded rifles received the Spencer carbine. While it smacked of poor planning to be issued weapons on the eve of battle, those who got them chatted at length about the desirable qualities of the new arm.[23]

At three A.M. on the fifth the march resumed in the direction of Ely's Ford, one of the crossings the army had taken to Mine Run. At about ten o'clock Custer began moving horsemen, artillery, and the cumbersome wagons across the stream. On the south bank, he led the way into the Wilderness, a fifteen-mile square of second-growth pine and tangled thicket that stretched almost as far south as Spotsylvania Court House. Shortly after noon his column came to a halt at the Chancellorsville crossroads where, almost exactly one year ago, Joe Hooker had lost his nerve and, effectively, his command. Sounds of fighting to the west were already hours old: out there—somewhere—Meade's infantry, preceded by Wilson's horsemen, had clashed with the Army of Northern Virginia, which had come up on the run from the west. The noise told the cavalrymen that Grant and Meade had been unable to clear the trees before giving battle; their plan to sneak into Lee's rear had failed as signally as it had in November.[24]

Custer's command took no direct part in the day's action, remaining in bivouac about a mile below Chancellorsville. Early the next morning, with musketry and cannon-fire rising again in the west, Torbert ordered the brigade down the Catharine Furnace Road toward one of the few commodious trails in the Wilderness (Custer mistook it for a turnpike), the Brock Road. In a clearing adjacent to that intersection the Wolverines dismounted and advanced pickets, under Captain Maxwell of the First Michigan and Captain Manning D. Birge of the Sixth, toward the scene of fighting. Meanwhile, Custer established contact with Gregg's division, deployed farther south near Todd's Tavern.[25]

The tavern, situated at the junction of the Brock and Catharpin Roads, was a strategic landmark that Gregg, at Sheridan's order, had seized as a place in which to anchor Meade's forward flank. There Gregg had also reinforced Wilson's division, which had been throttled and forced to fall back—much to the chagrin of the First Vermont, who, when they saw their old Michigan comrades, wished aloud they might return to Custer's brigade. While he sympathized with the Vermonters, the general took a certain amount of satisfaction in his rival's misfortune. As he told his bride in a letter, Wilson, in his first outing with Meade's army, "proved himself an imbecile."[26]

Wilson may have been overmatched this day, but not his golden-locked colleague. Custer was preparing to head south, ready to pitch into the Rebels who had bested the Third Division, when Thomas Rosser's brigade of Hampton's division came slicing through the trees. Driving in the picket line of the First Michigan, Rosser's men made for Custer's clearing only to be taken head-on by Peter Stagg, with the main body of the regiment, supported by Kidd's Sixth. Both outfits counterattacked to the bracing accompaniment of the brigade band, playing "Yankee Doodle" with all its might. The headlong charge sent Custer's old classmate scurrying down the woodland trails he had taken to the front. When Rosser attempted a comeback, Custer moved the Fifth and Seventh Michigan toward the Rebel right; impressed by the show of strength, Rosser stayed put—for a time.

Later in the day the Confederates launched a series of frontal attacks—mostly on foot, for the paucity of clearings prevented mounted charges of more than a few hundred yards in any direction. Later still, part of Fitz Lee's division came up in hopes of crumpling the Union right. Custer stopped Lee's drive in mid-stride, then sent the Sixth Michigan to outflank and silence a battery that was shelling the brigade's position.[27]

When the Sixth fell back to avoid being flanked in turn by the battery's supports, Custer sent the Fifth Michigan to its aid, seconded by a regiment from the brigade of Colonel Thomas Devin, which had come up on Custer's lower flank. As Kidd noted, "with Spencer carbines full shotted, the two magnificent regiments deployed into line on our right. Then moving forward, by a left half wheel, [they] turned the tables on the exultant foe, and he was forced slowly but surely back." Kidd believed that "no one who witnessed it, can ever forget the superb conduct of Colonel Alger and his men when they swung into line on the right of the Sixth Michigan and turned a threatened reverse into a magnificent victory."[28]

The Sixth and its supports pursued the retiring enemy for a short distance before rushing back to the clearing under a cannonade. "It was their artillery that caused us to fall back at first," wrote Dexter Macomber, who saw Custer ride up and heard him assure the brigade that all was well: "In four minutes our artillery will be here." True to his word, eight cannon sent up from Todd's Tavern by General Gregg were soon answering the Rebel artillery "as rapidly as they could be loaded and fired." With branches and leaves cascading upon them, the enemy gunners pulled back, their retreat ensured by a counterattack from a single dismounted squadron under Captain Maxwell. Instead of launching a full-scale pursuit, Custer withdrew in response to an order from Torbert and went into bivouac near the woodland forge that gave the Furnace Road its name.[29]

The fighting between Grant and Lee on the sixth had ended as a tactical draw, but the strategic advantage seemed to belong to "Marse Robert." One of many footholds he had gained inside his enemy's lines was Todd's Tavern, a position that Sheridan had relinquished in response to an ill-advised order from Meade. Early on the seventh, as Grant prepared to resume his search for open ground toward

Spotsylvania, Meade's cavalry found it necessary to reclaim the lost position. It had to do so amid the decomposing carcasses of horses that littered the woods near the junction, the stench of which "seemed nearly strong enough to arrest the course of bullets...."[30]

Several portions of Gregg's and Torbert's divisions (the latter now under Brigadier General Wesley Merritt, Torbert having become unwell) operated at and near the tavern. Ranging south of the crossroads he had occupied the previous day, Custer fulfilled Sheridan's expectations by chasing away infantry and cavalry that had dug in above Todd's. The critical maneuver was a dismounted advance along both sides of the Brock Road by a portion of the First Michigan under Lieutenant Colonel Stagg while the rest of his regiment, under Captain William M. Brevoort, attacked mounted on the road itself. Just as Sheridan envisioned, when Custer's opponents were thrust back to Todd's Tavern they arrived off-balance, vulnerable to overthrow. With little effort Gregg drove them out of the area, reoccupied the lost ground, and reconnected his line with Custer's.[31]

As if cowed by the Wolverine Brigade's ability to fight afoot and mounted with equal power, neither infantry nor horsemen challenged Custer through the balance of the day. Dawn of 8 May brought an order to move northeastward to Silver's, a plantation along the road from Chancellorsville, near which Meade's trains were parked. Upon reaching that point, far in rear of the firing lines, the Michigan Brigade took stock of the tactical situation. It concluded that after two days of heavy fighting, neither Grant nor his adversary had gained a pronounced advantage. What the brigade did not know at the time was that, unlike other commanders whom Lee had fought to a standstill, the lieutenant general would not retreat. Not till after sunrise on the ninth, when the army resumed its claustrophobic journey through the Wilderness, was the resolve of the new man at the top manifest.

The main army marched alone. In the small hours of 9 May Sheridan led his divisions not to Spotsylvania but toward the Richmond, Fredericksburg & Potomac Railroad. Details were sketchy, but rumor had it that Little Phil had been given authority to mount an independent mission. The rumor proved true: late the previous day, Sheridan's Irish temper had got the best of him, he berating Meade for issuing orders to the cavalry without consulting, or even informing, its commander. The most recent upshot had been a traffic snarl on the road to Spotsylvania, foot soldiers and horsemen crowding together and no one getting anywhere. When Meade replied with criticism of the cavalry's performance to date, Sheridan vowed that, if Meade would stop meddling in its affairs, the mounted arm would be used as it should be used, as a strategic weapon to locate, engage, and destroy J.E.B. Stuart.[32]

Meade was incensed by Sheridan's behavior, but Grant backed up his long-time subordinate, giving him the opportunity to make good on his boast. Thus, early on the ninth the entire Cavalry Corps, 10,000 strong, began to retrace the steps of Judson Kilpatrick toward Richmond—a maneuver sure to draw Stuart from Meade's front and into a fight. This was something the Michigan Brigade eagerly anticipated. If a showdown were in the making somewhere north of the Confederate capital, every man under Custer wanted a role in it.[33]

* * *

From the first day out, the troopers liked the way this operation was being conducted. Unlike previous superiors such as Wyndham, Stahel, and Kilpatrick, Sheridan preferred to move at an easy pace, one that conserved both manpower and horseflesh. One reason was obvious: his intent being to lure Stuart after him, Sheridan did not wish to outpace his opponents, discouraging pursuit. Regardless of the strategic considerations, the Wolverines found it an agreeable change to be led by one more intent on killing his enemy's cavalry than his own.[34]

The early stages of the operation proved memorable for another reason. On the afternoon of the ninth, the Michiganders, leading Sheridan's thirteen-mile-long column, crossed the North Anna River and struck the railroad that would carry them to the city Kilpatrick should have captured and which Sheridan surely would if he set his mind to it. Major Brewer, with a large body of the First, was sent ahead to seize and hold Beaver Dam Station. Just short of the depot, the detachment found perhaps two dozen Rebels escorting nearly 400 Union prisoners, taken in the Wilderness, to the railroad. Brewer "gallantly charged the enemy," wrote Custer, "and succeeded in recapturing all our men and quite a number of their captors." Some of the freed soldiers fell in with their liberators, a few finding mounts or wagons to carry them. Others made their way on foot, as best they could, toward the reported location of the army.[35]

Continuing south, Custer's vanguard charged into Beaver Dam, overwhelming its guard and capturing three trains laden with food, forage, and other supplies worth several million dollars. The troopers broke open boxcars and cheerfully appropriated their contents—barrels of bacon, flour, sugar, molasses, and (until provost guards confiscated it) liquor. Once his men were provisioned, Custer ordered the cars burned to their trucks and hundreds of feet of track levered up. He camped his men on the scene of their spoils-taking, from which, during the night, enemy bands tried unsuccessfully to drive them.[36]

Early on 10 May the brigade was back on the road, angling southeastward with the rest of the corps toward Hanover Junction. Several miles short of that depot, the column curved down across the South Anna River, then cut northeastward toward Ashland Station on the R, F, & P. Below the South Anna Sheridan's main body bivouacked while its rear guard engaged Rebel troopers who had made contact with it. Many Federals suspected that the pressure applied in that quarter masked an effort by Stuart to overtake them, placing himself between Sheridan and Richmond.

Suspicions were confirmed early on the eleventh when, having struck the Mountain Road at Allen's Station, the raiders moved down that thoroughfare toward its junction with the old Telegraph Road. Along wooded ridges and astride fields east of and along that historic road, Stuart's main body had deployed for battle. Four Virginia regiments formerly led by Fitz Lee, commanded today by Brigadier General Williams C. Wickham, comprised an east-west-running line, its left flank resting on the Telegraph Road. Extending the line southwestward along the road were the three outfits of Virginians under now-General Lomax.[37]

Sheridan embraced the confrontation now at hand—after all, Stuart, not Richmond, had been his objective all along—although he may have been mystified by his adversary's decision to give battle with only a third of his command. Covered by a heavy line of skirmishers including many from the Michigan Brigade, he spent the better part of the morning making his dispositions. By early afternoon, he had extended his line as far south as Yellow Tavern, a dilapidated public house just below the point at which the Mountain and Telegraph Roads merged to form the Brook Pike. Wilson's two brigades held the top of that line, with Merritt's three on the southern end, Custer forming Merritt's upper flank. Gregg's division remained in the rear, opposing the pesky North Carolinians of Brigadier General James B. Gordon.[38]

Fighting began with an advance by various elements of Merritt's division. When Custer's men were sent forward they were careful to maintain contact on the right with the "Reserve Brigade" of Colonel Alfred Gibbs. Thus supported, the Fifth and Sixth Michigan moved eastward through an open field fringed in front and on the left by woods; those ahead were teeming with Confederate cavalry, also afoot. The two sides traded skirmish fire in the middle of the field until pent-up energy prompted the Fifth, on the left of the line, to charge the enemy. Kidd noted that his regiment "caught the infection" of this spontaneous offensive but held back when its comrades came under fire from the woodlot on the left. The unexpected opposition caused some confusion, which ended when a portion of the Fifth changed front, advanced against their new assailants, and put them to flight. The remainder of the regiment then joined Kidd's men in charging east, clearing the woods in that direction as well.[39]

At about this point Custer appeared on the field, re-forming the line and leading it through the woods just cleared. At the edge of the trees the Wolverines entered a field that, by Kidd's calculation, stretched for 400 yards toward a ridge on which Lomax's men had deployed, their left flank guarded by a battery that immediately began shelling the Federals. They darted back into the trees, where they remained for some hours, trading long-distance fire with the gunners and their supports. Finally, late in the afternoon, word came that Sheridan wished the Confederate position carried by a mounted charge, followed up by a dismounted advance—Custer's brigade to lead the effort. Custer was equal to the assignment. Although

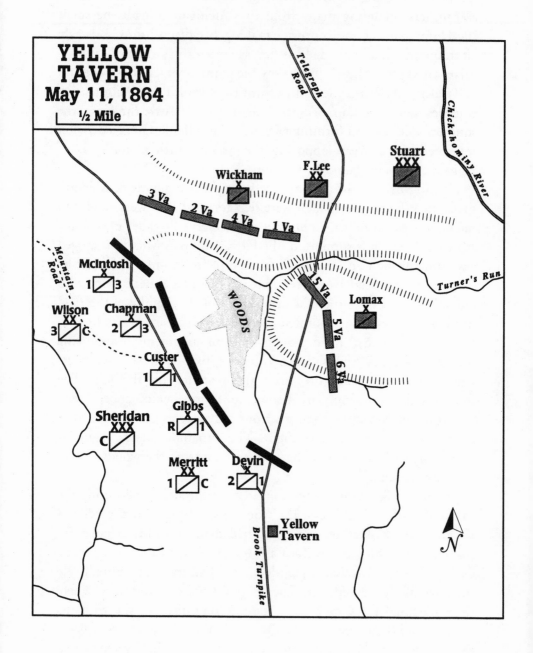

YELLOW
TAVERN
May 11, 1864
½ Mile

Stuart
XXX

F. Lee
XX

Wickham
X

Chickahominy River

Telegraph Road

3 Va
2 Va
4 Va
1 Va

Turner's Run

Mountain Road

McIntosh
X
1 3

5 Va

Lomax
X

WOODS

5 Va

Wilson
XX
3 C

Chapman
X
2 3

6 Va

Custer
X
1 1

Gibbs
X
R 1

Sheridan
XXX
C

Merritt
XX
1 C

Devin
X
2 1

Yellow
Tavern

Brook Turnpike

N

charging artillery was a risky business, his people had done so successfully at Brandy Station and if anyone could duplicate the feat it was his own First Michigan. "There is good ground over there," Dexter Macomber heard Custer tell Lieutenant Colonel Stagg, "and I think we can take their battery."[40]

Directing Alger and Kidd, along with Lieutenant Heaton, to keep up their fire, Custer sent his most veteran regiment forward over terrain replete with obstacles: five fences and a bridge so narrow that only three horsemen could cross abreast. With characteristic panache, Stagg and his troopers threaded their way through the field, deploying for the charge 200 yards from the gun-crowned bluff. They made a formidable impression on Asa Isham, whose Seventh Michigan had closed up in their rear. The lieutenant calculated that Stagg's outfit "in squadron front... covered over two hundred and fifty feet by one hundred and twenty in depth, and it formed a weight of six hundred tons that was about to be hurled across the fields and ravines upon that battery and its supports. It was a magnificent engine of warfare, and I somehow began to feel a contempt for the Rebel cannon, which had inspired me with profound solicitude but a few minutes before...."[41]

At a signal, the First spurred toward the left flank of the battery, everyone screaming what Custer called "a yell which spread terror before them." Distracted by the cannon- and carbine-fire steadily raking their center and right, the enemy gunners were slow to swing their pieces toward the charging mass. This gave the First Michigan—two squadrons under Major Howrigan in front, followed by Stagg with the rest—time to gather irresistible momentum. The First was so quickly upon them that the gunners could not depress the barrels of their cannon enough to strike back. Half the battery quickly went under, gunners and teams falling beneath the sabers of the attackers. Besides several prisoners, Stagg and Howrigan combined to take two cannon and two limbers filled with ammunition.[42]

While the guns were being captured, Wickham's troopers were withdrawing from their bluff and crossing a ravine to a new position about a quarter of a mile beyond the first. Their line imperiled by the First Michigan's success, Lomax's regiments fell back and re-formed at right angles to Wickham. From his new perch Lomax poured musket balls into the ranks of the First Michigan, preventing a farther advance.

To spell the exhausted First, Custer sent in its "understudy." Major Granger's outfit made an enthusiastic attempt to extend the day's success, sweeping down a hill, across a brook, and up the Telegraph Road toward the refused enemy line. Just before closing with Lomax, however, the second-in-command, Major Walker, inexplicably wheeled about. Most of his troopers followed him to the rear, leaving only a few to accompany Granger to "the very muzzles of the enemy's guns."[43]

Of this group, Lieutenant Isham, along with another officer and six men, rode into the arms of the enemy and were taken prisoner. Their leader was shot out of the saddle, felled by three bullets. Custer, visibly shaken by Granger's death, told a sergeant in the Seventh: "I never saw a man go more gallantly about the work before him than he did. He was a splendid man; too bad, too bad!" Later he eulogized the major as one who "fell as the warrior loves to fall, his face to the foe."[44]

Forced to resort to dismounted tactics, Custer sent up the Fifth and Sixth, supported by Heaton's battery and joined on the run by their old comrades of the First Vermont, charging simultaneously on Wilson's front. The combined effort carried the day, the Confederates racing for the rear. The triumph, pronounced Custer, "was complete."[45]

More complete, in fact, than anyone at the time suspected. One of those rushing forward during the final attack, Private John A. Huff of Company E, Fifth Michigan, a forty-four-year-old native of New York, more recently a resident of Armada, Michigan, came within pistol range of an officer in a plumed hat, sitting his horse in the midst of his retreating men, calling on them to rally. Huff, a veteran of the Second U. S. Sharpshooters, took careful aim (laying his Colt pistol across a fence rail, by some accounts) and at a distance of about eighty rods put a 44-calibre ball into the rider's abdomen. At the time he did not know—perhaps he never knew for certain—that he had struck down the Beau Sabreur himself. J.E.B. Stuart would succumb to the wound the next day, plunging his army and his nation into mourning.[46]

When the news of Stuart's death circulated and the Fifth Michigan's connection with it became apparent, some of Huff's comrades advanced another claimant for the honor of felling the most famous cavalry commander of the war. This soldier, whose carbine is supposed to have brought down Stuart, was identified only as "Private Dunn"—quite possibly, Charles Dunn, a thirty-year-old Kalamazoo resident in Company L. Other alleged observers identified Stuart's killer as Sergeant R. M. Bellinger of the Seventh Michigan; still others credited unidentified or partially identified marksmen in the First Michigan, First Vermont, and Ninth New York. The conflicting claims were never resolved, in part because both Huff and Dunn would die in battle within a few months of Stuart. Almost without exception, however, latter-day historians would recognize Huff as Stuart's slayer, undoubtedly because he was featured prominently in the earliest recorded versions of the deed and because his regimental commander, Russell Alger, avidly supported his claim.[47]

* * *

Following the overthrow of Stuart's troops, the balance of the Richmond Raid seemed to all involved almost anticlimactic. The Federals spent the remainder of the day and half the night burying their dead and treating their wounded—a goodly percentage of both having been suffered by the Michigan Brigade. Some time after midnight the march resumed along the Brook Pike toward the Rebel capital, Wilson's division in the lead, Merritt's in the center, Gregg's still in the rear. The layover near Yellow Tavern had failed to dispel the accumulated fatigue of the journey. Yet the troopers were fortified by the knowledge that again they had beaten "Stuart's Invincibles"—even fight or not—and by the thought that they were going to do the same to the bureaucrats and clerks of the Richmond defense battalion.[48]

By early morning of the twelfth, with rain pouring down, the advance guard came up to Meadow Bridge, which carried the turnpike across the Chickahominy River five miles above the city. It found that Stuart's men, who had been chased beyond the stream and were peppering the column from the far side, had partially unplanked the bridge to deny them access to the capital.

Stalled in their tracks, under fire from artillery as well as from sharpshooters, mired in the mud of unfamiliar roads, and menaced by subterranean torpedoes planted by the enemy, the raiders appeared to be in a position most precarious. At this point, if not before, Sheridan reevaluated his chances of succeeding where Kilpatrick had failed. Even if he took Richmond, would that accomplish anything beyond freeing prisoners who would still be far from freedom? How long could he hope to hold the place with infantry support so far away? He had already accomplished what he set out to do, having put the run to that ostrich-plumed egomaniac and his overrated cavaliers. In the end, Little Phil decided that any benefits accruing from the temporary seizure of Richmond would not compensate for the possible sacrifice of the Cavalry Corps, Army of the Potomac.[49]

Having made up his mind to bypass the city, he still had to fight his way across the river. At his order, Merritt and Custer sent riders splashing toward Meadow Bridge in the pelting rain. Alger's regiment dismounted and, with Kidd's men close behind, started across the railroad trestle that continued to stand a short distance below the dismantled span. Against natural and man-made resistance, the regiments advanced far enough to lay down an effective fire. Shielded by the fusillade, engineer and pioneer teams worked feverishly to repair the upper bridge using timber from nearby trees and lumber from nearby houses.[50]

By mid-morning the bridge had been sufficiently restored to permit a crossing by a limited number of mounted men. The Seventh Michigan, which Custer had temporarily entrusted to Melvin Brewer, moved cautiously across the span, followed by two regiments of Devin's brigade of Merritt's division. Gaining the far shore, the force dismounted to fight under the continuing downpour. Atoning for its conduct at Yellow Tavern, the Seventh made a major contribution to the small-scale offensive, which slowly pried the enemy loose from their advantageous position. In the end they fled so precipitately that their assailants, caught far in advance of their horses, could not pursue. Reacting quickly, Custer sent Peter Stagg and the First, accompanied by two outfits of Reserves, after the escapees; they returned with several prisoners.[51]

Satisfied with the results of the fight, Sheridan crossed Merritt's division to the far side, accompanied by Wilson. Last came Gregg, disengaging from a fierce rear-guard struggle that had taken the life of General Gordon. On the north bank of the Chickahominy the Federals were out of sharpshooter range as well as beyond pursuit by any portion of what used to be Stuart's corps. Thus Sheridan bivouacked his troopers not far from Meadow Bridge, allowing them to feed their horses and themselves and enjoy whatever sleep the elements would permit them. On the morrow, their job well done, they would turn toward the James River and then homeward. Even without having taken Richmond, they could expect a warm welcome from Grant—perhaps even from that rheumy-eyed curmudgeon, George Meade.[52]

CHAPTER ELEVEN

Custer's Third Stand

*A*fter spending the night near Gaines's Mill, site of once and future battles, Sheridan's raiders trudged along the upper bank of the Chickahominy, crossing the Richmond & York River Railroad and recrossing the river via Bottom's Bridge. On the afternoon of the fourteenth, after what James Kidd called an "uneventful" ride from Meadow Bridge, the head of the column pulled up on the banks of the James River near Malvern Hill. There, suddenly, the day became eventful: a Union gunboat in the river, mistaking the new arrivals for Stuart's cavalry, opened fire on horses and riders. The barrage ended only when the troopers draped the Stars and Stripes from the roof of a house in clear view of the navy.[1]

Peace having been restored, Sheridan opened communication with friendly troops across the river at Bermuda Hundred, the peninsula that constituted the operating base of Major General Benjamin F. Butler's Army of the James. Although Butler had led most of his command northward against the defenses of Richmond, numerous support personnel remained behind. To resupply his men and replace those horses that could not continue the journey, Sheridan received permission to draw on Butler's quartermaster's and commissary stores via Haxall's Landing.

The refit took three days, a period of "placid contentment" for the Michigan Brigade and its comrades. "The soldiers smoked their pipes," Kidd recorded, "cooked their meals, read the papers, wrote letters to their homes, sang their songs and, around the evening camp fires, recalled incidents, humorous, thrilling or pathetic, of the march and battle-field. There was not a shadow on the scene." The collective peace of mind was buttressed by the knowledge that in the recent fighting Sheridan's men had clearly gotten the better of their long-superior enemy. As one of General Merritt's subordinates observed, "our loss in this expedition was between six and seven hundred men and officers. The enemy's, I should judge to have been about the same, but we certainly secured the advantage in morale, as we were successful in every encounter, and proved conclusively, to our own satisfaction if not to theirs, that the Rebel cavalry could not hope for success without the help of its infantry."[2]

Custer's troopers had special reason to be light-hearted; they basked in the praise of colleagues who had witnessed their performances at Yellow Tavern and Meadow Bridge. Their leaders likewise commended the Wolverines for their aggressiveness and tenacity. Writing to his beloved Libbie from Haxall's Landing, Custer exulted that "*our* brigade has far surpassed all its previous exploits." He relayed Sheridan's comment that more than once over the past three weeks Custer and his command had "saved the Cavalry Corps." In his after-action report, Wesley Merritt—like Wilson, a personal rival of Custer's—praised the Michigan Brigade warmly if not effusively for its many contributions to Sheridan's debut campaign in Virginia.[3]

While Custer and his men soaked up the tributes, Sheridan and his staff crossed the river and travelled to Drewry's Bluff, seven miles below Richmond, to pay a courtesy call at Butler's new headquarters. During the meeting, Sheridan's host sounded him out on the subject of attaching his people to the Army of the James. When the cavalryman explained he must return forthwith to his own army, Butler hinted that he might compel his visitors to remain until his own horsemen returned from a raid around Petersburg. Lest Butler make good on his threat, Sheridan hustled back to Haxall's Landing and late on the seventeenth—shortly before the Army of the James returned to Bermuda Hundred, having been attacked and routed at Drewry's Bluff—Little Phil pointed his refreshed column toward home.[4]

The return route led westward to Charles City Court House, northward to the Chickahominy at Long Bridge, and on to Baltimore Cross Roads, where the command spent the night of the eighteenth. En route, Sheridan sent Major Kidd to destroy the column's recent crossing-site, Bottom's Bridge, as well as an adjacent trestlework. The following day, the Sixth Michigan led the brigade in wrecking another bridge, this over the South Anna River near Hanover Court House. On this errand the brigade also flanked a Rebel guard at Hanover Station on the Virginia Central, captured a cache of commissary stores, and tore up a long stretch of the railroad.[5]

On 22 May the raiders crossed the Pamunkey River and the following day, Herring Creek. On the twenty-fourth, after resting at King William Court House, they came within sight of the Army of the Potomac at Concord Church. Next morning the head of the column drew rein at Chesterfield Station on the R, F & P, where it linked with Union infantry for the first time in more than a fortnight.[6]

Sidling westward, the cavalry reestablished contact with Meade's army, now dug in along the North Anna River. The prodigals learned that in their absence Meade and Lee had met violently and often outside Spotsylvania Court House. Both armies had shed a great deal of blood to no strategic purpose, persuading Grant to head south and east—as he had after Todd's Tavern—in hopes of skirting Lee's right flank in the direction of Richmond. The latest sidestep had produced another stalemate, and more casualties, along the North Anna. Now the army was poised to move southeastward yet again. This time Sheridan's men would lead the way, drawing from Meade's path the cavalry under Stuart's temporary successor, Wade Hampton.[7]

The new move, begun on the afternoon of the twenty-sixth, sent the divisions of Torbert (who, fresh from minor surgery, had resumed command) and Gregg, supported by a few thousand foot troops, back to the Pamunkey River at Hanovertown, where the entire army would cross. Meanwhile, Wilson's division feinted toward the Confederate left, causing Lee to wonder if that area, not Hanovertown, were Meade's destination. Late on that rain-soaked day, Custer conducted a lone reconnaissance to Hanovertown, returning to his brigade under a hail of musketry. Obviously, Lee was hedging his bets, covering every route his enemy might take come morning.[8]

In the predawn darkness of the twenty-seventh the real movements commenced. The men of Torbert and Gregg marched down to the Pamunkey and dismounted to cover the laying of a pontoon bridge. Under fire from Rebel pickets on the south shore, Custer sent a body of the First Michigan, led by the resourceful Captain Maxwell, across the stream in a pontoon boat. Leaping ashore, Maxwell's team charged and routed the enemy, taking a half-dozen prisoners.

Opposition gone, a New York engineer regiment laid the floating span that would accommodate Meade's infantry, artillery, and wagons. About ten A.M., with the span complete, the balance of the Michigan Brigade, Custer and Lieutenant Colonel Stagg in the lead, crossed the Pamunkey, followed by Merritt's and Devin's brigades, then by Gregg's division. Next to cross was a division of the VI Corps, which remained at the river while the horsemen pushed inland. Per orders, Custer proceeded to Hanovertown, where he divided his force, sending the First and Sixth Michigan northward on a return trip to Hanover Court House and the Fifth and Seventh farther south toward a smithy's establishment known as Haw's Shop. Trouble began soon after the force split, when Stagg's and Kidd's regiments were fired on by a substantial force of Rebels—cavalry formerly under James Gordon, now led by Colonel Rufus Barringer—who brought their advance to a halt. Custer countered by ordering the Fifth and Seventh up from Haw's Shop and into the Rebel rear.[9]

The lead regiment, the Fifth Michigan, came to the rescue in two parts, four companies under Smith Hastings riding in advance, the main body close behind led by the senior line officer, Captain William T. Magoffin (Russell Alger had gone to Washington on sick leave the previous day and Lieutenant Colonel Gould remained on detached duty as commander of a dismounted cavalry unit at Meade's headquarters). Both segments of the Fifth charged Barringer's men, exchanged shots and saber strokes with them, and, in Custer's words, "drove them in great disorder." The Fifth and Seventh pursued to within sight of a narrow stream called Crump's Creek, on the near side of which Barringer's men had dug in to shower their antagonists with rifle balls. Undaunted, Custer dismounted Magoffin's outfit and placed it on the right of the creek road. At his signal, the men of the Fifth advanced, their Spencers crackling. Simultaneously, Major Walker—undoubtedly hoping to atone for his inexcusable behavior at Yellow Tavern—led the Seventh in a saber charge across an open field on the left.[10]

Before the attackers could reach them, Barringer's men mounted and splashed across the stream, Walker's regiment in frenzied pursuit ("such a chase I never saw before," wrote a member of the Seventh). The race continued for three miles; when Walker rejoined the rest of the brigade, he had forty prisoners in tow. With men and mounts reeling from their exertions and the heat of the day, Custer bivouacked along the creek.[11]

The men lounged by the water until some time after ten o'clock on the twenty-eighth, when sounds of battle drifted up from the direction of Haw's Shop and nearby Enon Church. Soon came word that Gregg's division, reconnoitering Lee's movements, had attacked Wade Hampton. Mounting up, Custer led his force along a southward-running road roughly parallel to the Virginia Central Railroad, then east to Haw's Shop. It was well after noon before the Michigan Brigade came up in rear of Gregg's hard-pressed troopers, then engaged with elements of three Rebel divisions. An agitated Sheridan rode up to meet the brigade leader, jabbed a stubby finger toward the enemy, and said, "Custer, I want you to go in and give those fellows hell!"[12]

His words made the task sound simple—it was not. For an hour or more Custer attempted to maneuver into supporting range of his colleague, but the land west of the blacksmith shop was so thick with trees and underbrush that not till after four P.M. could the Michiganders move up, dismounted, in Gregg's rear. By then the adversaries had been fighting so long and hard that casualties exceeded 200 on both sides and numerous carbines had fouled from overuse.

When Custer added his weight to the fight, the balance appeared to shift to his side. The true reason was that Hampton had learned from prisoners what General Lee had sent him to Haw's Shop to find out: at least part of Meade's infantry had crossed the Pamunkey (in truth, the entire army was across by now) and the movements of Wilson's and other Yankee forces opposite the Confederate left had been feints. Their job done, Hampton's men had begun to disengage at about the time Custer advanced. Unaware that the enemy was falling back, the Michiganders moved into place in the middle of Gregg's line, the First Cavalry on Custer's right, the Sixth farther south, the Seventh still farther to the left, the Fifth at the lower end of the line.[13]

Custer's arrival persuaded many of Hampton's men to stay and fight. Suddenly a deadly crossfire tore into the left flank of his brigade. Time and again, Brewer's and Magoffin's men fell back before the firestorm, each time regrouping and advancing "with courage and determination." Those subjected to the barrage would describe the experience as "equal to the heaviest infantry fights." Facing somewhat less resistance, Stagg's and Kidd's regiments poured an equally destructive fire into Hampton's line at close range, forcing their opponents to yield terrain. As more and more Rebels withdrew, the First and Sixth Michigan moved up to occupy the abandoned ground, by now covered with bodies in gray and butternut.[14]

This success enabled the outfits on the left to advance as well, until they too cleared the front. In doing so, however, they had to fight their way past several raw regiments from South Carolina, armed with Enfield rifles, that constituted Hampton's reserve force. For all their inexperience, the reserves proved to be, in James Kidd's estimation, "the most stubborn foe Michigan ever had met in battle.... The sound of their bullets sweeping the undergrowth was like that of hot flames crackling through dry timber."[15]

By the time the South Carolinians had been overwhelmed, each of Custer's units had felt the effects of what many considered their most difficult fight of the war. All told, the brigade suffered forty-one casualties, the majority in the ranks of the Fifth and Sixth Michigan. As usual, the officer corps had been hit hard: among the several seriously wounded were Captain Maxwell of the First and Captains David Oliphant and Horace W. Dodge of the Fifth (Oliphant would die of his wound a week later). Along with their riders, dozens of horses including Custer's had attracted enemy bullets. One observer counted this the seventh time the general had lost a mount in battle; the figure seems conservative. Two of Custer's aides were wounded in the fight, and three were unhorsed in the same manner as their boss.[16]

The brigade buried eighteen of its men on or near the battlefield, eight in the cemetery at Enon Church, and ten at Newton's Farm, three and a half miles to the east. While the burial details labored, stretcher-bearers scoured the field for wounded who could not walk. Among the "bleeding, mangled multitude [who] covered the surrounding grounds" moved Chaplain Greely of the Sixth Cavalry, dispensing comfort and counsel where he could, and sharing a last prayer with the dying.

One with whom he prayed was a young Rebel, a member of those South Carolina reserves who had taken such a toll of their more experienced opponents. "There is no enmity between you and me as you lie here," Greely told the Carolinian, promising to send to his wife of one year—this day was their wedding anniversary—the blood-stained testament he handed up. "God bless you, God bless you," whispered the Confederate, grasping the chaplain's hand. Greely sat with the youngster until he died. Then he offered his services to the regimental surgeons who labored long after the last shot was fired at Haw's Shop. "There were amputations," he reported, "until midnight."[17]

* * *

Relieved after dark by Meade's infantry, the Michiganders fell back to the Pamunkey, camping a mile or so from the mouth of Totopotomoy Creek. Early on the twenty-ninth Custer led them across the creek to New Castle Ferry, downriver from Hanovertown. He and his men were permitted to rest there until midday on the thirtieth. The respite was much appreciated; the brigade needed a goodly amount of time to recover from their most costly engagement of the campaign.[18]

Once they broke camp at the ferry, however, it was back to business. Moving southwestward toward noises of battle near Old Church, Custer's men came up behind Merritt's brigade, which they found tangling with the Rebels across a little creek. In obedience to an order from Torbert, Custer dismounted every regiment but the Sixth—which he kept in the rear as a mounted reserve—and advanced their men along both sides of the Old Church road. The three outfits went in "with a yell," vying with each other to make first contact with the enemy, a race won by Captain Magoffin and the Fifth. As the enemy staggered backward, Custer readied Kidd's people for a saber charge—only to learn one was not needed, the Rebels having fled, leaving their dead and wounded behind. One prisoner informed Magoffin that his outfit had disrupted a carefully planned attack on Merritt's flank: "We were just getting ready for a sword charge when you all came out of the woods yelling so [loudly that] we thought there was 5,000 of you!"[19]

At three P.M. on the last day of May, after spending the night along the disputed creek, the men of Michigan turned south to Old Cold Harbor, a small cluster of dwellings by a crossroads nine miles northeast of Richmond. Grant wished the junction held as a stepping-off place for a new attempt to pass Lee's flank. Since Meade's infantry could not be expected to arrive for some hours, the cavalry must seize Cold Harbor and hold it for as long as necessary.

Once again, the Wolverines reached a battlefield to find Merritt's brigade hotly engaged, this time against Fitz Lee's division, the original occupiers of Cold Harbor, backed by some foot troops. Custer fed his regiments, one after the other, into the firing line, but for upwards of two hours he failed to drive Lee's men or their friends from the log breastworks they had erected on high ground beyond the crossroads. Frustrated, the brigadier sent the Fifth Michigan creeping along an enemy flank; the well-directed carbine-fire the regiment unleashed pried many of the Rebels loose. To exploit the breakthrough, Major Brewer led a battalion of his old outfit, the First Cavalry, in a saber charge up the hill toward the works. Not willing to retreat just yet, the enemy raked the head of the unit with musketry and shell, causing a part of it to break from the rest and flee. By strenuous efforts Brewer re-formed the battalion, but before it could make a new attempt to carry the works Custer found them abandoned.[20]

Sheridan sent portions of Torbert's and Gregg's divisions in pursuit, but when they ran into a wall of infantry he began to doubt the advisability of holding Cold Harbor without infantry support of his own. Only hours after evacuating the place, however, Little Phil returned his troops to the crossroads in response to Grant's order that Cold Harbor be held at all hazards.[21]

The first day of June found Custer's people sleeping on their arms behind the breastworks they had captured. Fighting resumed early in the morning as Confederate infantry, cavalry, and artillery tested Sheridan's position. That part of the line held by the First Michigan received an especially heavy pounding that took several lives including that of Captain Brevoort, whom Custer eulogized as "one of the most gallant officers in the corps" (an enlisted man agreed that Brevoort was "one of our best Officers"). Casualties among the other regiments included John Huff, Stuart's slayer, his skull creased by a rifle ball. Invalided home to Armada, the celebrated marksman would die of his wound three weeks later.[22]

Despite the heavy pressure, the captured defenses held—barely. After what seemed an eternity of waiting, shortly before noon members of the VI Corps began to relieve the cavalry all along the line. "Never were reinforcements more cordially welcomed....," Major Kidd recalled. "The tension was relaxed and for the first time since midnight the cavalrymen drew a long breath."[23]

Once Torbert and Gregg fell back to Old Church, their men began a vacation from battle that lasted almost a week. For five days—while the rest of the army attacked Lee's lines outside Cold Harbor, spawning horrific carnage—the most taxing duty required of the cavalry was picketing from its base at New Castle Ferry to Haw's Shop to Old Church. During the interlude, Russell Alger returned to the Fifth Michigan, replacing Captain Magoffin, and Melvin Brewer was permanently installed as commander of the Seventh with the rank of lieutenant colonel.[24]

By 6 June, the first entirely quiet day the Michigan Brigade had spent in weeks, a new mission came to hand. Through morning and afternoon quartermaster's and commissary officers swarmed over the cavalry's camp at New Castle Ferry, stocking a caravan of supply wagons and replenishing haversacks, forage bags, and cartridge boxes. Early the next day Sheridan formed Torbert's and Gregg's divisions, plus a half-dozen units of horse artillery including Pennington's Battery M, into a column that he guided across the Pamunkey to Aylett's, on the south bank of the Mattapony River. By the humid morning of the eighth the troopers were heading west by northwest, bound for some point on the railroad to Fredericksburg. Soon the ten-mile line was alive with rumors as to

Little Phil's intentions. No one claimed to know their destination, but even the greenest recruit could see they were off on another raid.[25]

In fact, Grant had directed Sheridan to strike the Virginia Central Railroad in the vicinity of Louisa Court House and Trevilian Station, almost sixty miles from where the raiders had crossed the Pamunkey. In sending his cavalry so far from its main army, the lieutenant general trusted that Wade Hampton would follow. Hampton's departure would give the Army of the Potomac a clearer path to its next destination, Petersburg, the support center twenty-two miles below Richmond via which the capital's defenses and Lee's army received the bulk of their supplies. By breaking the Virginia Central, Sheridan would also disrupt the flow of food and forage that reached Lee from the Shenandoah Valley. Finally, Grant hoped that when he neared Charlottesville Sheridan would link with a Union army, under Major General David Hunter, operating on the edge of the Shenandoah Valley. If he did so, Sheridan should team with his associate to destroy further the railroad and the adjacent James River Canal.[26]

As Grant foresaw, Sheridan's counterpart rode hard to overtake him short of his objective. Hampton's determination to hurt his enemy as much as possible, while minimizing the damage Sheridan could do to Lee's communications, would set up a classic confrontation. Ahead lay the first planned encounter between the leaders of the eastern cavalries during the post-Stuart era.

* * *

The journey to Trevilian Station was made at the same loping pace Sheridan had set during the Richmond raid. During the four days thus consumed, the troopers inflicted damage of one kind or another on a section of Virginia that had not felt the hard hand of war. As their route paralleled the Virginia Central, detachments had to travel south only a few miles in order to demolish ties and dislodge rails—a small-scale tuneup for the more extensive job of railroad-busting that lay ahead. Near towns such as Chilesburg and New Market, other troopers left the column with tacit permission to loot kitchens, barns, and smokehouses. Roving bands also combed the area for remounts, the need for which was becoming critical. The relentless campaigning of the past month and the torrid weather of early June were causing horses to play out by the dozen.[27]

On 10 June, homing in on their target and alert to signs that Hampton was moving to gain the head of their column, the raiders turned en masse toward the railroad. Fording two branches of the North Anna River, Sheridan's advance marched to a point about four miles above Trevilian Station. There his outriders discovered that the hard-riding Confederates—a good part of Hampton's corps, if not all of it—had stepped between them and their target.

As at Yellow Tavern, Sheridan would enjoy a pronounced numerical advantage in the fighting that lay ahead. His opponent had also been obliged to leave a third of his command with the main army. But whereas Sheridan, even without Wilson's division, could call on nearly 8,000 effectives, Hampton had only sixty percent as many; moreover, one third of his disposable force, under Fitz Lee, lay at Louisa Court House, almost four miles east of Trevilian, at the time of Sheridan's approach.[28]

Hoping to overcome the disparity by taking the offensive, Hampton planned to butt head-on into the Yankees with his old division while Lee's slammed into their flank at a propitious time. Instead, it was Sheridan who seized the initiative. Just after sunrise—perhaps five-thirty A.M.—Merritt's Reserve Brigade came pounding down to the depot via the Clayton's Store Road, shoving in Hampton's skirmishers. Hampton hastened to the scene with two brigades under Brigadier General M. Calbraith Butler and Colonel G. J. Wright, and a pitched battle broke out on heavily wooded ground two miles above the railroad.[29]

As the combat heated up, Custer's Wolverines remained well east of the action. Sheridan had placed them in that sector to guard his left and cover the roads from Louisa Court House, where he suspected part of Hampton's force to be lurking. His vigilance was rewarded as early as three-thirty A.M., when Custer's rear regiment, the Seventh Michigan, took blows from Wickham's brigade of Lee's division. When reinforcements hastened to the Seventh's assistance, Wickham backed off. His withdrawal permitted Custer, some time after sunrise, to move in the general direction of Merritt's fight. Via a narrow trail that intersected the Clayton's Store road just east of

Trevilian Station, the boy general headed southwestward through a woods so thick it shielded his men from Hampton's sight. Fortuitously, the trail brought the column to a point safely in rear of the Confederates engaging Merritt.[30]

Instead of hastening to his comrade's assistance, Custer heeded information brought him by a breathless Captain Hastings, whose advance guard of the Fifth Michigan had crept to within sight of the railroad station before doubling back. Hastings had spied dozens—perhaps hundreds—of supply wagons moving in column along a road that led westward from Trevilian. Unable to resist the urge to grab spoils, Custer ordered Russell Alger and the rest of the Fifth to follow Hastings's scouts. In Alger's rear would move Pennington's battery—once again serving with Custer's command, to the delight of all involved.[31]

After Alger and Pennington moved off, Custer decided to send James Kidd and the Sixth Michigan to Trevilian as well. This day the major was riding a fractious steed, a powerful black charger that a fellow-officer had asked him to break. Instead, the horse nearly broke its rider: when Rebels lurking in the woods suddenly opened on Kidd's regiment, the horse ran away with him, racing past his outfit and into the midst of the enemy. Visions of Libby Prison danced in the major's head, but after having been escorted only a hundred yards toward the rear he was rescued through the effects of a charge led by Captain Birge's battalion of the Sixth. Recalling his brief captivity more than forty years later, Kidd insisted that "to no man on this earth am I under greater obligations than to Manning D. Birge."[32]

While Kidd was being liberated, Alger, followed closely by Captain Vinton's battalion of Kidd's regiment (which had passed Battery M), charged south in an effort to overtake the wagon train, whose drivers were lashing their teams in a desperate attempt to escape capture. Spurred on by what Custer called "the impulses of a pardonable zeal," the colonel raced well past the depot, "hoping to increase his captures." Eventually he rounded up not only scores of wagons but some 1,500 horses as well as 800 horse-holders and train guards. Almost every prize, however, would be recaptured before battle's close.[33]

The spoils were temporarily secured, but only minutes after Alger

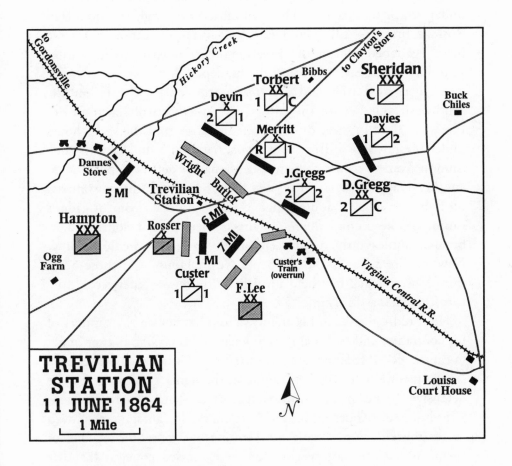

to Gordonsville

Hickory Creek

to Clayton's Store

Torbert
XX
1 C

Bibbs

Sheridan
XXX
C

Devin
X
2 1

Buck
Chiles

Merritt
X
R 1

Davies
X
1 2

Dannes
Store

Wright

Butler

J.Gregg
XX
2 2

D.Gregg
XX
2 C

5 MI

Trevilian
Station

6 MI

Hampton
XXX

Rosser
X

7 MI

1 MI

Custer's
Train
(overrun)

Virginia Central R.R.

Ogg
Farm

Custer
X
1 1

F.Lee
XX

Louisa
Court House

TREVILIAN
STATION
11 JUNE 1864

1 Mile

N

231

passed Trevilian a wave of dismounted Confederates, alerted by the ruckus in their rear, disengaged from Merritt's front and poured south, effectively isolating the Fifth Michigan and Vinton's detachment of the Sixth from Custer, Pennington, and the rest of the brigade. Casting about for an outlet, Custer tried to retrace his steps along the woods trail, only to learn from a courier that his rear was under attack by Fitz Lee. The trap closed even tighter when Tom Rosser's brigade—till then held in Hampton's rear as a reserve force—galloped up from the direction of Gordonsville to box Custer into open fields east and south of the depot.[34]

Assailed by Butler and Wright on the north, Rosser on the southwest, and Lee on the east, Custer was virtually surrounded. Forced to fight in three directions at the same time, he spent hours under the hot sun shifting squadrons, battalions, and Pennington's cannon from one part of his crescent-shaped defensive position to another. Dexter Macomber termed the proceedings "the most mixed up fight I ever saw," adding that "a large number of our brigade is captured," he among them. As the desperate fight continued, it became unpleasantly reminiscent of the brigade's predicament at Newby's Cross Roads and Culpeper Court House. On those occasions Custer's luck had held until he withdrew to safety; could he turn the trick a third time?[35]

He could—thanks to his enemy's faulty tactics, to the support of his comrades, and to his ability to keep his collapsing pocket intact (a captured Confederate later admitted that Custer's regiments were "most splendidly handled" throughout the fight). Even when on the defensive, Custer managed to counterattack. Late in the afternoon, after hours of peppering him at long range, his antagonists moved in for the kill. Some made for Pennington's guns, seizing one of them. When the battery commander expressed concern that the Rebels would haul the piece to the rear, Custer shouted, "I'll be damned if they do!" In a few minutes he was leading thirty troopers—men of the Seventh Michigan plus members of the brigade staff—in retaking the prize.[36]

The temporary capture of the gun marked the zenith of Confederate success at Trevilian Station; thereafter the gray tide began to ebb. Like Captain Thompson's supports at Hunterstown, by moving to within easy rifle-range of Custer his assailants fired into each other instead of the enemy. Once their comrades began to topple from friendly fire, the Confederates pulled back, giving the Wolverines breathing room.

Late in the afternoon, Sheridan engineered a major effort to rescue the embattled brigade and its leader. Backed by a portion of Gregg's division—whose involvement till then had been minimal at best—Merritt's brigade, followed closely by Devin's, charged with what one Regular called "an Indian war whoop." The Reserves pierced the mass of Rebels north of Custer's position and, after some of the most vicious close-quarters fighting of the war, linked with the shot-torn Michiganders. The junction reversed the enemy's situation, catching some 500 of them in a giant pocket. Meanwhile, Davies's brigade of Gregg's division attacked Fitz Lee, further easing the pressure on Custer. Soon the worst was over. By the narrowest of margins, Custer's luck had held.[37]

Yet he could have been luckier. During the engagement, the general had sustained minor wounds to the shoulder and arm, while being struck temporarily senseless by a spent ball. Some of his most trusted staff officers had also gone down, as had his personal color bearer, Sergeant Mitchell Beloir (Custer had saved the flag from capture by wrapping it around his waist).[38]

Then too, before Davies shoved it back, Lee's division overran the brigade wagon train, which had taken a wrong road in search of a safe haven. At the head of a detachment of the Seventh Michigan, Custer tried to retrieve the vehicles but rescued only a few. For the second time in eight months the general's headquarters wagon, containing his personal belongings, had been lost. This time, he winced at the thought of Rebels sitting around the campfire, reading Libbie Custer's letters to her husband. Of equal regret, the enemy had made off with Custer's prized cook, a freed slave named Eliza Brown. Thankfully, "Aunt Eliza" wandered into camp after dark, having escaped her captors although unable to retrieve any of her employer's property.[39]

By early evening, Hampton's men had drawn off, abandoning Trevilian Station and the surrounding area. Soon Custer would be able to reunite Alger and Vinton with their comrades in the main body. The brigade would then bind up its wounds, inter its dead, interrogate its prisoners, and make plans for the morrow.

* * *

Another who planned ahead was Phil Sheridan. Although elated at forcing Hampton to withdraw, Little Phil was concerned by the many casualties his divisions had taken—400 of them in the Wolverine Brigade alone. Thus he wondered whether he should continue west come morning, or start for home. One factor that helped him decide was the news, extracted from prisoners, that instead of moving to meet him David Hunter had turned in the opposite direction, toward Lynchburg. Moreover, Rebel forces had occupied Charlottesville and Gordonsville, interposing between the Union commanders. Sheridan began to doubt that pushing along the Virginia Central would pay dividends, especially when Fitz Lee was known to have made a roundabout march to join Hampton, Butler, and Rosser west of Trevilian.[40]

By the morning of the twelfth, Sheridan had decided to go no farther. Rather, he would head east at a pace slow enough to keep Hampton on his trail, and away from Petersburg, for several days. His battle-weary men spent the morning and half the afternoon destroying the railroad from Louisa Court House to a point about a mile west of Trevilian. When the demolition ended at three P.M., Torbert moved out along the Gordonsville Road, planning to turn right and cross the North Anna at Mallory's Ford. Well short of the road to the ford, however, the First Division came upon a solid line of dismounted Confederates, Hampton's division (today under General Butler) facing the Union right and Fitz Lee's opposite the left, blocking the way west. Although the gray troopers appeared well entrenched—part of their line protected by the railroad embankment, all of it by breast-works—Sheridan dismounted and moved to the attack.[41]

Custer's brigade, backed by part of Devin's, was tasked to keep Fitz Lee occupied while Merritt's Reserves attempted to flank Hampton and gain his rear. Custer had no fear that his men would accomplish their mission, but today his confidence was misplaced. When he moved up the dismounted Sixth and Seventh Michigan, Lee tossed them back with relative ease. He then sent in the First and Fifth, farther to the right, but they too were stopped short of the enemy line. Next, Lieutenant Colonel Stagg attacked mounted across an open field, making for Lee's flank—and was repulsed less than halfway to his target. Looking on from the south, James Kidd could hardly credit his eyesight: "When the First Michigan could not stand before a storm of bullets, no other regiment in the cavalry corps need try."[42]

Instead of Fitz Lee being held in place, half of his division—Lomax's brigade—kept Custer's men rooted to their position while the brigade of Williams Wickham moved north to help Hampton stymie Wesley Merritt. In his after-action report Merritt—figuratively shooting a cold glance at Custer—claimed that his men "vigorously" engaged Butler but could not handle Wickham too. Wickham's counterthrust was so strong, in fact, that it came close to flanking Merritt and rolling up his line.[43]

Fighting continued into the evening, producing a butcher's bill nearly as large as the previous day's, although Custer's brigade suffered far less than it had on the eleventh. When Sheridan saw that progress toward Mallory's Ford must be measured in feet if not in inches, he abandoned his plan: in the morning he would depart the railroad by the same way he had come. After another night filled with the cries of broken men—almost 500 had been wounded this day—the raiding force backtracked to Carpenter's Ford and headed slowly east, its march encumbered by dozens of ambulances filled to, and in some cases beyond, capacity. Sheridan had accomplished his mission to keep Hampton from Grant's and Meade's heels, but at shattering cost.[44]

Nowhere did that cost come higher than in the ranks of the Michigan Brigade, where the toll of the Trevilian Raid was not confined to casualty statistics. Custer's luck appeared to survive, his brigade having escaped encirclement and potential destruction for the third time in less than a year. Yet the fighting of 12 June suggested that the losses of the past six weeks—over 700 officers and men killed, wounded, or missing—had reduced the offensive power of the command. It was too soon to tell whether the erosion was temporary or long-lasting. Still, Custer had cause to wonder if somewhere between Todd's Tavern and Trevilian Station his Wolverines had lost their storied ability to prevail in any situation, on any day, against any odds.[45]

CHAPTER TWELVE

Back to the Valley

For a number of reasons the return march was even longer, the pace slower, than the journey to Trevilian Station. The horses "were actually reduced to skin and bone," as one raider wrote, "and were greatly in need of shoeing." Many gave out on the homeward leg and had to be shot; thereafter their riders kept up with the column as best they could, many carrying their saddles. The heat was more intense than the week before, and many men keeled over from sunstroke and dehydration. Almost 400 prisoners and about 2,000 runaway slaves who had fallen in with the raiders also impeded the march.[1]

Above all, the pace was slowed by the long line of ambulances that accompanied the column across the North Anna at Carpenter's Ford, then eastward along the upper bank of that stream. Among the 400 wounded they transported, nearly half came from Custer's brigade. When added to the 41 killed or mortally wounded and the 242 missing as result of the battle, the command had lost almost a quarter of the strength it had taken into that two-day slugging contest. Once again the brigade had lost heavily in officers as well as enlisted men: Captain Alpheus W. Carr and Lieutenants Andrew J. Pulver and Robert Warren, all of the First Michigan, had been killed; the wounded included Lieutenant Colonel Brewer of the Seventh, Captains Duggan and Lieutenant Joseph L. Bullock of the First, Captains Hastings and Dodge of the Fifth, and Captain Lovell and Lieutenant Luther C. Kanouse of the Sixth Michigan.[2]

Although spared a close, damaging pursuit, the journey to Grant's new address outside Petersburg lasted fifteen days. Via Shady Grove Church, Guiney's Station on the Fredericksburg Railroad, Spotsylvania Court House, Bowling Green, Walkerton, King and Queen Court House, Dunkirk on the Mattapony River, White House on the Pamunkey, Tunstall's Station on the Richmond & York River Railroad, Jones's Bridge over the Chickahominy, and Charles City Court House, on 25 June the raiders reached the James River, camping near the pontoon bridge that Ben Butler's army had thrown across to Deep Bottom four days before. On the twenty-eighth Custer led his troopers across the bridge and into camp near Light House Point. The following day, however, the weary brigade was moving again, crossing the railroad to Norfolk in rear of the fighting lines at Petersburg. On the last day of the month it was bivouacking, along with the rest of Sheridan's force, at Reams's Station, seven miles below the city Grant had set out to capture three weeks ago.[3]

The fact that the Army of the Potomac (now enlarged by a part of Butler's command) occupied trenches east and southeast of the "Cockade City" told Custer's people that Grant's offensive had fallen short. While Sheridan had done his part to make the surprise assault a success, other generals had not. At critical times between 15 and 18 June subordinate commanders had failed to march in timely fashion, to cooperate with one another, and to attack thinly held defenses before they could be reinforced by Lee's army. The upshot was a lost opportunity of monumental proportions.

In the end, even Sheridan's long-suffering raiders had been tainted with failure, for as they limped home Hampton's cavalry used interior lines of movement to forge ahead of them. Not only had the less-encumbered Rebels attacked the wagon train of the Army of the Potomac at White House—a train Sheridan not only rescued but escorted south of the James—on the twenty-fourth they had also assaulted Gregg's division at Saint Mary's Church, eight miles above the river, inflicting heavy loss. Worst of all, from Grant's viewpoint, Sheridan had failed to prevent Hampton from leading many of his troopers against another Union raiding force: Wilson's division, augmented by Butler's cavalry, which Grant had dispatched on the twenty-second to cut the railroads south and west of Petersburg. Sheridan's returnees had marched to Reams's Station on 30 June because there, the previous day, Hampton had joined Confederate infantry in encircling and mauling Wilson's column.[4]

The rescue effort had accomplished nothing beyond adding an extra layer of fatigue to men and animals. When Sheridan's column reached Reams's Station, it found no one there. Wilson's raiders had scattered, every man for himself, and Hampton and the infantry, their job done, had returned to their lines at Petersburg. Again, Custer could not resist gloating over his enemy's misfortune, writing Libbie that the mishap of the twenty-ninth was the fault of "the upstart and imbecile Wilson... [and] the result of consigning several thousand cavalry to the charge of an inexperienced and untrained officer."[5]

The would-be rescuers returned glumly to Light House Point, within easy reach of Meade's supply coffers. These yielded up all manner of replacement weapons, ammunition, equipment, and attire ("the men's clothing was in rags," one of the raiders observed). The horse corrals behind the Petersburg lines also furnished the men with badly needed remounts. When not drawing horses, rations or supplies, the men lolled about, rested, and otherwise recruited their strength.[6]

Recuperation was a time-consuming process, but fortunately—after weeks of ceaseless toil—Sheridan's men had time to spare. James Kidd noted that "from July 2, when we returned to Lighthouse Point on the James river, to July 26 was quiet and uneventful. Many hundred convalescent wounded and sick men returned from hospital to duty; many also who had been dismounted by the exigencies of the campaign returned from dismounted camps...." The latter included Lieutenant Colonel Gould, whose unhorsed troopers were reassigned on 4 July from Meade's headquarters to Sheridan's. These additions, plus the return of most of Wilson's fugitives in the first days of July, improved the emotional as well as the physical condition of the corps.[7]

Another advantage to life at Light House Point was the camp's accessibility to visitors, including those of the female persuasion. On 5 July the famous Michigan *vivandiere* and nurse Annie Etheridge paid a call on the sick of the brigade; during her stay she must have compared notes with her counterpart in the First Michigan, Bridget Divers. At about the same time, Mrs. Custer came down from Washington, where she had been lodging, aboard the presidential yacht *River Queen* in company with Congressman Kellogg and other notables. Accompanied by her "Autie" as well as by Phil Sheridan, Libbie also visited City Point on the Appomattox, where Grant had established his headquarters. At an impromptu party hosted by the general-in-chief, Libbie waltzed with Little Phil as well as with her considerably more graceful husband.[8]

If the rank-and-file of the Michigan Brigade enjoyed neither sightseeing nor dancing, they did not seem to mind. Resting was their main priority, and they continued to enjoy it. As Major Kidd observed, along the James "the [only] duty performed was to picket the left flank of the army," and the work was not taxing enough to vitiate the effects of the rest and recuperation all enjoyed in camp.[9]

Even when the idyll ended and the brigade returned to active operations, it marched rather than fought. On 26 July Sheridan's again-intact command trotted back to Deep Bottom, where it recrossed the James. On the Northside, in company with the II Corps of Meade's army, the cavalry encountered Confederate infantry along the New Market Road south of Richmond. The offensive, planned as a diversion for a powder-mine set to be exploded under a Confederate salient east of Petersburg, lasted three days but featured minimal involvement by Custer's men. By morning of the thirtieth, the demonstration over, the cavalry returned to the Southside and veered west to Prince George Court House. The following day, twenty-four hours after the mine exploded as planned but failed to achieve a breakthrough, Sheridan's men were at City Point, awaiting a new assignment.[10]

They did not wait long. That afternoon the first contingent of Torbert's division was taken aboard transports docked near army headquarters. The vessels carried men and horses to the James, then down that historic river to Hampton Roads. Passing equally historic Fort Monroe, the little flotilla ascended Chesapeake Bay, entered the mouth of the Potomac, and steamed up to Washington.[11]

As ever, rumors as to destination and mission flew fast among the seaborne cavalrymen; most proved to be vague, inconsistent, and false. Not until 3 August, when they disembarked at the remount camp at Giesboro to complete the refit begun at Light House Point, did the troopers gain a better understanding of where they were heading.

They found Washington still quaking from its recent invasion by 14,000 Rebels under Major General Jubal Anderson Early. Seven weeks ago, Lee had dispatched the feisty corps commander to the Shenandoah Valley, where Early had driven the less-than-formidable David Hunter into the mountains and beyond range of Lee's communications. Then, with dramatic flair, Early turned his sights, and his army, north. Departing Staunton on 27 June, he moved to Winchester on 2 July, bypassed the garrison at Harpers Ferry, and crossed the Potomac to Frederick, Maryland. Near Frederick on the ninth he defeated a hastily assembled force in what became known as the Battle of the Monocacy. Two days later a confident Early reached the northern outskirts of Washington to find the capital's fortifications reinforced by Meade's VI Corps and miscellaneous forces including 600 dismounted troopers from Giesboro Point under Major Briggs of the Seventh Michigan. After a daylong fight, the invaders withdrew on the evening of the twelfth, eventually returning to the Shenandoah where they were reinforced by Lee.[12]

Early may have failed to take Washington but he had made the worst nightmare of many a bureaucrat come true. His audacious offensive added fuel to the national suspicion that the war to save the Union was being lost. That perception boded ill for the beleaguered Lincoln, who was facing a difficult reelection effort. (Adding near-injury to insult, Early's men had shot at Lincoln on the twelfth as he observed the fighting near Fort Stevens, north of the capital.)

The government and the army would not let such an embarrassment as Early's raid happen again. On 1 August Grant formally designated his most energetic subordinate, Phil Sheridan, to take command of an army based in the Shenandoah and composed of the VI Corps; the VIII Corps, formerly of Hunter's command; most of the XIX Corps, fresh from duty in the Southwest; plus three cavalry divisions, two of them—Torbert's and Wilson's—from the Army of the Potomac, and the third, from Hunter's army, under Brigadier General William Woods Averell. Sheridan had a single overriding mission: rid the Valley of Jubal Early, once and for all, by means moderate or extreme.[13]

* * *

On the evening of 6 August Torbert's division trooped from the remount camp through the streets of Georgetown and into the Maryland countryside around Tennallytown. "The march through Maryland was delightful," wrote an officer of Merritt's brigade. "The weather was cool, as compared with the hot, stifling temperature of Southern Virginia, the farms were neat and well kept, and there was an air of thrift and comfort delightful to contemplate, after four years' experience of poor Virginia,—war-torn and battered as it was." The men of the Michigan Brigade shared these sentiments. As Henry G. Lewis of the Sixth Cavalry put it, "to say that we are pleased with our change of base, would be too dull an expression—*we are more than pleased.*"[14]

The advance of Sheridan's column reached Harpers Ferry on the eighth; there General Torbert, who had been detached from his division, reported for duty. By seniority, he assumed command of every cavalry unit, while Merritt again succeeded him as leader of the First Division. When he learned of Merritt's promotion, the ambitious and envious Custer, who reached Harpers Ferry with his brigade on the tenth, redoubled his resolve to win promotion at the earliest opportunity.[15]

Early on the eleventh, his Wolverines led Merritt's division down the Valley Pike via Halltown, toward Early's headquarters at Winchester. Scenes familiar to the First Michigan loomed up on all sides: the verdant pastures, the compact valleys, the picturesque villages the regiment had not seen—except for brief and infrequent excursions—in more than two years. Not every sight called forth pleasant memories. Too many landmarks reminded Thornton Brodhead's veterans of defeat at the hands of Stonewall Jackson and Turner Ashby—recollections best left to molder in the back rooms of the mind.

Late in the day, the march provided the Michigan Brigade with its first combat service as members of what would become known as the Army of the Shenandoah. Crossing Opequon Creek, shoving in Rebel pickets, and pressing to within two and a half miles of

Winchester, portions of the First Michigan, backed by units of the Sixth, clashed with some of Early's infantry near Sulphur Springs Bridge. The fight, which featured a charge against the flank of the First and a counterattack by a battalion of the Sixth, resulted in the deaths of five Michiganders including Captain James Mathers, and the wounding of eighteen. The mission, however, was a success, for captive Confederates told Custer what he had been sent to find out: that Early had moved up the Valley, evacuating Winchester. Clearly, the Confederate leader would not wait for Sheridan to bring him to battle.[16]

The following day Sheridan commenced his pursuit of Early's army, tangling with the Rebel rear at Fisher's Hill, between Cedar Creek and Strasburg. Mountain walls sheltering the well-entrenched enemy made their position impregnable to direct assault. "For three days," recalled James Kidd (recently promoted to full colonel), "we remained face to face with Early's infantry, constantly so close as to draw their fire and keep them in their intrenchments."[17]

On the fifteenth Sheridan ended his confrontation and sent the cavalry eastward toward another of the First Michigan's old haunts, Front Royal. Little Phil had received a report that reinforcements from the Army of Northern Virginia—Major General Joseph B. Kershaw's infantry division and Fitz Lee's cavalry, all under Lieutenant General Richard H. Anderson—were approaching Front Royal from the east, planning to take the Federals in flank. The report proved true, although Custer learned this only after ranging beyond Front Royal, crossing and then recrossing the Shenandoah, and camping next to Tom Devin's brigade on the turnpike to Winchester.

There, on the afternoon of 16 August, as Custer's men tried to polish off a midday meal, the picket line they shared with Devin's troopers came under attack from foot soldiers, horsemen, and cannoneers. At once Custer took charge of the defense and made a rousing success of it. At his word, a newly attached horse battery from the Third U. S. Artillery, under Captain Dunbar R. Ransom, traded shells with an equal number of enemy cannon, giving better than it got. Galled by the fire, the gray cavalry suddenly charged. Custer beat them back with a counterthrust by Kidd's regiment,

CUSTER AND HIS WOLVERINES

assisted by Colonel Alger and the Fifth Michigan as well as by a pair of Devin's regiments.[18]

The Rebel horse neutralized, Custer turned north to confront a phalanx of foot troops making for his left flank via a ford across Crooked Run. Again he dosed the enemy—part of Kershaw's command—with shells from Ransom's battery, then ordered a dismounted advance by Alger. Attacking out of a ravine that shielded them from enemy view, the Fifth Michigan opened on the enemy line with such effect that, according to James Kidd, "the head of Kershaw's column was completely crushed." Minutes later the Rebels were returning to the ford on the double. To help them along, a battalion of the First Michigan under Angelo Paldi galloped past the Fifth and slammed into Kershaw's rear, cutting down luckless footmen and capturing almost 150 of them. Custer's casualties numbered close to fifty; fatalities included Lieutenant Lucius Carver of the Seventh, who the previous evening had informed a reporter from the *New York Times* that he would gladly sacrifice his life if it would hasten the day when "every enemy to the Union has been disarmed."[19]

When some of Lee's re-formed troopers tried to rescue their comrades at the ford, elements of Paldi's First and Melvin Brewer's Seventh Michigan, thrown forward in precise combination, blocked them, encircled them, and took additional prisoners. By day's end Custer was minus one of his golden locks, shorn by a stray bullet, but otherwise in excellent condition as well as high spirits. Today he had demonstrated what Kidd called a "marvelous intuition." The mealtime assault had taken him by surprise, "but he was alert, and equal to the emergency." Furthermore, he had shown himself "as bold to act as his perceptions were keen."[20]

When Sheridan learned from Custer that the reports of enemy reinforcements were true, he reacted as if alarmed that Early might overwhelm him—a disaster sure to have serious military and political repercussions. Already he had fallen back from his advance positions, heading for Berryville. Now he determined to go as far north as Charles Town. At the outset of the movement he issued a drastic order, one that originated with Grant. As the army moved down the Valley to Berryville and beyond, its cavalry would sweep the countryside, confiscating every serviceable horse as well as every bite of food and every ounce of forage it could find. That done, it would put the torch to all crops growing along a line south of Winchester, effectively eradicating the Breadbasket of the Confederacy.[21]

Sheridan's campaign of devastation lasted for weeks and stirred such resentment among his enemy that atrocities were committed in the name of retaliation. Even with revenge to spur him on, however, Early failed to harass Sheridan's withdrawal—which the Michigan Brigade covered—through a lack of both manpower and nerve. Although his opponent's movements suggested otherwise, Early's additions had failed to redress the imbalance of power in the Valley: Sheridan continued to outnumber him at least two-to-one. Had Little Phil halted his retreat, turned about, and struck at full strength, he might have mashed Early flat.

After Sheridan left Berryville on the eighteenth, his cavalry spent a week of what James Kidd called "marching and countermarching, picketing, reconnoitering and skirmishing... maneuvering for position and advantage." On the twenty-fifth, however, maneuvering turned into fighting as Torbert, at Sheridan's directive, led Merritt's and Wilson's divisions northwestward to investigate reports that Fitz Lee had moved toward the Potomac fords near Williamsport, perhaps on a raid into Maryland. Encountering a small force of riders near Kearneysville on the Baltimore & Ohio Railroad, Torbert drove it south toward Leetown, where he stumbled upon the infantry division of Major General John C. Breckinridge, former Vice President of the United States and future Confederate Secretary of War. Likewise taken by surprise, Breckinridge sent a mere regiment to swat the bluecoats aside. Torbert's men retaliated with enough carbine-fire to compel a much larger force to deploy against them.[22]

Belatedly concerned that he had angered a gray-clad Goliath, Torbert abruptly turned south, leading Wilson's division and much of Merritt's out of harm's way. Custer he left behind to safeguard his withdrawal via a fighting retreat—a gesture that many members of the Michigan Brigade forever regarded as abandonment. Late in the day, with his Wolverines falling back to the Potomac at Shepherdstown, Custer found that Breckinridge had trapped him at river's edge. The young general was forced to choose between fighting his way through an infantry line or turning his back to his foe while attempting to ford the stream. "Of course there was no thought of surrender," wrote Colonel Kidd, "and Custer was not much given to showing his heels."[23]

Adopting a middle course, Custer formed line of battle well in advance of the ford, the Sixth Michigan on the right, the Seventh on the left, the other regiments grouped in the center on either side of Ransom's battery. Every carbineer blasted away at Breckinridge, who, unused to such opposition from a cavalry force, hung back from the river long enough for Custer to leapfrog his units to the rear. For hours, Custer deployed his units from line into column and back into line, confusing Breckinridge's men and keeping them off-balance. Though the situation retained "a critical look" until the end, before evening every Wolverine and artillerist was safely across the river. They would remain in Maryland for three days before rejoining Sheridan via Harpers Ferry. Just as the brigade left the lower bank, a line of enemy troopers appeared on the Virginia side. James Kidd reported that "so astounded were they to see how we had escaped from their grasp, that some of them actually cheered...."[24]

* * *

Sheridan's withdrawal down the Valley had the opposite effect of what had been intended. Northern editors and politicians heaped scorn on the Army of the Shenandoah for fleeing a toothless opponent. Grant and Lincoln, as well as Sheridan, felt the sting of criticism, and on 16 September—as soon as he could confirm that Anderson and Kershaw had returned to Petersburg—Grant hastened to the Valley for a meeting with his suddenly timid-looking subordinate. Happily, he found Sheridan spoiling for a fight, eager to show Early and everyone else what his veteran army could do. The lieutenant general merely told Sheridan to "go in" against his foe.[25]

Sheridan planned a multi-pronged advance against Early's scattered army, cavalry forces to strike north of Winchester via Stephenson's Depot, the infantry to move directly on the city from the east along the Berryville Road. After imparting the details to his ranking subordinates, Sheridan moved swiftly to make amends for six weeks of relative inactivity. At two A.M. on 19 September Custer's camp near Summit Point stirred into life, and before two-thirty his men were moving southwestward to Locke's Ford on Opequon Creek. The advance contingent of Merritt's division, the Michigan Brigade met its timetable by completing the six-mile journey before daylight.[26]

As Custer had anticipated, recent reconnaissances in this area had prompted Early to bolster his pickets on the far side of the ford. Obliged to cross regardless, Custer moved to do so at sunrise. Meanwhile, almost five miles downstream at Berryville Crossing, Sheridan's foot soldiers, preceded by Wilson's cavalry, were wading the creek prior to advancing through a long ravine toward Early's headquarters. Wilson and the infantry appeared to have an unobstructed road to the front, but Custer's path was not so clear. Troubles began when the Seventh Michigan followed the inexperienced Twenty-fifth New York (which had been temporarily added to the casualty-depleted brigade and whose commander had petitioned to lead the movement) toward the ford. When fired on by dismounted cavalry holding well-concealed rifle pits, the New Yorkers halted short of the crossing-point, bunched up in confusion, then broke for the rear. Caught up in their flight, most of the Seventh Michigan circled back to its starting point, to the mortification of Lieutenant Colonel Brewer. Looking on from the north bank, Custer must have wondered again if his command had lost the resiliency, the power to overcome adversity, on which its reputation was based.[27]

While the already-dismounted Sixth Michigan laid down a cover fire for their stampeding comrades, Custer called up the old timers of the First. Determined not to repeat his predecessors' mistake, Peter Stagg sent Major Maxwell and two squadrons partway across the stream to deflect fire from the bulk of the regiment, which fought its way to the south bank, gouged the defenders from their trenches, and took many prisoners. Immediately thereafter the rest of the brigade crossed, pushing east toward Stephenson's Depot. At the depot it found Brigadier General Gabriel C. Wharton's infantry of Breckinridge's division drawn up in line of battle.

To test Wharton's strength, Major Maxwell advanced at the head of his own regiment, followed by the Seventh Michigan and Twenty-fifth New York, with the Reserve Brigade of Merritt's division (now commanded by Colonel Charles Russell Lowell) covering his flanks and rear. Maxwell's charge came within "a few feet" of the enemy line before overwhelming numbers of marksmen sent it reeling east.[28]

Custer was checked only momentarily. By now he was aware that Sheridan's advance had stalled and that the struggle farther south was "being contested with the utmost energy upon both sides." Intent on helping his side prevail, he kept up a heavy fire against the infantry in his front, hoping to keep it in place as long as possible. Shortly after one P.M., however, Early recalled his outlying detachments and Wharton began to shuttle regiments south. Custer quickly moved to take advantage. Attempting to flank Wharton's men and gain their rear, he again moved toward Stephenson's Depot—and this time came under a ragged fire from half of Early's cavalry, under Lunsford Lomax. Lomax, who had been tangling with blue horsemen to the north—General Averell's division—was so startled by Custer's appearance that his command "broke and fled" almost at first touch.[29]

As Lomax fell back to link with the division of Fitz Lee, Custer joined his Wolverines with Averell's two brigades. The columns remained in close contact as they headed down the Martinsburg Pike toward Winchester. Beyond Custer's left, the rest of Merritt's division moved in the same general direction, creating a mobile line more than a half-mile long and three ranks deep.

Three miles from the town, the Federals spied their re-formed counterparts under Lomax and Lee, drawn up in a mounted column that appeared on the verge of charging. Custer braced himself for the coming blow. When it hit, his skirmishers were pushed in but his main body promptly counterattacked, bouncing the Confederates backward and severely wounding General Lee. Lee's subordinates rallied the fugitives about a quarter-mile from the scene of the collision, but at Custer's signal, all five of his regiments, supported by Averell's people, galloped south in a thunderous charge that scattered their opponents in every direction.[30]

After pausing to secure prisoners and treat casualties, Custer resumed his descent upon the town. When a Rebel battery loomed up in his path, he sent detachments of each regiment to take it.

Infantry forces intervened, however, and the attackers withdrew with loss. But the rescue effort so weakened the enemy that minutes later two of Lowell's regiments made trophies of the Rebel guns.

Again resuming his advance, Custer looked south, where Sheridan's infantry, having overcome its earlier troubles, was emerging from the ravine to drive the overmatched Confederates toward the town. Hoping to strike in flank and rear while Sheridan plowed ahead, Custer led the head of his column to within 500 yards of Early's principal fortified position northeast of Winchester. Although directed by General Merritt to attack at once, the brigade leader withheld his blow until, as expected, the gray troops abandoned their works under the pounding of the VI, VIII, and XIX Corps. At that point, Custer moved in for the kill.[31]

Giving the word to his regimental commanders—Stagg, Hastings, Kidd, and Brewer—he spurred forward, shouting, gesticulating, waving his sword. Behind him four regiments of Michiganders tossed red neckties over their shoulders and, followed by their new allies from New York, careened down upon Early's half-demoralized infantry, ignoring a cannonade that passed just above their heads. In a minute or less they were among the Rebels, driving them, scattering them, riding them down, laying them flat with saber strokes, firing into them at point-blank range, lashing them again and again with anything that would serve as a weapon, caught in a frenzy that shook assailants as much as victims. The fury of the assault was nothing less than overwhelming; it robbed the Confederates of the ability to do anything but flee. Heedless of officers' orders to stand and fight, they threw down their weapons and raced toward Winchester in abject terror, all hope of resistance, every vestige of self-respect, gone.[32]

The few who stood and fought took a toll; among their victims were Captains Albert T. Jackson of the First and William O. North of the Fifth Cavalry. Another who fell, mortally wounded, was Lieutenant Colonel Brewer ("a soldier *sans peur et sans reproche*," intoned Custer). But the casualties the brigade absorbed could not compare with the losses it inflicted: by day's end it had killed or wounded hundreds of Early's people while taking more than 700 prisoners, along with seven battle-flags, two caissons, and enough rifles and pistols to rearm every Wolverine twice over. At least one participant, the Sixth Michigan, secured more prisoners than it had men engaged.[33]

Custer could only marvel at the all-consuming zeal of the attack, which sealed Early's defeat. As he noted in his report, "instances of personal daring and gallantry" were too numerous to mention. This fact helped assure him that despite reduced numbers the Michigan Cavalry Brigade retained the strength and spirit he feared it had left on some midsummer's battlefield.[34]

* * *

Not content to send the panic-stricken Confederates "whirling through Winchester," Sheridan staged a vigorous pursuit. Three days later he overtook his still-reeling enemy at Fisher's Hill. On the high ground he delivered a new flurry of punches that knocked the breath out of Early's army and sent it staggering off toward Woodstock, dazed, demoralized, and trailing blood.[35]

The greater part of the cavalry did not witness this latest pummeling, for Sheridan, anticipating victory, had sent Torbert, with most of Merritt's division, to join Wilson in his advanced position at Front Royal. Via the Luray Valley and a pass through Massanutten Mountain Torbert was to intercept Early's column and cut off its retreat. This the mounted leader attempted to do, but when he overtook what he supposed to be the rear of a demoralized mob he found instead Fitz Lee's cavalry, now under Williams Wickham, resolutely holding a position along the South Fork of the Shenandoah River. Every bridge for miles around had been destroyed, precluding a frontal assault, and the Luray Valley ran so narrow at that point that there seemed little hope of flanking Wickham.

Torbert made a half-hearted attempt to prove otherwise, sending Custer and his troopers across the Shenandoah west of Wickham's line, then by a roundabout route toward his rear. Detecting the maneuver, Wickham blocked it by dropping down toward Milford. His new position, enclosed by steep mountain walls, was even more formidable than the old, and so Torbert gave up the effort and retreated. An angry and disappointed Sheridan ordered him to return and try again on the twenty-fourth. Torbert did so and this time, thanks to a "gallant charge" by Custer and his Wolverines, dispersed Wickham's people, opening the road toward New Market, which Early's still-retreating army was approaching. "Even then," wrote a disapproving James Kidd, "the march was [made] leisurely, and the two big divisions arrived in Newmarket on the 25th only to find that it was too late. Early had escaped again." By failing to find a way to attack Wickham the first time and by failing to follow up his second-time success, Torbert had so displeased his superior that his relief from command was a matter of time.[36]

Another cavalryman who performed less than brilliantly in the aftermath of Fisher's Hill was General Averell, whose rather small division remained with Sheridan throughout the fight on the twenty-second, then pursued the defeated Rebels toward Woodstock. When the pursuit ended several miles short of Early's new position, Sheridan was so furious he fired Averell on the spot and replaced him with a much more reliable and combative subordinate, Armstrong Custer. The assignment lasted only a week, for Custer preferred a command that had come from—and was expected to return to—the Army of the Potomac. An opportunity of this nature presented itself, and Custer availed himself of it, on 1 October, when James Wilson, at Grant's recommendation, was transferred from Virginia to command the cavalry of Grant's successor in the West, Major General William T. Sherman.[37]

Custer's permanent separation from the brigade he had led since its inception—a command he had organized, staffed, inspired, and molded into one of the most powerful strike forces in the Union ranks—was a wrenching experience for all concerned. As his hand-picked successor, James Kidd, expressed it, "the Michigan brigade without Custer... was like the play of Hamlet with the melancholy Dane left out." Many of the troopers Custer left behind petitioned for transfer to his new command, hoping to trade places with a Third Division brigade. (Custer boasted to Libbie that "some of the officers say they would resign if the exchange were not made.... Some of the band threatened to break their horns"). Conversely, Wilson's old command gave his successor a hearty welcome; one trooper later noted that until Custer's coming his division "had no reputation, or but little.... The 'Mich Brig, 1st Div' bore the palm, every soldier in it glorying in its proud reputation while under the command of Genl Custer."[38]

In terms of personnel turnover, Custer's departure came at a bad time for the Wolverine Brigade. It saddled the command with a leader, James Kidd, who considered his elevation "an unsought and an unwelcome responsibility." It also created bad blood between him and Peter Stagg, who had made colonel almost three months after Kidd but who appears to have considered himself senior by virtue of his additional year of field service. Moreover, Custer's departure occurred at a period when the First Michigan was frequently without a leader (a chronic intestinal ailment intermittently placed Stagg on the sick list) and when the Seventh was still reeling from the loss of its commander (the day after Winchester, Melvin Brewer was succeeded by the capable but less popular Major Darling, who would be succeeded in turn by the recently promoted Lieutenant Colonel Briggs). Then, too, the Fifth Michigan was in the hands of a very junior field officer: only a week before Custer's departure, Smith Hastings had been mustered in as major. Hastings had succeeded to command not only because Lieutenant Colonel Gould was recuperating from a more virulent form of the disease that afflicted Stagg, but because Russell Alger had left the regiment for good—and under a cloud.[39]

On 20 September the War Department had accepted Alger's resignation, which he claimed to have submitted "on account of the health of my family." According to Custer, however, on 28 August, when the Fifth Michigan passed through Harpers Ferry en route from Shepherdstown to Sheridan's headquarters, Alger had dropped out of formation "owing to some indisposition" never identified. Soon afterward, Alger had been granted sick leave for reasons Custer considered unjustified. When the colonel attempted to extend the leave, Custer rejected his request. Alger left the brigade anyway, travelling to Baltimore, then to Washington where he was later assigned to court-martial duty.[40]

By mid-September Generals Torbert and Merritt were accusing Alger of being absent without leave, an offense that (according to Torbert) the colonel had committed on two previous occasions. The cavalry commander urged Sheridan to adopt "stern measures... to prevent a recurrence of this evil." Although he had long considered Alger a "good officer," Sheridan endorsed Torbert's suggestion that he be dismissed from the service. The acceptance of Alger's resignation ended all efforts to punish him, and at war's end the War Department awarded him the brevets of brigadier and major general of volunteers for meritorious conduct. Even so, charges that he had gone A.W.O.L. left a stain on Alger's record that political foes exploited when he ran for governor of Michigan in 1884. Thirteen years later, when Alger was named secretary of war by William McKinley, the record continued to dog him. Even former-General Wilson, a fellow-Republican, denounced the appointing of "any man over the Army who had virtually been kicked out of the service during the Civil War."[41]

* * *

Jubal Early's Confederates had been ravaged and routed, but not destroyed, at Winchester and Fisher's Hill. Sheridan made amends for the lapse during two October battles. The first resulted in the defeat and humiliation of Early's cavalry; the second ended with Old Jube's army in bloody fragments.

Having chased the Confederate leader into virtually inaccessible depths of the Shenandoah, Sheridan on 6 October began another retreat along the Valley Turnpike toward Harpers Ferry. As he moved, Torbert's people redoubled their efforts to "leave the Valley a barren waste." The success of this campaign so angered Early's cavalry, which followed Sheridan's column, that the divisions of Thomas Rosser and Lunsford Lomax began to pummel the Federal rear, killing and wounding several troopers, taking more than fifty prisoners, and carrying off supply wagons, ambulances, and horses. When his own cavalry appeared unable or unwilling to end the harassment, Sheridan on the evening of the eighth gave Alfred Torbert an ultimatum: "Whip the rebel cavalry or get whipped."[42]

The implied criticism in Sheridan's directive so stung his subordinate that next morning Torbert turned about and lit into his pursuers. On the Back Road, Custer's new command, fewer than 2,000 strong, charged Rosser's larger division, handled it with exceeding roughness, and drove it twenty miles up the Valley. In two hours of action the Third Cavalry Division had achieved more success under its new commander than in six months under James Wilson.[43]

While Custer was adding to his laurels, James Kidd, in his initial outing in brigade command, was enjoying similar, though less dramatic, success. Originally positioned southeast of Custer's command along Tom's Brook, the Michiganders teamed with Devin's brigade in ramming head-on into General Lomax's force along the Valley Pike, while Lowell's Reserves moved against the Rebel right. It was the flank drive that undid Lomax, but Kidd's and Devin's strikes made the success possible. Minus the First Michigan (picketing in rear of the division) but still augmented by the Twenty-fifth New York, the Wolverine Brigade pierced the Rebel center (which Kidd admitted was "rather thin") and tore through to the rear of the line.[44]

Lomax, his command collapsing around him, ordered a retreat toward Woodstock. His enemy pursued with a grim determination unusual at this stage of a cavalry battle. When mounted forces broke contact, ordinarily the loser was permitted to regroup and salve his wounds beyond harm's reach. Today things were different: each time Lomax attempted to collect his scattered ranks, Kidd and his colleagues struck again, uprooting the Confederates and sending them hurtling south. On Merritt's front, the relentless pursuit lasted several hours and covered twenty-six miles. By sundown the "Woodstock Races" had reached their devastating conclusion. While suffering fewer than sixty casualties, Merritt and Custer killed many more, while taking 350 prisoners, all but one of the twelve cannon the Rebels had brought into the fight, and everything else on wheels. "It was a square cavalry fight," a Northern newsman reported, "in which the enemy was routed beyond my power to describe."[45]

Only ten days later Early's infantry met a similar fate, although at the outset it appeared that Sheridan, not his enemy, would feel the sting of defeat. That Little Phil's army recovered so fully from its shaky start was due mainly to his personal leadership, but also to the retaliatory capabilities of his horsemen.

Nearly exhausted from their running fight of the ninth, Torbert's divisions spent that night and the next day near Woodstock, on the eleventh falling back to Cedar Creek. On the twelfth Sheridan made preparations to send a part of his army, at Grant's direction, to Petersburg, as though the effort to both devastate and pacify the Valley was a settled issue (the VI Corps would go as Grant wished, but not as soon as he expected). By 15 October Sheridan was heading east to confer with his military and civilian overlords, having issued instructions for his cavalry to make another raid on the Virginia Central Railroad, this time via Gordonsville and Charlottesville.[46]

Before Sheridan could return to the Valley, and before his horsemen could leave it, Jubal Early, having again been reinforced, sallied forth from Fisher's Hill to challenge the Yankees who considered the Valley campaign over. Using surprise as a shield, he slipped down the Valley Pike toward the left flank of the army commanded in Sheridan's absence by Major General Horatio G. Wright. Further aided by a morning fog that cloaked his movements, Early's advance took the VIII Corps unawares—most of its men were asleep when the shooting started—and overran its position. Then the Rebels forged westward, forcing the XIX Corps, then the VI Corps, down the pike, the former in some disorder. By midmorning, the army to which Sheridan was now returning was teetering on the brink of collapse.[47]

Stationed well to the north and west of the infantry's line along Middle Marsh, Merritt's division was not caught up in the initial retreat. Even so, its men were as shocked by Early's audacity as the rest of their army. Topping a ridge that offered a broad view of the battlefield, members of the Michigan Brigade stared open-mouthed at the sight of hundreds if not thousands of men in blue rushing to the rear, "dazed by the surprise in their camps... chagrined, mortified, mad at their officers and themselves—demoralized; but, after all, more to be pitied than blamed." The brigade took heart, however, when it spied, in its front, sections of Wright's VI Corps safeguarding the right flank: "Neither shot nor shell nor volleys of musketry could break them."[48]

About nine A.M. General Merritt ordered his division to move from behind the VI Corps to what remained of the Union left, there to link with Custer. The Reserve Brigade started off in that direction, Colonel Kidd's Wolverines immediately behind. As they crossed the Valley Pike, the Michiganders came under fire from one of Early's batteries. "One shell took an entire set of fours out of the Sixth Michigan," Kidd recalled, but "not a man left the ranks." Arriving in the position designated for it, the brigade formed line in front of Custer, its flank guarded by Captain Joseph W. Martin's Sixth New York Battery.[49]

As it prepared to meet an anticipated onslaught, the brigade watched its old leader "riding along the front of his command, chafing like a caged lion, eager for the fray." While Custer paced, the VI Corps, having withdrawn in good order from its original position, extended the cavalry's line westward, the re-formed XIX Corps on its other flank. Once properly aligned, cavalry and infantry unleashed long-range volleys at Early's troops, many of whom had suspended their advance to plunder the abandoned camps of their opponents.[50]

For an hour or more, Merritt's division held its new line, most of it—including the entire Michigan Brigade—mounted. On Kidd's front, every outfit but the Fifth Michigan, which had been deployed in rear as a reserve, waited in columns of squadron, a heavy line of skirmishers thrown out in front. Kidd, who was experiencing his first full-scale battle as an acting brigadier, was gratified when General Merritt rode up to approve the dispositions he had made.

Close to two o'clock, a great commotion went up from the right rear, and a common cry ran along the lines with the speed of heat lightning: "Sheridan has come; Sheridan has come... there is to be an advance all along the line!" Indeed, Little Phil had galloped twenty miles from his evening lodgings in Winchester to divert the course of battle. As he rode past the VI Corps, dispensing advice and encouragement, he was answered by what Kidd called "a shout that sent a thrill across the valley and whose ominous meaning must have filled the hearts of the Confederates with misgivings."[51]

Within an hour of Sheridan's arrival, Torbert had sent Custer's men westward yet again, while forming Merritt's division into waves of counterattack. Along the Michigan Brigade's line, the First Cavalry, today under Major Maxwell, held the right, the Seventh, under Lieutenant Colonel Briggs, the left, Charles Deane's Sixth and Smith Hastings's Fifth Michigan the center. Each outfit was now in column of battalions, "making three lines of two ranks each."

About mid-afternoon, a several-hour lull in the fighting ended when buglers all along the line blared out the call to advance. In minutes massed ranks of horsemen were rumbling south, heading toward the unsteady lines of Rebel soldiers who had become as much demoralized in victory as the VIII Corps in defeat. "It was a glorious sight," Kidd remembered, "to see that magnificent line sweeping onward in the charge.... There were no reserves, no plans for retreat, only one grand, absorbing thought—to drive them back and retake the camps."[52]

When the attackers came within rifle range, a blizzard of missiles ripped into Devin's brigade on the right flank, shoving it back and breaking the momentum of the entire division. Riders pulled on their reins, fell back a short distance, and re-formed. A second time they spurred forward, only to be halted when an errant detachment of the VI Corps stumbled across their path, blocking the way south. Again Merritt's division sorted itself out, formed for the attack, and started toward the enemy, again in proper alignment with the infantry.

Despite having to clear a wide depression as well as a creek and two ravines, this time the attackers gained their objective, which they struck with tremendous force. Like rotted wood, Early's line split apart, chips flying everywhere. Penetrating the gray mass, charging men spread out to right and left, tearing jagged holes in ranks that Early would never be able to rally. At some point, Wolverine regiments went their separate ways. Maxwell's First pounded along the Valley Pike, Briggs's Seventh tore through an open field crowded with panic-stricken fugitives, Deane's Sixth raced as far as Buckton on the north fork of the Shenandoah River, and the impulsive Major Hastings led the Fifth Michigan toward a Shenandoah ford so far in advance of the rest of the brigade that many of his men would not circle back till the next day. Each element of the brigade drove herds of demoralized Confederates before it, enabling Sheridan's infantry not only to regain the ground it had lost but to sweep Early's remnants completely off the field.[53]

While it may have lacked the wild abandon of the final charge at Winchester, this day's assault gained the Michigan Brigade a more complete, longer lasting, triumph. The earlier attack had robbed an army of its will to resist; this one took that army's life, and by extension, perhaps, the life of its nation. "His prestige was gone," James Kidd declared of Early, "his army destroyed and, from that moment, for the Confederacy to continue the hopeless struggle was criminal folly."[54]

CHAPTER THIRTEEN

The Last Pursuit

The day after Early's rout, Merritt's horsemen pursued as far as Woodstock but found so few organized bodies of the enemy that they went into camp. For several days they picketed the roads leading up the Valley and scouted in all directions. After taking part in some of these reconnaissances, the Michigan Brigade accompanied the division as it retraced its steps to Cedar Creek. During the return trip it was led not by Colonel Kidd but by the recently promoted Colonel Stagg, whom General Torbert had placed in command, overriding Kidd's seniority. For some time Kidd had made no secret of his less than hero-worshipful attitude toward Torbert, whom he continued to blame for abandoning Custer's command at Shepherdstown. Quite possibly, Torbert had learned of Kidd's feelings toward him and decided to punish him for it. Or he may simply have preferred a more experienced officer for a brigade leader.[1]

On 10 November the Michigan Brigade broke camp at Buck's Yard along Cedar Creek and, with the rest of the division, moved to Sheridan's headquarters at Winchester. There it would remain, except for short trips into the surrounding countryside, for the balance of the fall and for much of the winter as well. Winter, in fact, was lurking in the wings: two days after the Wolverines reached Winchester, a weekend of frigid winds made Chaplain Greely exclaim that in all his life "I never suffered as I did last Saturday afternoon and Sabbath. Our tents were [blown] down, and the wind blew like a tornado, and it grew dreadfully cold. Fires would not warm us, for the heat was carried by the wind everywhere...."[2]

Despite the unwelcome change in weather, strenuous campaigning was required of Sheridan's cavalry. On 14-15 November Stagg and his men followed General Merritt to Mount Jackson, where they skirmished with some of Early's more combative remnants. On the twenty-first Merritt's division, temporarily under the recently promoted Brigadier General Devin, scouted about Front Royal and Milford in coordination with Custer's division and the brigade of Brigadier General William H. Powell, Averell's permanent successor. On the twenty-eighth the Michiganders ranged into the Loudoun Valley on a different mission altogether—to burn the barns and crops of Southern-sympathizing farmers.[3]

Grant's requirement to destroy provisions and confiscate resources of value to the enemy was more or less rigidly enforced by Sheridan and his subordinates, especially Wesley Merritt, and the Michigan Brigade was a frequent instrument of that policy. By year's end, the Seventh Cavalry alone was responsible for forty-two barn burnings, the torching of 131 stacks of hay, and the confiscating of 700 hogs, 200 head of cattle, 250 sheep, and countless horses and mules; a Detroit newspaper placed the total damage at more than one hundred thousand dollars. But if the Wolverines were good at their work, it did not follow that they enjoyed it. Indeed, in common with almost everyone tasked with carrying it out, they considered this campaign of devastation a disagreeable, cowardly, and inhumane business. James Kidd undoubtedly spoke for the brigade as a whole when he described what he saw and felt on one of these incendiary missions:

"Women with children in their arms, stood in the street and gazed frantically upon the threatened ruin of their homes, while the tears rained down their cheeks. The anguish pictured in their faces would have melted any heart not seared by the horrors and 'necessities' of war. It was too much for me and at the first moment that duty would permit, I hurried away from the scene. General Merritt did not see these things, nor did General Sheridan, much less General Grant."[4]

In addition to causing pangs of guilt and remorse, such wanton destruction left Sheridan's troopers vulnerable to drastic forms of retaliation. At least partly in response to the burning of the lower Shenandoah, guerrillas and bushwhackers took an increasing toll of Sheridan's pickets, outposts, and wagon trains. Many of these punitive strikes were delivered by the Michigan Brigade's old nemesis, John Mosby.

Mosby had begun sniping at Sheridan's rear and flanks soon after the Federals reached Harpers Ferry in August. Early on, the partisan leader appeared to single out the Michigan cavalry for special attention. As early as 18 August his men—several of them disguised as civilians—attacked an isolated detachment of the Fifth Cavalry near Snicker's Gap, killing one trooper, wounding another, and capturing two. Operating under Grant's blanket instructions, Custer retaliated by burning the homes of local citizens.[5]

The following day, near Berryville, Mosby—his men concealed in blue uniforms—struck at a moving column of the Fifth Michigan, cutting off its rear guard, capturing several of its members, and reportedly shooting sixteen of them in cold blood while slashing the throats of two others. The incident fostered among the victims' comrades "an undying hatred, a desire for revenge, which the blood of Mosby and his gang alone can satisfy." Again the regiment lay waste to a section of the lower Valley, while vowing to take no more of Mosby's people prisoner.[6]

The blood feud between Mosby and the Wolverines simmered for a few weeks but caught fire in the aftermath of another atrocity. On the morning of 23 September a band of partisans, this time wearing Confederate gray but unaccompanied by their leader, ambushed a supply train and its escort on the road to Front Royal; the attackers were accused of gunning down an unarmed lieutenant of Regular cavalry who had tried to surrender. When reinforcements overtook Mosby's band, six fell into the hands of members of the slain officer's command. Their leader, Wesley Merritt, avenged his subordinate by shooting four of the prisoners and hanging the others. To the bodies of those hanged he affixed a note proclaiming this "the fate of Mosby and all his men."[7]

When he learned of the summary executions—which rumor mistakenly laid at the feet of Custer—Mosby escalated the feud. He spent weeks attacking detachments of Custer's old brigade and taking prisoners. On 6 November he assembled twenty-seven of these near Berryville and forced them to draw lots. Seven unlucky Wolverines thus condemned themselves to die. Some managed to escape before the sentence was carried out, others may have been pardoned, but at least three and possibly as many as seven were hanged as close to

Custer's headquarters as Mosby could safely penetrate. Like Merritt (or, as he supposed, Custer), Mosby tagged his victims, announcing that they had died "measure for measure" for Yankee barbarism.[8]

The inhumane cycle of atrocity and reprisal continued until cold weather curtailed the field operations of both armies. In its later stages, this war-within-a-war appears to have produced nothing on the scale of the executions at Front Royal and Berryville, but the bitterness it created endured long after Sheridan ended his scorched-earth campaign, some time after Thanksgiving. Whether the confrontation hearkened back to the warfare of primitive times or anticipated the total-war ethos of the next century, the excesses of which both sides were guilty stained the honorable record of competition between Mosby and the Wolverines dating back at least to late 1862.

* * *

Some aspects of service outside Winchester during the long winter of 1864-65 were well worth forgetting, but others would provide Sheridan's troops with years of pleasant memories. To be sure, the local weather remained unusually severe; by late January, according to Corporal Stephen Thompson of the Fifth Michigan, temperatures dipped so low that sentinels could not walk guard for more than a half-hour at a time without being frostbit. Even so, most of Sheridan's men managed to stay tolerably warm inside the cabins and stockaded tents they erected late in December and early in January, as did their horses in the stables and lean-tos common to every camp. An anonymous member of the Seventh Michigan boasted that, warmly attired and flushed with victory, his regiment remained in a "flourishing condition" throughout the winter. The men also ate well; so did their animals. Sergeant Hiram Rix, Jr., insisted that the mounts of the Sixth Michigan were "fed better than we are," explaining that "we get enough of bread and meat, coffee and sugar...." The ample fare helped him and his comrades get through "the usual routine of duties" that even the foulest weather could not postpone: "Get up at daylight, [go] to roll call, then take care of our horses, get breakfast, [and join] the detail for guard... duty, also the pickets...."[9]

With Early's shattered army unlikely to cause trouble in any season, furloughs were issued on a regular basis, permitting soldiers to escape outdoor duty for rest and refreshment in Harpers Ferry, Washington, or—if they could afford the cost of transportation—in Detroit and Grand Rapids. Even those who could not escape the harsh weather tried to make the best of it, sleighing along snow-capped ridges and "snowballing" with comrades and occasionally in competition with other regiments.[10]

Numerous events kept the troopers' spirits as high as possible under the conditions then obtaining. The "hard-war" members of the brigade—and even after three years of hardship and privation there were any number of these—applauded Lincoln's reelection in November and his defeat of the Peace Democrat candidate, former General McClellan. "I am Rejoicing to think Uncle Abraham is Re-Elected," Joseph Gillet of the First Michigan told his brother and sister. "May the Angels Strew Flowers in his Path...." Told of the electoral results, Trooper George Dennis of the First shouted out "Three Cheers for Old Abe." Other Michiganders had their spirits lifted and their resolve strengthened by news, received throughout the winter, of Union triumphs in other theaters: the defeat of Confederate forces at Franklin, Tennessee, late in November, and at Nashville the following month; Sherman's capture of Savannah, in late December; the January seizure of Fort Fisher, North Carolina; and the February occupation of Charleston, scene of the war's opening salvos.[11]

Still other morale-raising events of the winter were available only to officers, such as the dinners and parties thrown by General Custer and his wife, who weathered the season in a "fine old Virginia mansion" four miles south of Winchester. In the first week of February, the Custers hosted a "Michigan Brigade Ball" at a local academy, the York Institute. The occasion paired local ladies of unionist persuasion and Custer's subordinates. As snow drifted down outside, the officers and their partners waltzed the night away to the accompaniment of the Michigan Brigade band.[12]

By mid-February men were returning from leave in large numbers, signalling an early end to winter quarters. On the twenty-first, with the snow that had long covered the Winchester area fast disappearing, Sheridan firmed up plans to pass the Blue Ridge and attack the Virginia Central Railroad and James River Canal, objectives General

Grant had been recommending to his attention ever since the Trevilian Raid.[13]

Already Sheridan had attempted to appease the lieutenant general. In late December he had dispatched General Torbert, with Merritt's and Powell's divisions, from Front Royal to Gordonsville with orders to damage the railroad as far south as Lynchburg. Snow, sleet, and bottomless roads had hampered the operation from the outset, making everyone involved miserable. When reinforcements rushed up from Richmond to secure Gordonsville, Torbert gave up the raid as a lost cause.[14]

Now Sheridan planned to head to Lynchburg, from which point he would destroy railroad track "in every direction." This time his cavalry commander would not take part. Torbert had a habit, which Sheridan tolerated but did not appreciate, of taking frequent leave far from the scene of his army's operations. He was absent in Delaware when Sheridan made final preparations to march, and Little Phil—still rankled by Torbert's failures in the Luray Valley as well as by the Gordonsville fiasco—decided not to recall him. Instead, Wesley Merritt would lead the cavalry on the upcoming expedition, with Tom Devin moving up to take Merritt's division.[15]

Another officer who would not accompany Sheridan from Winchester was James Kidd, who had been on court-martial service since December. Though the colonel asked to be relieved of that duty so he might join his regiment in time for the march, Sheridan refused, perhaps fearing the friction Kidd's return to the Michigan Brigade might produce. Early in December, the long-simmering feud between Kidd and Peter Stagg had boiled over when Stagg arrested and confined his colleague for alleged disobedience of orders. Kidd insisted that the infraction was "supported by a very trivial specification" and claimed that Stagg had acted out of concern "that I stood in his way for promotion to Brig. General, which he is exceedingly ambitious to be...." When Kidd went over Stagg's head by bringing his arrest to the attention of General Devin, commanding the division, he was immediately released, to the irate displeasure of his jailor. From that time on, the two men had been unable to serve together without rancor; on the coming expedition, at least, they would not have to.[16]

*   *   *

When reveille was blown in the camps outside Winchester on the raw, rainy morning of 27 February it signalled Sheridan's farewell to the Valley. Before noon, almost 10,000 troopers and horse artillerymen in or attached to the divisions of Devin and Custer were clip-clopping up the Valley Turnpike toward Woodstock. The command included the forty-some officers and 950 men of Stagg's brigade: the Fifth Michigan under Major Hastings, the Sixth under Lieutenant Colonel Vinton, Lieutenant Colonel Briggs and the Seventh, and a small detachment of the First led by Lieutenant Colonel Maxwell, the unhorsed remainder of the regiment having been left—much to its chagrin—in the remount camp at Harpers Ferry.[17]

Considering how long and hard the regiments had served—considering, too, the lack of a concerted recruiting campaign this winter—the Wolverines were not abnormally understrength. Most of the other brigades in Sheridan's column had been similarly reduced by hard campaigning, harsh weather, and a host of other influences. The men who remained, however, were veterans in the truest sense of the term, not only experienced but accepting of the most onerous burdens, and worthy of Sheridan's implicit trust. Then, too, even in their diminished state they made for a powerful-looking column. Years later a New York officer recalled the commencement and first leg of the march:

"Under wintry skies, with the snow lying in shrunken drifts by the roadside, and in great masses on the mountains, with a drizzling rain, which froze as it fell, the dark column stretched to its full length, and wound slowly up the familiar pike.... We marched thirty miles to Woodstock and bivouacked for the night on a sloping hillside half covered with ice and snow. The blazing fires set little rills of water running, which added to the picturesqueness but not to the comfort of the situation."[18]

Sheridan's first item of business was not to cross the mountains to Lynchburg but to pay his final respects to the tattered remains of Jubal Early's army. Whether or not absolutely necessary, Little Phil was determined to ensure that his opponents—however many of them were left—would cause no mischief after he exited the Valley.

He looked forward to the confrontation, doubting that Early would prove a match for the mighty host heading toward him. The initial encounter between the two suggested that Sheridan was correct. On the third day of the journey, 1 March, what remained of Tom Rosser's cavalry tried to prevent the Federals from crossing the bridgeless Middle Fork of the Shenandoah near Mount Crawford. Without breaking stride, Sheridan's advance swam the icy river, outflanked the flabbergasted Rebels, and chased them away. That same day, with almost laughable ease, the Michigan Brigade pried a part of Early's main body loose from Staunton, chased it eastward to Waynesboro, and burned a railroad bridge between the towns.[19]

When the final showdown occurred on 2 March, victory came too quickly to be truly satisfying. That morning Custer advanced on Early's hastily prepared defenses northwest of Waynesboro, moved one of his brigades around an exposed flank, and attacked frontally with the other two. Almost effortlessly he dislodged Early's infantry, compelling much of it to surrender; the rest he pursued across the South Fork of the Shenandoah. Custer's trophies included 1,600 prisoners, seventeen battle flags, eleven cannon, and 200 wagons. The brief but decisive encounter ended any speculation that Early's army might rise from the ashes of Cedar Creek to fight on.[20]

On the morning of the third, having left behind a party of 1,200 troopers to escort his prisoners to Winchester, Sheridan led his column through Rockfish Gap in the Blue Ridge, heading for Charlottesville. The next day, after slogging through what the historian of the Seventh Michigan called "the rain-soaked roads of red Virginia clay, churned into thin mortar by the hoofs of many thousands of horses," the men dried and rested in the dormitories and faculty quarters of the University of Virginia. On the sixth, having foraged off the local populace and torn up stretches of the railroad back to Staunton, the raiders returned to the road. While the main column headed south to damage the James River Canal, Lieutenant Colonel Maxwell led the detachment of the First Michigan southeastward, destroying bridges, mills, and supply depots along the Rivanna River, before rejoining Sheridan near Columbia.[21]

At Columbia, where the Rivanna and James Rivers met, Sheridan found he had forged as far south as possible. Local Confederates had destroyed the only bridges by which the column could cross the wide and treacherous James. Thus Sheridan had ample reason to abort his Lynchburg mission, which had been imposed on him by Grant, and turn north and east, as he preferred, rejoining Meade's army at Petersburg for what would surely be the final campaign of the war in Virginia.[22]

The last leg of Sheridan's march consumed two weeks, during which his men wrecked strategic sections of the Virginia Central and the canal toward Richmond, burned bridges, destroyed supply depots, liberated hundreds of slaves from surrounding plantations, eluded forces sent by Lee to run them down, and crossed a series of familiar rivers: the South and North Anna, the Pamunkey, the Chickahominy, and, at Harrison's Landing on 26 March, the James. When, later that same day, Sheridan reported at City Point, his troopers had compiled a memorable resume of destruction, to which the Michigan Brigade, by Peter Stagg's account, had contributed the following: five miles of railroad, four rail bridges totaling 400 feet of trestlework, one depot (Hanover Junction), one aqueduct, nineteen canal locks, four canal boats, nineteen canal and road bridges, one combination boat house and lumber yard, seven flour mills, one cotton mill with three tons of raw cotton, and five warehouses containing 500 bushels of wheat, 400 barrels of flour, 1,500 pounds of wool, and sixty hogsheads of tobacco. According to General Sheridan, the Wolverines had also taken seventeen prisoners of war and 120 horses and mules.[23]

The record of accomplishment lent the brigade a deserved sense of satisfaction, a feeling that a disagreeable but necessary job had been done well. To a man, however, the Wolverines were relieved that the march was over, its difficulties and perils behind them. Captain Rockafellow of the Sixth Michigan knew of "no human language that can describe the rain, the mud and the raging, foaming rivers that we have waded through." Thus he understood and appreciated the reaction of the chattels his command had led out of bondage, who, upon crossing the James, raised "a song of thanksgiving like Israel of old on the escape from Egypt."[24]

*   *   *

If indeed the war's closing scenes were about to be played out, the Michigan Brigade and its comrades under Sheridan quickly took their places on stage. After talking Grant out of his long-held notion that the cavalry should swing south to link with Sherman's armies in the Carolinas, Little Phil accepted a new set of instructions, much more to his liking. In response to it, early on 29 March, at the head of Devin's and Custer's divisions (both grouped under Wesley Merritt) as well as the Second Division, Army of the Potomac (once David Gregg's, now Major General George Crook's), Sheridan looped below Petersburg past infantry commands preparing for a coming, final assault on Lee's lines. Turning westward, he and his troopers crossed Rowanty Creek, then forged toward Five Forks, a fortified crossroads twenty-two miles below Petersburg that weighted the extended right flank of the Army of Northern Virginia.[25]

By five P.M., despite being funnelled into roads that spring weather had not fully dried, Sheridan's men were at Dinwiddie Court House, five miles from Lee's flank. Behind them foot soldiers were moving up in accordance with Grant's strategy. A heavy rain came down that night, and it continued the next morning when Sheridan sent some of Devin's and Crook's men to scout the strategic crossroads to the north.

One of the few units of the Michigan Brigade engaged on the thirtieth was the Seventh Cavalry, with which Merritt supported the advance to Five Forks of one Regular and one volunteer regiment of the Reserve Brigade. Detecting a force of Rebel cavalry along the White Oak Road east of Five Forks, the Reserve regiments charged without ascertaining the strength of the opposition, only to be stopped and thrown back. The Confederates, obviously "confident of success," pursued the Reserves, their pistols spitting, until running into Lieutenant Colonel Briggs and the Seventh, drawn up in column of squadrons astride the muddy road. Though now composed of fewer than 300 officers and men, Briggs's outfit could not refuse an opportunity to get to know its enemy at close range. Counterattacking, it broke the oncoming force, scattering bits and pieces of it across the fields. Several members of the Seventh and supporting units were wounded in the melee including Major Duggan of the First Michigan, who received a gunshot wound in the thigh. To salve their injuries the regiments fell back in good

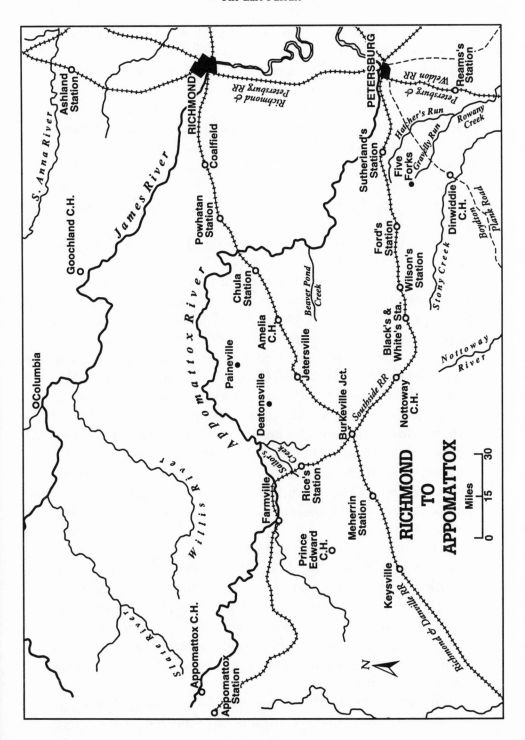

RICHMOND
TO
APPOMATTOX

Miles

0 15 30

order to Dinwiddie Court House, where they were complimented by General Merritt for a charge well conducted.[26]

Intelligence gathered by Devin and Crook on this stormy day enabled Merritt to inform Sheridan—and Sheridan to inform Grant—that Five Forks was held by several thousand infantry, cavalry, and artillery under the Gettysburg hero, George Pickett. Late that night Grant told Sheridan to return to Five Forks on the morrow, this time in full force. At first opportunity he should turn Pickett's right, sneak into his rear, and force him out of his works. Pickett dislodged, the entire length of the Confederate line at Petersburg would be vulnerable to attack.[27]

Before dawn on the overcast morning of 31 March Sheridan returned Devin's and Crook's divisions to the strategic crossroads (Custer's division had been left in the rear to escort a bogged-down supply train to the front). Per Grant's instructions, the cavalry took aim at Pickett's right flank. As they moved north, however, the much larger enemy left their defenses and made for Sheridan's left.

Pickett's offensive packed an unexpected punch. In midmorning his cavalry and infantry crossed Chamberlain's Creek, between Five Forks and Dinwiddie Court House, and sliced through Sheridan's force, isolating Stagg's Wolverines and two other brigades north of the creek from three brigades on the south side of the stream. Not only was Pickett now in position to defeat the cut-off forces in detail, he was within striking range of an infantry force positioned northeast of the courthouse, Major General Gouverneur K. Warren's V Corps, portions of which were already under attack by Lee's infantry below Petersburg.

As Pickett's force moved toward Dinwiddie, however, it exposed its right flank and rear—just those points Sheridan had been directed to strike. At Sheridan's order, the cavalry below the creek loosed a powerful fusillade that brought Pickett's advance to a halt and caused it to face southward. Sheridan exploited this temporary success by calling up Custer, along with several horse artillery units, and sending word that the forces above Chamberlain's Creek should fall back to the courthouse.[28]

In trying to comply with Sheridan's directive, Stagg's Michiganders and the other outflanked brigades had a rough time of it. Since morning they had been tangling with a much heavier foe, supported by artillery; the contest had left the Wolverines "in much disorder." Under the circumstances, disengaging and withdrawing might turn disorder into chaos. The men, however, were equal to the task. One of them, Captain John Clark of the Seventh Michigan, had been in tougher scrapes before: captured on the Kilpatrick-Dahlgren Raid, he had escaped from prison in South Carolina after ten months of captivity and by almost superhuman efforts had rejoined his regiment. This day he helped his regiment rejoin its division, keeping the enemy at arm's length with its rapid-fire carbines, all the while moving to the rear. Clark boasted that "we fought & fell back about 2 miles but they [Pickett's infantry] Payed [sic] dearly...."[29]

As soon as they were able to remount, Stagg's Wolverines joined their comrades in a roundabout ride to Dinwiddie, which they reached late in the day to find a desperate fight in progress. Inside a semicircular defense line three-quarters of a mile above the courthouse, Sheridan's troopers and cannoneers were fighting for their lives, "the carbines of five brigades... blazing in the twilight, the repeating Spensers [sic] puffing out their cartridges like Roman candles." As soon as the new arrivals entered the line, the firepower they added turned the tide. Pickett's men could make no inroads; when the weather-shortened day came to a close Sheridan's people remained rooted inside their works.[30]

For a time Pickett remained in place as well, making Sheridan see him as vulnerable to counterattack if Union infantry could come up in time. Learning of Sheridan's situation, Grant assured him that Warren's corps would join him by midnight to assist in attacking Pickett. But by three A.M. on 1 April Warren was not up and Pickett was gone, having retired to his strong line at Five Forks. Angry that an opportunity to destroy the Rebel right had been lost to a lack of marching speed on the part of the V Corps, Sheridan nevertheless intended to strike Pickett come morning, with or without infantry support.[31]

By sunrise, only one of Warren's three divisions had reached Dinwiddie; the rest of the corps was moving down from the northeast as fast as foot soldiers and gunners could negotiate roads so muddy as to be beyond hope of firming up. An impatient and frustrated Sheridan decided to move out with Devin and Custer and the small infantry force on hand. Stagg's Michiganders, leading the march on the right, passed over ground "from which," they noted sourly, "we had been driven the day before." In the murky light the advance-guard encountered infantry from Pickett's command along the swampy bottoms of Chamberlain's Creek. The force proved to be sizable enough to discourage a head-on attack, so Devin dismounted his Second Brigade, Colonel Charles L. Fitzhugh's, and pushed it across the stream opposite the enemy's left flank. The Rebels' attention thus diverted, Stagg, at Devin's order, sent George Maxwell with the First Michigan, plus the Sixth Michigan under Lieutenant Colonel Vinton, splashing through the creek on Fitzhugh's left, the First U. S. Cavalry of the Reserve Brigade close behind. At the same time, Smith Hastings—himself recently promoted to lieutenant colonel—led the Fifth Michigan across on Fitzhugh's other flank.[32]

The maneuver was bold enough to invite loss. Lieutenant Colonel Maxwell's career ended when a rifle slug buried itself in his left knee; the wound would require amputation of the leg. But the multiple crossings were effective enough to force the suddenly demoralized enemy to retire to the shelter of a woods. Members of Fitzhugh's brigade and the Reserves promptly drove them from the trees and pursued them to within twenty yards of their works along the White Oak Road. When the defenders opened with musketry and cannon, Devin's division fell back a short distance, then dug in and returned fire. Captain Clark noted that through the rest of the day the Rebel infantry "did not expose themselves" to the men of the Michigan Brigade: "If they did they got a shot."[33]

With Devin and, farther west, Custer in place opposite Pickett's works, Sheridan began to implement his strategy. Custer's men would threaten the enemy's right, holding Pickett's attention until the rest of Warren's infantry—when and if it arrived—could overwhelm the Rebel left. The plan was both simple and viable but it hinged on close infantry-cavalry coordination, something noticeably lacking thus far. In fact, not until four P.M., with another day of limited daylight almost spent, did the head of Warren's main body

reach the jumping-off point for the assault Sheridan had mapped out for it.[34]

By then Devin's and Custer's divisions—Crook's was farther south, protecting the rear—had been maneuvering, demonstrating, jockeying for position for upwards of two hours, raising the possibility they would soon run out of ammunition. And when Warren finally formed an assault column and ordered it forward, he failed to strike the angle, just above Stagg's position, where Pickett's front and left flank met. Instead of engaging the defenders, many foot soldiers blundered into the ranks of the Wolverine Brigade. An angry Sheridan rode forward, straightened out the attack formation, led it toward the critical point—and made use of authority given him by Grant to relieve Warren from command, replacing him with Brigadier General Charles Griffin.[35]

With infantry cooperation finally assured, Merritt's horsemen stopped feinting and began attacking. They rushed up—some mounted, some afoot—to Pickett's line, scaled his works, and on the other side grappled with the enemy. "Hardly halting to reform," Sheridan wrote, "the intermingling infantry and dismounted cavalry swept down inside the intrenchments, rushing to and beyond Five Forks, capturing thousands of prisoners." Many Rebels did not wait to be taken. Captain Clark observed with satisfaction that the force opposite the Michigan Brigade "showed as clean a pair of heels as you could wish to see."[36]

Sheridan's victory, completed by nightfall, resulted in the dissolution of Pickett's command. Nearly 6,000 Confederates surrendered inside their works; a few thousand others fled north across Hatcher's Run. Some tried to make their way back to the Petersburg front; many others started for home, their war over. Of greater importance than Pickett's overthrow, Lee's right flank had not only been turned, it had been obliterated, exposing to capture his last line of supply, the Southside Railroad. As a defensive position, Petersburg was no longer tenable, and with the Cockade City evacuated, Richmond must be abandoned. Five Forks had sealed the fate of the Confederacy; ultimate defeat was a week away.[37]

* * *

Within hours of the loss of his lower flank, Lee made plans to lea

both Petersburg and the capital, marching southwestward in search of a safe haven that neither he nor his opponents knew to exist. The next morning Meade's army, exploiting Sheridan's breakthrough, attacked all along its lines, gaining footholds that guaranteed Petersburg's seizure and occupation. Hours later Lee's retreat got underway, the remnants of his once-formidable army—now fewer than 30,000 including the troops that had held the Richmond defenses—streaming out along the railroads leading into the Confederate interior.

Having anticipated Lee's flight, Phil Sheridan moved to curtail it as quickly as possible. Early on 2 April he sent Merritt's cavalry, including the Michigan Brigade, across Hatcher's Run to secure the Southside and tear up some of its track. En route to the rail line, the Wolverines bagged dozens of Pickett's stragglers and at a few points tangled with the still-combative but overmatched Confederate cavalry. In every instance, the Southern troopers gave way and galloped off.[38]

Late in the morning of the third Grant ordered Sheridan and the cavalry to lead the pursuit south of the Appomattox River. Thereafter Sheridan was guided by a simple strategy: to overtake the enemy and to strike their flank and rear until they halted and faced about to defend their trains and artillery. Little Phil's strategy meant that his troopers faced a long, hard road. As Hiram Rix of the Sixth Michigan noted, his brigade required the rest of 3 April to align itself with Lee's rear. The march left the troopers not only fatigued but ravenous, for no rations had been issued them in four days and they had outdistanced their commissary trains. To aching muscles and hunger pangs, the Michigan Brigade next day added combat duty: it drove a line of enemy sharpshooters, part of Lee's rear guard, from a ridge and the upper stories of a house atop it.[39]

For the Seventh Michigan, at least, the action ended on a happy note. Upon entering the house where the Rebels had taken refuge, John Clark was accosted by its secessionist owner, who demanded that a guard be posted on the premises because "he had provisions stored there." The man had barely spoken before Clark's men were helping themselves to everything that looked remotely edible. It was well they took the opportunity, for early that evening, after a strenuous ride to Beaver Pond Creek, just east of Amelia Court

House, Merritt's men were forced to strike camp, dump coffee pots, and make an all-night march to reach Sheridan. With a small escort Little Phil had pushed ahead of the main column to Jetersville, which he correctly assumed was Lee's next destination.[40]

The blocking maneuver should have stopped Lee in his tracks, but it did not. His path south barred by cavalry, with infantry forces known to be closing up in Sheridan's rear, Lee on 5 April decided to lead his remnants westward to strike the railroad to North Carolina, via which he hoped, somehow, to join General Sherman's opponent, Joseph E. Johnston. The next morning, the cavalry was again pushing westward, hoping to get ahead of their quarry at Deatonsville and Rice's Station.[41]

Upon reaching Deatonsville that morning, the cavalry of George Crook overtook a part of the enemy column—a long line of supply wagons, well guarded by foot and horse soldiers. In rear of the wagons, along the banks of Little Sailor's Creek, marched what remained of Lieutenant General Richard S. Ewell's infantry corps, with the tiny division of Joseph B. Kershaw—the Wolverines' antagonist at Front Royal the past August—leading the column. While Crook's men maneuvered toward the head of the supply train, Sheridan left the Michigan Brigade in position almost three miles south of Deatonsville, supported by a section of a light battery, to await the imminent arrival of the VI Corps. Stagg also had orders to demonstrate against the wagon train, buying time for Crook to assault farther along the line.[42]

Stagg did his job well, leading his men up to the wagons, where they blazed away at close range, then falling back, "thus keeping," Sheridan reported, "a large force of the enemy from moving against the rest of the cavalry...." Then General Merritt sent word that Stagg should make a mounted attack on the head of Kershaw's command. By now Kershaw had placed his men behind hastily erected breastworks along the creek, facing northeastward. Remounting the Seventh Michigan, Stagg sent it toward the right flank and rear of the enemy, its own right secured by the advance echelon of the VI Corps and its path cleared by a covering fire from the balance of the brigade. Captain Clark, whose squadron led the charge, summarized the result: "As we advanced, their [the Confederates'] rear guard &

skirmish line retired on the main boddy [sic] which were on the side of a hill sloeping [sic] toward a small stream.... A part of their line was hid by woods & bushes. The 6th Corps advanced down the hill & across the stream & commenced ascending the other.... They had to face a storm of bullets & did it bravely. We were on their left & advanced with them mounted. The 3rd Division of Cavalry [i.e., Custer's] charged the enemy in rear at the same time & what was not killed we captured...."[43]

The combined cavalry-infantry assault began an offensive that destroyed Ewell's command. When the shooting ended Ewell was a prisoner along with five other generals and some 6,000 men, and the survivors were fleeing across the creek, utterly demoralized. Meanwhile, Crook's attack captured 300 or more vehicles plus three artillery batteries. The captures along Sailor's Creek symbolized the fate that awaited the rest of Lee's ragged column.[44]

* * *

The fighting of the sixth so fragmented and scattered the Confederates that the next day the Michigan Brigade "found no enemy to fight." That night, after another hard ride that put them close to blocking Lee's path, they bivouacked near Prince Edward Court House. Throughout the eighth, too, the brigade marched rather than fought, hitting the railroad at Prospect Station, then curling south and west to Appomattox Station, two and a half miles southwest of the county courthouse of the same name. By now the Michiganders had come almost eighty miles since leaving Petersburg five days ago, making this the most grueling, sustained march the brigade had conducted since Gettysburg. The men's spirits, however, were at their highest level since the war's earliest, rosiest days. Every man under Sheridan, Merritt, Devin, Crook, and Custer sensed that the goal toward which they had striven so long, and which had taken so many years, dreams, and lives, was at hand. It lay, perhaps, around the next bend, over the next ridge, just a mile or so up ahead....[45]

Toward evening on the eighth, as their division turned north to Appomattox Station, the men could hear firing at the head of the column, where Custer's command was riding. John Clark recalled that "we went forward at a rapid gait & when we reached the R.R. saw 3 trains well laden with supplies in our hands. [We] went in &

assisted in capturing a waggon [sic] train, [and] a quantity of Artilery [sic] which kept us busy until midnight." In actuality, four trains full of rations and forage had fallen to Custer, all misdirected from their famished enemy by Sheridan's scouts, who had intercepted the orders of Lee's commissary general. After helping secure the spoils, the Michigan Brigade remained at Appomattox Station, relieving one of Custer's brigades, which rode off toward Appomattox Court House to block Lee's route of retreat, the road to Lynchburg.[46]

The cavalry's position at and north of the railroad meant that it had finally passed Lee's flank, gaining the road in his front. Everyone realized he must hold this ground until the nearest infantry—troops not of Meade's command but of Major General Edward O. C. Ord's Army of the James—arrived to relieve them. On the evening of the eighth, Ord's people were several hours to the rear. The Michigan Brigade could only hope they would move faster than Lee.

Not surprisingly, despite the long hours they had devoted to the road Stagg's men remained awake throughout the night, standing to horse in columns of squadrons. Vigilance was rewarded at about four o'clock on the morning of the ninth when a line of dismounted cavalry from Fitz Lee's command moved slowly in from the east, leading the Rebel column. While Sheridan strengthened his position along the Lynchburg road, the Michiganders, still south of the thoroughfare, were on their own. At first, they enjoyed a measure of success. Lieutenant Isham of the Seventh observed that "under the steady stream of lead poured out by our Spencer carbines the advance of the enemy was checked, held for a time, and then forced slowly back." The enemy, however, did not retire. When horse artillery was sent up to support the brigade, dismounted Confederates posted on high ground rained minie balls on both troopers and cannoneers, keeping the early hours lively for everyone.[47]

Then infantry appeared in rear of the enemy horsemen, "greatly outnumbering us," wrote John Clark. He added that "our flanks were greatly exposed. But our 7 shooters kept them back for a long time until finally they were around us like a horse shoe.... We were forced to fall back, but slowly & in good order, going but a short distance at a time.... The men seemed determined to contest every foot of ground." As they retired, the Wolverines kept glancing over their shoulders, hoping for a sign that Ord's infantry had arrived. For several minutes no sign appeared; presently, Sheridan's line began to tear at the seams under pressure from the swelling mass of soldiers to the east.[48]

Shortly after nine o'clock bugles began to blow in the cavalry's rear and the hard-pressed troopers offered up thanks for the sight that met their eyes the next time they turned about: files of Union infantry, white and black, coming up from the south on the double. A brigade of United States Colored Troops began to form behind Stagg, making many of his men, heretofore skeptical of the policy, avid supporters of the government's decision to enlist freedmen and former slaves. Relieved—in more ways than one—by the new arrivals, the Wolverines and their comrades under Devin and Custer remounted and galloped toward the flanks of the infantry.

As they moved off, the Michiganders passed through a woods and into a wide clearing that looked out across the disputed road. Suddenly "Lee's whole army, deployed for action, came into view and our bugles were sounding the charge." So there was to be an attack after all—one last, violent encounter that would change the tactical situation not at all but would take the lives of many good men on the brink of peace.[49]

Shortly before the brigade could be formed into columns of attack alongside Custer's men, members of the Seventh Michigan witnessed a sight they had waited for what seemed like a lifetime to see, and feared they never would. Across the fields came a party of horsemen, an officer in front carrying a white flag. This man rode up to Lieutenant Colonel Briggs, before whom he halted. Saluting smartly, the flag-bearer announced that he bore a message from General Lee to the Union officer commanding, proposing a cessation of hostilities. The news began to spread and soon, as Captain Clark noted, "cheer upon cheer went up" along the line. Past that joyous throng rode the colonel and his staff, escorting the truce party not to Phil Sheridan nor to Wesley Merritt nor to Thomas Devin, but to the general every Wolverine still regarded, deep in his heart, as his commander—George Armstrong Custer.[50]

CHAPTER FOURTEEN

Unwilling Frontiersmen

With a tremendous lurch and a blast of steam, three passenger trains, followed by a freight train hauling cavalry horses, left Washington shortly after ten o'clock in the evening of 24 May, heading west. From the start the going was slow and by the time the trains reached Harpers Ferry, at two o'clock the following afternoon, the rusty, overage locomotives were barely moving. Each was creaking and squealing as if ready to blow a boiler at any moment.

Ordinarily, the passengers would have been put out by such poor accommodations. As a matter of fact, the several hundred soldiers crammed into the coaches were "very much disgusted" by their situation. Their disgust, however, transcended such mundane annoyances as cramped quarters and an engine on the verge of exploding. To these veterans of the Michigan Cavalry Brigade, their present conveyance was nothing less than a prison train, operated by a government they had risked their lives to preserve, time and again, over the past four years.[1]

After Lee's surrender at Appomattox Court House, the members of the brigade had logically expected, some time during the next few weeks, to be mustered out, discharged, and returned to their homes where families and occupations awaited them. That is precisely what happened to the great majority of the units in the Army of the Potomac as well as to most Union veterans in every theater of operations. Their enlistment papers had specified that each soldier would serve a certain fixed term unless sooner discharged—a clause that virtually every recruit took to mean "unless the war ended first." The war had surely ended; within days of Appomattox Confederate soldiers from Virginia to the New Mexico Territory—their armies broken up, their weapons confiscated, their paroles signed—had made their weary way home. By late May 1865 no one remained for the average Union soldier to fight. And yet the Michigan Cavalry Brigade, and select other units of the volunteer army, remained in service, very much against their will. Even worse, they were compelled to go forth against a new enemy, one most of them had no reason to hate, much less a desire to fight: the American Indian.

The decision to keep the Michigan cavalry in service beyond the close of hostilities had been made less than a week after the command came east from Appomattox and north from Petersburg. On 21 May General Grant had decreed that the four regiments under Brevet Brigadier General Peter Stagg would "proceed at once with horse equipments and arms complete to report to Maj. Gen. John Pope at Saint Louis, Mo." Whether or not the men would have appreciated it, there appeared to be a legitimate basis for Grant's action. The Regular Army garrisons on the western frontier had been denuded of troops in 1861-62, and the militia and state troops who had replaced them were too few and not professional enough to suppress the Indian uprisings that had broken out in many corners of the territory beyond the Mississippi. Until the Regulars returned in force to the forts that guarded the routes of settlement and commerce—indeed, until the Regular Army was recruited beyond its too-small pre-war strength—volunteer forces, especially highly experienced cavalrymen, were urgently needed in the Nebraska, Colorado, Utah, Dakota, and New Mexico Territories.[2]

Grant must have known the hardships his edict would occasion, but the only gesture he felt constrained to make in the Wolverines' behalf was to defer their transfer until after the twenty-third. This would permit the brigade to join thousands of other Potomac Army veterans in parading through the streets of Washington past crowds bestowing on the saviors of the Union the gratitude of the Northern people. The Grand Review of the Union Armies—which figured to be the last formal service the unsuspecting participants would be called on to perform in uniform—had been an emotional high point for the Michigan Brigade, one eclipsed only by the sight of that truce flag crossing the lines on the morning of Appomattox.

Not only had the celebration in Washington provided material for happy memories, it had marked the final time the Michiganders would parade with (though not under) their beloved Custer, who rode at the head of his Third Division. The boy general—a well-deserved second star on his shoulder straps—had riveted spectators' eyes on himself and his men even before his horse, apparently spooked by the crowd, carried him through the streets at breakneck speed until he could regain control. Even now, as they rode west—their commander left behind in Washington, soon to depart for a new assignment in Texas—Custer's veterans debated whether the flamboyant general, an expert horseman, had staged the incident for its effect on the crowd.[3]

When they boarded the waiting trains late on the twenty-fourth some of the Wolverines had supposed they were going home. Assurances to that effect had been given them earlier in the day by a visitor to their camp outside Washington, Governor Henry H. Crapo of Michigan, Austin Blair's successor. Other troopers, however, had heard ugly but credible rumors to the contrary. These men also noted that only comrades who had several months remaining on their enlistments were boarding. The freight cars waiting on the siding, crammed with the brigade's mounts, also indicated that further duty lay ahead.[4]

By the afternoon of the twenty-eighth, when the trains reached the Ohio River at Parkersburg, West Virginia, and the men saw the fleet of seven steamboats waiting to take them downriver to Guyandotte, some recruits held out the faint hope they those conveyances would turn north at some point. But when the boats carried them and their horses past Cincinnati, even the most self-delusive trooper realized he was not homeward bound.

The voyage continued across the southern extremity of Indiana, then around the tip of Illinois. Chaplain Greely of the Sixth found the weather throughout the trip "perfectly entrancing," although every day was intensely hot. Rations were few—they consisted mainly of pork, biscuits, and coffee—and the drinking water was not only "horrid" but promotive of dysentery. The chaplain's boat, which carried not only his own regiment but a part of the Fifth Cavalry as well as (below decks) the horses of both, was too crowded by half, "and there seemed to be little care on the part of the managers of the concern, whether the men had any comforts or not."[5]

At Cairo, Illinois, the steamers departed the Ohio for the muddy waters of the Mississippi, up which they churned until nosing into the docks of Saint Louis on the evening of 1 June, eight days out of Washington, D.C. This being their first landfall since reaching the Ohio, the men were more than a little eager to debark and stretch their legs. When officers tried to keep them on board, trouble began. Stagg and his regimental commanders, especially the hard-bitten Colonel Hastings of the Fifth, kept most of their people in tow, but the officers aboard the Seventh Michigan's steamer were not so successful. On the main deck Major Darling "stood guard... [and] told the boys that they could not get off." When several made a break for shore, Darling barred their path—whereupon hands laid hold of him, lifted him over the side, and deposited him in the river. By the time he floundered to dry ground, dozens of veterans were heading for the gaslights of Saint Louis, many never to be seen again.[6]

Those who could not escape ship spent their forty-eight-hour layover in Saint Louis pondering their ultimate destination. One rumor had them bound for Texas, there to sew up pockets of Confederate resistance; another would send the brigade even farther west: Fort Union, New Mexico Territory, to guard army trains. As the shipborne cavalrymen gossiped, the issue was being settled by the First Michigan's old army commander. On 2 June General Pope, who after the debacle at Second Bull Run had gone west to fight Indians and now commanded the Military Division of the Missouri, ordered General Stagg to "proceed without delay" with all of his regiments to Fort Leavenworth, Kansas, reporting there to Pope's ranking subordinate, Major General Grenville M. Dodge.[7]

The following morning the transports steamed into the mouth of the Missouri and paddled westward across the state whose entrance into the Union in 1821 had ignited a crisis that took forty years to explode. On the sixth, the 160-mile voyage from Saint Louis ended with the steamers depositing their human and equine cargo on the right bank of the Missouri twenty-some miles above its confluence with the Kansas River. At that point sat the venerable post erected to protect emigrants on the Santa Fe Trail and to provide supply for installations as far west as the Rocky Mountains.

Beyond the fort lay the city of Leavenworth, which the incurably romantic Chaplain Greely described as "the most populous, wealthy and important city west of St. Louis." Impressed by the prosperous look of local civilization, the home of the "universal Yankee," the good chaplain discerned in this budding metropolis of 20,000 the rise of "the tried and proved and redeemed Republic...."[8]

It is doubtful that Greely's enthusiasm for the local venue was shared by the enlisted men of his brigade. The veterans knew they were here only because Leavenworth was a staging base for a journey—quite possibly a one-way journey—into Indian-infested wilds. Within days of their arrival, despite the best efforts of officers to corral them, hundreds of enlisted men had gone A.W.O.L., more than 100 of them in the Seventh Michigan alone. It was not an auspicious start to a major campaign to secure the byways of westward settlement.[9]

* * *

On 9 June, ten days after leaving Washington, Colonel (soon to be Brevet Brigadier General) James Kidd arrived at the newly pitched camp of the Michigan Brigade three miles beyond Fort Leavenworth. Kept at Winchester on court-martial duty until after the close of hostilities, the commander of the Sixth Michigan had rejoined his regiment in Washington just before the Grand Review, only to fall ill as the outfit entrained for the west. His recuperation complete, he had traveled by train, riverboat, and stagecoach to overtake the brigade, whose executive officer he had become. A brevet brigadier since March, Peter Stagg clearly outranked him, removing the seniority problems that had plagued their relationship in the war's latter months.[10]

Kidd was less than enthralled by his new surroundings. He viewed the frontier that lay beyond the fort as a hideous dustbowl lacking even the rudiments of polite civilization and which harbored a multitude of threats to one's well-being, Native Americans in war paint being only one. The post itself, while historic and even important, was "simply a collection of barracks... and a depot of supplies." He could appreciate the distaste his men felt at being made to serve in such a desolate, dangerous place, and he certainly understood their resentment at being kept in service beyond what they had understood to be their effective term of enlistment.[11]

While he may have sympathized, he could not allow discontent to impair soldiering. A few days after arriving at Leavenworth, attempting to clear the air and at the same time forestall a possible mutiny, he assembled a group of veterans and made what one of them called "a short but good speech... concerning the state of things. He says we will have to stay our time out now & he said that it was orders from the war Department that we should. it dont look right but we must stand it it seems for [a] *few* months longer. then we hope they will be content to let us go home in piece [sic]...." Everything considered, Kidd's speech "has made the boys feel a good deal better & I for one feel some[what] better than at first...."[12]

Two days after Kidd made his appeal, the brigade received marching orders. Though expected, the news was unsettling to many men, especially when word came that the brigade would serve in isolated detachments rather than together at a single duty station. Unsettling in a different way was the news, which came at about the same time, that one of the regiments would not have to share the duties and hardships imposed on the others. The Fifth Michigan having a preponderance of men whose original three-year terms were nearing expiration, the government had determined that the outfit would be mustered out en masse. The discharge process—denied to only a few new recruits in the outfit—was completed in early July. A few days afterward, Colonel Hastings led the delighted men back to the steamboat landing for another excursion on the wide Missouri—this time heading north.[13]

The rest of the brigade—those members of the Sixth and Seventh with several months remaining on their service terms, and the First, with its many re-enlistees and recent recruits—prepared to make the best of their unfortunate situation. Having no choice, they went forth. On 17 June, James Kidd led the way west at the head of the main body of the Sixth, followed by a line of supply wagons carrying thirty days' rations.[14]

The provisions indicated a long campaign. In fact, Kidd's regiment had been assigned to a three-column expedition that Brigadier

General Patrick E. Connor, commanding the District of the Plains at Fort Laramie, Dakota Territory, was about to launch against warlike tribes north of the Platte River. The native of County Kerry, a veteran of the Seminole and Mexican Wars who had fought in Utah against both Indians and Mormons, had begun to outfit his expedition at about the time the Michigan Brigade alighted at Fort Leavenworth. Connor's primary objective was the Powder River country in the western reaches of the vast Dakota Territory, home to Sioux, Arapahos, and Cheyennes. Each of these tribes, Connor had declared, "must be hunted like wolves" to extermination.[15]

From Fort Leavenworth Kidd led his column on a north-north-west heading toward Fort Kearny, Nebraska Territory, the army's principal presence on the Lower Platte River. Beyond lay Fort Sedgwick near Julesburg, in the northeastern corner of the Colorado Territory; and Fort Laramie, on the North Platte. Other elements of the brigade would join him at the end of the march. A week after Kidd's contingent set out, the balance of the Sixth Cavalry followed his trail in company with Stagg's First and George Briggs's Seventh Michigan.[16]

The journey left different travelers with different impressions. Kidd thought of the "barren plain" that stretched to infinity on all sides as a vast prison, while Trooper Charles P. Nash of the First Cavalry considered the territory a "delightful country" teeming with elk, antelope, bucktail deer, and grizzly bears. "Everything here," Nash concluded, "is wild, romantic, picturesque." More volatile was the reaction of Captain Rockafellow of Kidd's regiment, who, like Nash, left Leavenworth on the twenty-fourth. A few days out Rockafellow was rhapsodizing about the "splendid prairie country" he saw on every side, "the finest rolling prairie in the world." A week later his attitude had deteriorated. In place of majestic vistas and exotic animals he now saw rattlesnakes, pools of quicksand, and "nothing but prairie, prairie," a dull, static picture of the "most worthless country" ever seen.[17]

Kidd's contingent, which made an average of sixteen miles a day, reached Fort Kearny on 3 July. The following day he helped celebrate what he called "the dullest, most unenthusiastic 4th I ever saw." Unable to resist, he and his subordinates gave way to the same discontent Kidd had tried to suppress among his men: "Far away from everybody except ourselves and the few officers on duty at the Fort, with melancholy & bitter feelings we recalled the events of that day in years past and thought of the celebrations that... [others would] indulge in at the North, on the first anniversary of our independence after the downfall of the great rebellion." Perhaps after a few too many holiday libations, "many a muttered curse was heard as we ruminated in the solitude of the boundless western prairie, upon the fickleness of *justice*.... there was and is a bitter feeling among us against the authors of this wild goose chase," the latter a thinly veiled reference to General Connor's offensive.[18]

At six A.M. on 7 July, one day before Stagg's and Briggs's detachments reached Fort Kearny, Kidd's column started along the south bank of the Platte, heading for Julesburg. Throughout this leg of the journey the column was "blinded by dust and choked with thirst" as it struggled across the desolate plain, camping at night by "dirty little burgs of 'Adobe' huts" and reduced to buffalo chips to fuel their fires.[19]

Upon reaching Julesburg, Kidd found a telegram from General Connor, urging him to expedite his travel to Fort Laramie. In response, the brevet brigadier and his second-in-command, Major Storrs (Lieutenant Colonel Vinton was on sick leave) spent a brief layover at Fort Sedgwick before pushing on for Connor's headquarters, 200 miles away. Their outfit reached Laramie, within striking distance of the Powder River country, on 25 July—thirty-eight body-wracking, mind-numbing days out of Fort Leavenworth. Upon his arrival, Kidd found himself installed as commander of Connor's Left Expeditionary Column, to be composed not only of Kidd's regiment but other volunteer units that had been held to service after Appomattox.[20]

The other Michigan regiments would not join the Sixth. In late July, while the second column lay over at Julesburg, Connor called General Stagg to Fort Laramie and made him a sub-district commander. A detachment of Stagg's First Cavalry would later join him along the North Platte, but most of it, along with Briggs's Seventh Michigan, would report to Camp Collins on the South Platte near Laporte, Colorado, a garrison that safeguarded local settlers and

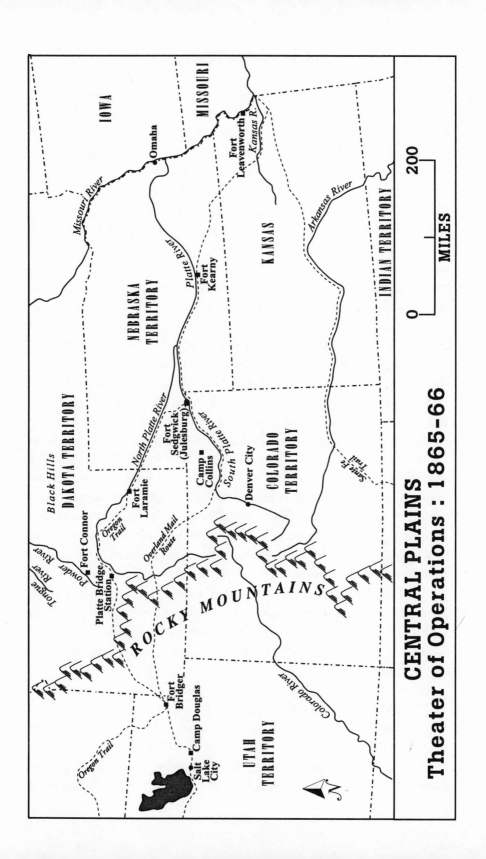

CENTRAL PLAINS
Theater of Operations : 1865-66

MILES

0   200

travelers on the Oregon Trail. By the end of July both regiments had ranged west of Collins to guard the overland mail and stage route from Julesburg to Denver City. Later, detachments of the Seventh would be sent through the Rockies to Sulphur Spring Station, Dakota Territory, fully 250 miles beyond Camp Collins.[21]

By not marching to Fort Laramie, the Seventh and most of the First Michigan escaped service on the Powder River Expedition. James Kidd was not so fortunate, although his participation was short-lived. The campaign was to begin soon after the main body of the Sixth reached Connor's headquarters. When they arrived, however, the commanding general found their members in a truculent mood. "Much dissatisfaction exists in [the] Sixth Michigan," he informed General Dodge. Already Connor had put down a mutiny in the First Nebraska Cavalry and had dealt harshly but effectively with a Kansas regiment whose men had demanded their discharge; he was confident that "I will manage" the Wolverines.[22]

Kidd came to view his superior as a "not... unpleasant man," but too strict a disciplinarian and unnecessarily heavy-handed in his dealing with volunteers who had legitimate grievances. His expressions of confidence notwithstanding, Connor never developed a smooth working relationship with the Sixth Michigan, officers or enlisted men. This fact may explain why, instead of taking the entire regiment to the Powder River, he selected only four companies to accompany him, three others to join him later but only in the role of wagon train guards. The remaining five companies of the regiment he originally dispersed to small outposts in the Dakotas, where they guarded settlers' trains and patrolled mail routes. By September, however, four of those companies were transferred to western Colorado to safeguard the military road to Salt Lake City, while Company K garrisoned Fort Laramie, designated headquarters of the regiment.[23]

On the last day of July, following weeks of planning and outfitting, the Powder River Expedition got under way. Kidd left Fort Laramie, accompanied by General Connor, at the head of a column consisting of four companies of the Sixth plus detachments of two other regiments of volunteer cavalry and a company of Pawnee Indian scouts. The long column, which would join two others descending from the Black Hills, proceeded briskly up the lower bank of the North Platte. Kidd had been versed in the work that lay ahead; as he informed his parents after the first day's march, "the Indians have been exceedingly troublesome of late and it is proposed to take vigorous measures against them." He was not, however, sanguine about the outcome: "I predict the Expedition will be a failure," not only because the horses were poor and the commanders of the satellite forces were of uncertain ability but because "this whole department has undoubtedly been mismanaged... by the Government... [in its] the belief that any sort of troops and the fewest... supplies could easily vanquish all the Indians in the Northwest."[24]

The weakest link of the expedition was its personnel—not because they were poor soldiers, but because they were volunteers "whose time is about out and who think they are near enough citizens to enjoy that prerogative that allows a civilian to do what he has a mind to...." Kidd knew that these citizen-soldiers had no heart for the mission; General Connor had compelled them to accompany him but he could not force them to take pride in their role as instruments of government retribution. Above all, the soldiers wanted to see Michigan, not western Dakota.[25]

Kidd was right to be pessimistic. While the left column experienced no major difficulties, the other wings encountered long delays that threw the expedition's timetable out of kilter. A major factor was an unexpected sleet storm that killed most of the columns' horses and left the troops easy prey to Sioux and Cheyenne ambushes. These obstacles to success doomed the whole campaign.[26]

The high point of the expedition may well have been 14 August, when Kidd laid out a military reservation, fully twelve miles square, along the east bank of the Powder River some 140 miles north of Fort Laramie. He christened the post—by order of his superior—Fort Connor. Primarily intended as a supply base for the expedition, Fort Connor would stand for less than a year before being replaced by a more permanent structure, Fort Reno, located a mile to the north on the opposite bank of the river.[27]

Connor deemed the fort's construction so critical to the success of his campaign that he left Kidd behind to supervise it. Most of the supply wagons that had accompanied the expedition remained with the colonel. For a labor force Kidd was assigned the four companies of his own regiment; later, three others were sent him from Laramie along with additional wagons. That the Sixth did not follow Connor into action further suggests the district commander failed to "manage" the disgruntled volunteers, at least to the extent of being able to rely on them in battle.[28]

Work on the stockade began the very day Kidd laid out the reservation. By early afternoon his troopers exchanged carbines for axes, which they applied to the small supply of suitable trees—eight feet tall and eight to ten inches thick—that would form the stockade.[29]

Neither Kidd nor any of his troopers was upset at being denied a role in Connor's confrontation on the Powder, which went ahead without them. Despite failing to link with his wing commanders, on the morning of 28 August the general led his main body in surprising and routing an Arapaho village on the Tongue River, a Yellowstone tributary north of the Powder River. In a five-hour battle, his troopers and their Pawnee allies destroyed 250 lodges, killed fifty inhabitants including several women and children, and confiscated more than a thousand of the tribesmen's ponies. After a mop-up operation, Connor pushed north, then doubled back to the Powder River where, early in September, he engaged several bands of hostiles. That month he was also ambushed by warriors seeking revenge for the massacre on the Tongue. These attacks cost Connor prestige as well as manpower. On the twentieth he returned to the fort that bore his name, having failed signally in his quest to "attack and kill every male Indian over twelve years of age."[30]

Especially after word got out that many of his victims had not been warriors, Connor's expedition became stigmatized as an embarrassment to the Military Division of the Missouri. Within a fortnight of his return the War Department sent him back to Utah. It would be his next-to-last assignment; Connor would be out of the army in less than a year.[31]

The Sixth Michigan was not sorry to see him go, and not only because of his treatment of volunteers. Connor had been indirectly responsible for the death of one of the regiment's most popular officers. In mid-August the general had provided a military escort from another volunteer outfit to a civilian-led wagon train traversing Arapaho country. Supposedly the travelers were seeking to open a new overland route; in reality they were bound for the gold fields of the Montana Territory. At the last minute Connor had assigned the train an extra escort of twenty men under Captain Osmer F. Cole, commander of Company G, who had risen through the wartime ranks by virtue of conspicuous service, having lost an arm in the process. Three days after the fight on Tongue River a vengeful war party attacked the goldminers' train. They surrounded Cole, who had been scouting in advance of the column; when his body was found it bore five arrows. "He was a young man of fine talents," wrote a close acquaintance, "brave, and genial in his manners, and was much lamented by the command." Equally valorous were two of Cole's men, Sergeant William Hall and Trooper Henry E. Evans, who, when the hostiles lay siege to the train, escaped to bring word of their comrades' plight to the nearest garrison. To rescue troopers and miners, the pair had been forced to cover fifty miles on foot "through a wild and to them an unknown country, swarming with hostile Indians...."[32]

* * *

Although the command was not involved in its finale, the Powder River Expedition was the largest Indian-fighting operation in which the Michigan Cavalry Brigade participated during its frontier service. While other units saw action against hostiles, most of these occasions were limited, localized encounters. On 12 August a detachment of the First Michigan—which included a few veterans of the Fifth Cavalry not mustered out at Fort Leavenworth—fought a band of warriors at Willow Springs in the Dakotas. By the end of that month, units of the First and Seventh Michigan stationed at Camp Collins had engaged in more than half a dozen fights with Cheyennes and Shoshonis along the mail and stage route to Denver.[33]

Despite a greater likelihood of their isolation from support, more and more detachments of the Michigan Brigade moved farther and farther west. By the fall of 1865 detachments of the First and Seventh were posted to the Utah Territory, where they guarded supply trains bound for Fort Bridger via the Overland Trail. In early November some units were sent to Camp Douglas, east of Salt Lake City, to protect the overland mail and telegraph while keeping watch over local Mormons.[34]

It is difficult to determine how many members of the Michigan Brigade became casualties of the early Indian wars. As far as can be determined, only one trooper fell into the hands of hostiles, to be tortured and killed by them. Early in August, warriors cut off a supply train near Little Laramie, not far from Camp Collins. They took prisoner a member of the escort unit, Corporal George Baker of Company B, Seventh Michigan, whom they tied to one of the captured wagons and set on fire.[35]

Baker's death, which "produced the greatest sensation and sorrow" among his colleagues, helped members of the brigade develop a perception of their enemy. A large percentage of Michiganders—like the majority of all troops who served during the Indian campaigns—considered their opponents savages beyond redemption, "a race of brutes," as one member of the Sixth put it, "nothing human about them.... they should be exterminated." Even friendly Indians were targets of disdain. Despite his liberal education and humanistic outlook, James Kidd alternately despised and pitied the Sioux, Arapahos, Cheyennes, and Shoshonis against whom he campaigned. He applied the same attitudes to the Pawnees who served with the army. Although brave and effective fighters when pitted against enemy tribes, they could be trusted only "until they catch a white man a long ways from home when they amuse themselves by scalping him and attributing the act to [the] Sioux." Kidd considered the Pawnees more backward and treacherous than some of the hostiles he had encountered. He even disparaged their attire: "They all wear the U S uniform decorated... with crow's quills, hen-feathers, corn-tails and other fantastic gee-gaws characteristic of 'ye poor Indian'."[36]

While such attitudes prevailed among the Wolverine regiments, some troopers expressed more ambivalent feelings. Though professing contempt for their social habits, these troopers considered most Native Americans to be worthy opponents. "The Indians are armed with bows & arrow & spears," Sergeant Henry Stewart of the Sixth Cavalry wrote from the Dakota Territory, "they can hit [a man] at 100 y[ar]ds with their arrows but they can not kill him very often but for 25 or 30 yds they will bother a fellow like the devil. they ride around you in circle and they will keep their arrows going about as fast as you can shoot a revolver." In battle they relied more often on intelligence than on brute strength: "They will not attack a party of men unless they are 8 or 10 to one," but they would make short work of any opponent "not cool [enough to]... make sure of every shot." With a cavalryman's eye, one of Stewart's comrades marveled at the Indians' "splendid horsemanship, so easy and graceful in all their actions." This man (and presumably others in the brigade) even expressed sympathy for the tribesmen's plight as perpetual targets of the army. The warriors, he opined, were "not... so much to blame for the present state of affairs" as were the government officials who broke treaties with impunity, the settlers and gold-seekers who trespassed on tribal lands, and the hunters who decimated the buffalo that provided the tribes with all manner of sustenance.[37]

* * *

By the time its units were being transferred to Utah, the Michigan Cavalry Brigade officially ceased to exist. As early as September 1865 the muster-out and discharge of numerous members of the First, Sixth, and Seventh Regiments had prompted General Pope to order a consolidation of the 1,216 remaining officers and men into a single regiment to be known as the First Michigan Veteran Cavalry. Under terms of the consolidation, all personnel with less than two years on their enlistments were to be immediately released from the service.[38]

Pope's subordinate, General Dodge, however, was concerned that a large-scale muster-out of brigade members would drastically deplete the garrisons in his domain. Through his efforts the consolidation was not immediately implemented (it was formally completed in late November) and those eligible to be discharged under Pope's decree were held in service until mid-December. Naturally, the men considered Dodge's action in abrogating the order of his superior an "unwarrantable and inexcusable" exercise of power. They had, however, no means of redress.[39]

By the later date set for their discharge, most of these unhappy but homeward-looking veterans, Brevet Brigadier General Kidd among them, had been returned to Fort Leavenworth, where they could readily obtain transportation to Michigan. Some were formally mustered out prior to 15 December—Kidd, by now thoroughly "sick of service," had signed his papers on 7 November—but all were held at Leavenworth in some vague active-duty status until the week before Christmas. Then and only then could they board the steamboats that would return them to the homes they had left back in 1861 and '62.[40]

Those members of the First Michigan Veteran Cavalry not eligible for "early" discharge remained on station for another three months. On 10 March 1866 these last survivors of what had once been the Michigan Cavalry Brigade of the Army of the Potomac were mustered out of service at Salt Lake City. That day, the already disgruntled veterans added yet another grievance: their separation from service had occurred so far from Michigan that the government allotment for travel home after discharge would not cover the cost of transportation. All who wished to avail themselves of local transport had to forfeit a substantial share of their final pay to make up the difference. Officers and men alike expressed outrage at their treatment but were forced to submit to it.[41]

Months later, they were reimbursed the cost of helping to pay their own way home. It took, however, a special enactment, sponsored by the Michigan congressional delegation, to grant each veteran discharged in Utah the full two hundred, ten dollars' compensation. This was a princely sum for the time, but the gesture was justified by the service these veterans had rendered—first as members of the Union army's premier mounted brigade, then as a major instrument of postwar military policy—as well as by the callous treatment they had endured at the hands of the army they had served so well, so faithfully, and so very long.[42]

Notes

Introduction

1. James H. Kidd, *Personal Recollections of a Cavalryman with Custer's Michigan Cavalry Brigade in the Civil War* (Ionia, Mich., 1908), 363.
2. *Ibid.*, 281-83; *R1MC*, 1-5; *R5MC*, 1-5; *R6MC*, 1-12; *R7MC*, 1-8.

Chapter One

1. Kidd, *Personal Recollections*, 5-11, 15-19.

2. James M. McPherson, *Ordeal by Fire: The Civil War and Reconstruction* (New York, 1982), 156, 177, 207-11.

3. Kidd, *Personal Recollections*, 24.

4. *Ibid.*, 123-24; James H. Kidd, "Address of General James H. Kidd, at the Dedication of Michigan Monuments Upon the Battle Field of Gettysburg, June 12, 1889," *JUSCA* 4 (1891): 45; *Detroit Advertiser & Tribune*, 2, 6, 10 Sept. 1862; *Kalamazoo Gazette*, 12 Sept. 1862; Francis F. McKinney, "Michigan Cavalry in the Civil War," *Michigan Alumnus Quarterly Review* 43 (1957): 137.

5. Kidd, *Personal Recollections*, 24, 395; Ezra J. Warner, *Generals in Blue: Lives of the Union Commanders* (Baton Rouge, La., 1964), 92; Asa B. Isham, *An Historical Sketch of the Seventh Regiment Michigan Volunteer Cavalry from Its Organization, in 1862, to Its Muster Out, in 1865* (New York, 1893), 71; Asa B. Isham, *The Michigan Cavalry Brigade* [broadside] (Ionia, Mich., 1911), 1.

6. Stephen Z. Starr, *The Union Cavalry in the Civil War* (3 vols. Baton Rouge, La., 1979-84), 1: 65-68; Moses Harris, "The Union Cavalry," *War Papers: Wisconsin MOLLUS* 1 (1891): 350-51; *Report of the Secretary of War, December 1, 1861* (Washington, D.C., 1861), 4.

7. Starr, *Union Cavalry*, 1: 64; *OR*, I, 2: 315, 393; George Armstrong Custer, "War Memoirs," *Galaxy* 21 (1876): 629.

8. *New York Times*, 1 June 1861; *OR*, III, 1: 380-83.

9. McKinney, "Michigan Cavalry in the Civil War," 136.

10. *Grand Rapids Weekly Enquirer*, 7, 14 Aug. 1861; John Robertson, comp., *Michigan in the War* (Lansing, 1882), 553; Dexter Macomber diary, 21 Sept. 1861, CMUL.

11. Bert Wood, *Franklin's Yesteryear* (Ann Arbor, 1958), 90-92.

12. *Ibid.*, 92; Dexter Macomber diary, 21 Sept. 1861, CMUL; Kidd, *Personal Recollections*, 24-25; Edward M. Watson to "Dear Pen," 1 Sept. 1861, UML.

13. Minnie D. Millbrook, ed., *Twice Told Tales of Michigan and Her Soldiers in the Civil War* (Lansing, 1966), 80-81.

14. Wood, *Franklin's Yesteryear*, 92.

15. *Ibid.*; Order #1, HQ, 1st Mich. Cav., 24 Aug. 1861, RG-94, NA.

16. Frederic Schmalzried to "Dear friend," 11 Sept. 1861, UML; Wood, *Franklin's Yesteryear*, 92.

17. Order #5, HQ, 1st Mich. Cav., 24 Aug. 1861, RG-94, NA; Smith H. Hastings, "The Cavalry Service, and Recollections of the Late War," *Magazine of Western History* 11 (1890): 261.

18. Frederic Schmalzried to "Dear friends," 10, 11 Sept. 1861, UML.

19. Edward M. Watson to "Dear Pen," 1 Sept. 1861, UML.

20. Order #7, HQ, 1st Mich. Cav., 5 Sept. 1861, RG-94, NA; *Monroe Commer-*

cial, 7 Sept. 1861; *Battle Creek Journal*, 13 Sept. 1861; *Grand Rapids Weekly Enquirer*, 28 Aug., 11 Sept. 1861; *Kalamazoo Gazette*, 20 Sept. 1861.

21. Robertson, *Michigan in the War*, 553; Wood, *Franklin's Yesteryear*, 92.

22. *Detroit Free Press*, 10 Mar. 1864.

23. Elizabeth D. Leonard, *Yankee Women: Gender Battles in the Civil War* (New York, 1994), 174-75; Frank Moore, *Women of the War: Their Heroism and Self-Sacrifice* (Hartford, 1867), 109; Mary Livermore, *My Story of the War: A Woman's Narrative...* (Hartford, 1889), 116, 119.

24. Moore, *Women of the War*, 110.

25. *Ibid.*, 112; Leonard, *Yankee Women*, 175.

26. Wood, *Franklin's Yesteryear*, 93.

27. *Ibid.*; Dexter Macomber memoirs, 1, CMUL; Frederic Schmalzried to "Dear brother and friends," n.d. [Sept. 1861], UML; to his brother, — Sept. 1861, *ibid.*

28. Robertson, *Michigan in the War*, 554.

29. *Wolverine Citizen* (Flint), 12 Oct. 1861; Dexter Macomber diary, 18 Oct. 1861, CMUL; Thornton F. Brodhead to his mother, 8 Oct. 1861, DPL; Wood, *Franklin's Yesteryear*, 93.

30. *Jackson Citizen*, 28 Nov. 1861.

31. *Ibid.*; Thornton F. Brodhead to his mother, 8 Oct. 1861, DPL.

32. *Jackson Citizen*, 28 Nov. 1861; William S. Arnold to "Dear Mother & Brother," 24 Oct. 1861, MSUL.

33. Dexter Macomber diary, 28, 29 Oct. 1861, CMUL; Thornton F. Brodhead to his mother, 8 Oct. 1861, DPL; Frederic Schmalzried to "Dear brother, sister and friends," 27 Nov. 1861, UML.

34. Order #47, HQ, 1st Mich. Cav., 7 Oct. 1861, RG-94, NA; *R1MC*, 14.

35. Earl J. Coates and Dean S. Thomas, *An Introduction to Civil War Small Arms* (Gettysburg, Pa., 1990), 38, 93; Winthrop S. G. Allen to W. A. Tunnell, 17 Sept. 1862, Illinois State Historical Lib.

36. Dexter Macomber diary, 20 Nov. 1861, CMUL; Frederic Schmalzried to "Dear brother, sister and friends," 27 Nov. 1861, UML.

37. *Ibid.*

38. Wood, *Franklin's Yesteryear*, 93.

39. *Kalamazoo Gazette*, 27 Dec. 1861.

40. Wood, *Franklin's Yesteryear*, 94-95.

41. *Ibid.*, 94.

42. Fred Harvey Harrington, *Fighting Politician: Major General N. P. Banks* (Philadelphia, 1948), 59, 65, 229n.; *Kalamazoo Gazette*, 27 Dec. 1861.

43. Wood, *Franklin's Yesteryear*, 95.

Chapter Two

1. Robert M. Utley, *Cavalier in Buckskin: George Armstrong Custer and the Western Military Frontier* (Norman, Okla., 1988), 13-15; Jeffry D. Wert, *Custer: The Controversial Life of George Armstrong Custer* (New York, 1996), 23-45; James Harrison Wilson, *Under the Old Flag: Recollections of Military Operations in the War for the Union...* (2 vols. New York, 1912), 1: 101-02.

2. Wert, *Custer*, 26-38; Paul Andrew Hutton, ed., *The Custer Reader* (Lincoln, Neb., 1992), 8-9, 33-45; Tully McCrea, *"Dear Belle": Letters from a Cadet & Officer to His Sweetheart, 1858-1865*, ed. by Catherine S. Crary (Middletown, Conn., 1965), 42-43, 107, 214-15.

3. George B. Sanford, *Fighting Rebels and Redskins: Experiences in Army Life of Colonel George B. Sanford, 1861-1892*, ed. by E. R. Hagemann (Norman, Okla., 1969), 226, 316-17; *Detroit Advertiser & Tribune*, 11 Feb. 1864; Bruce Catton, *Mr. Lincoln's Army* (Garden City, N.Y., 1962), 42.

4. Wert, *Custer*, 45-46.

5. Frederic Schmalzried to "Dear friends, Brother and sister," 22 Dec. 1861, UML.

6. *Ibid.*; Delevan Arnold to his mother, 6 Jan. 1862, KPM.

7. Joseph H. Gillet to his sister, 14 Jan. 1862, WMUL.

8. Frederic Schmalzried to "Dear brother and sister," 29 Jan. 1862, UML.

9. *Ibid.*; Copy of telegram, 15 Nov. 1861, in CMSR of Charles H. Town, RG-94, E-519, NA; Surg. Alfred Nash to anon., 27 Jan. 1862, *ibid.*

10. Delevan Arnold to his mother, 6 Jan. 1862, KPM.

11. Delevan Arnold to his mother, 7 Feb. 1862, *ibid.*

12. *Ibid.*; Arthur Edwards, "Those Who Fought Without Guns," *Military Essays and Recollections: Illinois MOLLUS* 1 (1891): 443.

13. Harrington, *Fighting Politician*, 66; Robert G. Tanner, *Stonewall in the Valley: Thomas J. "Stonewall" Jackson's Shenandoah Valley Campaign, Spring 1862* (Garden City, N.Y., 1976), 44, 100-01.

14. Delevan Arnold to his sister, 19 Feb., 3 Mar. 1862, KPM; George K. Johnson, *The Battle of Kernstown, March 23, 1862...* (Detroit, 1890), 3-4.

15. Robertson, *Michigan in the War*, 554; *RIMC*, 12; *OR*, I, 5: 511-12, 733; 12, pt. 3: 136.

16. *Ibid.*, I, 5: 512-16; 12, pt. 1: 410-12, 499-502; pt. 3: 135-36; *Jackson Citizen*, 16 Apr. 1862.

17. Robertson, *Michigan in the War*, 554; "The Opposing Forces in the Valley Campaigns," *B&L* 2: 299.

18. Delevan Arnold to his sister, 3 Mar. 1862, KPM.

19. *Ibid.*; George H. Kilborn to Reuben MacArthur, 9 Mar. 1862, UML; Robertson, *Michigan in the War*, 554.

20. George H. Kilborn to Reuben MacArthur, 9 Mar. 1862, UML; Delevan Arnold to his sister, 3 Mar. 1862, KPM.

21. *Ibid.*; Robertson, *Michigan in the War*, 554.

22. *Ibid.*; George H. Kilborn to Reuben MacArthur, 9 Mar. 1862, UML; Nathan Kimball, "Fighting Jackson at Kernstown," *B&L* 2: 302; *OR*, I, 5: 739-40, 743.

23. Robertson, *Michigan in the War*, 554-55; *OR*, I, 5: 746-47.

24. Harrington, *Fighting Politician*, 229n.; Kimball, "Fighting Jackson at Kernstown," 302; Tanner, *Stonewall in the Valley*, 107.

25. *Ibid.*, 107-17; *OR*, I, 12, pt. 1: 355-56; George H. Kilborn to "Dear Sir," 16 Mar. 1862, UML.

26. *Ibid.*; *OR*, I, 12, pt. 3: 5.

27. *Ibid.*, pt. 1: 355; Tanner, *Stonewall in the Valley*, 118.

28. *OR*, I, 12, pt. 1: 355-56; Johnson, *Battle of Kernstown*, 5; *Mecosta County Pioneer* (Big Rapids), 17 Apr. 1862.

29. *OR*, I, 12, pt. 1: 356.

30. *Ibid.*, 378, 594; pt. 3: 7; Kimball, "Fighting Jackson at Kernstown," 303-04; Tanner, *Stonewall in the Valley*, 117-18.

31. *Ibid.*, 118-19; *OR*, I, 12, pt. 1: 356-57.

32. *Ibid.*, 355-57; Thornton F. Brodhead to his mother, 30 Mar. 1862, DPL; Robertson, *Michigan in the War*, 555; Johnson, *Battle of Kernstown*, 8; *Jackson Citizen*, 16 Apr. 1862; *Monroe Commercial*, 4 Sept. 1862.

33. Robertson, *Michigan in the War*, 556; Tanner, *Stonewall in the Valley*, 125-26.

Chapter Three

1. Robertson, *Michigan in the War*, 556; *OR*, I, 5: 515; 12, pt. 1: 349, 355; Thornton F. Brodhead to his mother, 30 Mar. 1862, DPL; Delevan Arnold to his mother, 3 Apr. 1862, KPM.

2. Robertson, *Michigan in the War*, 558.

3. *OR*, I, 12, pt. 1: 336-37.

4. *Ibid.*, 11, pt. 3: 46; Thornton F. Brodhead to his mother, 3 Apr. 1862, DPL.

5. *OR*, I, 11, pt. 3: 36; Robertson, *Michigan in the War*, 558.

6. *Ibid.*, 558-59.

7. *Ibid.*, 559; Tanner, *Stonewall in the Valley*, 140-44.

8. *Ibid.*, 144; Kimball, "Fighting Jackson at Kernstown," 308; *OR*, I, 12, pt. 1: 418-19; Starr, *Union Cavalry* 1: 279-80.

9. Tanner, *Stonewall in the Valley*, 145-46, 156, 160, 163; *OR*, I, 12, pt. 3: 99; Kimball, "Fighting Jackson at Kernstown," 308-09.

10. *OR*, I, 12, pt. 1: 448; Robertson, *Michigan in the War*, 559.

11. *OR*, I, 12, pt. 3: 121-22; Harrington, *Fighting Politician*, 67; Tanner, *Stonewall in the Valley*, 160-61.

12. *OR*, I, 12, pt. 3: 124-25, 134; Kimball, "Fighting Jackson at Kernstown,"

310; Stephen W. Sears, *To the Gates of Richmond: The Peninsula Campaign* (New York, 1992), 102-03.

13. Harrington, *Fighting Politician*, 68-69; Kimball, "Fighting Jackson at Kernstown," 310; *OR*, I, 12, pt. 3: 122-23, 126, 129, 132.

14. Harrington, *Fighting Politician*, 69; *OR*, I, 12, pt. 1: 554-56; Delevan Arnold to his mother, 9 May 1862, KPM.

15. *Ibid.*

16. Harrington, *Fighting Politician*, 69-70; Tanner, *Stonewall in the Valley*, 169-73; John D. Imboden, "Stonewall Jackson in the Shenandoah," *B&L* 2: 286-87.

17. *Ibid.*, 288-89; *OR*, I, 12, pt. 1: 536-37, 545-46, 555-66; Delevan Arnold to his mother, 23 May 1862, KPM; Alfred G. Ryder diary, 23-24 May 1862, UML; Kimball, "Fighting Jackson at Kernstown," 289.

18. *OR*, I, 12, pt. 1: 548, 579, 594; Harrington, *Fighting Politician*, 71.

19. *OR*, I, 12, pt. 1: 579-81.

20. *Ibid.*, 548, 579.

21. *Ibid.*, 579-80; Tanner, *Stonewall in the Valley*, 222-31.

22. *OR*, I, 12, pt. 1: 596-97.

23. *Ibid.*, 580, 597; Robertson, *Michigan in the War*, 560-61.

24. *OR*, I, 12, pt. 1: 580; Harrington, *Fighting Politician*, 76-77.

25. *OR*, I, 12, pt. 1: 580, 597; Tanner, *Stonewall in the Valley*, 231-33.

26. Harrington, *Fighting Politician*, 76.

27. *Ibid.*, 77-79; Tanner, *Stonewall in the Valley*, 238-40.

28. *Ibid.*, 286-310, 326-28; Sears, *To the Gates of Richmond*, 110-12.

29. Robertson, *Michigan in the War*, 563.

30. *OR*, I, 12, pt. 2: 95-96; pt. 3: 419-20.

31. *Ibid.*, 268, 273; Delevan Arnold to his mother, 3 Apr. 1862, KPM; Alfred G. Ryder diary, 27-28 May 1862, UML.

32. *OR*, I, 12, pt. 3: 268, 273, 300.

33. *Ibid.*, 268, 300, 313; Delevan Arnold to his mother, 3 June 1862, KPM.

34. Frederic Schmalzried to "Dear brother and friends," 10 June 1862, UML; Alfred G. Ryder diary, 1-26 June, *ibid.*; Develan Arnold to his sister, 20 June 1862, KPM.

35. Delevan Arnold to his mother, 29 June 1862, *ibid.*; Alfred G. Ryder diary, 26 June 1862, UML.

36. *OR*, I, 12, pt. 3: 460; Alfred G. Ryder diary, 6-13 June 1862, UML; Dexter Macomber diary, 23 July 1862, CMUL.

37. Order #6, HQ, 1st Mich. Cav., 11 July 1862, RG-94, NA.

Chapter Four

1. *OR*, I, 12, pt. 3: 435.

2. *Ibid.*, 473-74.

3. Starr, *Union Cavalry*, 1: 288-89; Catton, *Mr. Lincoln's Army*, 32-33.

4. *Ibid.*, 49-50; *OR*, I, 12, pt. 3: 475-76.

5. *Detroit Advertiser & Tribune*, 2 Aug. 1862; *OR*, I, 12, pt. 3: 481, 484.

6. Alfred G. Ryder diary, 17 July 1862, UML; Delevan Arnold to his mother, 25 July 1862, KPM; *Detroit Advertiser & Tribune*, 2 Aug. 1862.

7. *Ibid.*, 2, 12 Aug. 1862; Delevan Arnold to his mother, 25 July 1862, KPM.

8. *Detroit Advertiser & Tribune*, 2 Aug. 1862; *Philadelphia Inquirer*, 26 July 1862.

9. *Detroit Advertiser & Tribune*, 2, 12 Aug. 1862; *OR*, I, 12, pt. 3: 481-82.

10. Catton, *Mr. Lincoln's Army*, 50; *OR*, I, 12, pt. 3: 484-86; *Philadelphia Inquirer*, 26 July 1862; *New York Times*, 6 Aug. 1862; Alfred G. Ryder diary, 23-27 July 1862, UML; Delevan Arnold to his mother, 25 July 1862; to his father, 29 July 1862, KPM.

11. *OR*, I, 12, pt. 3: 514; Edward G. Longacre, *General John Buford: A Military Biography* (Conshohocken, Pa., 1995), 83-86.

12. *OR*, I, 12, pt. 1: 158, 201; pt. 2: 25, 55, 88-89; pt. 3: 544, 548; *Proceedings of the Buford Memorial Association...* (New York, 1895), 20.

13. *OR*, I, 12, pt. 2: 180-81; Delevan Arnold to his mother, 13 Aug. 1862, KPM; Longacre, *General John Buford,* 92.

14. "The Opposing Forces at Cedar Mountain, Va.," *B&L* 2: 495; *OR*, I, 12, pt. 2: 26; Delevan Arnold to his mother, 13 Aug. 1862, KPM.

15. *Ibid.*; *Detroit Advertiser & Tribune*, 6 Sept. 1862.

16. *OR*, I, 12, pt. 2: 28, 134, 240; 51, pt. 1: 121; Samuel J. Bayard, *The Life of George Dashiell Bayard...* (New York, 1874), 229; Delevan Arnold to his mother, 13 Aug. 1862, KPM.

17. *OR*, I, 12, pt. 2: 28-29; pt. 3: 589-90; 51, pt. 1: 740.

18. Ford H. Rogers, *"Jeb" Stuart's Hat...* (Detroit, 1893), 3; *Detroit Advertiser & Tribune*, 6 Sept. 1862.

19. *OR*, I, 12, pt. 2: 725-26; Dexter Macomber diary, 10[-17] Aug. 1862, CMUL; Rogers, *"Jeb" Stuart's Hat*, 4-6; *Detroit Advertiser & Tribune*, 6 Sept. 1862; Emory M. Thomas, *Bold Dragoon: The Life of J.E.B. Stuart* (New York, 1986), 142-44.

20. *OR*, I, 12, pt. 2: 28-29, 89; pt. 3: 592, 601, 604.

21. *Ibid.*, pt. 2: 89-90, 726-27; pt. 3: 603-04, 621.

22. *Ibid.*, pt. 2: 34, 334, 552-54, 564, 642-43, 730-32; Thomas, *Bold Dragoon*, 145-50; John J. Hennessy, *Return to Bull Run: The Campaign and Battle of Second Manassas* (New York, 1993), 74-79, 92-101, 107-22.

23. *OR*, I, 12, pt. 1: 263; pt. 2: 68, 271, 277, 333-34, 352; pt. 3: 657-58, 669, 685.

24. *Ibid.*, pt. 1: 263; pt. 2: 271, 277, 350.

25. *Ibid.*, pt. 1: 144; pt. 2: 277, 335, 564.

26. *Ibid.*, 271, 277; pt. 3: 658.

27. *Ibid.*, pt. 2: 91, 335-36, 383-84; Hennessy, *Return to Bull Run*, 141-42; *Buford Memorial Association*, 21.

28. *OR*, I, 12, pt. 2: 271-72, 277, 338; pt. 3: 729-30; *Buford Memorial Association*, 21; Hennessy, *Return to Bull Run*, 233.

29. *OR*, I, 12, pt. 1: 263; pt. 2: 338; Hennessy, *Return to Bull Run*, 234; Catton, *Mr. Lincoln's Army*, 29, 43-44.

30. *Buford Memorial Association*, 21; Alfred G. Ryder diary, 29 Aug. 1862, UML.

31. Hennessy, *Return to Bull Run*, 231-361, 430; *Buford Memorial Association*, 21.

32. *OR*, I, 12, pt. 2: 272, 274, 737, 746; *New York Times*, 2 Sept. 1862.

33. *OR*, I, 12, pt. 2: 274, 746, 748; Hennessy, *Return to Bull Run*, 431; Robertson, *Michigan in the War*, 565.

34. *Ibid.*; *OR*, I, 12, pt. 2: 746, 748; *Detroit Advertiser & Tribune*, 2, 5, 6 Sept. 1862; *Philadelphia Inquirer*, 2 Sept. 1862; Dexter Macomber diary [30 Aug. 1862], CMUL.

35. *OR*, I, 12, pt. 2: 746, 748, 752; Hennessy, *Return to Bull Run*, 432-33; *New York Times*, 2 Sept. 1862; *Philadelphia Inquirer*, 2 Sept. 1862.

36. Dexter Macomber diary [30 Aug. 1862], CMUL; *Philadelphia Inquirer*, 2 Sept. 1862; *Monroe Commercial*, 4 Sept. 1862; *Detroit Advertiser & Tribune*, 5, 6 Sept. 1862.

37. Robertson, *Michigan in the War*, 565; Dexter Macomber diary [30 Aug. 1862], CMUL; Alfred G. Ryder diary, 30 Aug. 1862, UML; Frederic Schmalzried to his brother, 24 Sept. 1862, *ibid.*; *Monroe Commercial*, 9 Oct. 1862; *Detroit Advertiser & Tribune*, 6 Sept. 1862; Delevan Arnold to his mother, 3 Sept. 1862, KPM.

38. Longacre, *General John Buford*, 108-09; *Monroe Commercial*, 9 Oct. 1862.

39. Thornton F. Brodhead to "My dearest Wife," n.d. [ca. 30 Aug. 1862], DPL; E.S. Williams, ed., "Col. Thornton Broadhead's [Brodhead's] Last Letter," *Michigan Historical Collections* 9 (1886): 208-09; *Detroit Advertiser & Tribune*, 12 Sept. 1862; *Mecosta County Pioneer*, 6 Oct. 1862; *Jackson Weekly Citizen*, 17 Sept. 1862.

40. *New York Times*, 3 Sept. 1862; Catton, *Mr. Lincoln's Army*, 49-52.

41. George A. Custer to his parents, 17 Mar. 1862, U.S. Military Academy Library, West Point, N.Y.; McCrea, *"Dear Belle"*, 106-07; Wert, *Custer*, 47-48.

42. *Ibid.*, 49-50; Gregory J. W. Urwin, *Custer Victorious: The Civil War Battles of General George Armstrong Custer* (Rutherford, N.J., 1983), 46.

43. Hutton, *Custer Reader*, 10-11; *OR*, I, 11, pt. 3: 198-99; Wilson, *Under the Old Flag*, 1: 101-02; Wert, *Custer*, 50-54.

44. *Ibid.*, 54.

45. Frederic F. Van De Water, *Glory-Hunter: A Life of General Custer* (Indianapolis, 1934), 42-43; Robertson, *Michigan in the War*, 575; Wert, *Custer*, 55-57.

46. *Ibid.*, 59-60, 66-67; Urwin, *Custer Victorious*, 51.

Chapter Five

1. Kidd, *Personal Recollections*, 30-31; *Jackson Eagle*, 7 June, 23 Aug. 1862; *Monroe Commercial*, 17 July 1862; Starr, *Union Cavalry* 1: 78n.

2. *Ibid.*, 1: 65.

3. Kidd, *Personal Recollections*, 31; *Wolverine Citizen*, 24 Aug. 1861; *Battle Creek Journal*, 23 Aug. 1861; *Jackson Citizen*, 5 Sept. 1861.

4. *Detroit Advertiser & Tribune*, 10 Sept. 1862; Isham, *Seventh Michigan Cavalry*, 8-9; William O. Lee, comp., *Personal and Historical Sketches and Facial History of and by Members of the Seventh Regiment Michigan Volunteer Cavalry, 1862-1865* (Detroit, 1904), 22.

5. *Detroit Advertiser & Tribune*, 14 July, 18 Aug., 13 Sept. 1862; *Jackson Eagle*, 23 Aug. 1862; *Wolverine Citizen*, 23 Aug. 1862.

6. Joseph T. Copeland to D. C. Ritter, 9 July 1863, Simon Gratz Coll., Hist. Soc. of Penna.; Robertson, *Michigan in the War*, 567-68; *R5MC*, 1.

7. *Detroit Advertiser & Tribune*, 26, 29 Aug. 1862; *Monroe Commercial*, 21 Aug. 1862; Lee, *Seventh Michigan Cavalry*, 22-23; William H. Rockwell to his wife, 14 Sept. 1862, WMUL.

8. Kidd, *Personal Recollections*, 31-32, 35.

9. *Ibid.*, 32, 36-37; F. W. Kellogg to James H. Kidd, 28 Aug. 1862, UML.

10. Kidd, *Personal Recollections*, 37-39; James H. Kidd to his father, 28 Aug. 1862, UML; *Monroe Commercial*, 17, 24 July 1862.

11. Kidd, *Personal Recollections*, 40-43.

12. *Detroit Advertiser & Tribune*, 4, 10 Sept. 1862; *Allegan Journal*, 4 Nov. 1862; Joseph T. Copeland to D. C. Ritter, 9 July 1863, Simon Gratz Coll., Hist. Soc. of Penna.; Coates and Thomas, *Civil War Small Arms*, 48; Kidd, *Personal Recollections*, 77-78; Order #9, HQ, 5th Mich. Cav., 10 Jan. 1863, RG-94, NA.

13. Joseph T. Copeland to D. C. Ritter, 9 July 1863, Simon Gratz Coll., Hist. Soc. of Penna.; Kidd, *Personal Recollections*, 51-53.

14. *Ibid.*, 51; Ella Lonn, *Foreigners in the Union Army and Navy* (Baton Rouge, La., 1951), 229; *Grand Rapids Daily Eagle*, 14 Nov. 1865.

15. Kidd, *Personal Recollections*, 53; James H. Kidd to his father, 25 Sept. 1862, UML.

16. Order #11, HQ, 6th Mich. Cav., 1 Nov. 1862, RG-94, NA; Russell A. Alger to T. S. Bowers, 18 Sept. 1865, Simon Gratz Coll., Hist. Soc. of Penna.; Donald L. Smith, "Booneville—Where Sheridan Won His Star," *CWTI* 1 (Oct. 1962): 32-34.

17. Kidd, *Personal Recollections*, 54-55; Frank B. Woodford, *Father Abraham's Children: Michigan Episodes in the Civil War* (Detroit, 1961), 280n.-81n.

18. Kidd, *Personal Recollections*, 383; Allen Johnson and Dumas Malone, eds., *Dictionary of American Biography* (11 vols. New York, 1964), 1: 179-80; *Biographical Directory of the American Congress, 1774-1971* (Washington, D.C., 1971), 503; George A. Custer to HQ, 1st Cav. Div., 16 Sept. 1864, in ACPF of Russell A. Alger, RG-94, E-297, NA; Endorsements on Note Forwarding Papers in Case of Russell A. Alger, 18 Sept. 1864, *ibid.*; Special Order #311, Adj. Gen.'s Office, 20 Sept. 1864, *ibid.*; Russell A. Alger to Lorenzo Thomas, 8 Feb. 1866, *ibid.*

19. Kidd, *Personal Recollections*, 57-58; *R6MC*, 1-2.

20. *Ibid.*, 1; Kidd, *Personal Recollections*, 45, 50-51, 55, 146-47; *Detroit Fress Press*, 21 July 1863; *Grand Rapids Daily Eagle*, 27 July 1863.

21. Kidd, *Personal Recollections*, 49; *R6MC*, 18, 22, 138.

22. *Ibid.*, 1-2, 81.

23. Kidd, *Personal Recollections*, 59-60.

24. *Ibid.*, 60-62.

25. *Ibid.*, 56.

26. *Ibid.*, 67.

27. Regimental Descriptive Book, 5th Mich. Cav., RG-94, NA.

28. Kidd, *Personal Recollections*, 44-45.

29. *Ibid.*, 55.

30. Robertson, *Michigan in the War*, 567-69; *R1MC*, 54-55; *R5MC*, 1; William Ball to his parents, — Dec. 1862, WMUL; John E. Clark to his wife, 11 Dec. 1862, Nebr. State Hist. Soc.

31. Order #5, HQ, 5th Mich. Cav., 6 Jan. 1863, RG-94, NA; Generals' Reports of Service, War of the Rebellion, 2: 232-33, RG-94, E-160, NA; Joseph T. Copeland to D. C. Ritter, 9 July 1863, Simon Gratz Coll., Hist. Soc. of Penna.

32. Order #6, HQ, 5th Mich. Cav., 6 Jan. 1863, RG-94, NA; Lee, *Seventh Michigan Cavalry*, 23; *R5MC*, 106.

33. Robertson, *Michigan in the War*, 570; *R6MC*, 3; Kidd, *Personal Recollections*, 69-70.

34. *Ibid.*, 70-73; Samuel Harris, *Personal Reminiscences of Samuel Harris* (Chicago, 1897), 12; John E. Clark to his wife, n.d. [ca. 15 Dec. 1862], Nebr. State Hist. Soc.; William V. Stuart to "Dear Friend," 21 Dec. 1862, DPL; William H. Rockwell to his wife, 14 Jan. 1863, WMUL; Gershom W. Mattoon to his sister, 22 Jan. 1863, MSUL; *Grand Rapids Daily Eagle*, 9, 11 Feb. 1863; Woodford, *Father Abraham's Children*, 115.

35. Kidd, *Personal Recollections*, 71; William H. Rockwell to his wife, 14 Jan. 1863, WMUL; William V. Stuart to "Dear Friend," 21 Dec. 1862, DPL.

36. Isham, *Seventh Michigan Cavalry*, 7; James H. Kidd to his father, 25 Sept. 1862, UML.

37. Lee, *Seventh Michigan Cavalry*, 22-24.

38. *Ibid.*, 24-25.

39. *Ibid.*, 25.

40. *Ibid.*

41. Isham, *Seventh Michigan Cavalry*, 9.

42. *Ibid.*

43. *Ibid.*, 10; Lee, *Seventh Michigan Cavalry*, 26; *Grand Rapids Daily Eagle*, 16 Apr. 1863.

44. Isham, *Seventh Michigan Cavalry*, 10.

45. *Ibid.*, 10-11.

46. *Ibid.*, 11-12.

47. *Ibid.*, 12.

48. Order #1, HQ, 7th Mich. Cav., 19 Feb. 1863, RG-94, NA.

49. Order #2, HQ, 7th Mich. Cav., 20 Feb. 1863, *ibid.*; Isham, *Seventh Michigan Cavalry*, iv, 13; Robertson, *Michigan in the War*, 572; Edward H. Harvey to "Brother John," 28 Feb. 1863, WMUL; *R7MC*, 1.

50. Isham, *Seventh Michigan Cavalry*, 12-13.

Chapter Six

1. Dexter Macomber diary, 2, 7 Nov. 1862, CMUL; Delevan Arnold to his mother, 5 Dec. 1862, KPM.

2. Charles H. Town to "E. Barnes, Esq.," 16 Jan. 1863, HQ, 1st Mich. Cav., RG-94, NA; George H. Kilborn to Reuben MacArthur, 16 Jan. 1862, UML.

3. Robertson, *Michigan in the War*, 565-66, 566n.; Delevan Arnold to his mother, 3, 15 Sept., 26 Oct., 24 Nov. 1862, KPM.

4. Order #43, HQ, 1st Mich. Cav., 30 Oct. 1862, RG-94, NA; *R1MC*, 12, 28, 96, 174, 184.

5. *OR*, I, 25, pt. 2: 31, 60.

6. Robertson, *Michigan in the War*, 565; Dexter Macomber to his parents, 19 Dec. 1862, U.S.A. Mil. Hist. Inst.; John S. Mosby, "A Bit of Partisan Service," *B&L* 3: 148-49; Jeffry D. Wert, *Mosby's Rangers*, 39-45.

7. Dexter Macomber diary, 16-20, 30 Nov., 4, 11, 17, 21, 23, 26-27, 30-31 Dec. 1862, CMUL; Dexter Macomber to his parents, 19 Dec. 1862, U.S.A. Mil. Hist. Inst.; Develan Arnold to his mother, 5, 30 Dec. 1862, KPM.

8. *OR*, I, 21: 711, 750-51.

9. Dexter Macomber diary, 31 Jan., 13 Feb. 1863, CMUL; Frederic Schmalzried to his brother, 22 Feb. 1863, UML.

10. *OR*, I, 25, pt. 2: 100-05; Wiley Sword, "Cavalry on Trial at Kelly's Ford," *CWTI* 13 (Apr. 1974): 33.

11. *OR*, I, 25, pt. 2: 102; Robertson, *Michigan in the War*, 565; Dexter Macomber diary, 23-25 Feb., 1863, CMUL.

12. Alfred Ryder to anon., 12 Mar. 1863, UML.

13. Dexter Macomber diary, 5 Mar. 1863, CMUL.

14. Kidd, *Personal Recollections*, 73.

15. *Mecosta County Pioneer*, 15 Jan. 1863; Frank L. Klement, ed., "Edwin B. Bigelow: A Michigan Sergeant in the Civil War," *Michigan History* 38 (1954): 201.

16. John E. Clark to his wife, 18 Dec. 1862, Nebr. State Hist. Soc.; James H. Kidd to his father, 27 Dec. 1862, UML; Kidd, *Personal Recollections*, 73-76, 203-04.

17. John E. Clark to his wife, 18 Dec. 1862, Nebr. State Hist. Soc.; James H. Kidd to his father, 27 Dec. 1862.

18. Robertson, *Michigan in the War*, 568; Klement, "Edwin B. Bigelow," 201; Order #9, HQ, 5th Mich. Cav., 10 Jan. 1863, RG-94, NA; James H. Kidd to "Dear Uncle Rich," 18 Jan. 1863, UML.

19. *Grand Rapids Daily Eagle*, 9 Mar. 1863; George L. Harrington diary, 10 Feb. 1863, WMUL.

20. William Ball to his parents, 31 Jan. 1863, *ibid.*; Percival S. Leggett to his mother, 31 Jan. 1862 [1863], DPL; David M. Cooper, *Obituary Discourse on Occasion of the Death of Noah Henry Ferry...* (New York, 1863), 21.

21. *Mecosta County Pioneer*, 15 Jan. 1863; *Grand Rapids Daily Eagle*, 9 Feb. 1863.

22. *Ibid.*

23. Dexter Macomber diary, 27-29 Jan. 1862, CMUL; Alfred G. Ryder to his parents, 27 Jan. 1863, UML; William H. Rockwell to his wife, 30 Jan. 1863, WMUL; Klement, "Edwin B. Bigelow," 203.

24. William H. Rockwell to his wife, 1 Feb. 1863, WMUL; *Grand Rapids Daily Eagle*, 9, 12 Mar. 1863.

25. William H. Rockwell to his wife, 1 Feb. 1863, WMUL.

26. Cooper, *Noah Henry Ferry*, 12-13.

27. *OR*, I, 25, pt. 2: 60-61; Klement, "Edwin B. Bigelow," 205.

28. *Ibid.*; Edward Corselius to his mother, 14 Feb. 1863, UML.

29. Klement, "Edwin B. Bigelow," 205n., 208 and n.; *R5MC*, 106; *Niles Republican*, 4 Apr. 1863.

30. Kidd, *Personal Recollections*, 87; *Grand Rapids Daily Eagle*, 9, 12 Mar. 1863; Klement, "Edwin B. Bigelow," 207; *History of the Eighteenth Regiment of Cavalry, Pennsylvania Volunteers* (New York, 1909), 35.

31. Kidd, *Personal Recollections*, 87-88; James H. Kidd to his mother, 6 Mar. 1863, UML.

32. *Ibid.*; James H. Kidd to his father, 6 Mar. 1863, *ibid.*

33. Harris, *Personal Reminiscences*, 16.

34. James H. Kidd to his father, 6 Mar. 1863, UML; Kidd, *Personal Recollections*, 94-96; *Grand Rapids Daily Eagle*, 12, 24 Mar. 1863; Klement, "Edwin B. Bigelow," 207-08; William Ball to his father, 5 Mar. 1863, WMUL; Hamilton Courson to Charles Hibberd, 9 Mar. 1863, CMUL; *OR*, I, 25, pt. 1: 38-39.

35. William H. Rockwell to his wife, 7 Mar. 1863, WMUL; *OR*, I, 25, pt. 1: 39-40.

36. *Grand Rapids Daily Eagle*, 9, 24 Mar. 1863.

37. Kidd, *Personal Recollections*, 96-97; James H. Kidd to his mother, 6 Mar. 1863, UML; Mosby, "A Bit of Partisan Service," 149; Dexter Macomber diary, 8-9 Mar. 1863, CMUL; Alfred G. Ryder to "Dear Friends," 12 Mar. 1863, UML; *OR*, I, 25, pt. 2: 183 and n.

38. Dexter Macomber diary, 17 Mar. 1863, CMUL; Starr, *Union Cavalry*, 1: 345-50; Sword, "Cavalry on Trial," 35-40.

39. Kidd, *Personal Recollections*, 96; George L. Harrington diary, 11-14 Mar. 1863, WMUL; William Ball to his parents, 18 Mar. 1863, *ibid.*; Klement. "Edwin B. Bigelow," 210-11.

40. *Ibid.*, 211; *Lansing State Republican*, 8 Apr. 1863; Kidd, *Personal Recollections*, 96; Joseph T. Copeland to D. C. Ritter, 9 July 1863, Simon Gratz Coll., Hist. Soc. of Penna.

41. *R7MC*, 2; Kidd, *Personal Recollections*, 76; Isham, *Seventh Michigan Cavalry*, 13; *Grand Rapids Daily Eagle*, 9, 12 Mar. 1863; Edward H. Harvey to "Brother John," 28 Feb. 1863, WMUL; Order #6, HQ, 7th Mich. Cav., 5 Mar. 1863, RG-94, NA.

42. Isham, *Seventh Michigan Cavalry*, 13.

43. Order #4, HQ, 7th Mich. Cav., 3 Mar. 1863, RG-94, NA; Order #5, HQ, 7th Mich. Cav., 11 Mar. 1863, *ibid.*

44. Isham, *Seventh Michigan Cavalry*, 14.

45. Order #10, HQ, 7th Mich. Cav., 9 Mar. 1863, RG-94, NA; Isham, *Seventh Michigan Cavalry*, 14.

46. *Ibid.*, 15; Order #17, HQ, 7th Mich. Cav., 26 Mar. 1863, RG-94, NA; Lee, *Seventh Michigan Cavalry*, 221.

47. Isham, *Seventh Michigan Cavalry*, 15.

48. *Grand Rapids Daily Eagle*, 16 Apr. 1863; *OR*, I, 25, pt. 2: 183 and n.

49. Lee, *Seventh Michigan Cavalry*, 221; Isham, *Seventh Michigan Cavalry*, 15-17; Klement, "Edwin B. Bigelow," 211; George L. Harrington diary, 31 Mar. 1863, WMUL.

50. *OR*, I, 25, pt. 1: 80; *Lansing State Republican*, 15 Apr. 1863; Cooper, *Noah Henry Ferry*, 13.

51. Dexter Macomber diary, 11 Apr. 1863, CMUL; Order #20, HQ, 7th Mich. Cav., 15 Apr. 1863, RG-94, NA; Order #7, HQ, 1st Mich. Cav., 18 Apr. 1863, *ibid.*

52. Starr, *Union Cavalry*, 1: 351-56.

53. Dexter Macomber diary, 27-29 Apr. 1863, CMUL; Kidd, *Personal Recollections*, 99-100; *OR*, I, 25, pt. 2: 257; Gilbert W. Chapman to "Friend Jane," 27 Apr. 1863, DPL.

54. *OR*, I, 25, pt. 2: 482; Isham, *Seventh Michigan Cavalry*, 17-18; George L. Harrington diary, 8 May 1863, WMUL; Asa B. Isham, "The Story of a Gunshot Wound," *Sketches of War History: Ohio MOLLUS* 4 (1896): 429-34; Isham, *Seventh Michigan Cavalry*, 18-19; Lee, *Seventh Michigan Cavalry*, 209-10; *Detroit Advertiser & Tribune*, 3 July 1863.

55. *OR*, I, 25, pt. 1: 1117-19; Lee, *Seventh Michigan Cavalry*, 91-95; Edwin R. Havens, "How Mosby Destroyed Our Train," *Michigan History Magazine* 14 (1930): 294-98; Isham, *Seventh Michigan Cavalry*, 19.

56. Starr, *Union Cavalry*, 1: 361-62; George A. Custer to Isaac P. Christiancy, 31 May 1863, U.S.M.A. Lib.

57. Cooper, *Noah Henry Ferry*, 14.

58. Klement, "Edwin B. Bigelow," 217; Edward Corselius to his mother, 5 June 1863, UML; George W. Barbour diary, 4 June 1863, *ibid.*; Frank Moore, ed., *The Rebellion Record: A Diary of American Events* (12 vols. New York, 1861-68), 7: 2 (Diary Sect.).

59. *OR*, I, 27, pt. 2: 785; pt. 3: 64-66; Dexter Macomber diary, 6-12 June 1863, CMUL; *Detroit Advertiser & Tribune*, 8 July 1863; *Detroit Free Press*, 12, 18 June 1863; *Grand Traverse Herald*, 19 June 1863; *Mecosta County Pioneer*, 2 July 1863; *Grand Rapids Daily Eagle*, 15 Aug. 1863; Alfred G. Ryder to his mother, 24 June 1863, UML; George L. Harrington diary, 6-8 June 1863, WMUL; Wilbur S. Nye, *Here Come the Rebels!* (Baton Rouge, La., 1965), 47-48, 69.

60. Starr, *Union Cavalry*, 1: 376-95.

61. Kidd, *Personal Recollections*, 106; Edward G. Longacre, *The Cavalry at Gettysburg: A Tactical Study of Mounted Operations during the Civil War's Pivotal Campaign, 9 June-14 July 1863* (Rutherford, N.J., 1986), 90, 93, 99.

62. *Ibid.*, 99-133; Starr, *Union Cavalry*, 1: 396-413.

Chapter Seven

1. *OR*, I, 27, pt. 1: 32, 575, 910; pt. 2: 689; pt. 3: 117, 175-77, 191, 195, 208; Luther S. Trowbridge, *The Operations of the Cavalry in the Gettysburg Campaign* (Detroit, 1888), 7-8.

2. *OR*, I, 27, pt. 3: 225, 232, 244-45.

3. Kidd, *Personal Recollections*, 111-12; *Battle Creek Journal*, 24 July 1863; *Detroit Advertiser & Tribune*, 3 July 1863; Klement, "Edwin B. Bigelow," 219; James H. Kidd to his father, 28 June 1863, UML; Dexter Macomber diary, 20-21 June 1863, CMUL; John H. Faxon diary, 21-22 June 1863, UML; George W. Barbour diary, 21 June 1863, *ibid.*; George L. Harrington diary,

21 June 1863, WMUL; John R. Morey diary, 21 June 1863, UML; William H. Rockwell to his wife, 20 June 1863, WMUL; John S. Farnill to his parents, 24 June 1863, UML.

4. *OR*, I, 27, pt. 3: 269-70; Dexter Macomber diary, 22-24 June 1863, CMUL; George W. Barbour diary, 22-24 June 1863, UML; John R. Morey diary, 22-24 June 1863, *ibid.*; George L. Harrington diary, 22-24 June 1863, WMUL.

5. Kidd, *Personal Recollections*, 112; James H. Kidd to his father, 28 June 1863, UML.

6. George W. Barbour diary, 16-17 June 1863, *ibid.*

7. Kidd, *Personal Recollections*, 107; Klement, "Edwin B. Bigelow," 216; Russell A. Alger to T. S. Bowers, 18 Sept. 1865, Simon Gratz Coll., Hist. Soc. of Penna.; Russell A. Alger to Adj. Gen.'s Office, 29 May 1863, in ACPF of Alger, RG-94, E-297, NA.

8. Isham, *Seventh Michigan Cavalry*, 20; Dexter Macomber diary, 25-26 June 1863, CMUL; *Detroit Advertiser & Tribune*, 8 July 1863.

9. Kidd, *Personal Recollections*, 97.

10. *OR*, I, 27, pt. 1: 143; pt. 3: 305-08, 312-13, 337-38.

11. Kidd, *Personal Recollections*, 115; James H. Kidd to his father, 28 June 1863, UML; *Detroit Advertiser & Tribune*, 8 July 1863; *Grand Rapids Daily Eagle*, 10 July 1863; George L. Harrington diary, 26 June 1863, WMUL; John M. Morey diary, 26 June 1863, UML.

12. *Grand Rapids Daily Eagle*, 15 Aug. 1863; *Mecosta County Pioneer*, 27 Aug. 1863; Kidd, *Personal Recollections*, 115.

13. *Ibid.*, 115-16; Dexter Macomber diary, 26 June 1863, CMUL; George W. Barbour diary, 26 June 1863, UML.

14. Kidd, *Personal Recollections*, 116; Edwin B. Coddington, *The Gettysburg Campaign: A Study in Command* (New York, 1968), 209-10.

15. *OR*, I, 27, pt. 3: 322, 333-38; *Grand Rapids Daily Eagle*, 10 July 1863.

16. *OR*, I, 27, pt. 3: 350-52; Coddington, *Gettysburg Campaign*, 124.

17. *OR*, I, 27, pt. 3: 370, 377.

18. Kidd, *Personal Recollections*, 119-21; James H. Kidd to his father, 28 June 1863, UML; George W. Barbour diary, 27-28 June 1863, *ibid.*; George L. Harrington diary, 26-28 June 1863, WMUL; Klement, "Edwin B. Bigelow," 219-20; Samuel Harris, *Michigan Brigade of Cavalry at the Battle of Gettysburg...* (Chicago, 1894), 5; Salome Myers Stewart Memoirs, 2-3, Adams Co. Hist. Soc.; Jennie S. Croll Memoirs, 2, *ibid.*; *Supplement to the Official Records of the Union and Confederate Armies* (Wilmington, N.C., 1995), I, 5: 270.

19. Kidd, *Personal Recollections*, 121-22.

20. *OR*, I, 27, pt. 3: 370, 377; Walter Kempster, "The Cavalry at Gettysburg," *War Papers: Wisconsin MOLLUS* 4 (1914): 399-400; Kidd, "Dedication of Michigan Monuments," 41-46.

21. Allen Rice, "A Letter from a Young Michigan Cavalryman...," *America's Civil War* 10 (Mar. 1997): 76; Samuel Harris, *Major General George A. Custer: Stories Told Around the Camp Fire of the Michigan Brigade of Cavalry* (Chicago, 1898), 1-2; Jennie S. Croll Memoirs, 2, Adams Co. Hist. Soc.

22. *OR*, I, 27, pt. 3: 376; Robertson, *Michigan in the War*, 574; Joseph T. Copeland to D. C. Ritter, 9 July 1863, Simon Gratz Coll., Hist. Soc. of Penna.; *New York Times*, 2 July 1863; Jay Monaghan, *Custer: The Life of General George Armstrong Custer* (Boston, 1959), 133.

23. Wert, *Custer*, 66-67; Urwin, *Custer Victorious*, 51.

24. Harris, *Michigan Cavalry Brigade at Gettysburg*, 3-4; Harris, *Major General George A. Custer*, 1.

25. *OR*, I, 27, pt. 3: 98; Edward G. Longacre, "Alfred Pleasonton, 'The Knight of Romance'," *CWTI* 13 (Dec. 1974): 14-18; George Armstrong Custer and Elizabeth Bacon Custer, *The Custer Story: The Life and Intimate Letters of General George A. Custer and His Wife Elizabeth*, ed. by Marguerite Merington (New York, 1950), 58-59; Wert, *Custer*, 65-80; Longacre, *Cavalry at Gettysburg*, 165-66.

26. *OR*, I, 27, pt. 3: 376; Robertson, *Michigan in the War*, 574; Joseph T. Copeland to D. C. Ritter, 9 July 1863, Simon Gratz Coll., Hist. Soc. of Penna.

27. Robertson, *Michigan in the War*, 574-75; Joseph T. Copeland to Adj. Gen., 30 Nov., 1 Dec. 1863, in General's Papers of Copeland, RG-94, E-159, NA; *OR*, I, 27, pt. 3: 520, 656.

28. Custer, *Custer Story*, 59-61; Wert, *Custer*, 82-83; *New York Times*, 26 Oct. 1863; *OR*, I, 27, pt. 1: 1000.

29. Monaghan, *Custer*, 134-35; Kidd, *Personal Recollections*, 129; Frederick Whittaker, *A Complete Life of Gen. George A. Custer...* (New York, 1876), 169; Henry C. Meyer, *Civil War Experiences Under Bayard, Gregg, Kilpatrick, Custer...* (New York, 1911), 48-49; Theodore Lyman, *Meade's Headquarters, 1863-1865: Letters of Colonel Theodore Lyman from the Wilderness to Appomattox*, ed. by George R. Agassiz (Boston, 1922), 17.

30. Whittaker, *Life of Custer*, 170.

31. *Ibid.*, 172; Dexter Macomber diary, 28 June 1863, CMUL; Monaghan, *Custer*, 134; Hutton, *Custer Reader*, 15-16.

32. Dexter Macomber diary, 29 June 1863, CMUL; Isham, *Seventh Michigan Cavalry*, 21; *OR*, I, 27, pt. 3: 400; Robertson, *Michigan in the War*, 574; Kidd, *Personal Recollections*, 125; Daniel Stewart to "Dear Margaret," 24 July 1863, WMUL; Wert, *Custer*, 85.

33. Kidd, *Personal Recollections*, 126; Wert, *Custer*, 86; Dexter Macomber diary, 30 June 1863, CMUL.

34. Kidd, *Personal Recollections*, 126; James Moore, *Kilpatrick and Our Cavalry* (New York, 1865), 85-86.

35. Kidd, *Personal Recollections*, 126; Longacre, *Cavalry at Gettysburg*, 174-75.

36. *Ibid.*, 155-59.

37. *Supplement to OR*, I, 5: 263, 271; Wert, *Custer*, 87.

38. *Supplement to OR*, I, 5: 263, 271.

39. Kidd, *Personal Recollections*, 125-27; *OR*, I, 27, pt. 1: 999.

40. Kidd, *Personal Recollections*, 127; George W. Barbour diary, 30 June 1863, UML; *Supplement to OR*, I, 5: 263.

41. Kidd, *Personal Recollections*, 127-28; Daniel Stewart to "Dear Margaret," 24 July 1863, WMUL; *Supplement to OR*, I, 5: 264.

42. William Anthony, *History of the Battle of Hanover...* (Hanover, Pa., 1945), 6, 9; John A. Clark to "My Dear Friend," 30 July 1863, UML; *Supplement to OR*, I, 5: 257, 267, 284.

43. Anthony, *Battle of Hanover*, 9; Longacre, *Cavalry at Gettysburg*, 177.

44. Kidd, *Personal Recollections*, 128-29.

45. *OR*, I, 27, pt. 1: 999; Anthony, *Battle of Hanover*, 9, 14; *Supplement to OR*, I, 5: 264.

46. Anthony, *Battle of Hanover*, 10; Longacre, *Cavalry at Gettysburg*, 177-78.

47. Luther S. Trowbridge to his wife, 7 July 1863, UML; *Supplement to OR*, I, 5: 261, 271.

48. Dexter Macomber diary, 28 June 1863, CMUL; Kidd, *Personal Recollections*, 132-33.

49. H. C. Parsons, "Farnsworth's Charge and Death," *B&L* 3: 394; Dexter Macomber diary, 1 July 1863, CMUL; Edwin R. Havens to his brother, 6 July 1863, MSUL; Robertson, *Michigan in the War*, 576; George W. Barbour diary, 1 July 1863, UML.

50. Longacre, *Cavalry at Gettysburg*, 178-79.

51. Kidd, *Personal Recollections*, 133-34; Dexter Macomber diary, 2 July 1863, CMUL.

52. Kidd, *Personal Recollections*, 133-34; Robertson, *Michigan in the War*, 586; W. C. Storrick, "The Hunterstown Fight," 3, Gettysburg Natl. Mil. Park; T. W. Herbert, "In Occupied Pennsylvania," *Georgia Review* 4 (1950): 109.

53. T. J. Mackey, "Duel of General Wade Hampton on the Battle-Field at Gettysburg with a Federal Soldier," *Southern Historical Society Papers* 22 (1894): 125-26.

54. Wilbur S. Nye, "The Affair at Hunterstown," *CWTI* 9 (Feb. 1971): 29-30; Mackey, "Duel of Wade Hampton," 125-26.

55. Wert, *Custer*, 88-89.

56. Longacre, *Cavalry at Gettysburg*, 200-01.

57. *OR*, I, 27, pt. 1: 998-1000; Dexter Macomber diary, 2 July 1863, CMUL; Luther S. Trowbridge to his wife, 7 July 1863, UML; Robertson, *Michigan in the War*, 586; John A. Clark to "My Dear Friend," 30 July 1863, UML;

New York Times, 21 July 1863; Edwin R. Havens to his brother, 6 July 1863, MSUL; *Supplement to OR*, I, 5: 257, 264, 267.

58. George W. Barbour diary, 2 July 1863, UML; James H. Kidd to his parents, 9 July 1863, *ibid.*; Rice, "Young Michigan Cavalryman," 78.

59. Kidd, *Personal Recollections*, 134; Nye, "Affair at Hunterstown," 33; *New York Times*, 21 July 1863; *Grand Rapids Daily Eagle*, 21 July 1863; *Supplement to OR*, I, 5: 285.

60. *OR*, I, 27, pt. 2: 724; Nye, "Affair at Hunterstown," 33; Wert, *Custer*, 89; Urwin, *Custer Victorious*, 70; Whittaker, *Life of Custer*, 173-74; *New York Times*, 6 Aug. 1863; Kidd, *Personal Recollections*, 134; *Detroit Free Press*, 15 July 1863.

61. Storrick, "Hunterstown Fight," 4, Gettysburg Natl. Mil. Park; Edwin R. Havens to his brother, 6 July 1863, MSUL.

Chapter Eight

1. Longacre, *Cavalry at Gettysburg*, 203-13.

2. *Ibid.*, 222-23; Kidd, *Personal Recollections*, 135; David McMurtrie Gregg, *The Second Cavalry Division of the Army of the Potomac in the Gettysburg Campaign* (Philadelphia, 1907), 10.

3. *Ibid.*, 11; Kidd, *Personal Recollections*, 136-38; Edwin R. Havens to his brother, 6 July 1863, MSUL.

4. Longacre, *Cavalry at Gettysburg*, 210-12, 223.

5. Kidd, *Personal Recollections*, 143; Russell A. Alger to John B. Bachelder, 8 Feb. 1886, Alger Coll., UML.

6. Kidd, *Personal Recollections*, 141-42; James H. Kidd to his parents, 9 July 1863, UML; *Supplement to OR*, I, 5: 264.

7. Gregg, *Second Cavalry Division*, 11; Hampton S. Thomas, "Notes as to the Cavalry Fight on the Right Flank at Gettysburg," William Brooke Rawle Coll., Hist. Soc. of Penna.

8. William E. Miller, "The Cavalry Battle Near Gettysburg," *B&L* 3: 402-03.

9. Kidd, *Personal Recollections*, 145-47; *Supplement to OR*, I, 5: 271; Russell A. Alger to John B. Bachelder, 4 Jan. 1886, Alger Coll., UML; Vincent A. Witcher to anon., 2 Aug. 1898, *ibid.*; *Detroit Advertiser & Tribune*, 17, 18 July 1863; Luther S. Trowbridge to his wife, 7 July 1863, UML; Cooper, *Noah Henry Ferry*, 20-22.

10. Miller, "Cavalry Battle," 402-03; Longacre, *Cavalry at Gettysburg*, 228-29; Luther S. Trowbridge to his wife, 7 July 1863, UML.

11. Kidd, *Personal Recollections*, 145.

12. Gregg, *Second Cavalry Division*, 11.

13. Kidd, *Personal Recollections*, 148; Trowbridge, *Cavalry in Gettysburg Campaign*, 12-13.

Notes

14. Thomas. "Notes as to the Cavalry Fight," William Brooke Rawle Coll., Hist. Soc. of Penna.; Trowbridge, *Cavalry in Gettysburg Campaign*, 12-13.

15. William O. Lee, "Michigan Cavalry Brigade at Gettysburg," *Gateway* 3 (1904): 46.

16. Kidd, *Personal Recollections*, 148-52; Isham, *Seventh Michigan Cavalry*, 22-23; Lee, *Seventh Michigan Cavalry*, 155; Meyer, *Civil War Experiences*, 50.

17. Lee, *Seventh Michigan Cavalry*, 155; Edwin R. Havens to his brother, 6 July 1863, MSUL.

18. John A. Clark to "My Dear Friend," 30 July 1863, UML; Andrew N. Buck to "Brother & Sister," 9 July 1863, *ibid.*; Kidd, *Personal Recollections*, 149-50; Lee, *Seventh Michigan Cavalry*, 56, 155, 158; *Battle Creek Journal*, 24 July 1863.

19. Kidd, *Personal Recollections*, 151-52; *Supplement to OR*, I, 5: 272; Russell A. Alger to William Brooke Rawle, 10 Nov. 1884, Alger Coll., UML; to John B. Bachelder, 8 Feb. 1886, *ibid.*; Luther S. Trowbridge to his wife, 7 July 1863, UML; Trowbridge, *Cavalry in Gettysburg Campaign*, 13; Edwin R. Havens to his brother, 6 July 1863, MSUL.

20. Meyer, *Civil War Experiences*, 52; Kidd, *Personal Recollections*, 153-54; James H. Kidd to his parents, 9 July 1863, UML; Harris, *Major General George A. Custer*, 6.

21. *Supplement to OR*, I, 5: 272; William Brooke Rawle to John B. Bachelder, 22 May 1878, Brooke Rawle Coll., Hist. Soc. of Penna.; Hampton S. Thomas to John B. Bachelder, 1 July 1886, Bachelder Coll., N.H. Hist. Soc.

22. Miller, "Cavalry Battle," 404.

23. Dexter Macomber diary, 3 July 1863, CMUL; Kidd, *Personal Recollections*, 154-55; Edward Corselius to his mother, 4 July 1863, UML; *Supplement to OR*, I, 5: 257-58.

24. George A. Custer to his sister, 26 July 1863, U.S.M.A. Lib.

25. Thomas, "Notes as to the Cavalry Fight," William Brooke Rawle Coll., Hist. Soc. of Penna.; Russell A. Alger to John B. Bachelder, 4 Jan. 1886, Alger Coll., UML; Meyer, *Civil War Experiences*, 50-51; *History of the Third Pennsylvania Cavalry... in the American Civil War, 1861-1865* (Philadelphia, 1905), 319.

26. *OR*, I, 27, pt. 2: 725.

27. *Ibid.*, pt. 1: 957; pt. 2: 699.

28. *Ibid.*, pt. 1: 186, 958; Kidd, *Personal Recollections*, 155-56; Robertson, *Michigan in the War*, 585; Isham, *Seventh Michigan Cavalry*, 28; *Battle Creek Journal*, 24 July 1863.

29. Kidd, *Personal Recollections*, 161-65; James H. Kidd to his parents, 9 July 1863, UML.

30. Kidd, *Personal Recollections*, 165-67; James H. Kidd to his parents, 9 July

1863, UML; Luther S. Trowbridge to his wife, 7 July 1863, *ibid.*; Isham, *Seventh Michigan Cavalry*, 29-30; Dexter Macomber diary, 4 July 1863, CMUL.

31. OR, I, 27, pt. 2: 322; Longacre, *Cavalry at Gettysburg*, 247-48.

32. *Detroit Advertiser & Tribune*, 13 July 1863; *Mecosta County Pioneer*, 27 Aug. 1863.

33. *OR*, I, 27, pt. 1: 993, 998; *Supplement to OR*, I, 5: 258; Kidd, *Personal Recollections*, 168.

34. *Ibid.*; *OR*, I, 27, pt. 1: 998; *Supplement to OR*, I, 5: 258-59; Dexter Macomber diary, 4 July 1863, CMUL.

35. *OR*, I, 27, pt. 1: 994; *Supplement to OR*, I, 5: 273; *New York Times*, 21 July 1863.

36. Russell A. Alger to L. G. Estes, 12 Feb. 1897, Alger Coll., UML; to S. L. Gillespie, 27 Apr. 1899, *ibid.*; Kidd, *Personal Recollections*, 169; James H. Kidd to his parents, 9 July 1863, UML; *Supplement to OR*, I, 5: 261, 264, 273.

37. Russell A. Alger to S. L. Gillespie, 27 Apr. 1899, Alger Coll., UML; Gilbert W. Chapman to "Jenny," 29 July 1863, DPL.

38. Russell A. Alger to L. G. Estes, 12 Feb. 1897, Alger Coll., UML; L. G. Estes to Secy. of War, 11 Feb. 1897, in ACPF of Alger, RG-94, E-297, NA; Kidd, *Personal Recollections*, 171; *Supplement to OR*, I, 5: 267-68, 273.

39. *Ibid.*, 286; Isham, *Seventh Michigan Cavalry*, 30; Andrew N. Buck to "Brother & Sister," 9 July 1863, UML; Luther S. Trowbridge to his wife, 7 July 1863, *ibid.*; Gershom W. Mattoon to his sister, 16 July 1863, MSUL; William V. Stuart to "Dearest friend," 9 July 1863, DPL; Dexter Macomber diary, 5 July 1863, CMUL; Rice, "Young Michigan Cavalryman," 79.

40. William Ball to his parents, 9 July 1863, WMUL; Edwin R. Havens to his brother, 6 July 1863, MSUL; John R. Morey diary, 5 July 1863, UML; *OR*, I, 27, pt. 1: 995.

41. *Ibid.*; *Supplement to OR*, I, 5: 260; Kidd, *Personal Recollections*, 198.

42. *Ibid.*, 174-77; *OR*, I, 27, pt. 1: 995, 999; *Supplement to OR*, I, 5: 265, 287; Klement, "Edwin B. Bigelow," 222; Dexter Macomber diary, 6 July 1863, CMUL; John R. Morey diary, 6 July 1863, UML.

43. *OR*, I, 27, pt. 1: 995, 1006, 1020; *Supplement to OR*, I, 5: 274.

44. *OR*, I, 27, pt. 1: 999; *Supplement to OR*, I, 5: 261.

45. Kidd, *Personal Recollections*, 178; Dexter Macomber diary, 7 July 1863, CMUL; John R. Morey diary, 7 July 1863, UML; Luther S. Trowbridge to his wife, 7 July 1863, *ibid.*

46. S. L. Gracey, *Annals of the Sixth Pennsylvania Cavalry* (Philadelphia, 1868), 186; Longacre, *Cavalry at Gettysburg*, 260.

47. Kidd, *Personal Recollections*, 178-81; *OR*, I, 27, pt. 2: 703; *Supplement to OR*, I, 5: 265, 268; *New York Times*, 12 July 1863; *Battle Creek Journal*, 24 July 1863; Dexter Macomber diary, 8 July 1863, CMUL; John A. Clark to

"My Dear Friend," 30 July 1863, UML; Edwin R. Havens to "Dear Father, Mother & Nell," 9 July 1863, MSUL; William Ball to his parents, 9 July 1863, WMUL.

48. Kidd, *Personal Recollections*, 181; *OR*, I, 27, pt. 1: 999; *Supplement to OR*, I, 5: 262, 274; *New York Times*, 12 July 1863; Luther S. Trowbridge to his wife, 7 July 1863, UML; Edwin R. Havens to "Dear Father, Mother & Nell," 9 July 1863, MSUL; William H. Rockwell to his wife, 9 July 1863, WMUL.

49. *OR*, I, 27, pt. 2: 704; Lee, *Seventh Michigan Cavalry*, iv.

50. *Allegan Journal*, 3 Aug. 1863; *Detroit Advertiser & Tribune*, 17 July 1863.

51. Longacre, *Cavalry at Gettysburg*, 262; Andew N. Buck to "Brother & Sister," 9 July 1863, UML.

52. *Supplement to OR*, I, 5: 259; Dexter Macomber diary, 12 July 1863, CMUL.

53. Kidd, *Personal Recollections*, 181; *OR*, I, 27, pt. 1: 996, 998-1000; *Supplement to OR*, I, 5: 262; Klement, "Edwin B. Bigelow," 223; Dexter Macomber diary, 12 July 1863, CMUL; Moore, *Kilpatrick and Our Cavalry*, 107; John R. Morey diary, 12 July 1863, UML; Surg. Lucius P. Woods to anon., 13 July 1863, in CMSR of Ebenezer Gould, RG-94, E-519, NA; Surg. John P. Wilson to anon., 16 Sept. 1863, *ibid.*

54. Longacre, *Cavalry at Gettysburg*, 266-67.

55. *OR*, I, 27, pt. 1: 990, 999; *Supplement to OR*, I, 5: 262; Kidd, *Personal Recollections*, 183-84; Klement, "Edwin B. Bigelow," 223; Willard Glazier, *Three Years in the Federal Cavalry* (New York, 1870), 290; John R. Morey diary, 14 July 1863, UML.

56. *Supplement to OR*, I, 5: 265; Kidd, *Personal Recollections*, 184-85; James H. Kidd to his parents, 16 July 1863, UML.

57. Kidd, *Personal Recollections*, 185; Starr, *Union Cavalry*, 1: 459.

58. *OR*, I, 27, pt. 1: 990; pt. 2: 705; *Supplement to OR*, I, 5: 265-66; Kidd, *Personal Recollections*, 186-89; James H. Kidd to his parents, 16 July 1863, UML; John R. Morey diary, 14 July 1863, *ibid.*; John O. Casler, *Four Years in the Stonewall Brigade...* (Guthrie, Okla., 1893), 264; Moore, *Kilpatrick and Our Cavalry*, 108-09; *New York Times*, 21 July 1863.

59. Kidd, *Personal Recollections*, 188; James H. Kidd to his parents, 16 July 1863, UML; Victor E. Comte to "Dear Elise," 16 July 1863, UML; Henry Heth, *The Memoirs of Henry Heth*, ed. by James L. Morrison, Jr. (Westport, Conn., 1974), 179.

60. *OR*, I, 27, pt. 1: 998, 1000; *Supplement to OR*, I, 5: 259-60, 268; Charles H. Town to L. G. Estes, 9 Sept. 1863, CMSR of Town, RG-94, E-519, NA; Lee, *Seventh Michigan Cavalry*, 278-79; Dexter Macomber diary, 14 July 1863, CMUL; Benjamin J. Clark to "Dear Brothers & Sisters," 17 July 1863, *ibid.*; Glazier, *Three Years*, 294; John R. Morey diary, 14 July 1863, UML.

Chapter Nine

1. Andrew N. Buck to "Brother & Sister," 9 July 1863, UML; *Battle Creek Journal*, 24 July 1863; Benjamin J. Clark to "Dear Brothers & Sisters," 17 July 1863, CMUL.

2. Victor E. Comte to "Dear Elise," 16 July 1863, UML; Edwin R. Havens to "Dear Father, Mother & Nell," 9 July 1863, MSUL.

3. George A. Custer to his sister, 26 July 1863, U.S.M.A. Lib.

4. William H. Rockwell to his wife, 9 July 1863, WMUL; Edwin R. Havens to "Dear Nell," 24 July 1863, MSUL.

5. *OR*, I, 27, pt. 1: 1004; *Supplement to OR*, I, 5: 262; Klement, "Edwin B. Bigelow," 223; Dexter Macomber diary, 16 July 1863, CMUL; *Detroit Free Press*, 30 July 1863; Moore, *Kilpatrick and Our Cavalry*, 113; George A. Custer to his sister, 26 July 1863, U.S.M.A. Lib.; *Grand Rapids Daily Eagle*, 25 July 1863.

6. *OR*, I, 27, pt. 1: 1001, 1004; John R. Morey diary, 17 July 1863, UML; Klement, "Edwin B. Bigelow," 223.

7. *Ibid.*

8. *Eighteenth Pennsylvania Cavalry*, 42; John R. Morey diary, 20 July 1863, UML.

9. Longacre, *General John Buford*, 224; E. B. Long, "The Battle That Almost Was: Manassas Gap," *CWTI* 11 (Dec. 1972): 21-22.

10. Dexter Macomber diary, 21-23 July 1863, CMUL; Klement, "Edwin B. Bigelow," 224; *Detroit Free Press*, 30 July 1863; Monaghan, *Custer*, 156; John R. Morey diary, 23 July 1863, UML.

11. *Ibid.*, 24 July 1863; Dexter Macomber diary, 23-24 July 1863, CMUL; *OR*, I, 27, pt. 1: 1002, 1004; pt. 3: 753-54; *Supplement to OR*, I, 5: 263.

12. *OR*, I, 27, pt. 1: 999, 1002-04; *Supplement to OR*, I, 5: 263, 266; Dexter Macomber diary, 24 July 1863, CMUL; Edwin R. Havens to "Dear Nell," 24 July 1863, MSUL; *Detroit Free Press*, 30 July, 2 Aug. 1863; *Eighteenth Pennsylvania Cavalry*, 42.

13. *OR*, I, 27, pt. 1: 1004; pt. 3: 765-66.

14. Rice, "Young Michigan Cavalryman," 79.

15. *Ibid.*; John R. Morey diary, 23 July 1863, UML.

16. *Detroit Free Press*, 8 Aug. 1863; *OR*, I, 29, pt. 2: 38-39, 63.

17. Dexter Macomber diary, 26 July 1863, CMUL; Edward H. Harvey to "Dear friends," 11 Aug. 1863, WMUL.

18. John R. Morey diary, 1-2 Aug. 1863, UML; Gershom W. Mattoon to "Dear Brother and Sister," 5 Mar. 1864, MSUL.

19. *OR*, I, 29, pt. 2: 448; Order #401, HQ, Provost Marshal, Washington, D.C., 20 Aug. 1863, in CMSR of Henry W. Granger, RG-94, E-519, NA; H. J. Kilpatrick to E. B. Parsons, 23 Mar. 1864, *ibid.*

20. *OR*, I, 27, pt. 3: 775; John R. Morey diary, 25 July 1863, UML; Lee, *Seventh Michigan Cavalry*, 78-79; Klement, "Edwin B. Bigelow," 224.

21. *OR*, I, 27, pt. 1: 1004; pt. 3: 775-76; John R. Morey diary, 30-31 July 1863, UML.

22. *OR*, I, 27, pt. 3: 792, 830; 29, pt. 1: 78; pt. 2: 43, 61, 66-67, 74; *Grand Rapids Daily Eagle*, 17 Sept. 1863; *Detroit Free Press*, 8 Aug., 2 Sept. 1863; John E. Clark to his wife, 31 Aug. 1863, Nebr. State Hist. Soc.; Klement, "Edwin B. Bigelow," 224-26; William V. Stuart to "Dearest Friend," 22 Aug. 1863, DPL.

23. *OR*, I, 27, pt. 3: 830.

24. *Grand Rapids Daily Eagle*, 20 Aug. 1863; *Monroe Commercial*, 27 Aug. 1863.

25. *OR*, I, 29, pt. 2: 167, 169, 172, 175; Monaghan, *Custer*, 159-60; Klement, "Edwin B. Bigelow," 227-28.

26. Monaghan, *Custer*, 160.

27. *OR*, I, 29, pt. 1: 120-21, 123-24; Glazier, *Three Years*, 314.

28. *New York Times*, 15, 17 Sept. 1863; Moore, *Kilpatrick and Our Cavalry*, 124-25; Klement, "Edwin B. Bigelow," 228; Wert, *Custer*, 109; *OR*, I, 29, pt. 1: 123-28; Hampton S. Thomas, *Some Personal Reminiscences of Service in the Cavalry of the Army of the Potomac* (Philadelphia, 1889), 15; Daniel H. Powers to his parents, 17 Sept. 1863, in possession of Mr. Alva Van Dyke.

29. *Grand Rapids Daily Eagle*, 25 Sept. 1863; *OR*, I, 29, pt. 1: 126-28; Lyman, *Meade's Headquarters*, 17.

30. *Ibid.*; Surg. D. G. Aleace to anon., 13 Sept. 1863, in General's Papers of George A. Custer, RG-94, E-159, NA; Wert, *Custer*, 112-13.

31. *OR*, I, 29, pt. 1: 126, 128; Charles H. Town to E. B. Parsons, 5 Sept. 1863, in CMSR of Town, RG-94, E-519, NA; Russell A. Alger to T. S. Bowers, 18 Sept. 1865, Simon Gratz Coll., Hist. Soc. of Penna.

32. *OR*, I, 29, pt. 1: 142-43; Klement, "Edwin B. Bigelow," 228-30; Henry E. Thompson to James H. Kidd, 30 Sept. 1863, UML; *Allegan Journal*, 12 Oct. 1863; Dexter Macomber diary, 29 Sept., 1, 5 Oct. 1863.

33. *Ibid.*, 9-10 Oct. 1863; *OR*, I, 29, pt. 1: 148-95, 389; pt. 2: 268, 279-80; Wert, *Custer*, 113-14.

34. *OR*, I, 29, pt. 1: 390; Robertson, *Michigan in the War*, 588.

35. *Grand Rapids Daily Eagle*, 28 Oct. 1863.

36. *OR*, I, 29, pt. 1: 390; Kidd, *Personal Recollections*, 206-09; Moore, *Kilpatrick and Our Cavalry*, 127.

37. *OR*, I, 29, pt. 1: 390.

38. Frank A. Burr and Richard J. Hinton, *"Little Phil" and His Troopers: The Life of Gen. Philip H. Sheridan...* (Providence, R.I., 1888), 249; *OR*, I, 29, pt. 1: 390-91; Harris, *Major General George A. Custer*, 7.

39. *New York Times*, 21 Oct. 1863; *Grand Rapids Daily Eagle*, 28 Oct. 1863; Glazier, *Three Years*, 328; Custer, *Custer Story*, 66.

40. Dexter Macomber diary, 11 Oct. 1863, CMUL; Dexter Macomber memoirs, 2-3, *ibid.*

41. Wert, *Custer*, 116-17; *Allegan Journal*, 26 Oct. 1863.

42. *OR*, I, 29, pt. 1: 390-91, 394-95; Custer, *Custer Story*, 66; *New York Times*, 21 Oct. 1863; *Grand Rapids Daily Eagle*, 28 Oct. 1863; Klement, "Edwin B. Bigelow," 231; Lee, *Seventh Michigan Cavalry*, 36-38.

43. *OR*, I, 29, pt. 1: 391; Klement, "Edwin B. Bigelow," 231; Dexter Macomber diary, 14 Oct. 1863, CMUL.

44. *OR*, I, 29, pt. 1: 391; Dexter Macomber diary, 17-18 Oct. 1863, CMUL; Kidd, *Personal Recollections*, 211.

45. *OR*, I, 29, pt. 1: 391; Kidd, *Personal Recollections*, 213-20; *Detroit Free Press*, 23 Oct. 1863.

46. Kidd, *Personal Recollections*, 221-22.

47. *Ibid.*, 221-23; Meyer, *Civil War Experiences*, 68; *Detroit Free Press*, 26 Oct. 1863; *Monroe Commercial*, 29 Oct. 1863.

48. *Detroit Free Press*, 30 Oct. 1863; Meyer, *Civil War Experiences*, 66-68; Starr, *Union Cavalry*, 2: 29-30.

49. Custer, *Custer Story*, 68; *OR*, I, 29, pt. 1: 392.

50. Jay Luvaas and Wilbur S. Nye, "The Campaign That History Forgot," *CWTI* 8 (Nov. 1969): 12-14; Dexter Macomber diary, 15-17 Nov. 1863, CMUL; *OR*, I, 29, pt. 2: 462.

51. *Ibid.*, pt 1: 655; pt. 2: 471; Charles H. Town to H. E. Davies, Jr., 18 Nov. 1863, in CMSR of Melvin Brewer, RG-94, E-519, NA.

52. Luvaas and Nye, "Campaign That History Forgot," 17; Starr, *Union Cavalry*, 2: 31.

53. *OR*, I, 29, pt. 1: 812, 815-16.

54. *Ibid.*, 811-13, 816; Isham, *Seventh Michigan Cavalry*, 35; *Lansing State Republican*, 16 Dec. 1863.

55. *OR*, I, 29, pt. 1: 812-13, 816.

56. *Ibid.*, 813; Luvaas and Nye, "Campaign That History Forgot," 31-36.

Chapter Ten

1. Kidd, *Personal Recollections*, 210; James H. Kidd to L. G. Estes, 6 Dec. 1863, in CMSR of Kidd, RG-94, E-519, NA; *Lansing State Republican*, 16 Dec. 1863.

2. Dexter Macomber diary, 20-21 Dec. 1863, CMUL; Robertson, *Michigan in the War*, 594.

3. *OR*, I, 33: 471, 474 and n., 475; Dexter Macomber diary, 28 Dec. 1863, 1-9 Jan., 28 Feb., 29 Mar. 1864, CMUL; Charles H. Town to James B. Fry, 30 Oct. 1863, in CMSR of Peter Stagg, RG-94, E-519, NA; *Detroit Advertiser & Tribune*, 17, 31 Mar., 19 Apr. 1864; George E. Dennis to Augustus Pomeroy, 9 Feb. 1864, UML; *Allegan Journal*, 28 Mar. 1864 .

4. Kidd, *Personal Recollections*, 233; Thomas W. Hill diary, 14 Jan., 8, 16 Feb. 1864, WMUL; *Wolverine Citizen*, 12 Mar. 1864.

5. Isham, *Seventh Michigan Cavalry*, 38; *Detroit Advertiser & Tribune*, 7 Mar. 1864; Special Order #566, Adj. Gen.'s Office, 22 Dec. 1863, in CMSR of Russell A. Alger, RG-94, E-519, NA; Copy of 5th Mich. Cav. recruiting poster, 1 Jan. 1864, in possession of Mr. Lou Clark.

6. Surg. Charles S. Tripler to anon., 21 Dec. 1863, in CMSR of Angelo Paldi, RG-94, E-519, NA; Surg. Levi Day to anon., 16 Dec. 1863, in CMSR of Charles E. Storrs, *ibid.*; Surg. B. F. Gilman to anon., 7 Jan. 1864, *ibid.*; Surg. H. O. Weston to anon., 17 Jan. 1864, *ibid.*; George K. Newcombe to Seth Williams, 10 Aug. 1863, in CMSR of Newcombe, *ibid.*; to Edwin M. Stanton, 8 Oct. 1863, *ibid.*; Special Order #456, Adj. Gen.'s Office, 12 Oct. 1863, *ibid.*; F. W. Kellogg to Edwin M. Stanton, 12 Oct. 1863, *ibid.*; Special Order #522, Adj. Gen.'s Office, 24 Nov. 1863, in CMSR of William D. Mann, *ibid.*; H. J. Kilpatrick to C. Ross Smith, 5 Nov. 1863, *ibid.*; William D. Mann, *Colonel Mann's Infantry and Cavalry Accoutrements...* (New York, 1864), 2-15.

7. *Ibid.*, 10, 41-44; R. Stephen Dorsey, *American Military Belts and Related Equipments* (Union City, Tenn., 1984), 25-26; Isham, *Seventh Michigan Cavalry*, 36-37; Special Order #99, Adj. Gen.'s Office, 1 Mar. 1864, in CMSR of William D. Mann, RG-94, E-519, NA.

8. *OR*, I, 29, pt. 2: 448-49; Starr, *Union Cavalry*, 2: 17; *Detroit Advertiser & Tribune*, 17 Mar. 1864; Coates and Thomas, *Civil War Small Arms*, 48.

9. *Detroit Advertiser & Tribune*, 29 Apr. 1864; Kidd, *Personal Recollections*, 232-33.

10. *Allegan Journal*, 21 Mar. 1864.

11. Longacre, "'Knight of Romance'," 19-20; Kidd, *Personal Recollections*, 261-63; Sanford, *Fighting Rebels and Redskins*, 223-24; Hinton and Burr, *"Little Phil" and His Troopers*, 240-49.

12. Longacre, *General John Buford*, 243-46; Kidd, *Personal Recollections*, 261; Sanford, *Fighting Rebels and Redskins*, 224, 265; James H. Kidd, *The Michigan Cavalry Brigade in the Wilderness* (Detroit, 1890), 4.

13. *OR*, I, 33: 893, 1033; *Detroit Advertiser & Tribune*, 29 Apr. 1864; Shirley A. Leckie, *Elizabeth Bacon Custer and the Making of a Myth* (Norman, Okla., 1993), 43; Wilson, *Under the Old Flag*, 1: 361-62; Edward G. Longacre, *Grant's Cavalryman: The Life and Wars of General James H. Wilson* (Mechanicsburg, Pa., 1996), 152-57.

14. Starr, *Union Cavalry*, 2: 57-67.

15. *OR*, I, 33: 161-63, 597-600, 615-16, 628, 783; *Detroit Advertiser & Tribune*, 11 Feb., 3 Mar. 1864; *Monroe Commercial*, 11 Feb. 1864; Whittaker, *Life of General Custer*, 217; Leckie, *Elizabeth Bacon Custer*, 36-37; Wert, *Custer*, 140-42; *New York Times*, 3 Mar. 1864; James O. Moore, "Custer's Raid

into Albemarle County: The Skirmish at Rio Hill, February 29, 1864," *Virginia Magazine of History and Biography* 79 (1971): 338-48; Virgil Carrington Jones, *Eight Hours Before Richmond* (New York, 1957), 34-35, 69.

16. *Ibid.*, 41-42; Robertson, *Michigan in the War*, 593-94; Samuel Harris, *A Story of the War of the Rebellion: Why I Was Not Hung* (Chicago, ca. 1895), 8-15; Samuel Harris to the Comm. of Pensions, 27 June 1888, in possession of Mr. Lou Clark; Isham, *Seventh Michigan Cavalry*, 38-39; Lee, *Seventh Michigan Cavalry*, 28-33, 171-72, 197-215; *Detroit Advertiser & Tribune*, 7, 16, 17, 26 Mar. 1864; Albert H. Fisher to Humphrey Fisher, 30 Mar. 1864, WMUL.

17. George A. Custer to his wife, 16 Apr. 1864, Marguerite Merington Coll., N.Y. Pub. Lib.; *Detroit Free Press*, 26 Mar. 1864.

18. *Detroit Advertiser & Tribune*, 1, 2, 17 Mar. 1864.

19. Dexter Macomber diary, 1 May 1864, CMUL; Isham, *Seventh Michigan Cavalry*, 41; Special Order #55, Adj. Gen.'s Office, 4 Feb. 1864, in CMSR of Charles H. Town, RG-94, E-519, NA; Surg. Charles S. Tripler to anon., 8 Feb. 1864, *ibid.*; Charles H. Town to Surg. S. B. W. Mitchell, 12 July 1864, *ibid.*

20. *Allegan Journal*, 30 Oct. 1863; Henry E. Thompson to James E. Kidd, 30 Sept. 1863, UML; *Grand Rapids Daily Eagle*, 8 Oct. 1864; Surg. J. W. Fitzpatrick to anon., 24 Sept. 1863, in CMSR of George Gray, RG-94, E-519, NA; Special Order #546, Adj. Gen.'s Office, 9 Dec. 1863, *ibid.*; H. J. Kilpatrick to E. B. Parsons, 23 Mar. 1864, and endorsement by Alfred Pleasonton, *ibid.*

21. *Allegan Journal*, 30 Oct. 1863; *Detroit Advertiser & Tribune*, 29 Apr. 1864.

22. *OR*, I, 36, pt. 1: 815-16; Dexter Macomber diary, 4 May 1864, CMUL; Thomas W. Hill diary, 4 May 1864, WMUL; Kidd, *Personal Recollections*, 264; Kidd, *Michigan Cavalry Brigade*, 10.

23. Asa B. Isham, Henry M. Davidson, and Henry B. Furness, *Prisoners of War and Military Prisons: Personal Narratives...* (Cincinnati, 1890), 3; Isham, *Seventh Michigan Cavalry*, 41.

24. Dexter Macomber diary, 5 May 1864, CMUL; Kidd, *Personal Recollections*, 264; *OR*, I, 36, pt. 1: 816, 827; Andrew A. Humphreys, *The Virginia Campaign of '64 and '65: The Army of the Potomac and the Army of the James* (New York, 1883), 36.

25. Daniel H. Powers diary, 5 May 1864, in possession of Mr. Alva B. Van Dyke; Dexter Macomber diary, 5 May 1864, CMUL; Kidd, *Personal Recollections*, 264-65; *OR*, I, 36, pt. 1: 816; Thomas W. Hill diary, 5 May 1864, WMUL.

26. Humphreys, *Virginia Campaign*, 35-36; *OR*, I, 36, pt. 2: 427-29; Kidd, *Personal Recollections*, 264-65; Custer, *Custer Story*, 97.

27. *OR*, I, 36, pt. 1: 816, 826-27, pt. 2: 466, 469; Kidd, *Personal Recollections*,

266-69; Kidd, *Michigan Cavalry Brigade*, 11-14; Humphreys, *Virginia Campaign*, 51; *Detroit Advertiser & Tribune*, 26 May 1864; *Lansing State Republican*, 15 June 1864.

28. Kidd, *Personal Recollections*, 269-71; *OR*, I, 36, pt. 1: 816, 827.

29. Dexter Macomber diary, 6 May 1864, CMUL; *OR*, I, 36, pt. 1: 816; Kidd, *Personal Recollections*, 278.

30. *OR*, I, 36, pt. 1: 816-17; pt. 2: 467, 470; Kidd, *Personal Recollections*, 272-78; Humphreys, *Virginia Campaign*, 52; Edward G. Longacre, "Cavalry Clash at Todd's Tavern," *CWTI* 16 (Oct. 1977): 15-16; Isham, *Seventh Michigan Cavalry*, 42-43; Isham, *et al.*, *Prisoners of War*, 10.

31. *OR*, I, 36, pt. 1: 817, 826, pt. 2: 514-16; Kidd, *Personal Recollections*, 278-84; Humphreys, *Virginia Campaign*, 52; Longacre, "Todd's Tavern," 16-18; Whittaker, *Life of General Custer*, 221.

32. Philip H. Sheridan, *Personal Memoirs of P. H. Sheridan, General, United States Army* (2 vols. New York, 1888), 1: 365-69; Longacre, "Todd's Tavern," 20-21.

33. Sheridan, *Personal Memoirs*, 1: 369-72; *OR*, I, 36, pt. 1: 817; Samuel Miller, "Yellow Tavern," *Civil War History* 2 (1956): 58-59; Isham, *Seventh Michigan Cavalry*, 43-44.

34. Louis H. Carpenter, "Sheridan's Expedition Around Richmond, May 9-25, 1864," *JUSCA* 1 (1888): 304.

35. *OR*, I, 36, pt. 1: 817, 826, 828; Kidd, *Personal Recollections*, 287-94; Dexter Macomber diary, 9 May 1864, CMUL; Daniel H. Powers diary, 9 May 1864, in possession of Mr. Alva Van Dyke; *Philadelphia Inquirer*, 18 May 1864; *Detroit Advertiser & Tribune*, 19 May 1864.

36. *OR*, I, 36, pt. 1: 817, 826; Isham, *Seventh Michigan Cavalry*, 44.

37. *OR*, I, 36, pt. 1: 817, 828; Dexter Macomber diary, 10 May 1864, CMUL; Miller, "Yellow Tavern," 70-73; Thomas, *Bold Dragoon*, 290; Kidd, *Personal Recollections*, 295-96, 300-01.

38. *Ibid.*, 296-97, 301-03; Miller, "Yellow Tavern," 73-74.

39. *OR*, I, 36, pt. 1: 817-18, 828; Kidd, *Personal Recollections*, 301-02.

40. *Ibid.*, 302-04; Dexter Macomber diary, 11 May 1864, CMUL.

41. *OR*, I, 36, pt. 1: 818; Isham, *et al.*, *Prisoners of War*, 18; Lee, *Seventh Michigan Cavalry*, 224-25.

42. *OR*, I, 36, pt. 1: 818, 826; Kidd, *Personal Recollections*, 305.

43. Isham, *Seventh Michigan Cavalry*, 44-45; Isham, *et al.*, *Prisoners of War*, 21.

44. *Ibid.*; Isham, *Seventh Michigan Cavalry*, 45-46; Lee, *Seventh Michigan Cavalry*, 125-26, 224-25; *Detroit Advertiser & Tribune*, 25 May 1864; *OR*, I, 36, pt. 1: 818.

45. *Ibid.*, 818, 828.

46. *Ibid.*, 819; Kidd, *Personal Recollections*, 305-06; Woodford, *Father Abraham's Children*, 168-70; Robertson, *Michigan in the War*, 597n.

47. Isham, *Seventh Michigan Cavalry*, 47-49; Lee, *Seventh Michigan Cavalry*, 99; *Detroit Advertiser & Tribune*, 3 June 1864; *Greenville Independent*, 7 June 1864; *Allegan Journal*, 13 June 1864; H. P. Moyer, comp., *History of the Seventeenth Regiment, Pennsylvania Volunteer Cavalry* (Lebanon, Pa., 1911), 75; *OR*, I, 36, pt. 1: 828-29.

48. *Ibid.*, 819; Sheridan, *Personal Memoirs*, 1: 380-81.

49. *Ibid.*, 384-87; *OR*, I, 36, pt. 1: 777, 819; Kidd, *Personal Recollections*, 307-10.

50. *Ibid.*, 310-12; *OR*, I, 36, pt. 1: 819, 828; Dexter Macomber diary, 12 May 1864, CMUL.

51. *OR*, I, 36, pt. 1: 819; Kidd, *Personal Recollections*, 312-13.

52. *Ibid.*, 313; *OR*, I, 36, pt. 1: 819.

Chapter Eleven

1. Kidd, *Personal Recollections*, 313-14; Sanford, *Fighting Rebels and Redskins*, 237; Dexter Macomber diary, 14 May 1864, CMUL.

2. *OR*, I, 36, pt. 1: 819; Sheridan, *Personal Memoirs*, 1: 387-88; Kidd, *Personal Recollections*, 314; Sanford, *Fighting Rebels and Redskins*, 237.

3. Custer, *Custer Story*, 97; George A. Custer to his wife, 17 May [1864], Marguerite Merington Coll., N.Y. Public Lib.; *OR*, I, 36, pt. 1: 811-15.

4. Benjamin F. Butler, *Autobiography and Personal Reminiscences of Major-General Benj. F. Butler: Butler's Book* (Boston, 1892), 653-54; Sheridan, *Personal Memoirs*, 1: 388.

5. *OR*, I, 36, pt. 1: 819, 829; pt. 3: 171; Kidd, *Personal Recollections*, 314-17; *Detroit Advertiser & Tribune*, 17 June 1864; Isham, *Seventh Michigan Cavalry*, 51-52; Dexter Macomber diary, 17-21 May 1864, CMUL; Thomas W. Hill diary, 21 May 1864, WMUL.

6. *OR*, I, 36, pt. 1: 819-20, 829; pt. 3: 82-83, 86, 98-99, 123, 171, 199-200; Dexter Macomber diary, 22-25 May 1864, CMUL; Kidd, *Personal Recollections*, 317; *Detroit Advertiser & Tribune*, 17 June 1864.

7. Sheridan, *Personal Memoirs*, 1: 394; Starr, *Union Cavalry*, 2: 116-17.

8. *Detroit Advertiser & Tribune*, 17 June 1864; Dexter Macomber diary, 26-27 May 1864; Custer, *Custer Story*, 99-100; *OR*, I, 36, pt. 1: 820.

9. *Detroit Advertiser & Tribune*, 17 June 1864; Dexter Macomber diary, 27 May 1864, CMUL; Kidd, *Personal Recollections*, 318-19; *OR*, I, 36, pt. 1: 820; Robert A. Williams, "Haw's Shop: A 'Storm of Shot and Shell'," *CWTI* 9 (Jan. 1971): 13-14.

10. Kidd, *Personal Recollections*, 319-20, 328; *OR*, I, 36, pt. 1: 820, 829; Isham, *Seventh Michigan Cavalry*, 52-53; *Detroit Advertiser & Tribune*, 17 June 1864; Surg. L. L. Morris to anon., 22 May 1864, in CMSR of Russell A. Alger, RG-94, E-519, NA; Russell A. Alger to Charles Kingsbury, Jr., 22 May 1864, *ibid.*

11. *OR*, I, 36, pt. 1: 821; *Grand Rapids Daily Eagle*, 20 June 1864; *Detroit Advertiser & Tribune*, 12 Nov. 1864; Kidd, *Personal Recollections*, 320.

12. *Detroit Advertiser & Tribune*, 10, 17 June 1864; Kidd, *Personal Recollections*, 322-24.

13. Williams, "Haw's Shop," 16-18; *Detroit Advertiser & Tribune*, 17 June 1864; Kidd, *Personal Recollections*, 325; Humphreys, *Virginia Campaign*, 164-65.

14. *OR*, I, 36, pt. 1: 821; *Philadelphia Inquirer*, 3 June 1864; *Detroit Advertiser & Tribune*, 17 June 1864; *Grand Rapids Daily Eagle*, 20 June 1864.

15. Williams, "Haw's Shop," 18; Kidd, *Personal Recollections*, 326-27.

16. *Detroit Advertiser & Tribune*, 10 June 1864; *OR*, I, 36, pt. 1: 821, 830-31.

17. *Grand Rapids Daily Eagle*, 1 July 1864, 5 Jan. 1866.

18. *OR*, I, 36, pt. 1: 821-22.

19. *Ibid.*, 822; Dexter Macomber diary, 30 May 1864, CMUL; *Detroit Advertiser & Tribune*, 17 June 1864.

20. *OR*, I, 36, pt. 1: 822; pt. 3: 411-12; Kidd, *Personal Recollections*, 330-32; Dexter Macomber diary, 31 May 1864, CMUL; *Detroit Advertiser & Tribune*, 17 June 1864.

21. *OR*, I, 36, pt. 1: 822; Sheridan, *Personal Memoirs*, 1: 402-03; Kidd, *Personal Recollections*, 332.

22. *OR*, I, 36, pt. 1: 822; Kidd, *Personal Recollections*, 333-34; Dexter Macomber diary, 1 June 1864, CMUL; Woodford, *Father Abraham's Children*, 176; *R5MC*, 75.

23. Isham, *Seventh Michigan Cavalry*, 54; Kidd, *Personal Recollections*, 335.

24. *Ibid.*, 336, 343; Isham, *Seventh Michigan Cavalry*, 50; Dexter Macomber diary, 2-5 June 1864, CMUL; *Detroit Advertiser & Tribune*, 25 June 1864; *OR*, I, 36, pt. 1: 831.

25. *Ibid.*, 823, 830; Dexter Macomber diary, 7 June 1864, CMUL; *Grand Rapids Daily Eagle*, 20 June 1864; Kidd, *Personal Recollections*, 342-43.

26. Roy Morris, Jr., "Sweltering Summer Collision," *Military History* 9 (Feb. 1993): 42-45; Edward G. Longacre, "The Long Run for Trevilian Station," *CWTI* 18 (Nov. 1979): 28-31; Sheridan, *Personal Memoirs*, 1: 413-18.

27. *OR*, I, 36, pt. 1: 823; Dexter Macomber diary, 8-10 June 1864, CMUL; Thomas W. Hill diary, 8-10 June 1864, WMUL; Kidd, *Personal Recollections*, 345; Longacre, "Long Run for Trevilian," 32-34.

28. *Ibid.*, 34; M. C. Butler, "The Cavalry Fight at Trevilian Station," *B&L* 4: 237.

29. Theophilus F. Rodenbough, "Sheridan's Trevilian Raid," *B&L* 4: 233; Kidd, *Personal Recollections*, 345-46; Sanford, *Fighting Rebels and Redskins*, 242.

30. *OR*, I, 36, pt. 1: 823, 832; Isham, *Seventh Michigan Cavalry*, 55; Lee, *Seventh Michigan Cavalry*, 53-54; *Detroit Advertiser & Tribune*, 7 July 1864; Kidd, *Personal Recollections*, 347; Morris, "Sweltering Summer Collision," 46-

47; Jay Monaghan, "Custer's 'Last Stand'—Trevilian Station, 1864," *Civil War History* 8 (1962): 249-50.

31. *OR*, I, 36, pt. 1: 823, 830; Monaghan, "Custer's 'Last Stand'," 250-51; Kidd, *Personal Recollections*, 350; *Detroit Advertiser & Tribune*, 7 July, 12 Aug. 1864; Russell A. Alger to T. S. Bowers, 18 Sept. 1865, Simon Gratz Coll., Hist. Soc. of Penna.

32. *OR*, I, 36, pt. 1: 824; Kidd, *Personal Recollections*, 351-57.

33. *OR*, I, 36, pt. 1: 823; Kidd, *Personal Recollections*, 351-55; *Detroit Advertiser & Tribune*, 7 July 1864.

34. Kidd, *Personal Recollections*, 350-51; *Detroit Advertiser & Tribune*, 7 July 1864; Morris, "Sweltering Summer Collision," 47.

35. *OR*, I, 36, pt. 1: 823-24; Dexter Macomber diary, 11 June 1864, CMUL; Monaghan, "Custer's 'Last Stand'," 252; Longacre, "Long Run for Trevilian," 36-37; Custer, *Custer Story*, 104; Isham, *Seventh Michigan Cavalry*, 58-59; Lee, *Seventh Michigan Cavalry*, 53-54, 149.

36. *Detroit Advertiser & Tribune*, 7 July 1864; *OR*, I, 36, pt. 1: 824, 832; Monaghan, Custer's 'Last Stand'," 253; Kidd, *Personal Recollections*, 360; Lee, *Seventh Michigan Cavalry*, 149, 230-31.

37. *OR*, I, 36, pt. 1: 808, 824, 855; Monaghan, "Custer's 'Last Stand'," 255; *Detroit Advertiser & Tribune*, 7 July 1864; Lee, *Seventh Michigan Cavalry*, 231.

37. Custer, *Custer Story*, 105; Lee, *Seventh Michigan Cavalry*, 231.

38. *OR*, I, 36, pt. 1: 824; Custer, *Custer Story*, 104-05; Thomas W. Hill diary, 11 June 1864, WMUL.

40. Kidd, *Personal Recollections*, 364-65; Wert, *Custer*, 165; Sheridan, *Personal Memoirs*, 1: 422-23.

41. *Ibid.*, 423-24; *OR*, I, 36, pt. 1: 824; Butler, "Cavalry Fight at Trevilian," 238.

42. *OR*, I, 36, pt. 1: 824, 831; Isham, *Seventh Michigan Cavalry*, 61-62; Monaghan, "Custer's 'Last Stand'," 256; Kidd, *Personal Recollections*, 362-63; Thomas W. Hill diary, 12 June 1864, WMUL; *Detroit Advertiser & Tribune*, 7 July 1864.

43. Butler, "Cavalry Fight at Trevilian," 238-39; Kidd, *Personal Recollections*, 362-63; *OR*, I, 36, pt. 1: 850-51.

44. Sheridan, *Personal Memoirs*, 1: 425.

45. Robertson, *Michigan in the War*, 601.

Chapter Twelve

1. Longacre, "Long Run for Trevilian," 39; Rodenbough, "Sheridan's Trevilian Raid," 235; *OR*, I, 36, pt. 1: 785.

2. Kidd, *Personal Recollections*, 364-65; *OR*, I, 36, pt. 1: 824-25.

3. *Ibid.*, 825; Thomas W. Hill diary, 12-30 June 1864, WMUL; Kidd, *Personal Recollections*, 369; Isham, *Seventh Michigan Cavalry*, 62-63.

4. Sheridan, *Personal Memoirs*, 1: 429-44; *OR*, I, 36, pt. 1: 809-10, 843-44, 855-56, 859; Starr, *Union Cavalry*, 2: 176-207.

5. Sheridan, *Personal Memoirs*, 1: 444; Custer, *Custer Story*, 110-11.

6. *OR*, I, 36, pt. 1: 825, 831; Isham, *Seventh Michigan Cavalry*, 64; Longacre, "Long Run for Trevilian," 39.

7. Kidd, *Personal Recollections*, 370; *OR*, I, 40, pt. 2: 212, 463, 467, 632.

8. Cornelia Hancock, *South After Gettysburg: Letters of Cornelia Hancock, 1863-1865*, ed. by Henrietta Stratton Jaquette (New York, 1956), 131; Leckie, *Elizabeth Bacon Custer*, 50.

9. Kidd, *Personal Recollections*, 370-71.

10. *OR*, I, 36, pt. 1: 800-01; Sheridan, *Personal Memoirs*, 1: 446-52; Isham, *Seventh Michigan Cavalry*, 64-65.

11. Sanford, *Fighting Rebels and Redskins*, 256.

12. Isham, *Seventh Michigan Cavalry*, 65; Kidd, *Personal Recollections*, 373; Sheridan, *Personal Memoirs*, 1: 457-62; *OR*, I, 37, pt. 1: 231; *Detroit Advertiser & Tribune*, 28 Sept. 1864.

13. Sheridan, *Personal Memoirs*, 1: 462-63; Wesley Merritt, "Sheridan in the Shenandoah Valley," *B&L* 4: 500-01.

14. Sanford, *Fighting Rebels and Redskins*, 256; *Lansing State Republican*, 17 Aug. 1864.

15. *OR*, I, 43, pt. 1: 421, 501; Kidd, *Personal Recollections*, 373.

16. *OR*, I, 43, pt. 1: 464, 466, 769; Isham, *Seventh Michigan Cavalry*, 65; *Detroit Advertiser & Tribune*, 28 Sept. 1864; Sanford, *Fighting Rebels and Redskins*, 257; Kidd, *Personal Recollections*, 374; *New York Times*, 18, 20 Aug. 1864; Urwin, *Custer Victorious*, 170-71.

17. Kidd, *Personal Recollections*, 374; *OR*, I, 43, pt. 1: 464.

18. *Ibid.*, 464, 466; Kidd, *Personal Recollections*, 375-76; *New York Times*, 25 Aug. 1864.

19. *Ibid.*; Kidd, *Personal Recollections*, 376.

20. Urwin, *Custer Victorious*, 174; Kidd, *Personal Recollections*, 376-77.

21. Sheridan, *Personal Memoirs*, 1: 481-85; Sanford, *Fighting Rebels and Redskins*, 258; Merritt, "Sheridan in the Shenandoah," 503.

22. *OR*, I, 43, pt. 1: 464, 466; Kidd, *Personal Recollections*, 377-79.

23. *Ibid.*, 379-80.

24. *OR*, I, 43, pt. 1: 464, 466; Kidd, *Personal Recollections*, 380-83.

25. Sheridan, *Personal Memoirs*, 2: 8-9.

26. *Ibid.*, 11-14; *OR*, I, 43, pt. 1: 454, 467.

27. *Ibid.*, 454, 464, 467; Wert, *Custer*, 180-81; Kidd, *Personal Recollections*, 385-

88; Isham, *Seventh Michigan Cavalry*, 69; Lee, *Seventh Michigan Cavalry*, 168.

28. *OR*, I, 43, pt. 1: 454-55, 464-65, 467; Kidd, *Personal Recollections*, 388-89; Starr, *Union Cavalry*, 2: 272-73.

29. *OR*, I, 43, pt. 1: 455-56.

30. *Ibid.*, 456-57, 462; Kidd, *Personal Recollections*, 390-92.

31. *OR*, I, 43, pt. 1: 457-58.

32. *Ibid.*, 458; Kidd, *Personal Recollections*, 393; J. W. DeForest, *A Volunteer's Adventures: A Union Captain's Record of the Civil War*, ed. by James H. Croushore (New Haven, 1946), 189.

33. *OR*, I, 43, pt. 1: 455, 458, 462, 465; Kidd, *Personal Recollections*, 394-95; Isham, *Seventh Michigan Cavalry*, 70-71; *Detroit Advertiser & Tribune*, 12 Nov. 1864.

34. *OR*, I, 43, pt. 1: 458.

35. Sheridan, *Personal Memoirs*, 2: 34-42.

36. *OR*, I, 43, pt. 1: 463, 465, 467; *Philadelphia Inquirer*, 27, 29 Sept. 1864; Kidd, *Personal Recollections*, 395-96; Isham, *Seventh Michigan Cavalry*, 71-72; Sanford, *Fighting Rebels and Redskins*, 271-77; *Detroit Advertiser & Tribune*, 12 Nov. 1864.

37. Sanford, *Fighting Rebels and Redskins*, 274-75; Starr, *Union Cavalry*, 2: 280-85, 293; Kidd, *Personal Recollections*, 396, 408; *OR*, I, 43, pt. 1: 459; Longacre, *Grant's Cavalryman*, 159-60.

38. Kidd, *Personal Recollections*, 236; *OR*, I, 43, pt. 1: 463; Leckie, *Elizabeth Bacon Custer*, 56-57; W. G. Cummings, "Six Months in the Third Cavalry Division Under Custer," *War Sketches and Incidents: Iowa MOLLUS* 1 (1893): 297; Starr, *Union Cavalry*, 2: 294.

39. Kidd, *Personal Recollections*, 408; James H. Kidd to his parents, 5 Dec. 1864, UML; Isham, *Seventh Michigan Cavalry*, 72; *Detroit Advertiser & Tribune*, 12 Nov. 1864; *R5MC*, 68; Surg. George S. Gale to anon., 22 July 1864, in CMSR of Ebenezer Gould, RG-94, E-519, NA; Surg. Edmund Spare to anon., 8 Sept. 1864, *ibid.*; Surg. J. B. Barnes to anon., 29 Sept. 1864, *ibid.*

40. *R5MC*, 8; Kidd, *Personal Recollections*, 383; George A. Custer to HQ, 1st Cav. Div., 16 Sept. 1864, in ACPF of Russell A. Alger, RG-94, E-297, NA; Special Order #311, Adj. Gen.'s Office, 20 Sept. 1864, *ibid.*; Russell A. Alger to Lorenzo Thomas, 8 Feb. 1866, *ibid.*

41. Endorsements by Alfred T. A. Torbert and Philip H. Sheridan to note, 18 Sept. 1864, forwarding papers in Case of Russell A. Alger, *ibid.*; Johnson and Malone, *Dictionary of American Biography* 1: 179-80; Longacre, *Grant's Cavalryman*, 251.

42. Kidd, *Personal Recollections*, 399-400; Sheridan, *Personal Memoirs*, 1: 484-85; 2: 55-56; Sanford, *Fighting Rebels and Redskins*, 283.

43. Wert, *Custer*, 190-91; Starr, *Union Cavalry*, 2: 298.

44. *OR*, I, 43, pt. 1: 460-61, 465; Kidd, *Personal Recollections*, 401-02; *Detroit Advertiser & Tribune*, 12 Nov. 1864.

45. Merritt, "Sheridan in the Shenandoah," 513-14; Starr, *Union Cavalry*, 2: 299; *Philadelphia Inquirer*, 13 Oct. 1864.

46. Merritt, "Sheridan in the Shenandoah," 514; Sheridan, *Personal Memoirs*, 2: 59-68.

47. Kidd, *Personal Recollections*, 409-13; Merritt, "Sheridan in the Shenandoah," 515-18; Starr, *Union Cavalry*, 2: 303-11.

48. Kidd, *Personal Recollections*, 413-15.

49. *Ibid.*, 415-16.

50. *Ibid.*, 416; Sanford, *Fighting Rebels and Redskins*, 288-91.

51. Kidd, *Personal Recollections*, 418-21; Lee, *Seventh Michigan Cavalry*, 180, 217; Sanford, *Fighting Rebels and Redskins*, 291.

52. Kidd, *Personal Recollections*, 421-22.

53. *Ibid.*, 422-424; Sanford, *Fighting Rebels and Redskins*, 294-95; Merritt, "Sheridan in the Shenandoah," 519-20; *Detroit Advertiser & Tribune*, 12 Nov. 1864; Cummings, "Six Months in Third Division," 301; *Wolverine Citizen*, 12 Nov. 1864; Starr, *Union Cavalry*, 2: 316-20.

54. Kidd, *Personal Recollections*, 424-25.

Chapter Thirteen

1. *OR*, I, 43, pt. 1: 461.

2. *Detroit Advertiser & Tribune*, 21 Dec. 1864; Cummings, "Six Months in Third Division," 302; *Grand Rapids Daily Eagle*, 1 Dec. 1864.

3. Isham, *Seventh Michigan Cavalry*, 75; *OR*, I, 43, pt. 2: 649-52; Sanford, *Fighting Rebels and Redskins*, 300 and n.

4. *Detroit Advertiser & Tribune*, 21 Dec. 1864; Kidd, *Personal Recollections*, 399.

5. *New York Times*, 25 Aug. 1864; *Detroit Advertiser & Tribune*, 28 Sept. 1864; Moyer, *Seventeenth Pennsylvania Cavalry*, 211.

6. *New York Times*, 25 Aug. 1864; *OR*, I, 43, pt. 1: 466.

7. Wert, *Custer*, 184-85; Monaghan, *Custer*, 220-21; Lee, *Seventh Michigan Cavalry*, 258.

8. Starr, *Union Cavalry*, 2: 347; *OR*, I, 43, pt. 2: 566.

9. Stephen W. Thompson diary, 25 Jan. 1865, CMUL; John H. Hamlin to "My Dear friend B.," 1 Dec. 1864, *ibid.*; Hiram Rix, Jr., diary, 3, 4, 10 Jan. 1865, *ibid.*

10. Stephen W. Thompson diary, 2 Jan. 1865, *ibid.*; Hiram Rix, Jr., diary, 5 Jan., 6, 18 Feb. 1865, *ibid.*; *Detroit Advertiser & Tribune*, 1 Mar. 1865.

11. Joseph H. Gillet to "Dear Brother and Sister," 13 Nov. 1864, WMUL; George E. Dennis to his parents, 23 Nov. 1864, UML; Hiram Rix, Jr., diary,

23 Jan., 20, 21 Feb. 1865, CMUL; Stephen W. Thompson diary, 20 Feb. 1865, *ibid.*; Byron Fisher to his father, 22 Feb. 1865, WMUL.

12. George A. Custer to Daniel S. Bacon, 20 Nov. 1864, Marguerite Merington Coll., N.Y. Pub. Lib.; *Detroit Advertiser & Tribune*, 1 Mar. 1865.

13. Sheridan, *Personal Memoirs*, 2: 102.

14. *Ibid.*, 102-04; Starr, *Union Cavalry*, 2: 330-42; *Detroit Advertiser & Tribune*, 17 Jan. 1865; Merritt, "Sheridan in the Shenandoah," 520-21; Lee, *Seventh Michigan Cavalry*, 258.

15. Sheridan, *Personal Memoirs*, 2: 112; Sanford, *Fighting Rebels and Redskins*, 312.

16. James H. Kidd to his parents, 5 Dec. 1864, UML; Kidd, *Personal Recollections*, 434-35; James H. Kidd to George Lee, 6 Apr. 1865, in CMSR of Kidd, RG-94, E-519, NA.

17. *OR*, I, 43, pt. 2: 668; 46, pt. 1: 475, 495; pt. 2: 763; Stephen W. Thompson diary, 27 Feb. 1865, CMUL; Hiram Rix, Jr., diary, 27 Feb. 1865, *ibid.*; Starr, *Union Cavalry*, 2: 367-69; *Wolverine Citizen*, 8 Apr. 1865.

18. Hutton, *Custer Reader*, 71.

19. *Ibid.*, 71-72; *OR*, I, 46, pt. 1: 475, 489, 495; Sheridan, *Personal Memoirs*, 2: 113; Sanford, *Fighting Rebels and Redskins*, 314-15.

20. *OR*, I, 46, pt. 1: 476; Sheridan, *Personal Memoirs*, 2: 114-16; Starr, *Union Cavalry*, 2: 371-74.

21. Isham, *Seventh Michigan Cavalry*, 77-78; *OR*, I, 46, pt. 1: 477-78, 489, 495-96; Sheridan, *Personal Memoirs*, 2: 117-18; Sanford, *Fighting Rebels and Redskins*, 317-18; *Wolverine Citizen*, 8 Apr. 1865; Hiram Rix, Jr., diary, 3 Mar. 1865, CMUL.

22. Sheridan, *Personal Memoirs*, 2: 118-19; Starr, *Union Cavalry*, 2: 380-81.

23. *Ibid.*, 382-85; *OR*, I, 46, pt. 1: 481, 496.

24. *Detroit Advertiser & Tribune*, 4 Apr. 1865.

25. *OR*, I, 46, pt. 1: 1101-02; Sheridan, *Personal Memoirs*, 2: 124-39; Starr, *Union Cavalry*, 2: 424-33; Hiram Rix, Jr., diary, 29 Mar. 1865, CMUL; Frances R. Reece, ed., "The Final Push to Appomattox: Captain [John A.] Clark's Account of the Seventh Michigan Cavalry in Action," *Michigan History Magazine* 28 (1944): 456.

26. Isham, *Seventh Michigan Cavalry*, 80; Robertson, *Michigan in the War*, 608-09; Surg. D. O. Ferrand to anon., 12 May 1865, in CMSR of Andrew W. Duggan, RG-94, E-519, NA.

27. Sheridan, *Personal Memoirs*, 2: 142-45.

28. *Ibid.*, 149-151; *OR*, I, 46, pt. 1: 1102.

29. Reece, "Final Push to Appomattox," 459; Hiram Rix, Jr., diary, 31 Mar. 1865, CMUL.

30. *Ibid.*; Frederick C. Newhall, "With Sheridan in Lee's Last Campaign," *Maine Bugle* n.s. 1 (1894): 311-12.

31. Sheridan, *Personal Memoirs*, 2: 154-58.

32. *OR*, I, 46, pt. 1: 1123-24; Robertson, *Michigan in the War*, 608; Hiram Rix, Jr., diary, 1 Apr. 1865, CMUL.

33. Hospital Record, 14 Aug. 1865, in CMSR of George R. Maxwell, RG-94, E-519, NA; Reece, "Final Push to Appomattox," 459-60.

34. Sheridan, *Personal Memoirs*, 2: 155-62; *OR*, I, 46, pt. 1: 829-38, 1104-05; Starr, *Union Cavalry*, 2: 447-48.

35. Newhall, "With Sheridan," 105; Sheridan, *Personal Memoirs*, 2: 159-70.

36. *OR*, I, 46, pt. 1: 1105; Sheridan, *Personal Memoirs*, 2: 164; Reece, "Final Push to Appomattox," 460.

37. Starr, *Union Cavalry*, 2: 450-54.

38. *OR*, I, 46, pt. 1: 1106, 1118-19, 1124-25; Hiram Rix, Jr., diary, 2 Apr. 1865, CMUL.

39. *OR*, I, 46, pt. 1: 1106, 1119; Hiram Rix, Jr., diary, 3, 4 Apr. 1865, CMUL.

40. Reece, "Final Push to Appomattox," 461; *OR*, I, 46, pt. 1: 1106-07, 1119.

41. *Ibid.*, 1107, 1119-20, 1125; Hiram Rix, Jr., diary, 5, 6 Apr. 1865, CMUL.

42. Sheridan, *Personal Memoirs*, 2: 179-82; *OR*, I, 46, pt. 1: 1107, 1120, 1125.

43. Sheridan, *Personal Memoirs*, 2: 183; *OR*, I, 46, pt. 1: 1107-08; Hiram Rix, Jr., diary, 6 Apr. 1865, CMUL; Robertson, *Michigan in the War*, 609; Reece, "Final Push to Appomattox," 462.

44. Asa B. Isham, "The Cavalry of the Army of the Potomac," *Sketches of War History, 1861-1865: Ohio MOLLUS* 5 (1903): 326; Sheridan, *Personal Memoirs*, 2: 180; Starr, *Union Cavalry*, 2: 469-72.

45. Reece, "Final Push to Appomattox," 462; Hiram Rix, Jr., diary, 7, 8 Apr. 1865, CMUL; Isham, *Seventh Michigan Cavalry*, 83.

46. *OR*, I, 46, pt. 1: 1132; Reece, "Final Push to Appomattox," 462-63; *New York Times*, 20 Apr. 1865.

47. Isham, *Seventh Michigan Cavalry*, 83-84; *OR*, I, 46, pt. 1: 1109.

48. Reece, "Final Push to Appomattox," 463; Hiram Rix, Jr., diary, 9 Apr. 1865, CMUL; Lee, *Seventh Michigan Cavalry*, 173-74.

49. Isham, *Seventh Michigan Cavalry*, 84; Lee, *Seventh Michigan Cavalry*, 264-65.

50. *Ibid.*, 40-45; Isham, *Seventh Michigan Cavalry*, 84-86; *Detroit Advertiser & Tribune*, 20 May 1865.

Chapter Fourteen

1. Franklin P. Grommon diary, 24-25 May 1865, UML; Andrew N. Buck to "Dear Friends at Home," 22 Mar. 1866, *ibid.*; Lee, *Seventh Michigan Cavalry*, 206.

2. *OR*, I, 46, pt. 3: 1190; 48, pt. 2: 526; Russell F. Weigley, *The American Way of War: A History of United States Military Strategy and Policy* (New York,

1973), 155-58; Richard N. Ellis, "Volunteer Soldiers in the West, 1865," *Military Affairs* 34 (1970): 53-54.

3. *OR*, I, 46, pt. 3: 1190-91; Otto L. Hein, *Memories of Long Ago...* (New York, 1925), 37; Victor C. Wattles to "Friend Jasper," 11 June 1865, UML; *Philadelphia Inquirer*, 24 May 1865; Monaghan, *Custer*, 249-51.

4. Lee, *Seventh Michigan Cavalry*, 285; *Grand Rapids Daily Eagle*, 19 June 1865.

5. Franklin P. Grommon diary, 27-29 May 1865, UML; Isham, *Seventh Michigan Cavalry*, 87; Lee, *Seventh Michigan Cavalry*, 190, 285; *Grand Rapids Daily Eagle*, 3, 17, 19 June 1865.

6. Victor C. Wattles to "Friend Jasper," 11 June 1865, UML.

7. *Grand Rapids Daily Eagle*, 17 June 1865; *OR*, I, 48, pt. 2: 735.

8. Lee, *Seventh Michigan Cavalry*, 285; *Grand Rapids Daily Eagle*, 19 June 1865.

9. Victor C. Wattles to "Friend Jasper," 11 June 1865, UML.

10. Franklin P. Grommon diary, 9 June 1865, *ibid.*; James H. Kidd to his father, 31 May, 12, 16 June 1865, *ibid.*; *R1MC*, 174; *R6MC*, 81.

11. James H. Kidd to his father, 21 July 1865, UML.

12. Franklin P. Grommon diary, 15 June 1865, *ibid.*

13. *Grand Rapids Daily Eagle*, 19 June 1865; *OR*, I, 48, pt. 1: 346.

14. *Ibid.*, pt. 2: 975; "Uknohoo" to "Editor, [*Grand Rapids Daily*] Eagle," 1 July 1865, HQ, 6th Mich. Cav., RG-94, NA; James H. Kidd to his parents, 16 June 1865 [two letters], UML; *Grand Rapids Daily Eagle*, 18 Aug. 1865.

15. Warner, *Generals in Blue*, 87-88; H. E. Palmer, *The Powder River Expedition, 1865...* (Omaha, 1887), 6-12; *Daily Union Vedette* (Salt Lake City, U.T.), 29 May 1865; *Salt Lake Daily Telegraph*, 21 June 1865; Ellis, "Volunteer Soldiers," 54-55; Dee Brown, *Bury My Heart at Wounded Knee: An Indian History of the American West* (New York, 1970), 104-05.

16. Lee, *Seventh Michigan Cavalry*, 285; LeRoy R. Hafen and Ann W. Hafen, eds., *Powder River Campaigns... of 1865* (Glendale, Calif., 1961), 153; Andrew N. Buck to "Dear Brother and Sister," 3 July 1865, UML.

17. James H. Kidd to his father, 21 July 1865, *ibid.*; *Grand Rapids Daily Eagle*, 5 Sept. 1865; Hafen and Hafen, *Powder River Campaigns*, 154, 157, 169.

18. James H. Kidd to his father, 21 July 1865, UML.

19. *Ibid.*; Hafen and Hafen, *Powder River Campaigns*, 159.

20. Order #47, HQ, Dist. of the Plains, 25 July 1865, Kidd Coll., UML; Order #48, HQ, Dist. of the Plains, 26 July 1865, *ibid.*; G. W. Simonds to James M. Kidd, 1 Aug. 1865, *ibid.*; *OR*, I, 48, pt. 1: 1130.

21. Order #8, HQ, Dist. of the Plains, 26 July 1865, in CMSR of Peter Stagg, RG-94, E-519, NA; *OR*, I, 48, pt. 1: 1092, 1123; Lee, *Seventh Michigan Cavalry*, 285.

22. *OR*, I, 48, pt. 1: 1122-25.

23. James H. Kidd to "Dear Kate," 4 Aug. 1865, UML; G. W. Simonds to

James M. Kidd, 1 Aug. 1865, *ibid.*; Henry W. Stewart to his father, 16 July 1865, WMUL; *Grand Rapids Daily Eagle*, 18 Sept. 1865.

24. *Montana Post* (Virginia City, M.T.), 19 Aug. 1865; James H. Kidd to his parents, 30 July 1865, UML.

25. James H. Kidd to "Dear Kate," 4 Aug. 1865, *ibid.*

26. *Daily Union Vedette*, 30 Sept. 1865; James H. Kidd to his father, 24 Oct. 1865, UML; Ellis, "Volunteer Soldiers," 54; Brown, *Bury My Heart*, 113-14; *OR*, I, 48, pt. 1: 366-87.

27. Order #1, HQ, Left Column, Powder River Exped., 15 Aug. 1865, in James H. Kidd Coll., UML; P. E. Connor to James H. Kidd, 15 Aug. 1865, *ibid.*; Robert W. Frazer, *Forts of the West: Military Forts... West of the Mississippi River to 1898* (Norman, Okla., 1965), 180-81.

28. Order #5, HQ, Powder River Exped., 15 Aug. 1865, in James H. Kidd Coll., UML; Palmer, *Powder River Expedition*, 20; Henry W. Stewart to his father, 16 July 1865, WMUL.

29. Palmer, *Powder River Expedition*, 17-18; *OR*, I, 48, pt. 1: 336.

30. Generals' Reports of Service, War of the Rebellion, 8: 601-02, RG-94, E-160, NA; *Daily Union Vedette*, 5 Sept., 24 Oct. 1865; *Montana Post*, 30 Sept., 7 Oct. 1865; Hafen and Hafen, *Powder River Campaigns*, 192-93; Henry W. Stewart to his father, 21 Sept. 1865, WMUL; Palmer, *Powder River Expedition*, 24-29; Brown, *Bury My Heart*, 105, 110-13; *OR*, I, 48, pt. 1: 383-84.

31. Generals' Reports of Service, War of the Rebellion, 8: 602, RG-94, E-160, NA; Palmer, *Powder River Expedition*, 40-41; *OR*, I, 48, pt. 1: 337, 377, 382-83; *Daily Union Vedette*, 22 Sept., 24 Oct. 1865.

32. Robertson, *Michigan in the War*, 611-12; Hafen and Hafen, *Powder River Campaigns*, 192; Henry W. Stewart to his father, 21 Sept. 1865, WMUL; Palmer, *Powder River Expedition*, 33; *R6MC*, 9, 35.

33. *R1MC*, 5; George G. Briggs to John Robertson, 31 Aug. 1865, HQ, 7th Mich. Cav., RG-94, NA.

34. Lee, *Seventh Michigan Cavalry*, 192-93; Hafen and Hafen, *Powder River Campaigns*, 201-02; Order #178, HQ, 1st Mich. Cav., 16 Nov. 1865, RG-94, NA; *Daily Union Vedette*, 25 Nov., 12 Dec. 1865; Peter Stagg to G. F. Price, 1 Feb. 1865 [1866], in CMSR of Stagg, RG-94, E-519, NA.

35. Lee, *Seventh Michigan Cavalry*, 192; *Montana Post*, 23 Sept. 1865; Hafen and Hafen, *Powder River Campaigns*, 183; *R7MC*, 14.

36. Lee, *Seventh Michigan Cavalry*, 192; *Grand Rapids Daily Eagle*, 5 Sept. 1865; James H. Kidd to "Dear Kate," 4 Aug. 1865, UML.

37. Henry W. Stewart to his father, 16 July 1865, WMUL; "Uknohoo" to "Editor [*Grand Rapids Daily*] Eagle," 22 Aug. 1865, HQ, 6th Mich. Cav., RG-94, NA.

38. James H. Kidd to his father, 6 Sept. 1865, UML; Robertson, *Michigan in the War*, 612.

39. *Ibid.*; Hafen and Hafen, *Powder River Campaigns*, 202.

40. Henry W. Stewart to his father, 15 Nov. 1865, WMUL; James H. Kidd to his father, 24 Oct. 1865, UML; *R6MC*, 81; Isham, *Seventh Michigan Cavalry*, 87.

41. *Ibid.*; Robertson, *Michigan in the War*, 612; Andrew N. Buck to "Dear Friends at Home," 22 Mar. 1866, UML.

42. Robertson, *Michigan in the War*, 613.

Bibliography

Unpublished Materials

Manuscripts—General Officers, Michigan Cavalry Brigade

Copeland, Joseph T. Letter of 9 July 1863. Simon Gratz Collection. Historical Society of Pennsylvania, Philadelphia.

Custer, George Armstrong. Correspondence. Lawrence A. Frost Collection. Monroe County Historical Museum, Monroe, Mich.

_____. Correspondence. Marguerite Merington Collection. New York Public Library, New York City.

_____. Correspondence. Rochester Public Library, Rochester, N.Y.

_____. Correspondence. United States Military Academy Library, West Point, N.Y.

_____. Correspondence. Yale University Library, New Haven, Conn.

Manuscripts—Officers and Men, First Michigan Cavalry

Arnold, Delevan. Correspondence. Kalamazoo Public Museum, Kalamazoo, Mich.

Arnold, William S. Correspondence. Michigan State University Library, East Lansing.

Brodhead, Thornton F. Correspondence. Burton Historical Collection. Detroit Public Library, Detroit, Mich.

Bromley, John. Letter of 19 October 1864. Bentley Historical Library, University of Michigan, Ann Arbor.

Clark, Benjamin J. Correspondence. Clarke Historical Library, Central Michigan University, Mount Pleasant.

Corselius, Edward. Correspondence. Bentley Historical Library, University of Michigan.

Dennis, George E. Correspondence. Bentley Historical Library, University of Michigan.

Elliott, William R. Correspondence. Burton Historical Collection. Detroit Public Library.

Faxon, John H. Diary, 1863. Bentley Historical Library, University of Michigan.

Field, Frederick N. Correspondence. Bentley Historical Library, University of Michigan.

Gillet, Joseph H. Correspondence. Waldo Library, Western Michigan University, Kalamazoo.

Kilborn, George H. Correspondence. Bentley Historical Library, University of Michigan.

Leach, Morgan L. Correspondence. Bentley Historical Library, University of Michigan.

Macomber, Dexter M. Diaries, 1861-64, and Memoirs. Clarke Historical Library, Central Michigan University.

_____. Letter of 19 December 1862. U.S. Army Military History Institute, Carlisle Barracks, Pa.

Mathews, Amasa E. Letter of 6 September 1862. Bentley Historical Library, University of Michigan.

Maynard, Darius G. Correspondence. Wichita State University Library, Wichita, Kas.

Pistorius, Frederick. Correspondence. Bentley Historical Library, University of Michigan.

Rowe, James D. Memoirs. Bentley Historical Library, University of Michigan.

Ryder, Alfred G. Correspondence and Diaries, 1861-62. Bentley Historical Library, University of Michigan.

Schmalzried, Frederic. Correspondence. Bentley Historical Library, University of Michigan.

Watson, Edward M. Correspondence. Bentley Historical Library, University of Michigan.

Manuscripts—Officers and Men, Fifth Michigan Cavalry

Alger, Russell A. Correspondence. Bentley Historical Library, University of Michigan.

_____. Letter of 18 September 1865. Simon Gratz Collection. Historical Society of Pennsylvania.

Ball, William. Correspondence. Waldo Library, Western Michigan University.

Brown, Frank M. Correspondence. Bentley Historical Library, University of Michigan.

Chapman, Gilbert W. Correspondence. Burton Historical Collection. Detroit Public Library.

Clark, John E. Correspondence. Nebraska State Historical Society, Lincoln.

Comte, Victor E. Correspondence. Bentley Historical Library, University of Michigan.

Courson, Hamilton. Letter of 9 March 1863. Clarke Historical Library, Central Michigan University.

Doherty, William. Letter of 10 April 1865. Clarke Historical Library, Central Michigan University.

Franklin, William. Letter of 18 January 1865. Bentley Historical Library, University of Michigan.

Gould, Ebenezer. Correspondence. Clarke Historical Library, Central Michigan University.

Hickey, Myron. Correspondence. Library of Congress, Washington, D.C.

Jessup, Joseph. Correspondence. Bentley Historical Library, University of Michigan.

Leggett, Percival S. Correspondence. Burton Historical Collection. Detroit Public Library.

Morey, John R. Correspondence and Diaries, 1863-64. Bentley Historical Library, University of Michigan.

Rockwell, William H. Correspondence. Waldo Library, Western Michigan University.

Stone, Addison R. Correspondence. Bentley Historical Library, University of Michigan.

Stuart, William V. Correspondence. Burton Historical Collection. Detroit Public Library.

Thompson, Stephen W. Diary, 1865. Clarke Historical Library, Central Michigan University.

Townsend, George. Correspondence. Bentley Historical Library, University of Michigan.

Trowbridge, Luther S. Correspondence. Bentley Historical Library, University of Michigan.

Van Gieson, Lewis K. Correspondence. Bentley Historical Library, University of Michigan.

Wright, Francis M. Letter of 4 July 1864. Waldo Library, Western Michigan University.

Manuscripts—Officers and Men, Sixth Michigan Cavalry

Baird, William. Memoirs. Bentley Historical Library, University of Michigan.

Barbour, George W. Diary, 1863. Bentley Historical Library, University of Michigan.

Farnill, John S. Correspondence. Bentley Historical Library, University of Michigan.

Ford, Thomas J. Letter of 4 January 1865. Waldo Library, Western Michigan University.

Grommon, Franklin P. Diaries, 1864-65. Bentley Historical Library, University of Michigan.

Gross, Frank. Diaries, 1864-65. Bentley Historical Library, University of Michigan.

Harrington, George L. Diary, 1863. Waldo Library, Western Michigan University.

Hill, Thomas W. Diary, 1864. Waldo Library, Western Michigan University.

Holmes, Augustus B. Correspondence. Michigan Department of State, Lansing.

Kay, John B. Diaries, 1863-64. Bentley Historical Library, University of Michigan.

Kidd, James H. Correspondence. Bentley Historical Library, University of Michigan.

Mattoon, Gershom W. Correspondence. Michigan State University Library.

Powers, Daniel H. Correspondence and Diary, 1864. In possession of Mr. Alva B. Van Dyke, Nappanee, Ind.

Rix, Hiram, Jr. Diary, 1865. Clarke Historical Library, Central Michigan University.

Simonds, George W. Letter of 1 August 1865. Bentley Historical Library, University of Michigan.

Stewart, Daniel. Correspondence. Waldo Library, Western Michigan University.

Stewart, Frederick. Correspondence. Waldo Library, Western Michigan University.

Stewart, Henry W. Correspondence. Waldo Library, Western Michigan University.

Thompson, Henry E. Letter of 30 September 1863. Bentley Historical Library, University of Michigan.

Trego, David R. Correspondence. Bentley Historical Library, University of Michigan.

Manuscripts—Officers and Men, Seventh Michigan Cavalry

Buck, Andrew N. Correspondence. Bentley Historical Library, University of Michigan.

Clark, John A. Letter of 30 July 1863. Bentley Historical Library, University of Michigan.

Fisher, Albert H. Correspondence. Waldo Library, Western Michigan University.

Fisher, Byron. Correspondence. Waldo Library, Western Michigan University.

Hamlin, John H. Correspondence. Clarke Historical Library, Central Michigan University.

Harvey, Edward H. Correspondence. Waldo Library, Western Michigan University.

Havens, Edwin R. Correspondence and Diary, 1864. Michigan State University Library.

Monaghan, John W. Correspondence and Diaries, 1864-65. Bentley Historical Library, University of Michigan.

O'Brien, William H. Correspondence and Diary, 1864. Bentley Historical Library, University of Michigan.

Ralph, Oscar S. Correspondence. Bentley Historical Library, University of Michigan.

Wattles, Victor C. Letter of 11 June 1865. Bentley Historical Library, University of Michigan.

Michigan at Gettysburg. Detroit: Winn & Hammond, 1889.

Millbrook, Minnie D., ed. *Twice Told Tales of Michigan and Her Soldiers in the Civil War.* Lansing, Mich.: privately issued, 1966.

Monaghan, Jay. *Custer: The Life of General George Armstrong Custer.* Boston: Little, Brown Co., Inc., 1959.

Moore, Frank. *Women of the War: Their Heroism and Self-Sacrifice.* Hartford, Conn.: S. S. Scranton & Co., 1867.

_____, ed. *The Rebellion Record: A Diary of American Events.* 12 vols. New York: various publishers, 1861-68.

Moore, James. *Kilpatrick and Our Cavalry.* New York: W. J. Widdleton, 1865.

Moyer, H. P., comp. *History of the Seventeenth Regiment, Pennsylvania Volunteer Cavalry.* Lebanon, Pa.: *Sowers* Printing Co., 1911.

Murden, B. F. *A Sermon Preached at Milford on the Funeral Occasion of Lieut. Henry K. Foote of the Fifth Michigan Cavalry...* Pontiac, Mich.: Beardsley & Turner, 1863.

Nye, Wilbur S. *Here Come the Rebels!* Baton Rouge: Louisiana State University Press, 1965.

Palmer, H. E. *The Powder River Expedition, 1865...* Omaha, Nebr.: privately issued, 1887.

Proceedings of the Buford Memorial Association... New York: Buford Memorial Association, 1895.

Record Fifth Michigan Cavalry, Civil War, 1861-1865. Kalamazoo: Ihling Bros. & Everard, 1905.

Record First Michigan Cavalry, Civil War, 1861-1865. Kalamazoo: Ihling Bros. & Everard, 1905.

Record Seventh Michigan Cavalry, Civil War, 1861-1865. Kalamazoo: Ihling Bros. & Everard, 1905.

Record Sixth Michigan Cavalry, Civil War, 1861-1865. Kalamazoo: Ihling Bros. & Everard, 1905.

Report of the Secretary of War, December 1, 1861. Washington, D.C.: Government Printing Office, 1861.

Rhodes, Charles D. *History of the Cavalry of the Army of the Potomac...* Kansas City, Mo.: Hudson-Kimberley Publishing Co., 1900.

Robertson, John, comp. *Michigan in the War.* Lansing: W. S. George & Co., 1882.

Rogers, Ford H. *"Jeb" Stuart's Hat...* Detroit: privately issued, 1893.

Roster of Survivors of the Seventh Michigan Cavalry and Muster Out Rolls of the Regiment. Ann Arbor: *Register* Publishing Co., 1895.

Roster of the Survivors of the 1st, 5th, 6th and 7th Cavalry Regiments of Michigan... n.p.: privately issued, 1912.

Sanford, George B. *Fighting Rebels and Redskins: Experiences in Army Life of Colonel George B. Sanford, 1861-1892.* Edited by E. R. Hagemann. Norman: University of Oklahoma Press, 1969.

Manuscripts—Miscellaneous

Allen, Winthrop S. G. Correspondence. Illinois State Historical Library, Springfield.

Bachelder, John. Papers. New Hampshire Historical Society, Concord.

Croll, Jennie S. Memoirs. Adams County Historical Society, Gettysburg, Pa.

Gregg, David McMurtrie. Papers. Library of Congress.

Rawle, William Brooke. Papers. Historical Society of Pennsylvania.

Stewart, Salome Myers. Memoirs. Adams County Historical Society.

Storrick, W. C. "The Hunterstown Fight." Gettysburg National Military Park, Gettysburg, Pa.

Government Records

Appointments, Commissions, and Public Branch Document Files. Record Group 94, Entry 297, National Archives.

Compiled Military Service Records. Record Group 94, Entry 519, National Archives.

General's Papers. Record Group 94, Entry 159, National Archives.

Generals' Reports of Service, War of the Rebellion (13 vols.) Record Group 94, Entry 160, National Archives.

Records of Headquarters, Fifth Michigan Cavalry, 1862-65. Record Group 94, National Archives.

Records of Headquarters, First Michigan Cavalry, 1861-65. Record Group 94, National Archives.

Records of Headquarters, Seventh Michigan Cavalry, 1862-65. Record Group 94, National Archives.

Records of Headquarters, Sixth Michigan Cavalry, 1862-65. Record Group 94, National Archives.

Newspapers

Allegan Journal, 1861-65.

Battle Creek Journal, 1861-65.

Daily Union Vedette (Salt Lake City, Utah Terr.), 1865-66.

Detroit Advertiser & Tribune, 1861-65.

Detroit Free Press, 1861-65.

Grand Rapids Daily Eagle, 1861-65.

Grand Rapids Daily Enquirer & Herald, 1861-63.

Grand Traverse Herald (Traverse City, Mich.), 1861-65.

Greenville Independent, 1861-65.

Jackson Citizen, 1861-65.

Jackson Eagle, 1862-65.

Kalamazoo Gazette, 1861-65.

Lansing State Republican, 1861-65.

Mecosta County Pioneer (Big Rapids, Mich.), 1862-65.

Monroe Commercial, 1861-65.

Montana Post (Virginia City, Montana Terr.), 1865-66.

New York Times, 1861-65.

Niles Republican, 1861-65.

Philadelphia Inquirer, 1861-65.

Salt Lake Daily Telegraph (Salt Lake City, Utah Terr.), 1865-66.

Wolverine Citizen (Flint, Mich.), 1861-65.

Articles and Essays

Butler, M. C. "The Cavalry Fight at Trevilian Station." *Battles and Leaders of the Civil War* 4 (1887-88): 237-39.

Carpenter, Louis H. "Sheridan's Expedition Around Richmond, May 9-25, 1864." *Journal of the U. S. Cavalry Association* 1 (1888): 300-24.

Clark, S. A. "Brandy Station, October, 1863." *Maine Bugle* n.s. 3 (1896): 226-29.
_____. "Buckland Mills." *Maine Bugle* n.s. 4 (1897): 108-10.

Cummings, W. G. "Six Months in the Third Cavalry Division Under Custer." *War Sketches and Incidents: As Related by Companions of the Iowa Commandery, Military Order of the Loyal Legion of the United States* 1 (1893): 296-315.

Custer, George Armstrong. "War Memoirs." *Galaxy* 21 (1876): 319-24, 448-60, 624-32, 809-18; 22 (1876): 293-99, 447-55, 684-94.

Edwards, Arthur. "Those Who Fought Without Guns." *Military Essays and Recollections: Papers Read Before the Commandery of the State of Illinois, Military Order of the Loyal Legion of the United States* 1 (1891): 441-52.

Ellis, Richard N. "Volunteer Soldiers in the West, 1865." *Military Affairs* 34 (1970): 53-55.

Hanson, Joseph Mills. "The Civil War Custer." *Cavalry Journal* 43 (1934): 24-31.

Harris, Moses. "The Union Cavalry." *War Papers: Read Before the Commandery of the State of Wisconsin, Military Order of the Loyal Legion of the United States* 1 (1891): 340-73.

Hastings, Smith H. "The Cavalry Service, and Recollections of the Late War." *Magazine of Western History* 11 (1890): 259-66.

Havens, Edwin R. "How Mosby Destroyed Our Train." *Michigan History Magazine* 14 (1930): 294-98.

Herbert, T. W. "In Occupied Pennsylvania." *Georgia Review* 4 (1950): 109-15.

Merritt, Wesley. "Sheridan in the Shenandoah Valley." *Battles and Leaders of the Civil War* 4 (1887-88): 500-21.

Miller, Samuel. "Yellow Tavern." *Civil War History* 2 (1956): 57-81.

Miller, William E. "The Cavalry Battle Near Gettysburg." *Battles and Leaders of the Civil War* 3 (1887-88): 397-406.

Monaghan, Jay. "Custer's 'Last Stand'—Trevilian Station, 1864." *Civil War History* 8 (1962): 245-58.

Moore, James O. "Custer's Raid Into Albermarle County: The Skirmish at Rio Hill, February 29, 1864." *Virginia Magazine of History and Biography* 79 (1971): 338-48.

Morris, Roy, Jr. "Sweltering Summer Collision." *Military History* 9 (February 1993): 42-49.

Mosby, John S. "A Bit of Partisan Service." *Battles and Leaders of the Civil War* 3 (1887-88): 148-51.

Newhall, Frederick C. "With Sheridan in Lee's Last Campaign." *Maine Bugle* n.s. 1 (1894): 201-13, 297-317; 2 (1895): 1-7, 96-112, 236-56, 289-308; 3 (1896): 1-14.

Nye, Wilbur S. "The Affair at Hunterstown." *Civil War Times Illustrated* 9 (February 1971): 22-34.

"The Opposing Forces at Cedar Mountain, Va." *Battles and Leaders of the Civil War* 2 (1887-88): 495-96.

"The Opposing Forces in the Valley Campaigns," *Battles and Leaders of the Civil War* 2 (1887-88): 299-301.

Parsons, H. C. "Farnsworth's Charge and Death." *Battles and Leaders of the Civil War* 3 (1887-88): 393-96.

Reece, Frances R., ed. "The Final Push to Appomattox: Captain [John A.] Clark's Account of the Seventh Michigan Cavalry in Action." *Michigan History Magazine* 28 (1944): 456-64.

Rice, Allen. "A Letter from a Young Michigan Cavalryman..." *America's Civil War* 10 (March 1997): 74-79.

Rodenbough, Theophilus F. "Sheridan's Trevilian Raid." *Battles and Leaders of the Civil War* 4 (1887-88): 233-36.

Smith, Donald L. "Booneville—Where Sheridan Won His Star." *Civil War Times Illustrated* 1 (October 1962): 32-34.

Sword, Wiley. "Cavalry on Trial at Kelly's Ford." *Civil War Times Illustrated* 13 (April 1974): 33-40.

Williams, E. S., ed. "Col. Thornton Broadhead's [Brodhead's] Last Letter." *Michigan Historical Collections* 9 (1886): 208-09.

Williams, Robert A. "Haw's Shop: A 'Storm of Shot and Shell'." *Civil War Times Illustrated* 9 (January 1971): 12-19.

Imboden, John D. "Stonewall Jackson in the Shenandoah." *Battles and Leade* the Civil War 2 (1887-88): 282-98.

Isham, Asa B. "The Cavalry of the Army of the Potomac." *Sketches of War His 1861-1865: Papers Prepared for the Ohio Commandery of the Military Ord the Loyal Legion of the United States* 5 (1903): 301-27.

_____. "The Story of a Gunshot Wound." *Sketches of War History, 1861-1 Papers Prepared for the Ohio Commandery of the Military Order of the Loyal L of the United States* 4 (1896): 429-43.

_____. "Through the Wilderness to Richmond." *Sketches of War History, 1 1865: Papers Prepared for the Ohio Commandery of the Military Order of the Legion of the United States* 1 (1888): 198-217.

Kempster, Walter. "The Cavalry at Gettysburg." *War Papers: Read Befo Commandery of the State of Wisconsin, Military Order of the Loyal Legion United States* 4 (1914): 397-429.

Kibby, Leo P. "Patrick Edward Connor... First Gentile of Utah." *Journal of th* 2 (1963): 424-34.

Kidd, James H. "Address of General James H. Kidd, at the Dedication of Mi Monuments Upon the Battle Field of Gettysburg, June 12, 1889." *Jou the U. S. Cavalry Association* 4 (1891): 41-63.

Kimball, Nathan. "Fighting Jackson at Kernstown." *Battles and Leaders of th War* 2 (1887-88): 302-13.

Klement, Frank L., ed. "Edwin B. Bigelow: A Michigan Sergeant in the Civi *Michigan History* 38 (1954): 193-252.

Lee, William O. "Michigan Cavalry Brigade at Gettysburg." *Gateway* 3 45-50.

Long, E. B. "The Battle That Almost Was—Manassas Gap." *Civil Wa Illustrated* 11 (December 1972): 21-28.

Longacre, Edward G. "Alfred Pleasonton, 'The Knight of Romance'." *C Times Illustrated* 13 (December 1974): 10-23.

_____. "Cavalry Clash at Todd's Tavern." *Civil War Times Illustrated* 16 (1977): 13-21.

_____. "The Long Run for Trevilian Station." *Civil War Times Illust* (November 1979): 28-39.

Luvaas, Jay, and Wilbur S. Nye. "The Campaign That History Forgot." (*Times Illustrated* 8 (November 1969): 11-42.

Mackey, T. J. "Duel of General Wade Hampton on the Battle-Field at G with a Federal Soldier." *Southern Historical Society Papers* 22 (1894):

McClernand, Edward J. "Cavalry Operations: The Wilderness to the Jam *Journal of the Military Service Institution of the United States* 30 (1902)

McKinney, Francis F. "Michigan Cavalry in the Civil War." *Michigan Quarterly Review* 43 (1957): 136-46.

Books and Pamphlets

Anthony, William. *History of the Battle of Hanover...* Hanover, Pa.: privately issued, 1945.

Articles of Association and Roster of Survivors of "Gen'l Custer's" Michigan Cavalry Brigade Association... Detroit: privately issued, 1903.

Bayard, Samuel J. *The Life of George Dashiell Bayard...* New York: G. P. Putnam's Sons, 1874.

Biographical Directory of the American Congress, 1774-1971. Washington, D.C.: Government Printing Office, 1971.

Brown, D. Alexander. *Bury My Heart at Wounded Knee: An Indian History of the American West.* New York: Holt, Rinehart & Winston, 1970.

Burr, Frank A., and Richard J. Hinton. *"Little Phil" and His Troopers: The Life of Gen. Philip H. Sheridan...* Providence, R.I.: J. A. & R. A. Reid, 1888.

Butler, Benjamin F. *Autobiography and Personal Reminiscences of Major-General Benj. F. Butler: Butler's Book.* Boston: A. M. Thayer & Co., 1892.

Carroll, John M., comp. *Custer in the Civil War: His Unpublished Memoirs.* San Rafael, Cal.: Presidio Press, 1977.

Casler, John O. *Four Years in the Stonewall Brigade...* Guthrie, Okla.: State Capital Printing Co., 1893.

Catton, Bruce. *Mr. Lincoln's Army.* Garden City, N.Y.: Doubleday & Co., Inc., 1962.

Coates, Earl J., and Dean S. Thomas. *An Introduction to Civil War Small Arms.* Gettysburg, Pa.: Thomas Publications, 1990.

Coddington, Edwin B. *The Gettysburg Campaign: A Study in Command.* New York: Charles Scribner's Sons, 1968.

Cooper, David M. *Obituary Discourse on Occasion of the Death of Noah Henry Ferry...* New York: John F. Trow, 1863.

Custer, George Armstrong, and Elizabeth Bacon Custer. *The Custer Story: The Life and Intimate Letters of General George A. Custer and His Wife Elizabeth.* Edited by Marguerite Merington. New York: Devin-Adair Co., 1950.

DeForest, J. W. *A Volunteer's Adventures: A Union Captain's Record of the Civil War.* Edited by James H. Croushore. New Haven, Conn.: Yale University Press, 1946.

Dellenbaugh, Frederick S. *George Armstrong Custer.* New York: Macmillan Co., 1917.

Dorsey, R. Stephen. *American Military Belts and Related Equipments.* Union City, Tenn.: Pioneer Press, 1984.

Frazer, Robert W. *Forts of the West: Military Forts... West of the Mississippi River to 1898.* Norman: University of Oklahoma Press, 1965.

Freeman, Douglas Southall. *Lee's Lieutenants: A Study in Command.* 3 vols. New York: Charles Scribner's Sons, 1942-44.

Glazier, Willard. *Three Years in the Federal Cavalry.* New York: R. H. Ferguson & Co., 1870.

Gracey, S. L. *Annals of the Sixth Pennsylvania Cavalry.* Philadelphia: E. H. Butler & Co., 1868.

Gregg, David McMurtrie. *The Second Cavalry Division of the Army of the Potomac in the Gettysburg Campaign.* Philadelphia: privately issued, 1907.

Hafen, LeRoy R., and Ann W. Hafen, eds. *Powder River Campaigns... of 1865.* Glendale, Calif.: Arthur H. Clark Co., 1961.

Hancock, Cornelia. *South After Gettysburg: Letters of Cornelia Hancock, 1863-1868.* Edited by Henrietta Stratton Jaquette. New York: Thomas Y. Crowell Co., 1956.

Harrington, Fred Harvey. *Fighting Politician: Major General N. P. Banks.* Philadelphia: University of Pennsylvania Press, 1948.

Harris, Samuel. *A Curious Way of Getting Rid of a Cowardly Captain...* Chicago: Press of Adolph Selz, n.d.

_____. *In a Raid with the 5th Michigan Cavalry.* Chicago: privately issued, n.d.

_____. *Major General George A. Custer: Stories Told Around the Camp Fire of the Michigan Brigade of Cavalry.* Chicago: privately issued, 1898.

_____. *Michigan Brigade of Cavalry at the Battle of Gettysburg, July 3, 1863...* Chicago: privately issued, 1894.

_____. *Personal Reminiscences of Samuel Harris.* Chicago: Rogerson Press, 1897.

_____. *A Story of the War of the Rebellion: Why I Was Not Hung.* Chicago: Henneberry Press, ca. 1895.

Hein, Otto L. *Memories of Long Ago...* New York: G. P. Putnam's Sons, 1925.

Hennessy, John J. *Return to Bull Run: The Campaign and Battle of Second Manassas.* New York: Simon & Schuster, 1993.

Heth, Henry. *The Memoirs of Henry Heth.* Edited by James L. Morrison, Jr. Westport, Conn.: Greenwood Press, 1974.

Hickox, George H. *Remarks at the Funeral of Lieut. Percival S. Leggett, of Company I, Fifth Regt. Michigan Cavalry.* Detroit: O. S. Gulley's Presses, 1863.

History of the Eighteenth Regiment of Cavalry, Pennsylvania Volunteers. New York: Wynkoop Hallenbeck Crawford Co., 1909.

History of the Third Pennsylvania Cavalry... in the American Civil War, 1861-1865. Philadelphia: Franklin Printing Co., 1905.

Humphreys, Andrew A. *The Virginia Campaign of '64 and '65: The Army of the Potomac and the Army of the James.* New York: Charles Scribner's Sons, 1883.

Hutton, Paul Andrew, ed. *The Custer Reader.* Lincoln: University of Nebraska Press, 1992.

Isham, Asa B. *An Historical Sketch of the Seventh Regiment Michigan Volunteer Cavalry from Its Organization, in 1862, to Its Muster Out, in 1865.* New York: *Town Topics* Publishing Co., 1893.

_____. *The Michigan Cavalry Brigade* [broadside]. Ionia, Mich.: privately issued, 1911.

_____, Henry M. Davidson, and Henry B. Furness. *Prisoners of War and Military Prisons: Personal Narratives...* Cincinnati: Lyman & Cushing, 1890.

Johnson, Allen, and Dumas Malone, eds. *Dictionary of American Biography*. 11 vols. New York: Charles Scribner's Sons, 1964.

Johnson, George K. *The Battle of Kernstown, March 23, 1862...* Detroit: Winn & Hammond, 1890.

Jones, Virgil Carrington. *Eight Hours Before Richmond*. New York: Henry Holt & Co., 1957.

Kidd, James H. *The Michigan Cavalry Brigade in the Wilderness*. Detroit: Winn & Hammond, 1890.

_____. *Personal Recollections of a Cavalryman with Custer's Michigan Cavalry Brigade in the Civil War*. Ionia, Mich.: *Sentinel* Printing Co., 1908.

Lanman, Charles. *The Red Book of Michigan: A Civil, Military and Biographical History*. Detroit: E. B. Smith & Co., 1871.

Leckie, Shirley A. *Elizabeth Bacon Custer and the Making of a Myth*. Norman: University of Oklahoma Press, 1993.

Lee, William O., comp. *Personal and Historical Sketches and Facial History of and by Members of the Seventh Regiment Michigan Volunteer Cavalry, 1862-1865*. Detroit: Ralston-Stroup Printing Co., 1904.

Leonard, Elizabeth D. *Yankee Women: Gender Battles in the Civil War*. New York: W. W. Norton & Co., Inc., 1994.

Livermore, Mary. *My Story of the War: A Woman's Narrative...* Hartford, Conn.: A. D. Worthington & Co., 1889.

Longacre, Edward G. *The Cavalry at Gettysburg: A Tactical Study of Mounted Operations during the Civil War's Pivotal Campaign, 9 June-14 July 1863*. Rutherford, N.J.: Fairleigh Dickinson University Press, 1986.

_____. *General John Buford: A Military Biography*. Conshohocken, Pa.: Combined Books, 1995.

_____. *Grant's Cavalryman: The Life and Wars of General James H. Wilson*. Mechanicsburg, Pa.: Stackpole Books, 1996.

Lonn, Ella. *Foreigners in the Union Army and Navy*. Baton Rouge: Louisiana State University Press, 1951.

Lyman, Theodore. *Meade's Headquarters, 1863-1865: Letters of Colonel Theodore Lyman from the Wilderness to Appomattox*. Edited by George R. Agassiz. Boston: *Atlantic Monthly* Press, 1922.

Mann, William D. *Colonel Mann's Infantry and Cavalry Accoutrements...* New York: privately issued, 1864.

McCrea, Tully. *"Dear Belle": Letters from a Cadet & Officer to His Sweetheart, 1858-1865*. Edited by Catherine S. Crary. Middletown, Conn.: Wesleyan University Press, 1965.

McPherson, James M. *Ordeal by Fire: The Civil War and Reconstruction*. New York: Alfred A. Knopf, 1982.

Meyer, Henry C. *Civil War Experiences Under Bayard, Gregg, Kilpatrick, Custer, Raulston, and Newberry, 1862, 1863, 1864*. New York: Knickerbocker Press, 1911.

Sears, Stephen W. *To the Gates of Richmond: The Peninsula Campaign.* New York: Ticknor & Fields, 1992.

Sheridan, Philip H. *Personal Memoirs of P. H. Sheridan, General, United States Army.* 2 vols. New York: Charles L. Webster & Co., 1888.

Sheridan's Veterans: A Souvenir of Their Two Campaigns in the Shenandoah Valley... Boston: W. F. Brown & Co., 1883.

Starr, Stephen Z. *The Union Cavalry in the Civil War.* 3 vols. Baton Rouge: Louisiana State University Press, 1979-84.

Supplement to the Official Records of the Union and Confederate Armies. Wilmington, N.C.: Broadfoot Publishing Co., 1995.

Tanner, Robert G. *Stonewall in the Valley: Thomas J. "Stonewall" Jackson's Shenandoah Valley Campaign, Spring 1862.* Garden City, N.Y.: Doubleday & Co., Inc., 1976.

Thomas, Emory M. *Bold Dragoon: The Life of J.E.B. Stuart.* New York: Harper & Row, 1986.

Thomas, Hampton S. *Some Personal Reminiscences of Service in the Cavalry of the Army of the Potomac.* Philadelphia: L. R. Hammersly & Co., 1889.

Trowbridge, Luther S. *The Operations of the Cavalry in the Gettysburg Campaign.* Detroit: privately issued, 1888.

Urwin, Gregory J. W. *Custer Victorious: The Civil War Battles of General George Armstrong Custer.* Rutherford, N.J.: Fairleigh Dickinson University Press, 1983.

Utley, Robert M. *Cavalier in Buckskin: George Armstrong Custer and the Western Military Frontier.* Norman: University of Oklahoma Press, 1988.

Van De Water, Frederic F. *Glory-Hunter: A Life of General Custer.* Indianapolis: Bobbs-Merrill Co., 1934.

Warner, Ezra J. *Generals in Blue: Lives of the Union Commanders.* Baton Rouge: Louisiana State University Press, 1964.

War of the Rebellion: A Compilation of the Official Records of the Union and Confederate Armies. 4 series, 70 vols. in 128. Washington, D.C.: Government Printing Office, 1880-1901.

Weigley, Russell F. *The American Way of War: A History of United States Military Strategy and Policy.* New York: Macmillan Publishing Co., Inc., 1973.

Wert, Jeffry D. *Custer: The Controversial Life of George Armstrong Custer.* New York: Simon & Schuster, 1996.

_____. *Mosby's Rangers.* New York: Simon & Schuster, 1990.

Whittaker, Frederick. *A Complete Life of Gen. George A. Custer...* New York: Sheldon & Co., 1876.

Wilson, James Harrison. *Under the Old Flag: Recollections of Military Operations in the War for the Union...* 2 vols. New York: D. Appleton & Co., 1912.

Wood, Bert. *Franklin's Yesteryear.* Ann Arbor, Mich.: privately issued, 1958.

Woodford, Frank B. *Father Abraham's Children: Michigan Episodes in the Civil War.* Detroit: Wayne State University Press, 1961.

Appendix

Tables of Organization

Gettysburg
Appomattox
Powder River Expedition

Gettysburg
Cavalry Corps, Army of the Potomac
(Pleasonton)

1st DIVISION
(Buford)

1st Brigade
8th Illinois
12th Illinois
3rd Indiana
8th New York

2nd Brigade
6th New York
9th New York
17th Pennsylvania
3rd West Virginia

Reserve Brigade
6th Pennsylvania
1st U.S.
2nd U.S.
5th U.S.
6th U.S.

2nd DIVISION
(Gregg)

1st Brigade
1st Maryland
Purnell (Md.) Legion
1st Massachusetts
1st New Jersey
1st Pennsylvania
3rd Pennsylvania

2nd Brigade
2nd New York
4th New York
6th Ohio
8th Pennsylvania

3rd Brigade
1st Maine
10th New York
4th Pennsylvania
16th Pennsylvania

3rd DIVISION
(Kilpatrick)

1st Brigade
5th New York
18th Pennsylvania
1st Vermont
1st West Virginia

2nd Brigade
(Custer)
1st Michigan
5th Michigan
6th Michigan
7th Michigan

Appomattox
Army of the Shenandoah (Cavalry)
(Merritt)

1st DIVISION
(Devin)

1st Brigade
1st Michigan
5th Michigan
6th Michigan
7th Michigan

2nd Brigade
6th New York
9th New York
19th New York
17th Pennsylvania
20th Pennsylvania

3rd Brigade
2th Massachusetts
6th Pennsylvania
1st U.S.
5th U.S.
6th U.S.

3rd DIVISION
(Custer)

1st Brigade
1st Connecticut
3rd New Jersey
2nd New York
2nd Ohio

2nd Brigade
8th New York
15th New York
1st Vermont

3rd Brigade
1st New York
1st West Virginia
2nd West Virginia
3rd West Virginia

2nd DIVISION (Army of the Potomac)
(Crook)

1st Brigade
1st New Jersey
10th New York
24th New York
1st Pennsylvania

2nd Brigade
4th Pennsylvania
8th Pennsylvania
16th Pennsylvania
21st Pennsylvania

3rd Brigade
1st Maine
2nd New York
6th Ohio
13th Ohio

Powder River Expedition*
(Brigadier General Patrick E. Connor, Commanding)

Left Column	Center Column	Right Column
Col. James H. Kidd	Lt. Col. Samuel Walker	Col. Nelson Cole
6th Michigan Cavalry	16th Kansas Cavalry	2nd Missouri Lt. Arty.
7th Iowa Cavalry		12th Missouri Cavalry
11th Ohio Cavalry		
Pawnee Scouts		
Total: 475	Total: 600	Total: 1,108

With the exception of the 2nd Missouri Light Artillery (serving as cavalry) and the 16th Kansas Cavalry, the units involved were only detachments of regiments (200 men of 6th Michigan, 90 of 7th Iowa, 90 of 11th Ohio, and 311 of 12th Missouri). It is uncertain whether the numbers remained constant throughout the Powder River Campaign. By 23 July Kidd had not yet joined Connor, and he and the 6th Michigan dropped out before the expedition overtook the Indians.

A fourth ("West") Column, commanded by Captain Albert Brown and consisting of the 2nd California Cavalry (116 men) and Omaha Indian Scouts (84 men) made a sweep west of the Bighorn Mountains. Brown's force—actually a detachment of the Left Column—joined Connor's main force in late August, just before the fight on the Tongue River.

* The table of organization at the start of the Powder River Expedition, 23 July 1865—based on the commander's own report (Official Records, I, 48, pt.1:1130).

Index